HANK GREENBERG

HANK GREENBERG

THE HERO OF HEROES

JOHN ROSENGREN

NEW AMERICAN LIBRARY

New American Library
Published by New American Library,
a division of Penguin Group (USA) Inc.,
375 Hudson Street, New York, New York 10014, USA
Penguin Group (Canada), 90 Eglinton Avenue East, Suite 700, Toronto,
Ontario M4P 2Y3, Canada (a division of Pearson Penguin Canada Inc.)
Penguin Books Ltd., 80 Strand, London WC2R 0RL, England
Penguin Ireland, 25 St. Stephen's Green, Dublin 2,
Ireland (a division of Penguin Books Ltd.)
Penguin Group (Australia), 707 Collins Street, Melbourne,
Victoria 3008, Australia (a division of Pearson Australia Group Pty. Ltd.)
Penguin Books India Pvt. Ltd., 11 Community Centre,
Panchsheel Park, New Delhi–110 017, India
Penguin Group (NZ), 67 Apollo Drive, Rosedale, Auckland 0632,
New Zealand (a division of Pearson New Zealand Ltd.)
Penguin Books (South Africa), Rosebank Office Park, 181 Jan Smuts Avenue,
Parktown North 2193, South Africa
Penguin China, B7 Jiaming Center, 27 East Third Ring Road North,
Chaoyang District, Beijing 100020, China

Penguin Books Ltd., Registered Offices:
80 Strand, London WC2R 0RL, England

First published by New American Library,
a division of Penguin Group (USA) Inc.

First Printing, March 2013
1   3   5   7   9   10   8   6   4   2

 REGISTERED TRADEMARK—MARCA REGISTRADA

LIBRARY OF CONGRESS CATALOGING-IN-PUBLICATION DATA:
Rosengren, John.
Hank Greenberg: hero of heroes/John Rosengren.
p. cm.
ISBN 978-0-451-23576-3 (hardback)
1. Greenberg, Hank. 2. Baseball players—United States—Biography.
3. Jewish baseball players—United States—Biography. I. Title.
GV865.G68R67 2013
796.357092—dc23   2012027865
[B]

Set in Adobe Caslon Pro   •   Designed by Elke Sigal

Printed in the United States of America

PUBLISHER'S NOTE
While the author has made every effort to provide accurate telephone numbers, Internet addresses
and other contact information at the time of publication, neither the publisher nor the author
assumes any responsibility for errors, or for changes that occur after publication. Further, publisher
does not have any control over and does not assume any responsibility for author or third-party
Web sites or their content.

For Alison and Brendan,
with love

CONTENTS

———— ∞ ————

CHAPTER ONE

Leshono Toivo

Inside the Detroit clubhouse, Hank Greenberg sat slumped on a stool in front of his locker, still dressed in his street clothes. Around him, his teammates readied for that afternoon's game against the Boston Red Sox, buttoning jerseys, buckling belts, lacing spikes, but the Tigers' first baseman did not budge. It was September 10, 1934. Rosh Hashanah.

"What the hell's the matter with you?" asked third baseman Marv Owen, whose locker neighbored Greenberg's. "You sick?"

Hank shook his head. "No."

"Something bothering you?"

"I don't know what to do."

"You gotta play ball, that's what you gotta do," Owen said. He dressed and headed out to the field for batting practice.

Tradition dictated that Jews observe Rosh Hashanah solemnly in prayer; they were not to work or play. Greenberg spent the first morning of year 5695 at Congregation Shaarey Zedek, Detroit's oldest and largest conservative synagogue. When he entered the sanctuary, dappled with light streaming through the stained glass windows, those assembled turned their attention from the cantor singing with the choir. A murmur passed through the pews. *There he is.* Someone handed him a *talith* (prayer shawl), which he draped over his broad shoulders, and a *machzor* (holiday prayer book). The *shammes* (sexton) offered him the honor to serve as *hagbah*, to lift the Torah following the Reading of the Law. Hank declined.

"I am only a ballplayer," he said. "Give it to someone else who really deserves it."

Hank took his place in the section with the other men and joined in the prayers. He heard the shofar blown. The ancient ritual recalled Abraham's faith—so strong he was willing to sacrifice his son—and God's mercy in providing a ram instead. The whole time Hank stewed over his dilemma.

His parents had emigrated from Romania and raised their children in the strict tradition of their Orthodox faith. They spoke Yiddish at home, attended synagogue regularly and had Hank bar mitzvahed. Now twenty-three years old and a professional ballplayer, Hank Greenberg was old enough to make his own decisions, yet he knew his parents valued the Old World traditions over America's national pastime. When they had traveled to Philadelphia on the Tigers' last road trip to watch him, Hank promised them he would not play on the High Holy Days. Even as he was learning to live on his own in the gentile world, he still abided the commandments, including, "Honor thy father and mother."

About 12:30 that afternoon, Hank stood up to leave. The assembly buzzed again. *He's going to play.* A group of boys and girls rushed after him down the aisle. The cantor paused and turned to see what the commotion was about. *Leshono toivo!* the children called to him, Happy New Year! Some grabbed at his hands. They watched him descend the steps to his car and drive down Chicago Boulevard. He was still uncertain what to do.

Greenberg had not played on the High Holy Days last season, his rookie year with the Tigers, but no one noticed. A year later, everything had changed. Then, the Tigers had been twenty-eight and a half games back, en route to a dismal fifth-place finish. This year, they were in first place, fighting off the Yankees for the pennant.

In 1933, Greenberg had been a rookie, an inconsistent hitter and erratic fielder, the weakest in the league at first base. He had worked hard to improve both. This year, he had established himself as a fixture in the batting order and the infield. With growing confidence, he led the Tigers in runs batted in. His .335 batting average was second only to second baseman Charlie Gehringer's. He was third in runs scored. His league-leading 57 doubles had him within ten of the season record. His 21 home runs had earned the Tiger slugger comparisons to Babe Ruth, Lou Gehrig and Jimmie Foxx.

Come September, the Tigers led the Yankees by six games, but Greenberg had watched the Tigers' lead drop to four over the past week, when the team had faltered and lost half its games. The pennant no longer appeared a sure thing. Everybody on the team had slumped, except for Gehringer, who was challenging the Yankees' Gehrig for the batting title, and Greenberg, who was carrying the team. The sophomore sensation had not only sparked the '34 team's drive for the pennant, he had sealed its last two victories with his bat. Yesterday, with two strikes against him, he had singled to drive in Gehringer with the winning run in the tenth inning. Hank knew his team needed him.

He also knew the fans wanted him to play. They were delirious with the possibility of their Tigers clinching their first pennant since Ty Cobb's prime. Pennant hysteria had swept the city, intensifying as the team's drive neared the finish. With the Depression closing auto plants and lengthening soup lines, Detroit residents had little else to cheer. Yesterday's edition of the *Detroit Free Press* posted a headline in Hebrew with the English translation below, "Happy New Year, Hank." A large photo showed Greenberg swinging his mighty bat. That's how they wanted to see him observe the day: at bat, carrying the team. The Tigers needed the win that day. The thought that Hank might skip the game aggravated their anxieties. "Everybody waited in twisted anguish for the victory that would finally clinch it, and that victory simply wouldn't come," Kyle Crichton wrote in *Sports Illustrated*. "One more defeat at that particular moment would have been the signal for a mass suicide not equaled since the lemmings last marched into the sea." The three Detroit dailies issued extra editions with updates every half hour: "Hank has left his house"; "Hank has *not* left his house"; "Hank is headed for the synagogue"; "Hank is headed for the ballpark."

While fans streamed into the Navin Field grandstand and his team took batting practice, Hank sat alone in the clubhouse, still in his synagogue clothes. He knew the fans were wondering, just like his teammates, what Detroit's most prominent Jew was going to do on Rosh Hashanah. Some had talked behind his back, said things they wouldn't say to his face. Guys like outfielders Jo-Jo White and Gee Walker, good ole Southern boys, had groused about the Jew letting them down. Flea Clifton, a utility infielder, reprimanded them. "Where in the hell would you guys be if it wasn't for

Hank up to this time?" he snapped. "Hank has really been putting the bucks in our pockets. Hell, don't kick the horse you're going to ride."

These were not easy times for Jews. Adolf Hitler's crusade against the chosen people had gained momentum. The Nazi leader had already targeted German Jews as scapegoats and relegated them to second-class citizenship with restrictions on their commerce and education. Earlier that week at the National Socialist Party convention, Hitler accused Jewish intellectuals of creating spiritual confusion and cultural problems. The official convention program stated: "Without a solution of the Jewish question, there is no salvation for the German people."

The plight of German Jews was the central theme in temples and synagogues throughout Detroit on Rosh Hashanah. The situation prompted large turnouts, including some 4,000 faithful at Congregation Shaarey Zedek, where Greenberg had attended services. Jews in America worried about relatives in the old country and felt the sting of anti-Semitism at home. In Detroit, Henry Ford had published accusations purporting a Jewish conspiracy to bring down Christianity. From his Catholic parish in suburban Detroit, Father Charles Coughlin preached against "Jewish conspirators" and "moneychangers" to ten million rapt listeners on his weekly radio show.

Small wonder, then, that Jews would turn to Greenberg, the nation's first Jewish sports star, as a symbol of hope. The *American Hebrew* and *Jewish Tribune* had proclaimed him "that elusive Hebrew star." Jewish fans saw in his athletic prowess the ability to shatter stereotypes and secure for Jews their rightful place in America's Promised Land in the years before the nation of Israel galvanized ethnic identity. "I knew the Jewish people took pride in the fact I was Jewish," Greenberg said. Yet, still seeking his own footing, he bucked the role they had scripted for him.

Several days before Rosh Hashanah, Greenberg backed out of a banquet planned by a group of Detroit's prominent Jewish citizens to honor him. His gesture was front page news, indicative of his importance to Detroit and the curiosity over his Jewishness. The group had already sold tickets to the event slated for later that month. They expected to raise $1,500 to buy Hank a Cadillac. But Greenberg told them, "Listen, fellows, this is a swell thing you're trying to do for me, and I appreciate it, but I don't rate it. I have only been up in the big leagues a short time, and I really don't deserve anything like this. Wait till I really prove I'm a great ballplayer, and then maybe I'll go for a stunt like this."

Hank tried to hide his discomfort over being singled out as a Jew behind the modesty of a young ballplayer. Not that he wasn't modest, but his excuse for calling off the event was a convenient means to dodge attention from the Jewish community. He did not want to be pigeonholed by his religion. He also did not want to be beholden. "I knew that if I accepted an automobile," he wrote in his autobiography *Hank Greenberg: The Story of My Life*, "I would be obligated to every one of those fans who chipped in ten or twenty dollars, and I didn't want anyone to feel that they owned me."

At the same time, he did feel an obligation to the community. He was Jewish. He wouldn't deny that. Yet he was also a private man. It pained him that his team's pennant race with the New York Yankees thrust such a personal decision into the public spotlight. The national attention had taken him somewhat by surprise. But he was starting to understand that others— Jews and non-Jews alike—looked to him as not simply a Jew but representative of many. His actions had greater consequences beyond himself. He did not want to let down his people. Rosh Hashanah was no longer a personal decision.

The banquet planners accepted Greenberg's retreat gracefully, but the speculation over the young ballplayer's decision on whether or not to play on Rosh Hashanah polarized opinion within the Jewish community and among Tiger fans. Rabbis and other Jews from all over the country sent Greenberg telegrams advising him what to do. Some counseled him to rely on his conscience. Others told him it would be a mistake for him to play on the day when he should be observing the solemnity of the New Year in prayer. They reminded him that children were watching. If he played, it would not make it any easier for those Jewish children to stand up for their religion. Whether he liked it or not, he felt the burden of being a role model.

Detroit baseball fans grumbled, "Rosh Hashanah comes every year, but the Tigers haven't won the pennant since 1909." The goyim couldn't understand. Christians played on Easter, their holiest day, and regularly on Sundays. In fact, just earlier that season, on April 29, the Pittsburgh Pirates had become the final major league team to play a home game on a Sunday after the state repealed its "blue law," which prohibited Sunday games. By then, the notion of not playing on the day most Americans went to church had become antiquated. If Hank refused to play an important game for religious reasons, he risked their scorn and even his job.

Say Greenberg sat and the Tigers lost, the press might call for his hide. Even those writers seemingly sympathetic represented a certain danger. Their constant references to his heritage showed a preoccupation with his otherness, and they occasionally stumbled into the use of prevalent stereotypes. How far away were they from succumbing to bigotry if the Tigers' "Jewish first baseman" let them down? The sportswriters had emphasized his "duties to his teammates" and the New York *Evening Journal* wrote that his absence in the lineup would be a "loss to his companions."

Hank labored over his decision without any precedent to guide him. That very day, the Jewish boxer Barney Ross had decided not to fight in his welterweight title bout rescheduled for Rosh Hashanah in New York. But Ross's action was more economic than religious, knowing that his take of the gate would be light with a large percentage of his Jewish fan base in New York staying away to observe the New Year. Ross was also an individual athlete, not playing a team sport rooted in a city. You couldn't say his situation paralleled Hank's.

Absent the soul-searching Greenberg endured, four other Jews would play in the majors that day: Senators second baseman Buddy Myer, Giants catcher Harry Danning, and Indians catcher Moe Berg and outfielder Milt Galatzer. The only daily player among them was Myer, who had not considered taking the day off. Several other Jewish major leaguers did not play on Rosh Hashanah, not because of their conscience, but because they were pitchers or subs, relegated to the bench without a choice.*

---

* Thirty-one years later, Sandy Koufax, the Dodgers' dominating pitcher, would sit out the first game of the 1965 World Series to observe Yom Kippur. By then, American society was in the midst of a social revolution that opened latitude for personal decisions of conscience, morals or religion. Koufax, though under contract to the Dodgers, was free to do as he chose; his job and popularity were secure. By contrast, Greenberg lived in a black-and-white world that had not yet accepted varied shades of gray, a world which practiced social oppression habitually. If his employers or the press did not approve of his decision to play, there was not a sufficient level of tolerance guaranteed to save his job or place in the community. A generation later, Koufax and other players could refer to Greenberg's decision on whether or not to play on High Holy Days, but in 1934—before Koufax was even born—Greenberg shouldered the weight of breaking ground.

Perhaps no one wanted to see Greenberg play more than Elden Auker, the rookie Tiger pitcher scheduled to start that day against the Red Sox. Auker did not want to get stuck with the loss because the Detroit infield lacked a key cog. None of the four regulars—Marv Owen at third, Billy Rogell at short, Gehringer at second and Greenberg at first—had missed a game that season. They had been behind Auker for every start. He was upset not to spot Greenberg on the field for batting practice.

Auker was a twenty-two-year-old hayseed from Kansas. In his hometown of Norcatur, there were many wheat farmers but no Jews. Greenberg was the first Jewish person Auker met. Like the majority of his teammates from rural Southern areas, the young pitcher had no idea what Rosh Hashanah was until he read in the papers that the holiday might keep Greenberg from playing. Auker was so naïve that he didn't know the "Restricted" sign outside his Detroit apartment complex meant "No Jews." Tossing his warm-up pitches before the game, the Tigers' submariner hoped that Greenberg would somehow have a change of heart and join his team on the field.

Tiger owner and team president Frank Navin had called Hank before the game. So had his nephew Charles Navin, the team secretary. The Navins had not *ordered* him to play, but had made clear their interest. "This is a civic duty," they told him. "If Detroit is to win the pennant, you must play." Down the stretch, every loss seemed to count double against a team in a pennant race. If the Tigers lost without him, Hank would feel responsible. "We're only four games ahead of the Yankees now," he explained to Charles Ward of the *Detroit Free Press*. "Suppose I stay out of the game and we lost the pennant by one game? That will keep the boys out of the World Series after they have worked so hard all season to get into the Series. Would that be justice? What'll they think? And what will Detroit think?"

The *Detroit News* asked Rabbi Joseph Thumim, head of Detroit's Temple Beth Abraham and an authority on Orthodox Jewish law, for his learned opinion on Greenberg's situation. Rabbi Thumim found two references in the Talmud—one from Bitzo, 8:12, the other from Shulhan Aruch—that said, "It is allowed to play ball on a holiday in the street."

"You tell Henry Greenberg that he can play ball today and Saturday [the Sabbath] with a clear conscience," Rabbi Thumim said. "The Talmud gives him ample right."

Another Detroit rabbi, Dr. Leo M. Franklin of Temple Beth El, published a conflicting statement shortly before that day's game: "Mr. Greenberg, who is a conscientious Jew, must decide for himself whether he ought to play or not. From the standpoint of Orthodox Judaism, the fact that ball playing is his means of livelihood would argue against his participation in the Monday game. On the other hand, it might be argued quite consistently that his taking part in the game would mean something not only to himself but to his fellow players, and in fact at this time, to the community of Detroit."

This rabbi had left room for Greenberg to play or not, clarifying his dilemma but refusing to outright advise him what to do. The responsibility rested clearly upon the young ballplayer's conscience.

Greenberg didn't see either of these opinions before Monday afternoon's ballgame. The newspaper writers had consulted Thumim *after* Greenberg had already made his decision. He didn't read Franklin's statement until a reporter showed it to him in the clubhouse following the game.

When Hank arrived at the ballpark, he asked Mickey Cochrane if he would be required to play. Cochrane, the Tigers' catcher and manager, had ignited a competitive spark in the club when he joined it at the beginning of the season. He wanted Hank to play but did not want to trespass against Greenberg's religion. The Irish Catholic manager wasn't going to make the decision for him. No, this was a personal matter the young slugger had to decide for himself.

Sitting on his stool in his dress clothes, Greenberg thought about his promise to his parents. The shofar echoed in his mind. He looked around at the empty lockers. He had sweated through five months with these guys— Marv and Billy and Charlie and Mickey and Elden—bound by the common goal of making it to the World Series. When they had reached first place and the goal seemed possible, they had drawn tighter. He couldn't go back on his teammates. He stood, undressed and slowly began to pull on his uniform.

Elden Auker, the young submariner, was on that afternoon. After giving up a run in the opening frame, he settled into fine form, yielding only three hits. He relied heavily on his infielders, letting only half a dozen balls travel to the outfield. Greenberg had eighteen putouts at first. But Gordon Rhodes was equally good for the Red Sox. Mixing his lazy curve with a streaking fastball, the Boston pitcher messed with the Tigers' bats. Six of the starting lineup failed to touch him for hits. It looked like Detroit would take the loss even with its star Jewish first baseman in the lineup.

In the synagogues around Detroit, boys slipped outside to the parking lots, where they tuned in the game on car radios, and returned by the side doors. The adults followed them with their eyes for an indication of news. At one *shul*, the cantor broke off and asked pointedly, "How's Hank doing?"

The initial reports were not positive. He flubbed the first throw to him in the field. His first two at-bats against Rhodes, Hank grounded out weakly.

He came to bat again in the seventh inning with one out and his team behind 1–0. Rhodes fired a fastball. Hank couldn't keep pace. He swung late and missed. He worked the count to 2–2. Rhodes wound up and delivered a slow curve. Greenberg hesitated a split second, then swung heavily. He connected with a mighty *thwack*! The Navin Field crowd roared immediately. The ball rocketed toward the scoreboard in left-center. Red Sox outfielders Roy Johnson in left and Mel Almada in center simply watched. They didn't bother to chase the ball. It cleared the scoreboard easily. Greenberg had tied the game. His teammates congratulated him in the dugout.

Except for that one curveball, Rhodes continued his mastery of the Tigers lineup. Auker threw two more shutout innings himself. The score remained 1–1 headed into the bottom of the ninth with Greenberg due up first. He stopped in the dugout to get a drink of cold water. Then he grabbed his Louisville Slugger and climbed the steps.

Tiger outfielder Pete Fox watched Greenberg walk toward the plate. Feeling something special about to happen, Fox edged over the dugout steps and called, "Nice hit, Hank."

Greenberg sensed it, too. He could feel a hit coming. He settled into the batter's box and glared at Rhodes. The left field bleachers stood 339 feet away. *What a swell spot that would be for a hit,* Hank thought. *Give me a fastball, and that's where I'll send it.*

Rhodes surprised him with a slow curve. Hank hadn't expected to see another one of those after hitting the last one over the scoreboard. But this one was low, and Hank laid off.

He set for the next pitch, twirling the top of his bat in a tight circle. Rhodes went into his windup. *The hell with the bleachers,* Hank thought. *I'm not going to try to pull or steer this thing. I'm just going to swing.* The right-hander released a fastball. Hank saw it coming straight down his alley. He clobbered it.

Harry Salsinger described the moment in the *Detroit News*: "Greenberg drove the ball on a line. It looked like a Bobby Jones tee shot. It was rising when it neared the fence in left-center, just beyond the scoreboard. It cleared the fence with a few feet to spare and continued on its course, still rising. It was one of the most perfect hits we have ever seen delivered in baseball."

Even before the ball landed on Cherry Street, excited fans leaped over the low wall in front of the field boxes and swarmed the field to congratulate Greenberg when he crossed home plate. A gaggle of photographers crouched on the grass to capture the image. The fans thumped his back. He pressed through the swarm with his head down. In the clubhouse, his grateful teammates shook his hand.

The fans still in the stands grinned at one another and called, "Happy New Year!" The reporters drafted their game accounts. John M. Carlisle, the *Detroit News'* Tigers beat writer, composed: "Henry Greenberg is something more off the playing field than a first baseman who has been one of the sparkplugs in the Tiger drive for a pennant. He is a finely bred young man with a high sense of duty."

Carlisle's story ran under a front page head shot of Greenberg in the shower after the game, grinning sheepishly at the photographer.

His home run drew comparisons to the mighty Babe Ruth, which were becoming more common that season: "Ruth at his best never hit a baseball to more effect or never won a ball game more dramatically than the big, conscience-stricken youngster from the Bronx did Monday," Jack Carveth penned for the *Detroit Free Press*.

"You can bet all the money that you can count against a burnt match that Detroit would never have beaten Boston on Monday without the mighty bat of Henry Greenberg," raved Salsinger, the *Detroit News* columnist. "He will hit a great many more home runs before he retires . . . but there probably will never be another four-bagger from his bat that will carry the complete thrill that he produced in the ninth inning when he lined the ball over the distant fence in left-center field and delivered the run that beat

Boston. . . . It was a critical moment in Detroit's campaign, and Greenberg was the boy who came through."

Hank would indeed hit more thrilling home runs than this one—slugging home runs at dramatic moments characterized his career—but his ninth-inning, walk-off homer on Rosh Hashanah would stand as the most monumental in the context of his heritage. Bud Shaver encapsulated the moment's significance in the *Detroit Times*: "The traditional tenacity of the world's oldest and most beleaguered people today had played its part in a pennant race—winning a ball game. . . . There was more than the mighty bone and sinew of Hank Greenberg behind those two home runs which went whistling out of Navin Field. . . . They were propelled by a force born of the desperation and pride of a young Jew who turned his back on the ancient ways of his race and creed to help his teammates."

The legend of Hank Greenberg began to take shape. Newspapers in cities across the country were quick to pick up the story of the young Jewish star's heroics in a game he almost didn't play for religious reasons. Greenberg's hero status leaped to new proportions in Detroit and around the nation. His two Rosh Hashanah home runs became as celebrated as the stones flung from David's slingshot.

But Hank was not ready to step into the role of the anointed one. Back in front of his locker in the Tigers clubhouse, doubts lingered in his mind. He told the reporters without conviction, "The good Lord did not let me down."

Yet the thought that maybe he had let his people down troubled him. After finishing his shower documented in the newspaper, Hank dressed back in his street clothes and drove home Marv Owen. "You certainly banged that last one," said Owen, who would've filled in at first base had Greenberg not played.

"I hope I did the right thing," Hank confided. "Maybe I shouldn't have played. It's a sacred day. There wasn't any way of getting a dispensation or anything. . . . I got thinking about the team, and I didn't want to lay down on the team. But it's on my conscience."

Owen stepped out of Hank's roadster, paused, and said, "I wish I had a couple of home runs on my conscience."

The next time Owen saw Greenberg was the following day in the clubhouse. This time, Hank wore his uniform but again slumped on his locker stool.

"Goddamn it, Hank, you won the ball game with two home runs, what's wrong?"

"When I got back to my hotel my phone rang half the night," Hank said. "I caught hell from my fellow parishioners, I caught hell from some rabbis, and I don't know what to do. It's ten days until the next holiday, Yom Kippur."

A guilt-ridden Greenberg wrote a letter to his parents trying to explain his decision. He apologized for going back on his word but said that the team had needed him. His mother was more understanding than his father. David Greenberg made it clear to his son that he didn't want him to play on Yom Kippur. The Day of Atonement was the most sacred day of the year.

∞

CHAPTER TWO

Bruggy: The Pride of Crotona

They weren't human in Romania, the Jews, back then. Not in the government's eyes, not in the view of society. Romanian law stripped Jews of their political rights. Denied them jobs. Barred the children from public schools. Made citizenship nearly impossible to attain. Romanian Jews by the thousands—squeezed by legislated oppression and competition from a population boom in the last decade of the nineteenth century—joined Russians and Poles fleeing to America to escape persecution and embrace opportunity.

Sarah Schwartz, a determined eighteen-year-old girl, said good-bye to her parents in Falticeni, Romania, and boarded a ship in 1900 to pursue that better life. So, too, David Greenberg, age sixteen, left his family in Roman, about fifty miles southeast of Falticeni, with the same ambitions. Strangers to one another, the two Romanian teenagers passed through Ellis Island along with more than two million Jews between the assassination of Tsar Alexander II in 1881 and the beginning of the Great War in 1914, the period of largest immigration of Jews to the United States. David found work in a textile factory in Manhattan. In the early years of the twentieth century, he met Sarah, two years his elder, at a Lower East Side *landsmanshaft*, a place where Jewish immigrants socialized with others from the same area. They married in 1906, had four children, and discovered that the oldest prejudice in history had preceded them to the New World.

The majority of Jewish immigrants settled in Manhattan. Many didn't get farther than the Lower East Side ghettoes. David Greenberg made it to Greenwich Village, where he started his family on the second floor of a tenement house at 16 Barrow Street, between Bleecker and Fourth Street. The third of David and Sarah's children was born forty-five minutes past midnight on January 1, 1911. Sarah meant to call him Hyman, but the man filling out the birth certificate did not know that name, so he wrote down "Henry."

Through high school, he went by Hyman or Hymie or Hy. He signed his senior picture in his high school yearbook, "Hy Greenberg." It wasn't until he went to get his driver's license that he discovered his official name was "Henry."

A year after Hyman's birth, the Greenbergs moved a few blocks north to a sixth-floor walk-up on Perry Street. It was a tough neighborhood. "Kids down in the Village thought the national pastime was beating up kids of other nationalities," Greenberg wrote in his autobiography. On Halloween, they whapped one another with long black stockings filled with chalk, leaving a white mark. The Irish and Italian kids loaded their stockings with ash or coal, sometimes a rock, to smack the Jewish kids. To get to school, Hymie and his older brother and sister had to pass the Irish block and risk taking a loaded stocking to the head. "Look out," Sarah Greenberg told her children when they left the apartment. "Don't get the sock!"

Frugal and hardworking, David Greenberg bought shares in the Acme Textile Shrinking Works and eventually owned the company himself. When Hymie was six, David had saved enough to move his family to the Bronx countryside, into a sixteen-room, three-story house at 663 Crotona Park North. It was a step away from the bullying and a step up economically into a middle-class, predominantly Jewish neighborhood. Hymie looked out the large front windows, past the horse-drawn wagons in the road, and saw the lush hickory trees and rolling green hills of Crotona Park.

They played baseball there. Soon young Hyman had joined the group of boys on the sandlot a block away. Every day when classes let out at Public School 44, on Prospect Avenue and 175th Street, Hymie raced home, grabbed his glove, bat and ball, and dashed off to the park, where he and his buddies played until the evening darkness made it impossible to see the ball. Weekends and summers, he played baseball all day. The days began with Hymie shaking his younger brother Joe awake. "Let's go! Let's go! We have to get going!" The two boys would eat a quick breakfast in the kitchen, stuff fruit and candy in their pockets for lunch and dash off to the field to secure their spot. That was Hymie's routine from the time they shoveled the melting spring snow off the diamond to the days when winter reclaimed it. No matter how long they played, the darkness always seemed to come too soon.

Something else was happening on that Crotona Park sandlot. Hymie wasn't simply falling in love with baseball; he was becoming an American. "Baseball guaranteed second-generation Jewish boys admission to an American childhood and confirmed their American identities," writes historian Peter Levine in *From Ellis Island to Ebbets Field*. The national pastime ushered Hymie into the culture by a means his Romanian-born, Yiddish-speaking parents couldn't.

In winter, Hymie indulged another love: basketball. He played pickup games until the park's recreation center closed at 9:00 p.m. He walked home happy, his shirt drenched with sweat under his jacket. For young Hyman, the year was divided into two seasons: baseball and basketball.

David Greenberg enjoyed a cigar and a good laugh, but he also possessed firm beliefs about how things should be ordered. He provided for the family. His wife looked after the children and the house. She mended clothes, folded laundry and kept a kosher kitchen. She baked *challah*, cooked chicken soup and lit the candles on Shabbat. The family attended religious services at the neighborhood synagogue on Friday evenings and Saturdays. And they ate dinner together at 6:00 p.m. when Mr. Greenberg arrived home from work. If someone was late, they waited. David Greenberg, who had spent the past hour riding the streetcar from the Garment District, didn't want to have to wait for one of his children. Yet that's what happened some nights when Hymie was playing baseball across the street. While the food cooled, his father's stomach rumbled and his blood boiled. Baseball threatened the family structure.

During basketball season, when Hymie came home late and hadn't done his homework, he tried to sneak in the house past his father. David Greenberg let Hymie know he did not approve of him putting sports before ·

family and school. Some nights, he stressed his point with a belt across his son's backside. Hymie got it, but the pain soon subsided, and his love of sports persisted.

When Hymie was old enough, he played on P.S. 44's baseball and basketball teams. He became a first baseman in the Public School Athletic League. He had grown fast. By thirteen, he was already six-foot-three, but his coordination hadn't caught up with his growth spurt. The coach put him at first, where he didn't have much ground to cover and was less of a liability.

Sports made school and religious studies bearable. Like other Jewish boys in the neighborhood, Hymie learned to read Hebrew in preparation for his bar mitzvah, an event of much greater significance to his parents than to him. He was smart but studied only not to disappoint his parents. They had left their families and homeland to make a better life for their children—if he forgot, they reminded him. Some mornings Hymie dragged himself out of bed as early as 6:00 a.m. to finish his homework, though his mind was less on arithmetic than on box scores.

Raised in a home where his parents spoke Yiddish and English with thick accents, Greenberg sometimes misspoke himself. One winter day after a long session of three-on-three basketball in the park, he said, "I'm gruggy," meaning groggy. His buddies pounced on the malaprop, and Hymie suddenly had a new nickname. His high school baseball coach later thought the boys were calling Greenberg "Bruggy" and accidentally dubbed him that, a nickname that outlasted his days in the Bronx.

In high school, Bruggy became self-conscious about his fumblings with language and dedicated himself to a program of self-improvement with a notebook and a dictionary. Whenever he heard a word he didn't know, he wrote it down in the notebook. Later, he looked up the word, then committed it to his vocabulary. "He was a very determined guy," his brother Joe said. "If he made up his mind that he was going to do something, he would never quit until he had it accomplished."

Bruggy was also self-conscious about his size. Tall and gangly, he could barely fold into one of the school desks. When called up to the blackboard, he heard the other kids laugh at the way he dwarfed the teacher. In the hallways, they called him "Stretch" and asked repeatedly, "How's the air up there?" When guests visited the Greenberg home, they exclaimed, "My

God, he's grown two feet in a week!" It didn't help that he stuttered and developed a severe case of acne. He slouched around in a state of near-perpetual embarrassment.

Sports became an escape. Baseball players had undergone a transformation in the 1920s, generated by the fascination that surrounded Babe Ruth. Now a baseball player could captivate the nation's attention like Charles Lindbergh, who crossed the Atlantic in the *Spirit of St. Louis* in 1927, or Henry Ford, the great automaker. The Babe had become a national hero and elevated the others along with him. The newspapers mythologized baseball players, devoting endless columns of ink to the only real professional sport of the day, and Hymie was ripe to have these legends imprinted upon his consciousness.

The October that Hymie was ten—and when he was eleven, and again when he was twelve—the Yankees played the Giants in the World Series. For three consecutive seasons, 1921, 1922 and 1923, the crosstown rivals enthralled Gotham and riveted one young boy's attention. The Giants, who won the first two of those three Series, became his team. The Yankees played on the other end of the Bronx, but that might as well have been in a foreign country. Hymie had never been to a major league game, and no one he knew had gone to a World Series game. "That luxury seemed to be reserved for people who came from Manhattan," he wrote.

The World Series aired on the radio for the first time in 1921, but the medium was in its infancy, and hardly anyone had sets to pick up the broadcasts. Those October afternoons in the early Twenties, Hymie followed the games with hundreds of others in the street outside a neighborhood store that had posted an electric scoreboard in the window. The scoreboard listed the Giant and Yankee lineups with a small bulb lit next to the man at bat. The light flashed when he got on base. With the pulse of each bulb, the action on the field unfolded in Hymie's imagination.

His parents, meanwhile, had other, more frightful images occupying their minds. Pogroms swept across Europe, including Romania in 1924. They heard of attacks against Jews back home, where student mobs at the University of Bucharest hurled Jewish students down stairwells. Sarah and David Greenberg worried about the safety of their family members and former neighbors.

Hymie saw his first professional ballgame on Sunday, May 4, 1924, when David Greenberg, who casually followed the Giants, took his thirteen-year-old son to the Polo Grounds. John McGraw's nine played a double-header against the Philadelphia Phillies. Decades later, Hymie would remember that Frankie Frisch, schooled at Fordham University and known as "The Fordham Flash," collected seven hits in the Giants' double win. In fact, the Flash, batting third and playing second base, went three-for-five and stole a base in the first game and was two-for-three in the second. Even without the embellishment of Greenberg's memory, it was a good day for Frisch, one that made a lasting impression on young Hymie from his perch in the center-field bleachers. He heard the 42,000 fans roar their approval across the cavernous Polo Grounds for the local boy each time he made good with a hit. Such could be the culmination of those days at Crotona Park. Hymie did not envision himself as a professional ballplayer then, but the seeds of a dream furrowed into fertile ground that afternoon.

One day when he was fifteen, Hymie and his buddies heard that Hugh McMullen, one of the Giants, was visiting a woman in the Crotona Park North neighborhood. McMullen was a catcher of dubious ability who spent only one regular season with the Giants, but that didn't matter to Hymie and his friends. He was a *professional ballplayer* hanging out in *their* neighborhood. They waited around to catch a glimpse of him on the street. "We were awed by anybody in the major leagues," Greenberg said.

That would never be him. Summers, Hymie drove a delivery truck for his father. He figured he would work in the family business or do something similar, maybe run his own business, when he grew up. Besides, his size worked against him. He was slow and clumsy and had flat feet. Even at first base, he had trouble navigating the few square yards he was assigned to cover. "His feet played tag with each other on occasion, and he slid with the grace of a Rocky Mountain grizzly," Joe Williams later observed in the *New York World-Telegram*.

Hymie got frustrated easily when he stumbled or struck out. At James Monroe High School, Greenberg made the baseball team as a freshman but committed so many mistakes in the field and at the plate that it pained him. Irwin Dickstein, his varsity basketball coach, observed, "He was hard to handle because he'd get depressed at nothing at all. If he was free for a shot, for instance, and a teammate neglected to pass him the ball, Henry would brood about it all game. Another kid would figure the fellow hadn't seen him. Henry, abnormally shy and sensitive, suspected he had been overlooked deliberately."

But Greenberg had something in him that wouldn't let him wallow in self-pity; he had the drive to improve himself, that Horatio Alger spirit to work his way to the top. He devoted himself to overcome his flaws. His fear of embarrassing himself pushed him to work harder than anyone else. More than anything, he hated to lose, and he wasn't going to let his defects defeat him. "No one approached the game with the mixture of loving reverence and iron determination that Henry brought to it," Ed Fitzgerald wrote in a *Sport* profile.

To work on his fielding, he played pepper for hours in Crotona Park. A buddy hit or bunted the ball to him. Greenberg caught it. Tap, catch. Tap, catch. Tap, catch. Training his eyes to follow the ball, his hands to coddle it, his feet to move under him. Over and over, he had others hit the ball to him. He kept track of how many balls he gathered in without missing. When he muffed one, he made himself start over.

To work on his hitting, he coaxed his younger brother Joe and kids around the park to pitch him batting practice and chase down the balls he hit. After a while, they begged for a turn at the plate, but Hymie didn't surrender the bat until his hands got sore, and then only for a short time until he reclaimed the bat and resumed his batting practice. He hit the covers off the balls, so he had to wrap them in electrical or adhesive tape. When that came off—taking with it some of the string—he wrapped on more tape. He spent all of his allowance on tape. The balls became heavy, which strengthened his swing.

Bruggy was a case study in self-improvement. He squeezed a rubber ball to build his forearms. He did exercises to strengthen his flat feet until his arches were black and blue. He boxed at a gymnasium to improve his coordination. He practiced getting out of the batter's box quicker. "He couldn't run a lick, but even in high school he was practicing quick starts to overcome his handicap," Dickstein said.

To improve his base running on the other end, Hymie built a sliding pit in his backyard. He bought a load of sawdust at the butcher shop and spread it on the grass. Starting in front of the house, he ran down the alley about seventy-five feet to get to full speed, then cut left and slid into the pit.

He ran that route over and over, trying different slides to perfect his technique. When his father, who prided himself on his healthy plants and fine lawn, came home from work and saw Hymie's skid marks through the sawdust on his lawn, he was horrified.

David Greenberg angrily ordered his son to get the sawdust off his grass. Hymie complied, but the next day, after his father left for work, he spread the sawdust and resumed his sliding regimen. Only this time, and in the days that followed, he was careful to clean up the sawdust before his father returned home.

In high school, Hymie showed signs of impressive power. Stories circulated about him hitting the ball so far in some city parks that no one ever found the ball. Yet he struck out frequently, overstriding in his eagerness to crush the ball. He played in the shadow of the team's better players, Willie Rosen, a flashy shortstop, and Rudy Herzog, a promising pitcher. They had a strong team, but were a good pitcher away from making a run at the city championship. The James Monroe baseball coach, Tom Elliffe, recruited Izzy Goldstein, a twenty-year-old with a mesmerizing curve.

Goldstein, whose family had escaped Tsar Alexander III's anti-Semitic policies by emigrating to America, had dropped out of high school to play semipro ball. In 1928, Elliffe, who also taught physical education, enrolled Goldstein in the eleventh grade at James Monroe High. Greenberg, who had palled around with Izzy since their days at the same grade school, became a willing accomplice in the deception. He and several teammates completed Goldstein's homework and took his tests. Elliffe's team made it to the city finals at the Polo Grounds, where Goldstein pitched a fine game, but Hymie played poorly. He failed to get a hit and let a ball through his legs for a triple. He blamed himself for the team's 4–1 loss.

Hymie's passion for sports extended beyond baseball. He lettered in four others at James Monroe High. He was a solid fullback on the soccer team that won the city championship.* For the track and field squad, he put

---

* In that game against Thomas Jefferson High in 1928, a nail got stuck in his right shoe. He kicked it to the sideline but none of his teammates had a size 14 to lend him, so one was dispatched to find a hammer to remove the nail. Since impaired cleats didn't warrant a time-out, Greenberg stalled for ten minutes by kicking the ball over the fence with his bare foot until his shoe could be repaired. That's the story recounted by the *Saturday Evening Post* anyway.

the shot. Senior year, he went out for the football team to prove he wasn't a coward. He didn't like the practices or the weather, but he caught a touchdown pass in the final game of the season against Monroe's archrival, George Washington High, which boosted his social status.

Basketball was Hymie's best sport. He was a thinker on the court, as he was on the diamond, constantly analyzing the game, trying to figure it out. He was forever asking his coach why some plays worked when others failed. In those days, the team huddled after each basket, which was followed by a jump ball. Greenberg sometimes held up the game during those huddles, quizzing Dickstein about why things had happened the way they had.

Hymie was taller than the other players and, at 210 pounds, bigger. He did not have a shooter's touch, but he used his size well defensively and pulled down a lot of rebounds at both ends. Led by Greenberg, the team captain, and another Jewish star, Shikey Gotthoffer,* the James Monroe quintet were perennial Bronx champions and won the city championship Hymie's senior year. Greenberg was heralded as the best center in New York City, a noteworthy honor.

Hymie thought he might have a future in professional basketball. In the pre-NBA era, ad hoc teams representing a community center or YHCA or social club paid players modest stipends to play games. Honey Russell, from Brooklyn, who played in over 3,200 professional games and later became the Boston Celtics' first coach, paid Greenberg anywhere from five to twenty-five dollars a game to play on his teams. That wasn't bad in the days when a pound of chicken cost forty-two cents, but Hymie figured he could make more money playing baseball.

He knew it was a long shot. When Paul Krichell, the Yankee scout from the Bronx, had attended one of James Monroe High's games to watch

---

* Gotthoffer turned pro, playing for the dominant Philadelphia SPHAs (the South Philadelphia Hebrew Association, also known as the "Hebrews") of the American Basketball League. He discovered a hostile environment. Jews became lightning rods for the ignorance and hostility emerging in America. The opposition painted coffins and hangman nooses on the parquet to intimidate them. Locals at one gym hung signs around the balconies saying, "Kill the Christ-Killers." At Prospect Hall, home of the Brooklyn Visitation, fans threw beer bottles from the balcony at the Jewish ballplayers. Often, the bigots waited outside for visiting teams and greeted the Jewish players with stones packed inside snowballs.

pitcher Rudy Herzog, the big guy on first base had attracted Krichell's attention. He asked his name but did not show further interest. Still, Bruggy thought he might be able to get a look from the Giants.

By 1920, almost a third of New York's population was Jewish. Many had taken a liking to baseball, and John McGraw, the Giant manager, saw a great, untapped potential there. "A home run hitter with a Jewish name in New York would be worth a million dollars," he told the *New York Tribune*. He had signed several Jewish players to much fanfare, including Mose Solomon, hailed as the "Rabbi of Swat" and the "Jewish Babe Ruth," but they had not lived up to the hype nor produced the anticipated profits.

McGraw thought he had finally found his moneymaker in Andy Cohen, a Baltimore-born infielder whose Jewish parents had fled the pogroms in Eastern Europe. McGraw promised, "Cohen will draw like Ruth or Gehrig." The press called Cohen "The Great Jewish Hope." On Opening Day 1928, Cohen, the Giants' starting second baseman, went three-for-four, scored two runs and drove in two more. Thousands of Jewish fans poured onto the field, lifted Cohen on their shoulders and paraded him around the Polo Grounds. He batted .350 through May and achieved immense popularity. *Time* magazine put him on its cover. The Giants had to hire additional secretaries to handle his fan mail. But not everyone was happy to see a Jew succeeding on the field. Some of the letter-writers called him "you stupid Hebe," "you showy sheeny" and "you cocky kike." Players on other teams, especially the Chicago Cubs, renowned for their vicious bench jockeying, barraged him with verbal assaults. Cohen's batting average dropped to .274, though he did help boost attendance from 858,000 to 916,000 fans that season. He had another decent year in 1929, but McGraw, unhappy with Cohen's inconsistency, sold his contract to the Newark Bears.

The Giants' failure to find a star Jewish baseball player seemed to reinforce the prevailing stereotype of the day that depicted Jews as physically inferior and incapable. Despite their success in the boxing ring, they weren't cut out for baseball, or so the thinking went. Noted baseball writer Fred Lieb, who coined the term "The House That Ruth Built," said he had received more than one hundred letters asking why there had not been a standout Jewish ballplayer. He responded with his theory that "the race had been held back in developing along baseball lines by lack of opportunity. As a rule, Jewish boys are smaller than kids who spring from other races. The Jewish boy was pushed aside on the playground diamond by the bigger youth with an Irish, German or Scandinavian name. Also, it was my contention the Jew did not possess the background of sport, which was the heritage of the Irish. For centuries, the Jew, in his individual business, had to fight against heavy odds for his success. It sharpened his wit and made him quick with his hands. Therefore, he became an individualist in sport, a skillful boxer and ring strategist, but he did not have the background to stand out in a sport which is so essentially a team game as baseball."

While still in high school, Greenberg knew about McGraw's search for a Jewish turnstile attraction. He also knew the Giants sometimes let local kids shag balls when the backup players took batting practice in the morning. Hymie thought if he could just get the chance to do that, he might be able to catch someone's eye, impress them enough to give him a legitimate tryout. He convinced his father to help him.

The elder Greenberg had a friend, Max Schneider, who was president of the Sterling National Bank and well-connected with the Giants. David Greenberg asked his friend to arrange for Hymie to work out with the Giants. David was not keen on the idea of his son playing professional baseball, but he figured this would be a good way to assess his son's possibilities. Schneider passed along the request to McGraw. For two days, David Greenberg waited outside McGraw's office for a response. It finally came. No. McGraw said the Giants had already scouted Hymie at his James Monroe games and decided the boy was too big and awkward. Not only did he stand no chance of becoming the sought-after Jewish attraction, in McGraw's opinion, Hymie Greenberg would never be a ballplayer. That wounded David's pride and discouraged Hymie, but it did not crush him. He was still determined to make a ballplayer of himself.

First, he had to convince his parents. They wanted him to enroll in college after he graduated from high school in February 1929. He had won a scholarship for his academic and athletic achievements. They expected him to use it that spring. His older brother Ben had gone to St. John's College and was on his way to becoming a lawyer. His older sister Lillian was enrolled at Teacher's College. That was David and Sarah's plan for their children. They would go to college and become professionals—doctors, lawyers, business owners—not ballplayers. In his frustration, when Hymie made the family wait to eat dinner or he didn't show interest in his schooling, David had yelled at his son that he would never make anything of himself. Sarah also unleashed her frustrations on Hymie when she thought he had lost sight of priorities. "Why are you wasting your time playing baseball?" she said. "It's a bum's game."

Hymie faced not only his parents' skepticism; he fought the cultural tide of an entire generation. Those who had left behind their families in the Old World did not intend for their children to abandon their Jewish identity in the new country, especially through the frivolous pursuit of sport. "It makes sense to teach a child to play dominoes or chess," one father, a Russian Jewish immigrant, purportedly wrote in the early 1900s to an advice columnist at the Yiddish-language *Jewish Daily Forward*. "But what is the point of a crazy game like baseball? . . . Here in educated America adults play baseball. They run after a leather ball like children. I want my boy to grow up to be a *mensch*, not a wild American runner." The father captured his generation's derision toward baseball. They viewed it at best as a waste of time and at worst as an evil influence meant to divert their children's attention from religious studies, to tempt them away from professional pursuits and to sway them from traditional values. The comedian Eddie Cantor recounts that the worst put-down a parent or grandparent could administer a child was "you baseball player, you."

But Hyman was headstrong and persuasive. He managed to convince his parents to let him play ball for six months with the promise that he would attend college in the fall.

Early each morning, he headed across the street to Crotona Park and waited until some younger kids showed up who were willing to shag balls for him. He tossed the ball up and hit it until there was someone who would pitch to him. By late morning, there were ten kids scattered around the field to track down his line drives. That became his routine, working on his stride, his swing, his timing, until the bat became fluid in his hands. The constant swinging helped him develop tremendous strength in his shoulders, arms and wrists. He would make a ballplayer of himself yet.

Hymie's size impressed the Red Bank Towners, a semipro team in New Jersey that offered him seven dollars to play a pair of weekend games. He failed flamboyantly. He struck out in four consecutive at-bats. Placed in right field with his first baseman's mitt, he felt lost and made about eight errors. On one line drive, he ran back, and the ball bounced off his head. The Red Bank Towners wrote him off as a waste of money. But the next weekend they were short a player and asked him to play again without pay. Henry held out for cab fare, $3.03, and got it. That weekend, he hit three long home runs into the woods beyond the field. "That's how I was," he wrote. "Totally erratic and inconsistent."

He continued his morning workouts at Crotona Park, where he made an enemy in an Irish police captain, Pat McDonald. A mountain of a man at six feet, five inches and 275 pounds, McDonald was a two-time Olympic champion, winning gold at the 1912 Olympics in the shot put and again at the 1920 Games in the 56-pound weight throw. After finishing his police shift at 3:00 p.m., McDonald liked to put the shot at Crotona Park. Hymie was still there with his entourage, knocking flies across the grass. Sometimes, just as McDonald was about to release one of his throws, he spied a kid running into his path intent on one of Bruggy's drives, and the Olympic champion had to stop himself from clocking the kid with the iron ball. "When this happened, he was like a mad bull," Greenberg recounted. "He was so furious that he'd chase us from time to time. We'd always claim that possession was nine-tenths of the law, and since we got there first, we were entitled to the field. He felt otherwise."

Hymie managed to outrun McDonald but had endured plenty of his verbal wrath. When he heard the familiar Irish voice in the park call him over one day in April, he responded hesitantly. Turned out McDonald had been at Yankee Stadium for the '29 opener. "Young man," he said to Greenberg, "I just came from watching the Yankees play, and by God, you hit a ball better than Lou Gehrig."

It was a tremendous compliment to the eighteen-year-old's ears, especially coming from an adversary like McDonald. Heady stuff to be proclaimed superior to the Yankee star. But the significance of the comment went even deeper. It gave young Hymie a desperately needed affirmation that despite his parents' misgivings, the Giants' rejection and his own failings with the Red Bank Towners, maybe he did have what it took to become a professional ballplayer. Just maybe.

Izzy Goldstein, Hymie's elder high school teammate, secured him another chance with the Bay Parkways, a semipro team in Brooklyn. Goldstein was pitching for the Parkways, making thirty-five dollars a game, and he told the team about a first baseman he knew. Hymie was eager himself to get paid to play. The first game, though, he was hardly noticeable at the plate, and nobody offered to pay him. The next Sunday in Sheepshead Bay, Bruggy slugged three home runs in a doubleheader and expected to be compensated.

Afterward in the locker room, George Lippe, the manager, handed money to each of the players sitting on the benches—except Hymie. He stewed about it for a moment, then approached Lippe.

"I'm not coming back anymore."

"Why not?" Lippe asked.

"I didn't get paid."

"I thought you were an amateur."

"I am an amateur," Hymie said. "But, look, Mr. Lippe, it took me two hours to get out here, and it's going to take me that long to get home. I won't be home until about eleven tonight, and I left home at eight in the morning. Besides, I had a pretty good day. I expect to get paid, or I'm not coming back."

Lippe dug into his pocket and pulled out a five-dollar bill. "Here. You come back next Sunday for the doubleheader, and I'll pay you ten dollars."

Ten dollars was a handsome payday for a kid just out of high school. Hymie happily returned the next Sunday. While the other, older players worked their day jobs, Bruggy was at Crotona Park crushing fly balls. That practice paid off on Sundays, when he started hitting long balls regularly. One afternoon, in a game against the barnstorming bearded House of David team, Hymie slugged three home runs. Paul Krichell, the Yankee scout who had noticed Greenberg in high school, happened to be in the stands that day. After the game, Krichell offered Hymie $1,000 to sign a Yankee contract. Greenberg demurred, explaining that he planned to go to college. Much as he wanted to play professional ball, he didn't want to let down his parents.

Krichell knew Greenberg could be a prospect of sizable value to the Yankees, who were as eager as the Giants to find a Jewish star. During the period between the Wars, communities felt strong affiliation with their ethnic origins. Sportswriters reflected this but also, lazily, perpetuated stereotypes with their ethnic portrayals of "the fiery Frenchman, the even-tempered Bohemian, the Buffalo Irishman, the hardworking, likable Polish recruit, the mad Russian, the chunky Hebrew lad, the only Greek in the big show." The ethnic associations furthered the idea that baseball embraced all, come from where they may. They also identified heroes for those ethnic communities and, as historian William M. Simons observes, "generated pride in ancestral heritage even as they facilitated the Americanization of their partisans by participation in the baseball melting pot." That, in turn, stimulated interest, attendance and profits.

Krichell was not about to give up easily on a Jewish kid with an unmistakable name from the Bronx who could hit the long ball. A retired St. Louis Browns catcher, Krichell had built his reputation as a Yankee scout, recruiting Tony Lazzeri, Mark Koenig, Leo Durocher, and, of course, his first big find, Lou Gehrig. After watching Gehrig, a complete unknown to him, slug two home runs for Columbia University in April 1923, Krichell had phoned his boss, Ed Barrow, and gushed that he had found the next Babe Ruth. Now he was onto another New York kid near Gehrig's equal in size and potential.

Hymie had turned down Krichell's original offer, but he did tell his parents about it. The Greenbergs invited the Yankee scout and his wife to dinner. Krichell, a portly man with a big appetite, happily accepted the invitation, even if he was more accustomed to German cooking than kosher food. He urged David and Sarah to have Hymie sign a contract with the Yankees. They weren't ready for that. They were still intent upon their son going to college. The scout's offer of $1,000 to sign and $500 a year while Hymie was in college didn't win them over. But the Greenbergs did get along well with the Krichells and invited the couple back for several meals. The family even invited Krichell to a weekend party at their summer home in Atlantic Highlands, New Jersey. The Yankee scout returned from that trip confident that he would land his man.

Greenberg had made an indelible impression on another man in the stands that day he clobbered three homers against the House of David barnstormers. Jean Dubuc, a Detroit scout who had pitched for the Tigers, noted that Hymie continued to hit at an amazing clip. Through twenty-one games with the Bay Parkways, he was batting .454. Others noticed, too. After one strong day at the plate, the *New York Times* reported, "Hyman Greenberg, youthful first baseman for the Parkways, was largely responsible for his team's victory in the opener, six runs being scored on his two circuit clouts."

Jean Dubuc knew that he faced serious competition from other teams to sign Greenberg. In addition to the Yankees, the Senators and Pirates had picked up the scent. Dubuc arranged for Greenberg to play with the East Douglas, Massachusetts, team in the Blackstone Valley League. Dubuc explained to Hymie that he could lose his amateur status playing semipro ball and forfeit his college eligibility. The amateur East Douglas team would protect Greenberg's eligibility and allow Dubuc to shelter his prospect for a longer look. Hymie hadn't heard from Krichell for two weeks and thought the Yankees had lost interest. He liked Dubuc, a soft-spoken, low-key French-Canadian Catholic from Vermont, and accepted his suggestion to join the industrial league team.

Hymie, who had known nothing but his Crotona Park neighborhood and his family's summer place in Atlantic Highlands, experienced culture shock in East Douglas, a small Massachusetts mill town fifty miles southwest of Boston that might as well have been called Schusterville. The town revolved around Walter Schuster, a tobacco-spitting baron who owned the town from the Schuster Woolen Mills to the churches and school. The baseball team was his toy. He put Greenberg up in one of his hotels and let him eat at one of his restaurants. Yet there was little for the eighteen-year-old to do between weekend games. All of the other players, except two, worked in the mill during the week. Hymie's only amusements were the pool hall two blocks away and cribbage games at the hotel with a college star on summer break and a washed-up pitcher. They were mostly long, lonely days, far from home. The team was so good—with players like Gene Desautels, Gus Dugas and Bots Nekola, all of whom would go on to play in the majors, and the veteran Doc Couillard on first base—that Greenberg didn't get any playing time. After three idle weeks, Mr. Dubuc's plan didn't look so good anymore from Hymie's spot on the bench. On a Thursday, Hymie told Winfield Schuster, the owner's son, he was going home after that Saturday's game.

Winfield talked his dad into giving Hymie a chance to play. Greenberg doubled in his debut. He also hit a tape-measure home run, connecting on a shot that got up into the wind and carried. The ball sailed over the trees beyond left field. Walter Schuster jumped up from his spot on the bench before the ball landed and almost choked on his chewing tobacco. When Hymie returned to the dugout, the owner thumped him on the back. He suddenly knew Greenberg's name.

After the game, Schuster approached his new slugger. "I understand you're going home."

"Yes, sir," Hymie said.

"Now listen to me." The owner clutched Greenberg's arm. "You've got to promise to come back for next week's game. Promise!"

"Well, I, uh—"

"We need you," Schuster said. "We've got to have you!"

He plucked a pile of five- and ten-dollar bills from his wallet and handed them to Hymie, who continued to stammer in confusion.

Schuster told his driver to shuttle Greenberg the sixteen miles to Worcester, where he could catch the train to New York. The driver arranged a Pullman berth for the overnight trip.

Greenberg settled into his sleeper—he had never ridden in one before—drew the curtains and pulled out the stack of bills Mr. Schuster had given him. He counted $175. That's what Schuster paid one of his mill workers for two weeks. He didn't pay his ballplayers, other than room and board, yet here he had given Hymie a stack of money bigger than he had ever seen before. All for a single home run. Hymie put the cash under his pillow, convinced that if he fell asleep someone would rob him. He stayed awake the whole ride back to New York. And was happy to return for the games the following weekend.

Big Bruggy was more outer borough bumpkin than savvy city slicker. One weekend when the team stayed at a rural hotel, his teammates told him it was his turn to water the hotel's rooster. Hymie dutifully went to the coop out back, fitted a rope around the rooster's neck, led it reluctantly to the lake and pushed it in—much to the delight of his teammates.

The Washington Senator scout, Joe Engel, traveled to East Douglas one week when the Senators were in Boston for a series. Engel was another ex-player who made his mark on the game as a scout, discovering Joe

Cronin, Bump Hadley, Buddy Myer, Cecil Travis and Ossie Bluege, among others. Engel invited Greenberg to take batting practice with the Senators in Boston. Hymie suited up in the clubhouse and waited his turn on the bench, awestruck by the major league players around him that he had read about and terribly anxious, a pimply-faced teen feeling out of place among men. It did not help that Walter Johnson, no longer a player but now the manager, was pitching batting practice. The Big Train, who had won 417 games and fanned 3,509 batters over twenty-one seasons, still had plenty of jump left in his fastball. Hymie stepped into the batter's box palsied by nerves.

He swung and missed repeatedly at Johnson's pitches or lamely popped them foul. Greenberg heard the regulars crowded around the batting cage grumble after each huff, "That's it! Get him out of there!" That didn't help his nerves. He kept missing pitches.

Johnson finally waved him away. Hymie had taken twenty swings without managing to hit a fair ball. That ended his Washington tryout.

When Hymie returned to New York after his season with East Douglas, Paul Krichell intensified his efforts to sign him. He brought father and son to the Yankee offices on 42nd Street and Sixth Avenue to meet Ed Barrow, the Yankee general manager.

"How would you like to play for the Yankees?" Barrow asked Hymie.

The Yankees. Combs, Koenig, Ruth, Gehrig, Meusel, Lazzeri, Durocher, Grabowski and Dickey. World Champions the past two years. Hymie didn't have to think about that very long. "I'd like to very much."

Barrow offered the Greenbergs $4,000. They didn't bite. Barrow upped the offer. David Greenberg was beginning to understand that a man could make decent money playing baseball, but he still liked his son's prospects in the world better with a college education. Sensing that the Greenbergs had an affinity for another club, Barrow switched tactics. He warned the father about letting his son play for an out-of-town club. "There are many temptations that can befall a young man," Barrow said.

David Greenberg saw the specious advice for what it was. Even if his son played for a New York team, he would encounter those same temptations on the road. "My boy can take care of himself, thank you," he said.

Barrow raised his offer to $7,500. David Greenberg told him they would go home and think about it. But the money did not tempt him. He had seen that much before. "I say in all sincerity, I would not have jumped at $50,000," he said later. "I wanted Hymie to go to college."

Barrow handed Hymie passes to several Yankee games. "Here, take these."

Krichell joined Hymie for the Yankees' last regular season game on Sunday afternoon, October 6, 1929. A defining moment for Greenberg occurred in the bottom of the first inning. Babe Ruth stood at the plate, but the cleanup hitter captured Hymie's attention. From his box seat in the front row next to the Yankee dugout, Greenberg watched the Yankee first baseman climb out of the dugout and stride over to the on-deck circle. Lou Gehrig. The 1927 Most Valuable Player.* To that point, Gehrig had been only a name to Greenberg, one he had read in the papers, that strange spelling with the h before the r, and a name bandied about sandlot conversations, the hard g's at each end slurred into one syllable. Yet there, in the flesh, close enough for Greenberg to see the sunburn on the back of his neck, Gehrig made a tremendous impression. The broad shoulders thick with muscle. The legs solid as tree trunks. Gehrig's "sheer brute strength" awed him.

Krichell leaned over and whispered to his young prospect, "He's all washed up. In a few years, you'll be the Yankees' first baseman."

Hymie saw no way he could budge this man out of the lineup, even if McDonald the shot-putter thought Greenberg could hit the ball farther. Indeed, the twenty-six-year-old Gehrig was already four years into his 2,130–consecutive game streak that began June 1, 1925. He would play another nine full seasons before he missed a game. Much as Hymie liked the thought of himself in pinstripes, he did not want to have to wait in line behind Gehrig.

"That Lou Gehrig looks like he's got a lot of years left," Hymie said.

Krichell stayed in his huckster mode. "Look at how his batting average has slipped."

True, Gehrig's average had fallen from .374 year the before, but he had still slugged 35 homers and knocked in 126 runs. He finished the year at

---

* That was the year Ruth hit 60 homers, but Gehrig had led the league in doubles (52) and RBI (a record-setting 175), slugged 47 homers, hit 18 triples and batted .373, playing every game for the Yankees—one of the greatest all-around seasons ever.

an even .300. Hymie left Yankee Stadium convinced he would not be a Yankee.

Meanwhile, Jean Dubuc had sold Walter Briggs and Frank Navin, the Tigers' owners, on signing the Bronx kid with the big swing. Hymie felt slightly indebted to Dubuc for lining up his season in East Douglas. Plus, the Tigers' rookie first baseman in 1929, Moose Alexander, a weak fielder, seemed more realistic competition for Greenberg to unseat, even though Moose had enjoyed a strong year, leading the American League in hits (215), batting .343 and slugging 25 circuit clouts. "While his fence-busting blows were attracting attention, he [Alexander] certainly seemed to me on a humbler level in baseball society than Lou Gehrig, and I felt it would be easier for me to batter down his resistance," Greenberg told a reporter in 1933.

So, when Joe Engel of the Senators came back and surprised him with a signing offer of $10,000, Hymie felt torn. That was serious money. The hitch was that Clark Griffith, the Senators' owner, wanted Greenberg to report immediately to play for $800 a month in the Washington system, which, of course, meant no college. Hymie didn't think he could sell his parents on that idea, no matter how high the signing bonus. Also, he looked at the Senators' first base and saw Joe Judge, who had finished third in MVP voting the year before, 1928, his fourteenth season with the Senators. He had batted .306, knocked in 93 runs and played in every game except one. Moreover, he was the best defensive first baseman in the league. Judge was Gehrig's opposite in size—a mere five feet, eight inches and 155 pounds— but Greenberg didn't see the possibility of displacing the Washington veteran anytime soon either. Hymie told Engel, "No, thanks."

The Tigers offered Greenberg $3,000 cash immediately and another $6,000 when he reported to the team after his freshman year of college. But his parents remained reluctant to accept. Hymie, too, wanted to go to college, mostly because that's what his parents wanted for him. He told Dubuc he couldn't take his offer. Dubuc reversed the terms, promising him $6,000 up front and $3,000 in four years, allowing him to finish college. That appealed to Hymie. He just had to convince his father.

"Pop," Hymie asked. "Are you against baseball as a career?"

David Greenberg nodded.

"The Tigers offered $9,000," Hymie said.

"$9,000?" His father whistled softly. "You mean they want to give you that kind of money just to go out and play with the baseball?"

"That's right."

"And they'll let you finish college first?"

"Yes."

David Greenberg sat down. For a moment he didn't say anything. Nine thousand dollars was more than some people made in a lifetime. "I thought baseball was a game," he finally said. "But it's a business—apparently a very good business. Take the money."

When Krichell heard that the Tigers had offered $9,000, he upped the Yankees' offer to $10,000, but that didn't remove Gehrig from the equation. Hymie accepted the Tigers' offer and headed to college.

With the scholarship he had earned at James Monroe High, Greenberg intended to attend Princeton University, where the award had originally been designated. But Princeton did not grant him admission. Colleges and universities had strict quotas for admitting Jews in the Twenties and the Ivy League was no exception.* In 1924, Princeton's administration decided 3.6 percent of Jews in the student body was excessive and trimmed its quota to two percent. The school barred African-Americans outright. Instead, Hymie applied his scholarship to the School of Commerce, a division of New York University, in the fall of 1929.

David Greenberg invested his son's $6,000 signing bonus in the American Tobacco Company. The next day, it was worth $6,800. But by the end of October, after the market crashed, his stock was worth nothing. David Greenberg was devastated, but Hymie wasn't. The Tigers' belief that he could become a professional ballplayer meant more to him than paper futures.

Still looking for any way to improve himself, Hymie supplemented his academic studies with dance lessons. The lessons helped him with his coordination, or, as the *New York Post* later put it, they "made his feet behave."

---

* After Harvard's freshman class reached a 28 percent Jewish population in 1925, the school's administration imposed a 15 percent quota. Yale's administration imposed a 10 percent quota after the percentage of Jewish students reached 14 in 1924.

When the fall term at New York University ended, Hymie worked a couple of weeks for his father, driving the company delivery truck. But when he started reading in the papers about the coming baseball season, he didn't like the idea of going back to the School of Commerce. He itched to play ball, though not for the NYU Violets. He wanted to go to Florida for spring training with the Tigers.

"Pop," he told his dad. "I've got to go down there. I've got to play."

"What?" his father said. "What about college?"

"College can come later. Right now I want to play ball."

David reluctantly consented. Hymie wrote Frank Navin a letter asking permission to join the club. The Tigers' owner mailed him a railroad ticket to Tampa.

CHAPTER THREE

A Ballplayer Named Greenberg?!

In late February 1930, nineteen-year-old Bruggy kissed his parents good-bye and boarded a train for Tampa, 1,000 miles away, farther than he had ever ventured from home. The train carried him from the snow-etched hickories of Crotona Park down the eastern seaboard to the sun-kissed palm trees of Florida. He entered a land foreign to him in its geography, climate and culture. Far away from the provincial neighborhood where most people lived their lives within a three-mile radius—many of his high school classmates hadn't ventured to Manhattan. His journey was an evolution of the emigration his parents had undertaken as teenagers: they had sought opportunity in America; he sought opportunity in America's national pastime.

Hymie became Henry in this new land. He eagerly did his calisthenics and shagged balls at Plant Field, the combination ball field and racetrack on the old Florida state fairgrounds where the Tigers trained that spring, but no one seemed to notice him. Not even when he hit towering drives the few times he was allowed to take batting practice. The veteran players did not welcome new players out to take their jobs, especially not a teenager given $9,000—more than most of them made an entire season. Players competed intensely for the few spots on the sixteen major league teams, knowing that if they didn't perform, there was always someone behind them in the ranks ready to step in. So they ignored the new kid on the field and in the clubhouse.

Henry couldn't bring himself to initiate conversation. They were older, grown men, worldly men who had traveled the country regularly by train, who could rattle off the best steakhouses in Chicago and St. Louis and Philadelphia, men who wore suits and knew how to talk to women. Bruggy had never had a date, never tasted a beer, never been west of the Hudson. He wasn't even supposed to be there. The Tigers had signed him thinking he would finish college first, that he would report after four years, when he was twenty-three, a man himself, not when he was nineteen, still a child.

These men awed him. Charlie Gehringer, who led the American League in runs, hits, doubles, triples and stolen bases the previous season; Marty McManus, who hit two grand slams in three days last July; and Fatty Fothergill, the man who'd forced the great Ty Cobb into retirement. Moose Alexander, the twenty-seven-year-old coming off his sensational rookie season, was more formidable—and didn't seem so vulnerable—in person than he had been in Henry's imagination. The only person who talked to Henry was the clubhouse boy, Alex Okray, also away from home for the first time. Bruggy felt he had more in common with Alex than Gehringer, McManus and the others. He felt as out of place among them as he did that day in Boston facing Walter Johnson for batting practice.

Henry was surprised to find himself in the starting lineup for the first exhibition game. Johnny Cooney, the Boston Brave pitcher that day, felt sympathetic toward the youngster and took Greenberg aside before the game. "Kid, I'm going to give you one you can hit."

Sure enough, Cooney served up a fat pitch that Henry knocked over the fence. That tater and a couple of fortunate fielding plays impressed one Detroit sportswriter in Florida covering spring training: "Henry Greenberg, the prize rookie, stole the show. He made a couple of sensational plays at first base. His first chance was right in the dirt and he dug it up, and his trip to the plate resulted in a home run—Babe Ruth never hit a ball harder." Heralding Greenberg as "the greatest prospect in years," he wrote that the Tigers' discovery of the Bronx youngster "was a joke on Col. Jake Ruppert, owner of the Yankees."

That sort of hyperbole did not help endear the highly paid prospect to the veteran players. They suffered no sympathetic twinges watching Bruggy strike out and pop up as he did frequently over the next six weeks.

One day during batting practice at Plant Field, Henry lined a shot back at the mound—this in the days before the pitchers worked behind protective screens—that struck the lefty Phil Page sharply on the knee. Page, in pain, hurled a ball at Greenberg and yelled, "Goddamn Jew!"

Greenberg, who had grown up among mostly Jews, had not had many ethnic insults directed at him. Shaken, he resumed his place in the batter's box, while a doctor tended to Page and another pitcher took his place. After several pitches, Henry drilled a shot over the mound that narrowly missed the replacement pitcher's head. He could hear several of the regular players complain that he was taking out his frustration on the pitching staff.

That evening, Henry took a walk by the canal near the Tampa Bay Hotel, where the team stayed. Temperamental like he had been in high school, he brooded on the isolation and disappointment he felt. Suddenly, all of the frustration of those weeks—capped by Page's nasty fury and the veterans' criticism—overwhelmed him. He broke down in tears.

Billy Rogell, the shortstop who had just joined the Tigers himself that season, happened by. "What's the matter with you?"

"I'm leaving the Tigers," Henry said. "I'm gonna quit and go home."

"You're going to let that guy run you out of baseball?" Rogell said. "Don't be silly. Go out and outplay the bastards."

That was enough to keep Henry from quitting. But when the Tigers headed north for Detroit, he found himself assigned to Hartford in the Class A Eastern League. His contract stipulated that he could not be optioned lower than the highest minor league level, but Frank Navin, the Tigers' owner, convinced Henry that he was better suited to the level of play in the A league. Henry trusted him, a knowledgeable baseball man, believing that Navin wanted to see Henry succeed to make good on his investment. Henry was savvy enough to know he needed a couple, maybe three years of seasoning in the minors before he was ready for the big leagues, but he was still humbled to have to admit that he wasn't ready to face stronger competition.

When the nineteen-year-old Greenberg arrived in Hartford, fans there expected the second coming of Gehrig. The comparisons were inevitable. Both power-hitting first basemen came from New York City following abbreviated college stints. Gehrig had played a dozen games for the Hartford

Senators in 1921 under aliases, which had breached his amateur status and earned him a year's suspension from college ball. After signing with the Yankees in 1923, he returned to Hartford under his real name. The twenty-year-old quickly became a fan favorite as the best player on a good team. His 24 home runs, .749 slugging percentage and .304 batting average in fifty-nine games led the Senators to the Eastern League championship. The popular Gehrig returned the following year, again the team's best player, tops in every offensive category, including batting average (.369), slugging percentage (.720), home runs (37), doubles (40) and triples (13) in 134 games. In what would become a familiar situation throughout their parallel careers, Gehrig became the standard for measuring Greenberg's success.

Bruggy disappointed Hartford. Batting cleanup in the opener, he went one-for-four, but he did not remain a starter in that spot. Henry found it difficult to make the transition from playing weekend doubleheaders in a pseudo-amateur league to playing every day against professionals. Aware of the expectations in Hartford and from Detroit, he perhaps pressed too hard. At any rate, he managed only a dozen hits in seventeen games, unable to bat his own weight with a measly .214 average. He spent more time in the dugout than the batter's box. He was ready to quit again. "I'm not going to stay here if I am just a cheerleader on the bench," he wrote home. He did hit a home run and a triple in one game, but it turned out to be his last in Hartford. The Senators' management had given up on him and sent his contract back to Detroit. "Few of the inhabitants mourned his passing to other fields," *Baseball Magazine* reported.

Navin assigned his high-priced gamble to the Raleigh Capitals, a Detroit farm club that played Class C ball in the Piedmont League. One writer recounted that Henry "was sent far away from there [Hartford] to Raleigh, where he could no longer annoy the Hartfordites." Henry understood Class C was a considerable demotion, but he found the players there more polished and skilled than he expected. The talent pool ran deeper into the minor league levels back then. Henry remained determined to make good on his opportunity to play professional baseball. But he continued to have trouble hitting the ball. The fans in Raleigh razzed him.

His frustration erupted in rage one day on the diamond. There early to take batting practice, he was about to step into the box when his teammate

Flea Clifton cut in front of him. They argued about whose turn it was to hit. Though Flea was, as his nickname implied, small (160 pounds and half a foot shorter than Hank), he had a lot of fight in him. He raised his bat. Hank grabbed him in a headlock. Flea smacked Hank's shins with the bat.

The other players no doubt resented Greenberg's salary, especially as the Depression began to take its toll. His $500 monthly wage made him the highest-paid player in the Piedmont League, where the average take-home pay was $225 a month. Other scouts teased Jean Dubuc for what looked to be his $9,000 flop. Greenberg heard it from players on other teams. He tried to block out the older players' jibes with the thought that when he finally made it to the big leagues they would no longer be playing baseball.

But that didn't always work. On a bus ride to Durham, North Carolina, in early July, one of the veterans, a pitcher named Dusty, studied the team's batting averages in the newspaper. "Look at you, you big bum!" Dusty shouted the length of the bus to Henry. "I'm hitting .155 and you're slugging along at a terrific pace of .151!" The other Capital players took up the taunt and ribbed Henry mercilessly the rest of the way to Durham. The criticism stung. Henry smoldered silently in his seat.

That afternoon in Durham, Henry channeled his anger into achievement. He slapped four hits in four at-bats. Driven by humiliation and the fear of failure as he had been in high school, he continued to take extra batting practice, and he continued to hit the ball. His average soon climbed over .300.

Henry had other troubles fitting in with his teammates. He was the only one from New York City. Most of them were from the rural South. Farm boys weaned on Matthew, Mark, Luke and John. Being Jewish had not been a novelty in the Bronx, where nearly 90 percent of the families and three-quarters of his high school classmates were Jewish. That had sheltered him from ignorance and bigotry, but suddenly he felt exposed. One day when Henry was on the diamond, Jo-Jo White, a teammate from a small town in Georgia, walked slowly around him, gawking at Greenberg like he was a freak in a carnival sideshow.

"What are you looking at?" Henry asked.

"Nothing," White said. "I've never seen a Jew before. I'm just looking."

"See anything interesting?"

"I don't understand it," he said. "You look just like anybody else."

Henry became constantly aware of the way he was different, which troubled him, the way being tall had marked and troubled him as an adolescent. "I felt apart from the others," he said. That was common for a Jew as a minority, observed the American novelist E. L. Doctorow: "Of all the varieties of anti-Semitism, this is perhaps the most discreetly structural in form—the lingering widespread assumption of the irreducible otherness of someone of the Jewish faith."

Baseball had been the means for Greenberg to assimilate as the son of immigrants, but being a Jew made him stand out in the national pastime as in American society, targeted for criticism, prejudice and discrimination. In the Southern towns of the Piedmont League, the fans and opponents were not discreet with their slurs and insults. "No one would ever let you forget it," he said. "You'd hear it from the stands all the time: sheeny, Jew, kike, whatever." He took those comments personally but wrote them off as small-town ignorance, counted them as isolated incidents, and did not perceive them as part of something bigger brewing, an anti-Semitism gathering momentum in Europe and America after the Great War.

There had not been many Jews in the ranks of professional baseball. Including Andy Cohen and McGraw's other experiments, only thirty-three of the thousands of major league baseball players had been Jewish before 1930. Many Jews had embraced the game as fans but not as players. There were theories to explain this, like Lieb's, that said Jews weren't inclined toward team sports, or those who said Jews were physically inferior, bookish, weak, unathletic and so on. Henry Ford, perhaps the most famous man in the world, declared, "Jews are not sportsmen. This is not set down in complaint against them, but merely as analysis. It may be a defect in their character, or it may not; it is nevertheless a fact which discriminating Jews unhesitatingly acknowledge. Whether this is due to their physical lethargy, their dislike of unnecessary physical action, or their serious cast of mind, others may decide."

Discrimination throughout the country was widely practiced and mostly unchallenged, as socially acceptable as Jim Crow laws. Newspaper classifieds blatantly advertised jobs and housing openings for "Gentiles" or "Christians only." Certain apartment buildings or communities were "restricted," meaning no Jews. It was not uncommon to see signs on Miami beaches that read "No Dogs and No Jews." Those attitudes inspired Congress to pass and President Calvin Coolidge to sign into law the Immigration Act of 1924, which effectively closed America's doors to East European Jews.

Those same attitudes turned Jews away from baseball. Bob Berman was a promising catcher at DeWitt Clinton High School in the Bronx in 1918, when Branch Rickey, then with the St. Louis Cardinals, scouted him. Impressed by Berman's ability, Rickey gave him a contract, but then he found out Berman was Jewish. Almost thirty years before Rickey became the Great Emancipator who integrated baseball by hiring Jackie Robinson to break baseball's color barrier, he didn't think the Midwest was ready to embrace Jews on the ball field. So Rickey rescinded his offer. In 1921, the Cincinnati Reds wanted Sam Cohen to play second base but convinced him to change his family name to Bohne, because, unlike the Giants, the Reds' brain trust didn't think the Cincinnati public, with its heavy German population, would embrace a ballplayer named Cohen. Other Jewish ballplayers similarly changed their names to avoid discrimination and harassment: Hymie Solomon became Jimmie Reese, Joe Rosenblum became Joe Bennett, Henry Lifschitz became Henry Bostick, Michael Silverman became Jesse Baker and several other Cohens became Cooney, Corey and Kane.

The Black Sox scandal dominated front page headlines throughout 1920 and 1921 and eroded the American public's trust in the national pastime, in much the same way Watergate later erased a generation's faith in government. Though never convicted, the Jewish gangster Arnold Rothstein was widely believed responsible for organizing and bankrolling the 1919 World Series fix. Jewish involvement in the scandal reinforced prevalent attitudes about Jews as greedy and unscrupulous.

When questions of foul play first surfaced in October 1919, the inside baseball view was articulated by *The Sporting News*, "the baseball paper of the world": "There are no lengths to which the crop of lean-faced and long-nosed gamblers of these degenerate days will go." A week later, the baseball bible defended the integrity of the Series while further denigrating Jews, arguing that rumors of a fix had to be false even though "a lot of dirty, long-nosed, thick-lipped and strong smelling gamblers butted into the World Series."

Many believed that Jews had polluted not only baseball but the American way. "The scandal exemplified to bigots how Jews were insidiously destroying the inner fabric of American society by ruining the national pastime (not to mention motion pictures and Wall Street), and thereby subverting American institutions and undermining American morality," Steven Riess observes in *Sports and the American Jew*.* These attitudes greeted Henry Greenberg to the baseball world.

Being a minority also attracted attention to Greenberg from the Jewish community. After Henry had been in Raleigh for a couple of months, a Jewish baseball fan invited him to a Friday night Shabbat dinner. Henry had not received any other dinner invitations. He gladly accepted. When he arrived, he quickly realized the gentleman and his wife had not invited him simply to eat *challah*. They introduced Henry to their daughter and left the two alone after dinner. Henry graciously took the girl out for a movie and a soda. It was his first date. Still shy around girls, he did not ask her out again.

By the time the Raleigh Capitals' season ended, Henry had batted a respectable .314, with 26 doubles, 14 triples and 19 home runs. The home runs confirmed Greenberg's power, and the batting average showed he could hit consistently, but, more than anything, the three-baggers encouraged Detroit's management that Henry could overcome his liabilities. "If the big boy could get himself 14 triples, he wasn't dragging too heavy an anchor," Ed Fitzgerald wrote in his *Sport* profile. "He could move."

Navin summoned Greenberg to Detroit to join the Tigers for the final three weeks of their season. Henry happily packed up the Model A Ford he had purchased for $375. During the drive to Michigan, he no doubt thought about making an impression at Navin Field. The Tigers were in fifth place, twenty-five games out of first, their season virtually over, and Hank figured manager Bucky Harris would give him a lot of playing time.

Bucky Harris had other plans. Harris had been a scrappy second baseman for the Washington Senators discovered by the same Joe Engel who

---

* Ironically, the only Jewish owner of the day, Barney Dreyfuss, who owned the Pittsburgh Pirates and had conceived the World Series, was widely respected for his integrity.

had scouted Greenberg. Promoted to player-manager in 1924, the twenty-seven-year-old Harris led the Senators to a World Series victory as the youngest manager in the big leagues and was heralded as the "Boy Wonder." Navin recognized in Harris a kindred smart baseball man and hired him to lead the Tigers for the 1929 season. With his second season in Detroit drawing to a close, Harris was not interested in auditioning young players like Greenberg. He wanted to bump his fifth-place team up to the first division and into the year-end money. So Harris planted Greenberg on the bench and ignored him.

In a repeat of spring training, the veteran players snubbed him, too. When it was Henry's turn to take fielding practice at first base, Earl Whitehill, the thirty-one-year-old, red ass Tiger pitching ace, decided to work on covering the base. That left Henry to throw a ball against the outfield wall by himself, cussing Whitehill with each toss. In the clubhouse, Waite Hoyt, who had joined the Tigers that year midway through his twenty-one-year Hall of Fame career, had the locker next to Henry's but did not acknowledge him. It was part of the psychological warfare waged on the new guys. "That was the way they treated rookie ballplayers in those days," Greenberg wrote. "If anything, they made you feel as self-conscious and conspicuous as they possibly could because you posed a threat to their jobs."

After a week on the bench, Henry finally saw action on Sunday, September 14, when Harris picked him to pinch-hit for the pitcher in the bottom of the eighth, with the Tigers hopelessly trailing the Yankees 10–1. Henry picked up his bat and waited his turn in the on-deck circle. The Yankee players—Ruth, Gehrig, Lazzeri, Combs, Chapman—looked more imposing from the field than they had from the Yankee Stadium box seats that day almost exactly a year ago. Future Hall of Famer Red Ruffing towered above him on the mound. Henry felt hopelessly out of place. *What am I doing here?*

The crowd of nearly 22,000 at Navin Field got their first look at the "greatest prospect" that afternoon. Henry popped up weakly to Ben Chapman, the second baseman. He trotted back to the dugout once again feeling like a failure and certain everyone in the stands regarded him as a "gawky freak."

Henry hoped for another chance the final two weeks of the season. He figured Harris would put him in at least one or two games of the eleven left. But he didn't get in the next game or the one after that. He kept asking Jean Dubuc, who had become a coach with the Tigers in 1930, when Harris would give him a chance. "Don't worry," Dubuc told him. "You'll get in again."

But he didn't. Finally, the morning of the last day of the season, Henry loaded up his Model A for the long drive back to New York and headed to Navin Field. He dressed in good spirits. In a meaningless game like that afternoon's against the White Sox—with the first division out of reach—managers usually started their minor league players. Henry was surprised—and then angry—not to find his name in the lineup posted on the clubhouse bulletin board. He read instead Moose Alexander's name at first base and batting fourth. Alexander was having another solid season at the plate, batting .326, but it didn't make sense to Henry that Harris would start his regulars. He figured Harris would let Alexander bat once or twice, then put him in. That didn't happen either. Henry watched Moose bat three times, slugging his twentieth homer of the season. With each at-bat, Henry's anger intensified. Harris seemed to have no intention of giving him a chance.

Finally, before the start of the eighth inning, Harris said to Greenberg, "Get in there and play first base."

By then, Henry's anger was too far gone for him to think straight. He stood up hastily and banged his head against the dugout roof. "I ain't gonna play for this team," he snarled at the manager. Greenberg stomped past him and the team and down the runway. In the clubhouse, he quickly shed his uniform and pulled on his street clothes. He marched out to the parking lot and gunned his Model A toward New York.

"He had a short fuse," his brother Joe said. "A low boiling point."

Back in the Bronx, Henry encountered a variety of reactions. To his buddies and other young people around the neighborhood who knew he had been away playing professional baseball—but didn't know the particulars of how his season had ended—Greenberg was a celebrity. To his parents' generation, he was a failure, the only one of the four Greenberg children not to graduate from college. "Jewish women on my block would point me out as a good-for-nothing, a loafer, and a bum who always wanted to play baseball rather than go to school," Henry said. "Friends and relatives sympathized with my mother because she was the parent of a big gawk who cared more for baseball than school books. I was Mrs. Greenberg's disgrace."

To a local Irish policeman, he was simply an anomaly.

The cop pulled Henry over for running a red light. Giving the Model A with the North Carolina plates the once-over, he asked, "What do you do for a living, young man?"

"I'm a professional ballplayer."

The cop looked again at Henry's driver's license and laughed. "Who in the hell ever heard of a professional ballplayer named Greenberg?!"

Returning to familiar surroundings after eight months away from home, Henry felt himself changed, less the child who had left and more a man like those he'd been among. He spent that winter he turned twenty sleeping late, playing handball at the YMHA on 92nd Street in Manhattan and going out to dinner and the movies or theater in the evenings. There was no thought of returning to college; he was a ballplayer now. "It might seem a little premature to say, but at the time I felt I was becoming a man of the world," he wrote. Though he still had plenty to learn, he had broken from the provincial constraints of his neighborhood and realized that something greater awaited him beyond its limits, for better or worse.

In early 1931, Henry received Mr. Navin's orders to report to Beaumont, Detroit's Class A team, for the month of March, then to join Evansville, the Tigers' Class B team, when its season began in April. Enclosed was a contract for $300 a month—a 40 percent pay cut. Henry did not sign. Instead, he wrote the Tiger owner a letter. Henry told Mr. Navin he didn't think he had received a proper chance in Hartford to prove himself and that he belonged in Class AA ball. Also, he complained that Bucky Harris had not played him in Detroit during September.

Frank Navin was a sharp businessman passionate about baseball. He had been a thirty-one-year-old lawyer turned accountant in 1902 when his boss, Detroit insurance agent Samuel Angus, took over the Detroit Tigers and appointed Navin his business manager. In that role, Navin became the team's "secretary, treasurer, business manager, farm director, chief ticket seller, advertising manager, and any other position that demanded immediate attention." Navin, also an avid gambler, bought a $5,000 share in the team with his winnings from an all-night poker game. The following year Angus gave up on the Tigers as a losing venture, and Navin convinced lumber baron William Clyman Yawkey, the richest man in Michigan, to buy the team. When Yawkey died unexpectedly, Navin persuaded his son, Bill Yawkey to complete the deal and let him run the team.

In his first coup, Navin spent $750 on an eighteen-year-old outfielder from Georgia. The Tiger players had watched the youngster play some exhibition games and hadn't seen the promise Navin had. They heckled the young Georgian when he joined the team in late 1905, but eventually the kid, Tyrus Raymond Cobb, proved Navin's acumen for baseball and business. Navin wanted Baltimore's Hughie Jennings to manage his team, but Ned Hanlon, who controlled the Baltimore club, demanded $5,000 for the shortstop-manager. Noting that Baltimore had signed Jennings as a player before appointing him manager, Navin drafted him as a player for the standard $1,000 draft price and named him the Tigers' new manager in 1907. The man who became known for his shrill cry "Ee-Yah!" promptly led the Tigers to three consecutive pennants, helped, of course, by the competitive play and remarkable hitting of Ty Cobb.

The team's success stoked the city's interest in baseball, making the Tigers the best draw in the league. With his earnings, Navin purchased almost half of the company's stock from Yawkey. When Yawkey died of the Spanish flu in 1919, Navin enlisted automobile magnates John Kelsey and Walter O. Briggs as partners to buy out Yawkey's share. After Kelsey died in 1927, Briggs and Navin owned the team fifty-fifty, but Briggs stayed in the background while Navin ran the team.

Navin became famous for saving money wherever possible. He could be charitable, giving cash to players in need, but he did so out of the public eye. His players called him "hard-boiled" and "a nickel-nurser" with justification. In 1924, he fined Charlie Gehringer three days' wages for time missed on the field to attend his father's funeral. Many baseball owners had amassed their wealth in other businesses that could subsidize their ball clubs. Not Navin. "Navin's niggardliness in negotiating annual player contracts was legendary, but understandable," Richard Bak writes in *Cobb*

Would've Caught It. "His personal and business fortunes were tied directly to the number of fans who walked through his turnstiles and the number of peanuts and hot dogs they consumed."

Navin, who had invested his profits in the stock market, watched his worth plummet with the market in 1929 and 1930. He had tried to recoup his losses at the track, but lost there, too. The stress caused him ulcers and chest pains. His doctor recommended he sell the Tigers and retire to a calmer life. Navin refused to abandon his love, even if it cost him his life. "I'll stick around until we win a world championship," he told his friends.

Come 1931, when he received Greenberg's unsigned contract and letter, Navin had lost so much money that he had to borrow the funds to send his team to Sacramento, California, for spring training. He feigned no sympathy for the twenty-year-old's grievances. "I think it is foolish for you to talk about Double A baseball," Navin replied. "You would not have been retained at Raleigh last year were it not for the fact we are interested in that club and insisted that they keep you. . . . Relative to the bad treatment you received in Detroit, we took you to Detroit so you could get acquainted with major league surroundings and not to play ball, thinking it might help you. If it had come about that Manager Harris could have used you in a game, he would have undoubtedly done so. It seems to me it comes with rather poor grace from a boy who has just made good in Class C to criticize a manager of Harris' well-known ability. . . . So far as I am concerned, if you do not see fit to accept the contract tendered you by the Beaumont Club that is a matter entirely up to you."

Henry swallowed hard and signed. Come late February 1931, he once again left his home in the Bronx, this time driving his Model A Ford four and a half days southwest to Orange, Texas, about thirty miles east of Beaumont, where the Exporters trained. Henry wanted to make the Beaumont team and spend the summer in the Texas League playing Class A ball. But he found Ray Fritz on first base in Beaumont, two years his senior and coming off a strong season in Evansville. Henry quickly realized the Exporters did not intend to keep him. He was there just to get some extra practice time until the Evansville Hubs began play in April. Beaumont gave him three chances to pinch-hit—he failed to get a hit—then sent him north to Indiana.

Even though he had seen it coming, the demotion came as a blow. Had he stuck with Beaumont, Henry would have made an extra $100 a month. The privileged $500 monthly wage from the previous year was gone. He had been taken down several notches, put on par with his teammates and become "just another sweaty slave in the Tiger chain." But he wasn't discouraged only about the pay cut. Unlike most of the other players of those days in the minor leagues, for whom baseball was the bootstrap out of a dead-end mining town or off a struggling farm, Henry had come from a comfortable middle-class background. He was not motivated by economic necessity. No, he was inspired to overcome his size, which made him stand out, and the awkwardness that came with it. He burned with the desire not to fail. Especially at this, baseball, his passion, and the path he had chosen. Having forsaken college, he wanted to prove to himself and to his parents that he wasn't wasting his time in a quixotic pursuit. Now twenty, he considered that summer in Evansville his last chance.

Henry reported to the Evansville Hubs in the Illinois-Indiana-Iowa League, better known as the Three-I League, perhaps more driven than any other player on the team. He continued his practice of arriving early at the field to work on his fielding and batting. The extra work started to pay off. He began to hit with more consistency, including the long ball. But he also continued to make mistakes at the plate and in the field, which sent him into a funk. Unexpected situations tripped him up, and he berated himself for his mental errors. He tended to keep his frustrations to himself. While others noticed him moping, he was not one to talk about his troubles. Sometimes, though, his frustrations erupted, and others took the brunt of them.

That happened in the division championship in Quincy, Illinois. Cap Crossley, the Indians' older third baseman, had been jawing at Henry all day. He got under Greenberg's skin. When Henry slid into third base, he let Crossley know what he thought of his remarks. Soon the two were shouting in each other's faces. Their teammates broke it up before Henry clobbered the smaller Crossley, but he had incensed the Quincy fans. They jumped onto the field after the game and yelled viciously at Henry. His teammates rushed him into the dugout and, with the angry mob waiting for him outside the clubhouse, shielded him on the way to the bus.

In Evansville, Bob Coleman, who had been unspectacular as a catcher during sixteen seasons in the minors and parts of three in the majors but proved sympathetic as a manager, learned to handle his temperamental power hitter and first baseman with gentle instruction and regular encouragement. "I'd feel dismally blue, and he would come along with an optimistic pat on the back," Greenberg said. "When I blundered and made mental mistakes, [Coleman] could point out the errors without making me feel like a fool. We would go over these plays and discuss what should have been done and why, sanely."

That was an important part of Henry's maturation as a ballplayer, being able to trust and learn from his elders. He also became comfortable with his teammates. On long bus rides to games in Indiana, Iowa and Illinois, he often rode up top, with the luggage and several other players, where they napped or chatted. Other times, inside the bus, the players passed the miles singing tunes like "Let Me Call You Sweetheart" and "Sidewalks of New York." Evenings, they sought the coolness of someone's basement, where they drank beer and rehashed that day's game. This was during Prohibition, but the beer was easy to procure. "Looking back on it now, it was a great period in my life," Greenberg wrote.

When summer ended, Henry posed with his foot on the running board of his well-polished Model A, dressed in a snappy sport coat, pressed slacks and two-tone shoes, his hair slicked back smartly, looking every bit the successful young man he was becoming. He had made a respectable showing in Evansville, hitting .318 with 15 home runs, 10 triples and a league-high 41 doubles, and pacing the league in putouts and assists as the Hubs' regular first baseman. At the same time, he led the league in errors, making twenty-five in 126 games. In light of the Depression, the owners decided at their winter meetings to trim the active player rosters from twenty-five to twenty-three players, reducing their expenses but also reducing the number of jobs available in the big leagues. Henry had not sparkled enough to earn a spot on the parent club's shrunken roster, but his performance established him as one of the Tigers' legitimate prospects and secured a promotion to Beaumont the following summer.

Henry worked out over the winter playing handball. He ventured into Manhattan to amuse himself. And he ate the Shabbat dinner with his family. He knew how much that meant to his mother. "That was to her a good part of her joy in life," Henry's brother Joe said. "As boys, we were led to understand that on Friday night, regardless of what we were doing, we were supposed to be cleaned, washed up and ready to sit down for a traditional Friday night of Mother's cooked dinner. Even as we grew older, we would race back to get home to be sure we would be at the dinner table when my mother served the Friday night dinner."

Henry didn't like the contract that the Tigers sent him calling for a pay cut from the $400 promised him last season if he had made the Beaumont team to $350. In what would become a pattern over his career, Henry advocated for better pay, showing precocious skills in those days before agents dominated the scene. The twenty-one-year-old wrote Frank Navin a letter on March 5, 1932, threatening to quit if he did not pay him better.

Navin responded promptly. He reminded Greenberg that the country was in a Depression and the Tiger players—major leaguers—had taken pay cuts themselves. Then the gambler called Greenberg's bluff: "Now, I am going to tell you something for your own good. If you want to get out of baseball, do so and it will be all right with everyone concerned, but don't write to any club owner telling him you are going to quit unless you are satisfied because not one ballplayer in a thousand quits, no matter what their salary is, at least until they have reached the major leagues. The less said about quitting the game the better it will be for you unless you have actually made up your mind to quit."

So, that spring, Henry reported to Texas with a humbler contract, but not with misgivings. The Texas League was a rung up the ladder, that much closer to the major leagues. He was making steady progress, which gave him hope. He knew if he did well in the Texas League, he could make it to the big leagues. The Beaumont team traveled to games in distant cities like Dallas by train, which was better than by bus, but still carried the hardships of the minor leagues. In the days before air-conditioning, the train cars were hot and stuffy, yet when someone opened the windows for relief, cinders blew in, coating the passengers in soot. "But it was plush for us players traveling by train," Greenberg wrote. "It was one step closer to the dream of playing major league ball where all the teams traveled by train."

The competition was also better, which presented challenges for Henry, especially at the plate. He was almost defenseless against the chest-high fastball, a pitch other power hitters—at least those in the majors—crushed. New situations continued to confound him, prompting offensive and defensive blunders. He also continued to suffer bouts of frustration. He found in Del Baker, the Beaumont manager, someone equally as patient and nurturing as Evansville's Bob Coleman. Baker calmly discussed situations with Henry and provided opportune pats on the back.

Still, Henry's errors sometimes had costly consequences to his teammates. Twenty-two-year-old Lynwood Thomas Rowe had joined the Exporters that season bursting with confidence. The hard-throwing, lanky right-hander from Arkansas ripped off half a dozen straight wins. He boasted that he planned to win every start that season. Schoolboy, so named after outpitching his coach in a semipro game, was on the mound in Houston, bottom of the ninth, score tied, looking to extend his winning streak. With a runner on third and one out, Henry moved in with the rest of the infielders, prepared to cut off the run. The batter hit a sharp grounder to first. The play—as any Little Leaguer could tell you—was to throw home to stop the winning run from scoring. For a split second, though, Greenberg's mind wavered. He thought he could make the force at the bag, then throw home in time to catch the runner. He couldn't. By the time his throw reached the catcher, the Houston runner had crossed the plate to win the game. His gaffe had spoiled Schoolboy's winning streak.

Instantly ashamed, Greenberg headed off the field toward the third-base dugout. Schoolboy remained rooted on the mound. "C'mon, Schoolboy," Henry said. "The game's over."

"I ain't leavin'," the young pitcher muttered. "They can't beat Schoolboy Rowe on a play like that. Schoolboy don't lose games like that!"

Henry took him by the arm. "C'mon."

But Schoolboy stood firm. Tears leaked down his cheeks. "It can't be over."

The Houston fans that milled by the mound stared at the tall, sobbing pitcher and the equally tall bonehead consoling him. Henry already felt terrible; Schoolboy's reaction intensified his shame. He dragged Schoolboy off the field and into the clubhouse.

Other than Dallas, the eight teams of the Texas League played in small towns like Beaumont. Henry hadn't been sure what to expect in the Lone Star State, thinking maybe he would encounter cowboys and Indians. In fact, it wasn't unusual to see people strolling the sidewalks with guns tucked into holsters slung around their waists, but in places like Fort Worth, Houston, Tyler, Shreveport, Longview and Galveston, it was more common to come across small-minded people who had never seen a Jew. Many of them clung to the views propagated during the Twenties that the Jews were out to subvert Christian values. Such fears had bolstered the membership of the Ku Klux Klan throughout the previous decade to an estimated peak of six million members.* Beyond actual physical attacks against Jews, the Klan spread a pervasive spirit of animosity. Henry did not receive any direct threats, but he did feel conspicuous as a New York City Jew in the Texas League. Again, he felt acutely his "otherness."

Even though Beaumont was a town so small it had only two restaurants, it had a strong Jewish presence. Henry found a synagogue where he attended services. More than a thousand miles away from home, he went to *shul* voluntarily, finding there some familiarity from his past in an otherwise strange territory. He also continued to observe the holidays away from home, seeking matzo at Passover.

Oil money had filled the pockets of the townspeople, and they shared that with the players. When one made a good play—didn't matter whether he played for the home or visiting team—the fans tossed silver dollars on the field, and all of the players scrambled for the coins in a comical sight.

Henry continued to show up early for extra fielding and batting practice. You could take the boy out of Crotona Park, but you couldn't take Crotona Park out of the boy. Usually, he was the only player on the field. He couldn't figure out why the other players, who all fancied themselves as eventual major leaguers, weren't out there with him, working to make it to

---

* The summer of 1924, Orval Baylor, minister of the Richmond Street Christian Church in Cincinnati, wrote on church letterhead to the Reds, requesting a "Klan Day," when KKK members would present floral bouquets to the managers and players of the Reds and visiting Giants. Rev. Baylor boasted Klan membership exceeding 100,000 members in the southern Ohio, southern Indiana and northern Kentucky area. The Reds declined.

the next level. "There were other guys who had more ability, but he worked harder," says Allen Fox, a sports psychologist and author of *The Winner's Mind*. "That tells you something about the difference between the great athletes and the would-be great athletes. Henry had the mind of a champion, and the others didn't."

Having filled out to six feet, four inches and 215 pounds and found his stroke, Henry was developing a reputation as the slugger to see. He became an attraction not just in Beaumont, but on the road, as well, which was unusual in the Texas League during the early Thirties. "Back then, there were very few times when a minor league player would attract fans," said George Schepps, former owner of the Dallas Steers on the eve of Greenberg's induction into the Texas Baseball Hall of Fame in 1983. "Usually, it was a club or a rivalry that attracted the fans. But when Beaumont was on the road, Henry Greenberg was a drawing card. He was a tremendous home run hitter, and people came out to see him. He earned his paycheck."

Henry was also developing a reputation as an aggressive player. In the ninth inning of a muddy game in Dallas, Henry hit a ground ball to the left side that the Steers' shortstop fielded and flung to first, but his throw bounced to the left of the bag. Zeke Bonura, the Steers' six-foot, 210-pound first baseman from New Orleans, stepped into the base path to take the throw. Henry chugged down the line with nowhere else to go. He ran over Bonura. The former college football player got up and punched Greenberg in the face. Schoolboy Rowe, a big lad himself who'd been coaching first, decked Bonura with a right. "Within five seconds, fists are flying like snow in Switzerland," the *Laredo Times* reported. The benches emptied. The crowd jumped into it. The umpires needed more than five minutes to influence a truce. According to Del Baker, the Beaumont manager, "Greenberg was the last man to stop fighting."

The next day, an angry mob crowded the Dallas ballpark.* Someone warned Henry not to go into the home team's clubhouse, as was the custom, to

---

* "Dallas and Beaumont were mortal enemies," Flea Clifton recounted in *Cobb Would've Caught It.* "When we came to town, they always put us in hotel rooms where the most noise was. There'd be those bucket brigades outside your window, banging on pots and pans and buckets all night, trying to help their team out."

change his sweaty undershirt after taking infield practice. He might get hurt. The umpire kept the peace that day with a six-shooter strapped prominently to his side.

The Exporters had a strong team that season, stocked with future big league talent. In addition to Greenberg and Rowe, Flea Clifton, Pete Fox, Frank Reiber and Izzy Goldstein, Henry's childhood friend and high school teammate, wore Beaumont uniforms in 1932. Henry and Izzy roomed together early in the season until April, when the Tigers summoned Goldstein, who was 6–1 with a 1.58 ERA. The Exporters beat the Steers to win the league championship and face Chattanooga in the Dixie Series. On September 20, Henry hit a solo home run in the first game and backhanded a throw in the eighth to save Beaumont's 1–0 victory. His performance for the day was the biggest thrill of his young career, but the Exporters folded after that. Henry batted .200 and struck out four times in the remaining four games, all won by Chattanooga.

The season had been a success for Henry. He still missed often with his big swing—finishing with a respectable though not spectacular .290 average—but when he did connect, the ball knew it. With 344 total bases on 174 hits, he averaged two bases a hit. Playing every inning of the Exporters' season, he led the league in runs, total bases, extra bases, home runs and fielding chances. He was named the Texas League's Most Valuable Player. The Dallas sportswriters, still upset about Greenberg's fight with Bonura and perhaps reluctant to concede a Jew the best player in the league, refused to acknowledge their rival as the best, so they named one of their own, Steers' second baseman Byrne James, the league MVP.

The hope Greenberg had felt traveling by train, as though foreshadowing his days in the big leagues, seemed well placed. After three years in the minors, he had finally proven himself ready for a shot in the majors with his breakout season in Beaumont. But the contract sent by Frank Navin, which arrived the week Henry turned twenty-two, was not the birthday present Henry expected. It called for him to make $500 a month to play with the big league club, only $150 more than he had made the previous year playing Class A and the same amount he had made three years previous.

Baseball, like America itself, had fallen on hard times. In 1932, with the Depression peaking, 15 million workers were without jobs. Attendance at major league baseball games dropped from a then–twentieth century high of 10.1 million in 1930 to 8.1 million. It would plunge in the following year, 1933, to 6.3 million. The fan base in Detroit shrank when men and their families left to find work elsewhere—the city lost nine percent of its population. Some who stayed were so desperate to feed their families they stole biscuits from the dog pound. They could not afford to go to ball games. The Tigers would average little more than 4,100 fans per game at the 26,000-seat Navin Field. The obvious result was that owners like Navin had less to pay their players. The average player's salary dropped from $7,500 in 1929 to $6,000 in 1933. Commissioner Judge Landis took a $25,000 pay cut himself.* Still, Henry didn't like the terms Navin offered him.

Worse, though, was the bomb Navin dropped in his letter that accompanied the contract. Moose Alexander, once Henry's competition, had been traded to the Red Sox. The Tigers had invested an enormous amount, $75,000, to replace the error-prone Alexander with Harry Davis, a smooth fielder who'd batted .269 with 32 doubles and 13 triples and scored 92 runs in 1932. Since he was left-handed, Davis was not suited to play any position other than first base. Bucky Harris had lobbied for Davis and was committed to him. Navin's letter outlined Harris's plan to turn Henry into a third baseman. "I feel it would make considerable difference on our club if you can make third base, providing you can hit major league pitching the same as minor league pitching."

Third base?! Henry hadn't played third base since grade school, and then he had done so poorly. He was not a third baseman; he was a first baseman. Henry returned the contract unsigned with a terse letter of his own.

Navin's response was more conciliatory than his replies in previous years. He acknowledged that Jack Zeller, head of the team's minor league operations, thought Henry would make the Detroit team and admitted his

---

* The average wages for workers across all industries had fallen to $1,064 by 1933, a 25 percent drop from 1929.

weak negotiating position. "You know we could not put you out another year on option without losing title to you." He offered Greenberg a contract for $600 a month. Henry signed that one and headed to spring training in San Antonio, Texas, though his status with the club was still uncertain. It would also be the first time he faced the Tiger players since he had quit the team at the end of the 1930 season "in my great moment of shame."

CHAPTER FOUR

---∞---

The Elusive Hebrew Star

In January 1933, Adolf Hitler became Germany's chancellor. Two months later, Heinrich Himmler, the police president of Munich, commissioned the construction of a prison at a vacant Dachau munitions factory that would become the prototype for future Nazi concentration camps. Meanwhile, Henry Greenberg headed to San Antonio for spring training with the Tigers.

"Kid, I'm glad to see you," Bucky Harris welcomed the twenty-two-year-old. "You're gonna be my third baseman."

"I don't know how to play third base," Henry said.

"There's nothing to it," Harris said. The manager had no plans to move his pet Harry Davis off first. "You get out there and practice, and you'll do a great job."

What could Greenberg do? He borrowed a fielder's glove, which was too small, and headed out to third base, puzzling over how to work the fingers on the strange glove. In customary fashion, Henry worked hard to get the hang of playing third, but without much success. The ball comes off the bat differently at the opposite corner. That gave Greenberg problems. He stumbled over his flat feet, struggled to position his large frame and paddled ground balls with his unfamiliar glove. He threw the ball too hard at the second baseman, Charlie Gehringer, in his haste to turn double plays and was too slow in fielding bunts. Harris simply wired the Philadelphia Athletics to request a copy of Jimmy Dykes's glove, the largest of any infielder in the league.

Henry continued to work out at third but sat out spring training games, frustrated that Harris didn't give him a look at first base. "Why doesn't he give me a chance to fight for the job?" he asked. "I don't care how good this Davis is. I am willing to battle him for the position."

Harris finally played Henry at third in an exhibition against the University of Texas. On a ground ball into the hole, Henry cut in front of shortstop Billy Rogell, who had the ball lined up, and booted the grounder. On another ground ball with a force possible at second, Greenberg fired a throw that nearly blasted Gehringer into right field. The next day, Henry wasn't on the list to make the trip to an away game. Harris didn't talk to him for ten days.

Henry chafed under the silent treatment. "The hell with it," he said to his former Beaumont manager, Del Baker, who had become a Tiger coach. "I don't know how to play third base, I'll admit it. If they don't expect me to make errors there, they're crazy." He abandoned his fielder's glove for his first baseman's mitt and began working out at first base, fielding Baker's fungoes well after the other players had left. A newspaper reported asked him, "How long are you going to keep that coach out there hitting fungoes?"

"Until I can field first base as well as Harry Davis," Henry said.

"That'll be a long time," the writer said and walked off.

The week before Opening Day, the Tigers stopped in Norfolk, Virginia, on their way north to play a pair of exhibition games against the Giants. Harris visited his family in Washington and left Baker in charge of the team. Baker gave Greenberg the chance to play first base. Henry was flawless in the field and went three-for-eight, including two doubles, though he also struck out twice and got caught in a rundown between third and home after a base-running blunder. Still, he figured he had done well enough for Harris to play him at the Polo Grounds in two more exhibition games against the Giants. His parents came to watch with other family members and friends. But Harris was unmoved. He put Davis at first and left Greenberg on the bench.

To Greenberg's relief, none of the players who had witnessed his "great moment of shame" when he quit in a huff at the end of the 1930 season teased him about it. The only reference Harris made to the past was in his comment to the Detroit newspapers: "Greenberg is a much better ballplayer than when he was with us before. He will be a handy man to have around if anything happens to Harry Davis." Harris had abandoned his plans to use Henry at third—Marv Owen, back with the Tigers after a year of seasoning in the International League, where he was named MVP, had won that job.

Harris hadn't committed Greenberg to the Tigers' roster. There was no doubt about the young man's power, but his hitting had been inconsistent. Since Detroit couldn't farm out Greenberg again without losing him, the sportswriters speculated the team would trade its young prospect.

Tiger fans in Detroit read one sportswriter's assessment of Henry as "a big sweaty kid who looked pretty grotesque." He dismissed Greenberg as too large, a player destined to grow fat and slow. Even though Henry had some impressive hits, the writer figured that was only because the pitchers were rusty in spring training; once they found their groove, Henry wouldn't stand a chance against them. Greenberg arrived in Detroit with his confidence shaken and his place with the team tenuous.

The city of Detroit traces its beginnings to the day in July 1701 when Antoine de la Mothe Cadillac beached his fleet of canoes at one of the narrowest stretches of the Detroit River, a strategic spot to control the area's lucrative fur trade. The French explorer was also attracted to the bountiful chestnut and plum trees, grapevines and bears "by no means fierce and exceedingly good to eat." He built Fort Pontchartrain, and others settled there. Two hundred years later, in 1899, Ransom E. Olds built the country's first automobile factory, the Olds Motor Works, and men named Buick, Chevrolet, Chrysler, Dodge and Packard began to amass their fortunes in the industry that formed the economic backbone of the city and put Detroit on the map. In thirty years, the city's population boomed from 200,704 to 1,563,662 residents, many of them attracted from around the United States and other countries to the plentiful factory jobs, making Detroit America's fourth largest city in 1930.

But by 1933, when Greenberg's Model A joined over half a million automobiles on the streets of the Motor City, the Depression had hit Detroit hard. Auto production had dropped 75 percent, from 5,337,087 cars built in 1929 to 1,331,860 in 1931. General Motors laid off 100,000 of its workforce. The following year, unemployment was 25 percent nation-wide, but approximately 40 percent in Detroit. Auto industry workers who managed to keep their jobs saw their take-home pay shrink from $35 a week in 1929 to $20 in 1932. The city slashed salaries of municipal employees and drastically reduced welfare spending. By 1933, the municipal treasury ran dry; in April, the city paid its employees in scrip. Men warmed themselves by fires in barrels outside shuttered factories. Soup lines formed on the sidewalks. People desperate to make a few cents sold apples on street corners. Many lost their life savings when their neighborhood banks went belly up. A mood of despair clouded the city. Five hundred sixty-eight Detroit citizens took their lives in 1931.

Baseball was a welcome diversion from the hard times. "Major league baseball has done as much as any one thing in this country to keep up the spirit of the people," President Franklin Roosevelt said. But fewer could afford to part with a dollar to enjoy that diversion. When the Tigers opened their ticket windows at 8:00 a.m. on April 4 to sell tickets for the opener on the following Wednesday, the line was much shorter than in years past. Attendance plunged around the league in 1933 to just over six million fans. Owners of major league teams lost $1,651,00. The turnstiles clicked only 320,972 times at Navin Field, a 19 percent drop from the previous season, deepening Frank Navin's financial woes.

Baseball players still made far more than the average laborer, but the players felt the pinch, too, with their wage cuts. They pounced on discarded newspapers in hotel lobbies rather than spend three cents on a new copy. They crammed four or five to a taxi to reduce each player's share of the cab fare to the ballpark. They tipped only the minimum on their meals. Greenberg took a room for eight dollars a week at the Wolverine Hotel, several blocks from Navin Field, with a bed but no closet. He hung his clothes on the shower curtain rod. He was grateful to have a job, even if it wasn't ideal at the moment.

The Tigers opened their regular season at Navin Field against the Cleveland Indians on April 12 with the usual fanfare: Judge Kenesaw Landis, the commissioner owners put in place to restore baseball's image after the Black Sox scandal, was on hand. Mayor Frank Murphy threw out the first pitch. A marching band led a parade of soldiers and the players to the center field flagpole for the formal flag-raising. Almost 19,000 fans showed up, about twice as many as expected, thanks in part to dry skies. Owen was on third, Harry Davis on first and Greenberg on the bench. The Tigers lost in twelve innings, 4–1.

There was the promise that season of beer in the ballpark. Five days earlier, on April 7, Michigan had become the first state to repeal its Prohibition laws. That was a popular move with baseball fans and Frank Navin, who stood to earn more in concession sales once the breweries resumed production, but the repeal did not sit so well with the Purple Gang. The Jewish mob, comprised mostly of *shtarkers* from the ghetto near the Eastern Market, had thrived with the distribution of liquor to Detroit's 15,000 speakeasies, ten times the number of bars that had operated in the city prior to 1918, when Michigan banned the sale of alcohol a year before the Volstead Act outlawed booze nationwide. Monsieur Cadillac's decision to found the city on a narrow stretch of the river made smuggling booze from Canada on the other side convenient. Sometimes the Purple Gang simply stole the contraband from other bootleggers. The Purples basically controlled the flow of alcohol into Detroit, one of the wettest cities in the nation—and points beyond. It supplied Canadian whiskey to Chicago's Al Capone, who had decided not to contest the Purple Gang's grip on Detroit. The gangsters, known for their ruthless violence—police estimated the Purples were responsible for 500 murders, more than Capone's killers—ruled Detroit's underworld from 1927 to 1932, overseeing not just the liquor trade but also its gambling rackets. With witnesses too frightened to testify against them, the Jewish mob operated with nearly absolute immunity, though the police did, according to rumor, ask the gangsters "to please dump their bodies outside the city limits."

Prohibition hurt the gang's business, but its leaders, the Bernstein brothers—Abe, Joe, Ray and Izzy—found other illegal sources of income to keep it going for several years before self-destructing, undone by internal jealousies and weakened by an eventual conviction that sent Ray Bernstein, along with two other high-ranking gang members, to prison for life. The gangsters, especially Ray, were baseball fans, often seen at Navin Field. They became friendly with ballplayers and looked out for them. One day, a

Purple Gang member pulled Del Baker aside and said, "We know you shop at such-and-such grocery store. I would stay away from that store for a week. We've got some business there we need to attend to." A few days later, that grocery store was blown up. Over the years, Greenberg would become friendly with Abe Bernstein.

Though his parents still called him "Hymie" and his legal name remained Henry, the Detroit papers started referring to Greenberg as "Hank." He did not seem completely comfortable with the nickname. For years—even well beyond his retirement—he signed his name "Hank" with the quotation marks.

Harry Davis stayed on first and Greenberg stayed on the bench the opening week of the season. Hank, accustomed to playing every day for the past three years in the minors, grew restless. To get some action, he headed out to Belle Isle, an island park in the Detroit River just east of downtown, on Saturday and Sunday mornings to join the pickup games before he had to assume his place on the pine at Navin Field. The guys in the Belle Isle games didn't recognize the Tigers' reserve first baseman; they just saw a big, young guy who could pound the ball. But the pickup games didn't give Hank the playing time he desired. The longer he sat in the Tiger dugout without being sent onto the field, the more frustrated he became. Finally, he couldn't take it any longer. After another game on the bench, he showered, dressed and stomped upstairs to the front office and demanded to see Mr. Navin.

"Who are you?" the switchboard operator asked.

"Hank Greenberg. I'm on the team."

Frank Navin ushered him in.

"Mr. Navin, I can't play ball sitting on the bench." His voice quivered with anger. "I'm going to get fat. If people don't want me to play, then let me go someplace where I can."

"We can't do that, Hank." Navin regarded the angry young man before him calmly, without changing the expression on his poker face. "We've already optioned you three times, and if we do it again, we lose you."

"Lose me then," Hank said.

"No. We don't intend to lose you. You go sit on the bench and study what's going on and learn something. You're not wasting time, and you'll get your chance to play. I promise you that."

Hank left, hardly mollified. But Navin spoke to Bucky Harris. When the Tigers faced a left-handed pitcher, Lloyd Brown, on April 22, Greenberg finally found his name on the lineup card posted on the clubhouse bulletin board, playing first base and batting fifth. The big league pitching seemed to overwhelm him. He struck out twice in an oh-for-three effort. That put him back on the bench for eight days. Davis was not hitting either, batting only .170, so Harris gave Hank another chance on April 30 in the first game of a doubleheader, once again against the lefty Lloyd Brown. The rookie managed his first hit, which drove in his first run, but that was his lone hit in five at-bats, and he landed back on the bench for another week. His appearances were enough for the guys at Belle Isle to recognize him and disqualify him from their pickup games.*

That spring, workers had erected a twenty-foot screen over Navin Field's left field wall to keep fly balls from landing in Cherry Street, creating a thirty-six-foot-high barrier, which made it particularly difficult for right-handed pull hitters like Greenberg to hit four-baggers in his home park. On Saturday, May 6, Hank faced another lefty, Earl Whitehill, the former Tiger pitcher now with the Washington Senators. Hank hadn't forgotten how Whitehill treated him three years earlier, denying him practice time at first base. He got all of a Whitehill pitch and sent the ball over the screen in left for his first major league home run. That felt sweet.

Hank played the second game of a doubleheader the next day and went oh-for-four. Despite his home run, he was batting only .111. He was still overstriding, setting his body into motion and starting his swing early, making it difficult to adjust to pitches. He also had trouble keeping his head still, making it harder to focus on the ball. Curves undid him. He continued to arrive early at the park to take extra batting practice. He also took extra fielding practice.

The way he lumbered around the bag inspired one scribe to compare his fielding to "an elephant trying to pick up marbles with his toes." He had

---

* Another story contends that Navin heard about a young man walloping the ball in sandlot games. When he drove over to Belle Isle to check out the prospect, he discovered Greenberg. No more of that, Navin told him.

trouble with the footwork. Starting a double play and getting back to the bag in time gave him difficulties. So did pop-ups. "Every time he would try to catch a pop fly, he would throw his head back," his teammate Elden Auker remembered. "Those pop flies gave him fits." Hank had Del Baker hit him fungo after fungo in the mornings to work on his weaknesses. "Hank was determined to perfect the art of catching a pop fly," Auker said. "He got to the point where he could catch those things in his jockstrap."

By May, the implications of Hitler's anti-Jew agenda were beginning to take shape. The Nazis fed books by Jewish authors to bonfires on the streets of Germany. British Prime Minister Winston Churchill told the House of Commons that "the odious conditions now ruling Germany" would spread to Poland "and another persecution and pogrom of Jews would begin in this area."

That decade there would be more Jews playing in the big leagues (twenty-four) than ever before, but that did not mean they would be warmly accepted. In April, the Yankees' Ben Chapman, a noted anti-Semite, slid hard into the Senators' second baseman, the Jewish Buddy Myer, to break up a force play. Chapman—thirty pounds and two inches bigger than Myer—knocked the diminutive second baseman's feet out from under him while he waited for the shortstop's throw. Myer kicked Chapman in the leg. Enraged, Chapman leaped up and swung at Myer. The two traded punches until teammates and umpires separated them. *Washington Post* sportswriter Shirley Povich, himself Jewish, spun the incident as a hate crime, reporting that Chapman "cut a swastika with his spikes on Myer's thigh."

Chapman was a mean man. As a player, he mocked Jewish fans at Yankee Stadium with Nazi salutes and ethnic slurs. Years later, as the Phillies manager, he shouted anti-Semitic insults at a Giants fan in the Polo Grounds: a Jewish GI who had lost a leg in combat. "He [Chapman] was a genuine Jew-baiter," Greenberg wrote. "Whenever he would have a bad day in the outfield, the Jews at Yankee Stadium would get after him because he made remarks about Jews. Men like Ben Chapman, and there were a lot of men like him in baseball, hated my guts and resented my success all the more because I am a Jew."

Those men lit into the Tigers' Jewish rookie. Bench jockeys seized upon any trait—physical, ethnic or otherwise—to torment opponents. Yet while the Italians and Irish had other teammates to help them absorb the epithets of "wops" and "mics," Greenberg was usually the only Jew on the field to weather the cries of "kike!"* "I was singled out all the time," he said. "Being Jewish and the object of a lot of derogatory remarks kept me on my toes all the time. I could never relax and be one of the boys."

Fans, too, shouted ethnic insults at Greenberg at every ballpark, even Navin Field, where the close quarters amplified their voices. Those barbs, from opponents and fans, stung Greenberg. "I guess I had rabbit ears, because I often let what I heard bother me," he said. "During my first year in the big leagues, the remarks from the stands and the opposing bench about my Jewish faith made life for me a living hell."

Had Greenberg chosen to play in New York, he would have blended into the large Jewish community, but in Detroit, where less than five percent of the population was Jewish, Hank felt isolated. The city's environment was particularly hostile toward Jews, where country clubs, athletic clubs and law firms excluded them. Hospitals wouldn't hire Jewish physicians. Many corporations, like the Ford Motor Company, had glass ceilings that kept Jews off the executive floors. Not surprising, since the city's *paterfamilias*, Henry Ford, was its leading anti-Semite.

From 1919 to 1927, Ford published the *Dearborn Independent* and distributed it through his car dealerships nationwide, reaching an audience of nearly one million readers. He intended the weekly newspaper to rival the *New York Times* and the *Wall Street Journal* with its mix of news and commentary on social issues. The front page carried outlandish headlines: "Jewish Jazz—Moron Music—Becomes Our National Music" and "The Jewish Associates of Benedict Arnold." The editorial page became his forum to blame Jews for everything from the labor unions to the assassination of Abraham Lincoln. The organizing theme of Ford's editorials and articles was that Jews throughout history had conspired to subvert Christianity and topple capitalism.

The Black Sox scandal inspired him to publish a two-part series, "The

---

* His neighborhood pal and Beaumont roommate Izzy Goldstein was no longer with the Tigers.

Peril of Baseball—Too Much Jew," that suggested "American baseball can be saved if a clean sweep is made of the Jewish influence which has just dragged it through a period of bitter shame and demoralization." Ford's paper claimed "the bane of American sports today is the presence of a certain type of Jew, not as a participant but as an exploiter and corrupter. . . . The Jew saw money where the sportsman saw fun and skill. The Jew set out to capitalize rivalry and to commercialize the contestant zeal." The paper labeled the players involved in the 1919 World Series fix "Jewish dupes": "Every player on trial was there because he listened to the suggestions of a Jew." It further blamed baseball's other problems on Jews: "The rowdyism that has afflicted baseball especially in the East is all of Jewish origin—the razzing of umpires, hurling of bottles, ceaseless shouting of profane insults." The solution Ford proposed, since "American baseball has passed into the hands of the Jews," was for good Christians to reclaim the national pastime. "The disease is caused by the Jewish characteristic which spoils everything by ruthless commercial exploitation. . . . But there is no doubt anywhere, among either friends or critics of baseball, that the root cause of the present condition is due to Jewish influence."

Ford's views, whether about the state of baseball, jazz or cinema, found sympathetic readers happy to have a scapegoat exposed, particularly in small towns "where Ford's word is taken as gospel," according to Rabbi Leo Franklin of Detroit. In protest, Rabbi Franklin, Ford's former neighbor, returned the new Model T Ford gave him as an annual gift. The rabbi wasn't the only one who criticized Ford's commentary. President Woodrow Wilson, among others, asked Ford to temper his strident attacks.

Many Jews in Detroit and around the country refused to buy Ford cars because of the founder's philosophy. They also comforted themselves with humor, telling Henry Ford jokes like the one where a fortune-teller informs Ford that he will die on a Jewish holiday. "Which one?" Ford asks nervously. "Their new year? Their day of atonement? Their Passover? Which one?"

"Mr. Ford," the fortune-teller responds, "whatever day you die will be a Jewish holiday."

Ford eventually defended himself in a national radio broadcast, saying that he didn't dislike Jews—why, some of his friends were Jewish—he simply wanted to awaken "the boob gentile" to the evil influences at work in society.

Ford changed his tone but not his tune. He continued to publish articles that condemned Jews; they simply appealed more to the intellect rather than playing upon emotions. A *Detroit Jewish Chronicle* editorial suggested that the new spate of articles insinuated Jews were "fakers, liars and parasites." The editorial observed: "The cumulative effect leaves the reader with a definite picture that the Jew is a dangerous menace to American life and institutions." The dangerous one was actually the accuser. "We cannot be persuaded that the continuous, repeated fault-finding which has characterized every article concerning the Jews can emanate from any other than a thoroughly poisoned anti-Semitic mind. . . . Despite Mr. Ford's recantation, apologies and protests, we are convinced that Mr. Ford is the arch anti-Semite of America."

Ford's influence spread beyond America. Johannes Steel, a German with inside connections to the Nazi movement, charged in his 1933 book *Hitler as Frankenstein* that Ford funded a Nazi publisher that spread Hitler's rhetoric in Europe. From 1920 to 1922, Ford compiled his views from the *Dearborn Independent* into four pamphlets entitled *The International Jew* that were translated into foreign languages. He also published an autobiography, *My Life and Work*, in 1923, which dealt with "our work on the Jewish question." *Mein Leben und Werk* became a bestseller in Germany and influenced, among others, the author of *Mein Kampf*. Two years before he became chancellor, Adolf Hitler told a *Detroit News* reporter, "I regard Henry Ford as my inspiration." In his book *Explaining Hitler*, Ron Rosenbaum maintains that Ford did not call for the extermination of Jews but that he unwittingly shaped Hitler's views, rhetoric and policy. Rosenbaum calls Ford "one of the most vile and repulsive figures in American history . . . the spiritual godfather of mass murder."

Anti-Semitism gained traction in the United States in 1933. Ford's propaganda and Hitler's agenda inspired new Nazi organizations like the Silver Shirts, the Black Legion and the German-American Bund in American cities. The Ku Klux Klan flourished in rural communities. During the Klan's peak in the Twenties, Michigan had more members than any other state, somewhere between 80,000 and 120,000, with about half of those living in Detroit. "Taking their cues from Hitler, these outfits emphasized the dangers to the United States of 'Jewish bankers' and 'Jewish communists,'"

Everett Clinchy notes in his book *All in the Name of God*. As the Depression worsened, the verbal and physical attacks on Jews in the United States intensified. "Hitler's vicious assaults struck a responsive chord with many Americans who needed a scapegoat to explain their misery," historian Joe Dorinson writes in his essay "Jews and Baseball."

The voice of anti-Semitism in America belonged to Father Charles Coughlin, a Roman Catholic priest at the National Shrine of the Little Flower in suburban Detroit. Father Coughlin began broadcasting Sunday morning sermons in 1926 on WJR, and by 1933 the "Radio Priest" was at the peak of his power, heard by millions on his own national radio network. He preyed upon and stoked the country's economic anxiety, beginning with his rants against bankers and the rich. With his "vocal histrionics and oratorical trapeze acts," Father Coughlin was the Depression's radio equivalent of today's television evangelist, reaping huge sums from his flock's donations. When he orated at rallies in packed auditoriums, the fury of his words shook loose a wisp of hair that snaked over his forehead and he punctuated his statements with his fist—resembling in appearance and output a Roman collar version of the Fuhrer. Like Ford, Father Coughlin based his theories on half-truths and selective facts. He found a ready audience of ten million radio listeners nationwide. Dorinson observes, "Many adherents of Father Coughlin and Gerald L. K. Smith* linked Jews with either heartless capitalism or zealous communism—indifferent to the illogic of their rant."

This atmosphere made Detroit a lonely place for Hank Greenberg, the young Jewish transplant from the Bronx. When Harold Allen, a Jewish Detroit businessman, read in the local newspaper that the Tigers had a new Jewish first baseman, he understood. *That young man is going to be awfully lonesome around here.* Late on a Friday afternoon, Allen paid him a visit at the Wolverine Hotel.† The desk clerk told Allen that Greenberg was across the street in Grand Circus Park. Allen, in his thirties, "saw this big kid sitting on a bench with an apple and a banana." He introduced himself.

"What are you doing?" Allen asked.

---

* Another Christian crackpot with a radio show, Smith, a.k.a. the "Minister of Hate," teamed with Coughlin to found the Union Party in 1936 and later campaigned for the release of Nazi war criminals.
† Later demolished to build a parking ramp for Comerica Park.

"Eating my dinner," Hank said.

"You're coming with me," Allen said. "We're going to have a good dinner at my mother's."

So began Hank's lifelong friendship with Harold Allen and his brother, Sidney, who had transformed their father's bedding company into the world's largest manufacturer of automotive insulation materials and had box seats at Navin Field. Hank also became close with the Blumberg brothers, Louis and Irving. Other Jewish businessmen, such as Aaron DeRoy, Gus Newman, Maurice Caplan and Maury Aronsson, befriended him. Hank started receiving dinner invitations regularly to their and other Jewish homes. He was invited to join the two Jewish country clubs, Franklin Hills and Knollwood. He also joined the YMHA and the B'nai B'rith. He did not attend synagogue regularly, but he was a frequent guest at Jewish centers and other community events. Detroit's Jewish community embraced the Tiger rookie. That helped blunt the hostility he encountered elsewhere in Detroit and on the field.

Meanwhile, Hank was still struggling to break into the Tigers' lineup. On Wednesday, May 10, Harry Davis started the first game of a doubleheader; Hank started the second. He hit his first career double and then his second, going two-for-three and scoring twice. He also made his first error. The Tigers lost both games, putting their record at 10–13, a discouraging start for a team that Bucky Harris had promised would fare better than the previous year's fifth place.

After the opening home stand, the Tigers headed east, first stop New York. Hank's family came to Yankee Stadium to see him play. He started the opening game of the series on May 17 eager to put on a show. His family watched him go hitless in four at-bats, including a strikeout. With a dismal .160 batting average, he sat the next game. But his competition at first seemed determined to give away the job. Harry Davis, Harris's leadoff man, was batting only .234. The ordinarily sure-handed Davis had also been a disappointment in the field, guilty of seven errors in only twenty-two games.

Harris put Greenberg back in the lineup on Sunday, May 21, in Boston. Hank did not have a remarkable day—he smacked a double and struck out twice—but it was enough for Harris to let him play the following day.

Hank went two-for-four with another double and four RBI. Harris kept him in the lineup. Given the chance to play every day, Hank made good on the opportunity. In that six-game stretch, he collected eight hits in twenty-one at-bats, including a home run, two doubles and seven RBI. The first baseman's job was his.

In Washington, Hank had trouble with Heinie Manush, the Senators' hot-tempered left fielder. In those days, players kept their gloves on the field while they batted; Greenberg tossed his to the side, across the foul line, as other first basemen did. Manush, on his way off the diamond, kicked Greenberg's mitt. Hank yelled at him. Manush, a strong man himself at six feet, 200 pounds, yelled back. Their threats didn't blossom to blows, and it's not clear if Manush, the son of German immigrants, salted his words with ethnic slurs, but he sent a message to the rookie that was not welcoming.

In June, Max Baer, wearing the Star of David on his trunks for the first time, beat up the German Max Schmeling in a heavyweight bout at Yankee Stadium while the German's entourage shouted, "Kill the Jew bastard!" On June 16, President Franklin Roosevelt signed into law the National Industrial Recovery Act, which intended for industries to regulate themselves with minimum wages, price limits and collective bargaining rights for unions; Henry Ford was the only auto manufacturer not to comply. Also in June, Rabbi Jonah B. Wise reported on his recent trip to Germany. He told the audience at Detroit's Temple Beth El that Germany's 600,000 Jews "are hopelessly crushed and humiliated beggars in a country which they always have helped to build and which in time of war they helped to defend. . . . Hitler's program is to bring about the degradation of Jews—economic, social and moral. . . . They are leaving their hometowns and villages, fearing for the safety of their children—with no place to go.

"Not even in the darkest moments of the preelection campaign had a single Jew in Germany thought it conceivable that Hitler, if victorious, would actually put into effect his policy of Jewish disenfranchisement."

The rookie Greenberg may have earned the starting first baseman's job, but he still made mistakes typical of a newcomer's naïveté. In a game at Comiskey Park on June 9, Hank let a pitch go by with two strikes on him and the bases loaded. He thought the pitch was wide. Home plate umpire

George Moriarty called, "Strike three!" Bucky Harris charged out of the dugout to protest. The rookie didn't know the history between the two men: Moriarty had managed the Tigers until Harris replaced him. After Harris had exhausted his insults and headed back to the dugout, Hank yelled, "That goes for me, too!" Moriarty, who had ignored Harris, turned on Greenberg. "Get out of here, you fresh busher. You're out of the game."

In mid-July, the rookie landed in Harris's doghouse when he brashly defied the manager. Hank asked permission to skip an exhibition game in Albany, New York, so he could visit his parents. Harris, upset over a game the Tigers had lost after gaining the lead in the eleventh inning, said no. Hank went anyway. His mother cooked him his favorite meal. Harris fined the rookie fifty dollars, almost a full week's pay, and benched him.* Greenberg appeared in only one of the next nine games.

He was back playing daily in September when the High Holy Days arrived. Hank may not have felt drawn to attend religious services on the Sabbath, but he observed the holidays. He requested the day off on Rosh Hashanah, Thursday, September 21, and watched his teammates defeat the Athletics at Shibe Park. He also abstained from playing nine days later on Yom Kippur in another Tiger win.

Despite those victories without Greenberg, the Tigers lost more games than they won, surfacing above .500 only four times all season. Bucky Harris had given up in Philadelphia on a road trip during August when it became obvious the team would finish out of the money once again. He wrote Navin that he was going to quit. The Tigers' owner tried to talk him out of it when the team returned to Detroit. But after a doubleheader on September 24, with two games left to play in the season, Harris announced he was done. "If a manager cannot deliver in five years, he should resign," Bucky told the press. Del Baker skippered the team for the final pair of games.

About time, the press and fans concurred. Though Harris was generally liked and regarded as a good baseball strategist, Fred Lieb pronounced, "Bucky's five-year term as the head of the Tigers was one of the most dreary in Detroit history." After the team finished 75–79, in fifth place again, twenty-five games back, *Detroit Free Press* editor Milton Bingay articulated

---

* He told his mother in a letter her meal was worth it.

the fans' discontent under the headline: WE WANT TIGERS—NOT TAME KITTENS. In the twenty-four years since the Tigers won their last pennant, "Detroit, long one of the best baseball towns in America, has been steadily losing interest in the sport because of lifeless teams under lifeless management."

Hank had been disappointed that he had not done well at Yankee Stadium when family and friends showed up to watch, but when he returned to the Bronx he discovered he had become a hero. His family threw him a big party, followed by a neighborhood celebration. Mr. and Mrs. Greenberg, too, had become celebrities in the neighborhood, parents of the major league ballplayer. Their social status had risen with his success. Maybe he wasn't such a bum after all.

For the most part, Hank was pleased with his season. Not only had he established himself as the Tigers' first baseman, he had raised his average to .301, hit 33 doubles, 12 homers and knocked in 87 runs in 117 games. Yet he also set a team record for strikeouts (78). In the field, he still had trouble starting a double play and covering the base in time for the return throw. His footwork was not yet major league. "I've slipped and stumbled on fast bounders which other first basemen, of no greater speed of foot, have handled," he said after the season. "I haven't covered as much ground or got the jump on the ball as I should." Yet many, including Dan Daniel, one of the authorities of the day and often referred to as "Mr. Baseball," saw Hank on his way to stardom. In his *Baseball Magazine* analysis of the season's rookie crop, Mr. Baseball selected Greenberg as the best of five freshman first basemen: "Big, strong, a powerful hitter, he should develop into a great player within the next year."

Jews beyond the Bronx and Detroit also took note of Greenberg's success. Here was a young player with potential who might actually rise to that aspired status that had so long eluded other Jews. The *American Hebrew* called Greenberg "the elusive Hebrew star for whose discovery and acquisition John McGraw and Miller Huggins [of the Yankees]—canny ball club builders of New York—spent fortunes in vain." On the strength of one season alone, Greenberg was already assuming stature beyond that of another mere ballplayer.

CHAPTER FIVE

Bang, Bang, Bang, Go the Yiddish

Hank gained a deeper sense of his value in 1934. After establishing himself as a daily player in his rookie season, he believed he deserved a major league contract, rather than one that that would allow a minor league team to reduce his pay if he were sent down. He asked for $1,000 a month, $5,500 total for the five-and-a-half-month season. Tiger owner Frank Navin agreed that Hank had a good year but didn't think it was worth a $2,200 raise. He increased his offer to $4,500. In those days when the reserve clause defined baseball's labor negotiations, a player's only option was to not sign and not report to camp. Hank, who was honing his skills as a negotiator as well as a ballplayer, told Navin he would find other employment. The Tigers' new player-manager, Mickey Cochrane, visited Hank in Miami Beach, where he had spent part of the winter, to talk him into signing, but Hank didn't waver. He certainly didn't want to abandon baseball, having just gotten a taste of his potential, but he also didn't want to undersell his services.

A week before the season started, Navin phoned Greenberg at his Miami Beach hotel. "Listen, young man," he said. "If you don't want to play ball for us, you can just hang up your uniform and stay out of baseball."

He carried on for ten minutes from his Detroit office, but then said, "However, I'll tell you what I'll do. I'll give you $5,000 guaranteed, and if we finish one-two-or-three, I'll give you a $500 bonus."

Hank knew Navin wasn't likely to pay him more than the initial

$5,000. The Tigers hadn't finished higher than fourth place in nine years. But, with spring training scheduled to start in a week, Hank was eager to save face. "Thank you very much, Mr. Navin," he said into the hotel telephone. "I'll be there for spring training on March 1st, sir."

Navin had been busy with other negotiations that off-season. Replacing Bucky Harris was his first priority. He wanted to hire Babe Ruth, who had made clear his desire to manage. Navin asked Ruth to come to Detroit to discuss the possibility, but the thirty-eight-year-old home run king was headed to Hawaii to play some exhibition games. Ruth instead sent a letter stating his salary demands, which included a percentage of ticket sales. Navin liked the thought of having the Babe as a gate attraction but didn't like the idea of turning over the profits. Instead, he paid the Philadelphia Athletics $100,000 of his partner Walter O. Briggs's money for Mickey Cochrane.

Cochrane, a future Hall of Famer, was the best defensive catcher in the game and a reliable hitter in his prime who had batted .500 against the Tigers the previous season. Connie Mack, in need of cash to pay his Depression debts, let Cochrane go reluctantly. The Napoleonesque Cochrane was a leader with an infectious intensity that inspired those around him to play harder and better. Most significantly, he was a winner. He had spurred the Athletics' three consecutive first-place finishes from 1929–1931. "Winning was a way of life for him," Greenberg wrote. "He was the greatest fighting spirit on the field."

Cochrane's first move was to convince Navin to trade outfielder John Stone to the Washington Senators for Goose Goslin. Although Goslin was thirty-three years old, Cochrane recognized the "New Jersey farm boy noted for his blistering hitting and proboscis the size of a shade tree" still had some good years left in his Hall of Fame career. The left-handed hitting outfielder was another winner, a member of the Senators' World Series teams in 1924, 1925 and 1933. When the Tigers arrived at Henley Field Ball Park in Lakeland, Florida, their new spring training facility, Cochrane set the tone for the season. He enforced a midnight curfew and a 9:00 a.m. wake-up call. He started practices with twenty minutes of calisthenics. He emphasized fundamentals. He worked the players on advancing runners. And he told them, "We're going to win."

They had the talent. Charlie Gehringer, "The Mechanical Man," hoovered up everything hit his way at second base and ranked as one of the premier hitters in the league. Marv Owen at third and Billy Rogell at short wielded dependable gloves and bats. Goslin's hitting underwrote the speed of fellow outfielders Jo-Jo White, Pete Fox and Gee Walker. Three young arms formed the heart of the pitching staff: Tommy Bridges, a slight Tennessean with the best curve in baseball who had already thrown three one-hitters; Elden Auker, whose stone-skipping sidearm motion baffled batters; and Schoolboy Rowe, Hank's Beaumont teammate who could run and hit almost as well as he could throw. And then there was Greenberg at first, poised to make his presence known in a big way.

Hank continued to feel his otherness among his teammates. Most of them had never heard of a seder, let alone attended one. He lived in a Jewish boardinghouse during spring training so he could eat matzo at Passover.

Self-conscious and uncertain, he made up a middle name for himself—Benjamin, his older brother's name—so his suitcase could have three initials on the handle the way his teammates' did.*

Hank's moods continued to swing with his success—or lack thereof—on the diamond. Two or three hits on the day, and there wasn't a sweeter guy around. But oh-fers and errors soured him. Didn't matter if it was an exhibition game or the World Series, he played with an intensity that didn't know the difference. Once triggered, his rage could turn him against a teammate, which is exactly what happened in the final week of spring training.

The Cardinals had shut out the Tigers in an exhibition game. Hank had struck out and failed to get a hit. He brooded on the bus ride from Bradenton to Lakeland. Rip Sewell, who had been Hank's teammate in Beaumont and would eventually become best known for his eephus pitch,† was

---

* Even though posterity has adopted the name Henry Benjamin Greenberg, his birth certificate says simply "Henry Greenberg" and on his military forms he admitted to NMI—no middle initial.

† A slow, arcing lob that Sewell popularized. Sewell threw an eephus pitch to Ted Williams in the 1946 All-Star game. Williams missed and asked for another one. Sewell complied. Williams smashed it out of the park.

then a smart-ass rookie from Alabama. He made the mistake of engaging Greenberg in an argument. Hank called him a "Southern son of a bitch," fighting words to Sewell, who countered with "Big Jew bastard."

"When this bus reaches Lakeland, I'm going to beat the shit out of you," Hank said.

"You can stop the damn bus right now if you want to do that," Sewell said.

At the Lakeland Terrace Hotel, Hank got off the bus and waited for Sewell. According to Sewell, the two "fought and fought and fought." In Greenberg's version, Hank "grabbed Sewell and started pummeling him. He couldn't fight, so he grabbed me around the knees." Teammates remembered they quickly broke up the fight.

Hank had drawn the line on how much ethnic abuse he would tolerate. Cochrane sent Sewell to the minors, telling him, "We've got thirty pitchers but only one first baseman."

With his raise, Hank had upgraded his living arrangements, moving into the Leland Hotel, which not only had closets, but served full dinners complete with a live orchestra for an extra $1.25. Usually frugal like his father, Hank splurged on the meal and dropped a quarter for a tip to impress the attractive waitress.

Hank also wore a new number that season. He had worn 7 his rookie year but gave that number to Billy Rogell, who had been No. 7 in 1931. Hank took No. 5 for 1934.*

The way the regular season started for Hank put him in a foul mood. He went hitless in the Tigers' first four games, all played on the road. Cochrane had placed his faith squarely on Greenberg's shoulders, letting Harry Davis go. But Hank wasn't living up to the expectation. Through the first three weeks of the season, he batted .269 with only one home run. He heard the fans' displeasure at Navin Field, especially one young, shrill voice

---

* Infielder Billy Rhiel started the 1933 season wearing No. 5 for the Tigers, but he was sent to the minors in July. Catcher Johnny Pasek, promoted later that month, wore No. 5 for the rest of the season. He was sent to the Athletics in the deal for Cochrane, which made the number available for Hank in 1934.

from the upper deck after each of his plate failures, "Back to the minors, you busher!"

One day during his slump, Hank left the ballpark troubled by his lack of production and encountered Charlie Collins, a fourteen-year-old boy, waiting for him. Collins lived in sight of Navin Field with his grandmother, a huge Tiger fan. Greenberg was his favorite player. Collins nervously held out an official American League baseball and asked Greenberg to autograph it. Hank snatched the blond-haired kid's ball and flung it down the street.

Watching the boy run dejectedly after his ball, Hank immediately felt rotten. He waited for Collins to walk back. "Hey, Whitey, I'm really sorry," Hank said. "Things haven't been going so well. Come back here tomorrow, and I'll get you another ball and autograph it."

Good to his word, Hank gave the boy an autographed ball the next day. He also invited Whitey, as he called Collins, to shag balls for him before the team's regular batting practice. He paid Whitey and other neighborhood boys a dollar apiece to chase down his fly balls for two hours. He also paid American Federation pitchers like Ace Lee and Clarence Fuller several dollars each to show up at ten in the morning and pitch to him. While other players spent the mornings at the racetrack or golf course, Hank was on the ball field. His desire to make himself the best pushed him to spend whatever it took in time, money and effort.

Ever looking for more tangible ways to get an edge, Hank studied pitchers closely. In his second year in the league, he was getting to know them better. He looked for ways to predict what they might throw in certain situations and kept track of their tendencies. He also looked for indications of their pitches. If he spotted the white of the ball in the pitcher's glove, for instance, he figured the pitcher would throw a curve. He noticed that most pitchers wound up bringing their hands over their heads, then dropped them to about the top button to break them apart for a curve; they brought their hands back a littler farther for a fastball. He picked up how Rube Walberg, the Athletics' twenty-game winner that season, curled his wrist to throw a curve but kept it straight on his fastball. The book on Greenberg was that he couldn't hit the big curve—the *New York Post* called him a "sucker for a curveball"—but if he knew what pitch was coming, he had a better chance to hit it, even if it was a curve.

Hank was also wise enough to listen to advice. In one game, the umpire, Bill McGowan, a showman in his own right, helped correct Hank's tendency to overswing by telling him, "Hank, you don't have to hit the ball forty rows into the seats. Home runs count just as much if they only clear the fence by this much"—he held up his thumb and finger an inch apart. Hank sought out the advice of Jimmie Foxx, the Athletics' Hall of Fame–bound power-hitting first baseman. Foxx gave him pointers on his hands, his stance and his swing that Greenberg put to good use.

He also benefited from a conversation with Ty Cobb. The Tiger great revealed his psychology of hitting to Hank. Instead of worrying about choking, Cobb told him, he went to the plate thinking, *Look at that poor son-of-a-bitch pitcher out there, he's got to pitch to the great Ty Cobb with the bases full.* Adapting Cobb's thinking bolstered Hank's confidence and proved a turning point in his career.

By the time the Tigers played Cleveland for a July 4 doubleheader, Hank was batting .305. That day Greenberg had a pair of RBI, giving him sixty for the season, and hit his 27th double. The results quieted his critics, including the shrill voice from Navin Field's upper deck. "I sort of miss him, the little needler," Hank told his teammates in the dugout.

Others noted his improvement, which included his fielding. He had worked hard on that as well. "The development of Greenberg is one of the most amazing features of an amazing baseball season," Harry Salsinger wrote in the *Detroit News* three weeks later, with Hank leading the majors in doubles (37) and batting .332. "He has learned more about timing, developed a finer rhythm and has better leverage. He does not go after bad balls the way he did last season and he has a much wider knowledge of pitching. . . . The unusual feature of Greenberg's development is that Greenberg's fielding has improved with his hitting. . . . Today he makes with ease the plays he could not master a year ago." Salsinger asserted that Greenberg had reached the highest levels of achievement in the league: "Henry Greenberg's name must be added to the names of Jimmie Foxx, Lou Gehrig and Babe Ruth." In another article later that season, Salsinger marveled at the way Hank had molded himself into "the best-fielding first baseman in the American League" and one of "the leading home run hitters." "He arrived with more physical assets than hundreds of others who travel the same road, but where most of them stop at the point of arrival, Greenberg really started from there. He made use of his intelligence, his height, his reach, his wrist, forearm and shoulder power. He lifted himself above his fellows." Such were the fruits of his dedication to improve himself.

Long before the Internet and even television, radio became baseball's medium. Since the first game was broadcast in 1921, the cost of a set had come down, and by the midthirties two-thirds of all American households had a Philco or RCA or lesser brand, either perched on a living room table, a kitchen countertop or, if small enough, held in one's hand. Detroit fans tuned to WWJ to listen to Ty Tyson, the voice of the Tigers, deliver the action in his calm manner. His description sketched the scenes; their imaginations colored in the details. "We used to watch radio," said Max Lapides, a lifelong Tiger fan.

Radio forged an intimacy between the fans and ballplayers. The players took shape in the listener's mind, often swelling to larger proportions with their heroic feats. The fans felt a bond with the legends blooming in their imaginations.

Families gathered around their radio sets to listen to the Tigers split the July 4 doubleheader. Forty thousand fans showed up at Navin Field, the largest crowd there for a long time. It wasn't the holiday or weather that brought them out to the boxy white structure at the corner of Michigan and Trumbull. No, the Tigers had become a big draw. With his fighting spirit, Mickey Cochrane had transformed Bucky Harris's "tame kittens" into tough wildcats. Lo, the Tigers had become true contenders. They had spent half of June in first place and after July 4 trailed the Yankees by just one game. Eager to find something good to cheer in the dreary days of the Depression, Detroit fixated on the Tigers to lift them from their emotional despair. Ty Tyson declared, "The town was absolutely screwy."

The Yankees arrived in Detroit after the All-Star break for a four-game series with a half-game lead over the Tigers. The hometown team took two of the first three games at Navin Field to squeeze past the Bronx Bombers into first place. On July 15, Greenberg came to bat in the sixth inning of the fourth and final game. The Tigers had two men on with the score tied 2–2. The 26,000 "highly excited fans" at Navin Field knew the moment was ripe for a big hit. Greenberg delivered—as he so often did in the clutch. He "blasted a double that cleared the bases of two occupants," the *New York Times* reported. "The encouragement this hit provided sent the Tigers on to great heights, and they won the ball game 8–3."

That sent the Yankees away trailing the Tigers by one and a half games and further excited the fans with the possibility of their first pennant in twenty-five years.

The Tigers remained in first place in large part due to Greenberg's consistent play and clutch hitting. Schoolboy Rowe, a modest performer in 1933 (7–4, 3.58 ERA), exploded with success in 1934 with Cochrane nursing his confidence from behind the plate. Beginning on June 15 with a victory over the Red Sox, the big right-hander ripped off fifteen consecutive wins, longer than his Beaumont streak. That put him one away from the major league record shared by Walter Johnson, Joe Wood and Lefty Grove when he took the hill against the Senators in Washington on Saturday, August 25. "We were really breaking our backs for him," Gehringer said. "We wanted to see him make it."

Perhaps no one wanted to help Rowe make it more than Greenberg, whose boner had ended Rowe's Texas League winning streak. Schoolboy pitched well, but after eight innings the Tigers trailed 2–1, thunderheads threatened over the stands and it seemed Rowe would miss his chance to ink his name in the record books. Hank had one last chance when he came to bat in the top of the ninth with Billy Rogell on first and no outs. Hank took a bite of cheap candy for good luck—a superstition he had adopted before each at-bat—and dug in. He blasted a drive 400 feet over the right field fence, a rare opposite field homer for him that put the Tigers on top 3–2. Rowe finished off the Senators in the bottom of the ninth with the clouds darkening the field and dripping rain. Once again, Greenberg had come through in the clutch, this time with his twentieth home run of the season. His timely hitting would account for 40 percent of the Tigers' wins by tying the score or putting the team ahead. His WAR* rating was 6.7, second only to Gehringer. The way Greenberg carried the team to victory

---

* Wins Above Replacement: the number of wins a player added above what a replacement player would add.

on his back prompted Mickey Cochrane to call him the Tigers' most valuable player.

Greenberg wasn't the only Tiger playing well. Cochrane would bat .320 with 32 doubles, 76 RBI and be voted the American League MVP. Rowe, with his 24 wins, was the ace on a staff that would win 101 games. Gehringer would lead the league in hits (214) and runs scored (134) and finish with a .358 batting average, second only to the Yankees' Lou Gehrig. Goose Goslin, the aging addition in the outfield, played nearly every game, drove in 100 runs, scored 106 and batted .305. The Detroit press dubbed Gehringer, Goslin and Greenberg, the "G-men," after the special agents that brought down public enemies John Dillinger, Pretty Boy Floyd, Bonnie Parker and Clyde Barrow that summer. *Detroit Free Press* sports editor Charles Ward hung the moniker the "Battalion of Death" on the infielders— Greenberg at first, Gehringer at second, Owen at third and Rogell at short— who combined to drive in 462 runs, a record that still stands. The '34 Tigers, including four future Hall of Famers (Cochrane, Gehringer, Goslin and Greenberg), were proving themselves one of the best teams of all time, with Hank Greenberg the most consistent among them.

They called Greenberg "Greenie," "Lanky," "The Big Moose" or "King Kong," which was Ty Tyson's favorite handle for the big first baseman until he came up with "Hankus Pankus." By late '34, King Kong was an apt description not only of Hank's size but of his stature in Detroit. Fans swooned for the tall, handsome star winning ball games for their Tigers. "He is quite a guy, this fellow Greenberg, and well worthy of the adulation Detroit fans have showered upon him this season," the *Free Press*' Ward wrote. Salsinger declared Greenberg "one of the great men of sport," in the *Detroit News*. "He is also one of my favorite athletes." *Detroit Times* sports editor Bud Shaver appointed Greenberg to be Babe Ruth's successor as the game's most popular player: "Like Ruth, Greenberg's popularity is built upon sounder foundation than mere ability to hit a baseball. Greenberg has an attractive personality, crowd appeal." The press praised him for his modesty, intelligence, "driving ambition," "indomitable spirit," and all-around likability. The fans loved him for the same.

He became especially popular and important to the Jews that summer. For example, during a single week in Detroit that June, the Belcrest Campus

Club elected him an honorary member, the crowd at the Jewish Community Center gave him a "rousing reception" when he spoke to a group of boys and Wayne University's Campus Alumnae Club welcomed him as a guest speaker. In a national contest sponsored by the Jewish Telegraphic Agency, fans voted him "The Greatest Jewish Baseball Player of All Time."

In the days before multimillion-dollar contracts separated players from the general public, Hank lived among the Jewish community of Detroit. They saw him at Dorfman Drugs, the Dexter section institution whose soda fountain drew Hank for ten-cent strawberry sundaes; at Boesky's or Lieberman's, delis he frequented; they saw him shopping in J.L. Hudson's, walking down Elmhurst and buying fruit at Mr. Wall's Vegetable Stand. And, of course, they saw him at the ballpark, where he willingly chatted with fans in the box seats and posed for photos with a group or a youngster on his knee.

During a period of intense ethnic awareness, Jews paid close attention to Greenberg's progress and identified with his success. Even those who had not been baseball fans took an interest in Greenberg. Harvey Frank, a young Jewish schoolboy, listened to Tyson's broadcasts on the Zenith radio in his living room. His father was from Lithuania and his mother did not care for sports, but when they came home from work at the clothing store they owned, their first question was, "How did Greenberg do today?" Harvey recounted the game and Hank's part in it over dinner. It was a daily scene played out at dinner tables of Jewish families across Detroit. Through his own assimilation, Greenberg facilitated the assimilation of the generation that preceded him. "It's quite clear that until the immigrant population knew something about baseball, they didn't know anything about America," baseball scholar Rabbi Michael Paley said. "They were a population that lived by themselves." Greenberg became important to them because he helped them understand America through baseball, its national pastime.

Hank's parents had become baseball fans themselves. They had gone to watch him play at least once each summer when he was in the minors. Since he had been with the Tigers, they had seen every game he played in New York and Philadelphia, which were about an equal distance from their summer home on the Jersey shore. They were proud of him. So were his siblings, Ben, Lillian and Joe, a smaller version of Hank with big league ambitions of his own. Before the season started, Lillian's husband, Leon Golson, offered Hank ten dollars for every home run over fifteen he hit, which was starting to cost him. Hank's brothers and sister joined their parents, along with their spouses and Hank's uncle Cy Simon, who had played semipro ball himself, to watch Hank's games at Yankee Stadium.

When Hank saw his mother and father in Philadelphia for the series with the Athletics August 26–29, they talked about the upcoming holidays. Hank, knowing how his parents valued religious observance, promised them that he would not play on the High Holy Days.

Long before it became "Hockeytown," Detroit belonged to baseball. By September, with the Tigers in first place, the city was giddy with pennant fever. The press tripled the number of reporters it sent to games to keep up with the public's appetite to know how their boys were doing. On Tuesday, September 4, when the Tigers returned from a twenty-three-day road trip that stretched their lead over the Yankees to five and a half games, a huge crowd greeted their train at the Fort Street Union Station. A marching band led the players in their suits and hats out of the train station, and another band followed. Two detectives escorted the dangerously popular Schoolboy Rowe, whose winning streak had ended at sixteen in his last outing. The players shook hands and signed autographs for the fans. A man held up his baby for Schoolboy, who paused to pinch its chubby cheek. Young women pushed themselves toward the players. A contingent of photographers documented the celebration for the next day's front page, and movie cameras recorded the event for newsreels. "The throng cheered the conquering heroes as they left the terminal," one announcer intoned.

The intensity of the Detroit fans' desire to see their Tigers win another pennant upped the pressure on the players. "One of the things we'll all enjoy when the season ends is escape from the autograph craze," Hank told a reporter. "It's great to be popular, but there are penalties. Tiger players are safe only when they are right out in the field during a game."

In addition to the adjustments he had needed to make on the field, Hank also had to adjust to the pressures of celebrity, which challenged his temperament. "Learning to be agreeable to the public at all times and under all conditions isn't at all easy," he admitted.

In the future, he would sometimes duck the crowd but that evening, Greenberg was the first player off the train. A teenager named Sammy Kaufman grabbed his suitcase. "It's too heavy for you, isn't it?" Hank asked.

Sammy insisted it wasn't, so Hank draped his hand over the boy's shoulder and let him carry his suitcase. A porter tried to help, but Hank waved him off amiably. "If Sammy wants to lug it, he's going to," Hank said.

Hank had befriended Sammy earlier in the season when the fifteen-year-old boy had knocked on the door of his room at the Leland Hotel. He sheepishly told Hank he had come to apologize. He had been the shrill voice in the upper deck chastising Greenberg. Hank forgave him. "I guess you brought me out of a slump," Hank said. "How'd you like that home run yesterday?"

Sammy started to cry. He hadn't witnessed it. See, he'd been an usher, but his boss had fired him for yelling at Greenberg.

Hearing that, Hank took Sammy down to Navin Field, found the head usher and talked him into giving Sammy his job back.

Hank had worked his influence at the park in favor of another lad, Whitey Collins, whose ball Hank had thrown down the street. Hank introduced Collins to the clubhouse manager. "Take care of Whitey for me, okay?" Collins became a batboy and clubhouse attendant for Tiger opponents.

Since he had started playing minor league ball, Hank, like the majority of professional players in his day, had used Louisville Slugger bats manufactured by the Hillerich & Bradsby Company in Louisville, Kentucky. He experimented with hickory but preferred ash models. In 1932, he had increased his bat length from thirty-five to thirty-six inches. Over the course of his career, he would try a variety of lengths in that range, going as long as thirty-seven inches in 1933. His bats weighed between thirty-five and thirty-six ounces. He used seventeen different styles during his career, but the majority were thirty-six ounces. He liked the half-round barrel with large knobs.

His rookie year, the Hillerich & Bradsby company offered him a contract to make him a signature model bat and allow the company to use his name in advertising for twenty years. The standard contract paid one dollar. Hank knew that other players got more money, even before they played major league ball. That same year, the company paid a nineteen-year-old kid named DiMaggio twenty-five dollars with the promise of an additional twenty-five dollars if he broke any records—three years before he would play for the Yankees.* In 1918, Hillerich & Bradsby had paid Babe Ruth one hundred dollars. Hank figured he would be worth more himself in the future, so he said, "No, thanks," to the company's one-dollar offer.

The story goes that Greenberg's success during the 1934 season convinced company owner Bud Hillerich that Greenberg was worth more. He went up to Detroit in early September, after the Tigers had returned from their road trip and phoned Greenberg. Hank told him he wanted $200 to sign. (Bob Hill, author of *Crack of the Bat: The Louisville Slugger Story*, puts the figure at $500.) "What?!" Old Man Hillerich exclaimed. "We've got Babe Ruth, Lou Gehrig, and all of the other big name players. Young man, don't you know that's too much?"

Hank held firm. He invited Hillerich up to his room at the Leland Hotel before the game on Saturday, September 8. Hillerich pulled an envelope from his pocket and handed it to Hank. "We want you to sign our contract," he said.

Hank counted two hundred one-dollar bills (or five hundred, if you prefer that version) and signed the contract. Or maybe it was only twenty-five dollar bills and two bats. That's the notation on the bottom of the standard contract Hank signed in Detroit on September 8. At any rate, the company shipped the first order with his facsimile signature, "'Hank' Greenberg," two ash bats thirty-five inches long and weighing thirty-six ounces, three days later. Greenberg finally had his own Louisville Slugger signature bat, just like Ruth, Gehrig, Foxx and the others he was being compared to.

Tiger owner Frank Navin was enjoying the 1934 season as much as anyone. The fans' hysteria drew them to the ballpark in record numbers. After years of dismal performances, the Tigers led the major leagues in attendance, with 919,161 fans clicking the turnstiles. The $3.50 they paid for box seats

---

* That also happened to be the year Joe DiMaggio had a 61-game hitting streak with the San Francisco Seals.

and fifty cents for bleacher seats—along with the dimes they spent on hot dogs, pop and ice cream—added up to a profitable season. "Detroit went absolutely daft over its first pennant winner in a quarter of a century," Fred Lieb wrote. "The Depression had smacked industrial Detroit a hard right to the kisser, but people were having money again, and they spent it at Navin's ball orchard." Once it looked like the Tigers would capture the pennant, Navin invested his revenues in the construction of 17,000 bleacher seats in left field for the World Series that increased seating at the stadium by approximately 50 percent. He would happily pay Greenberg his $500 bonus.

Navin attentively watched the games from his box seat behind home plate and said he was getting more satisfaction out of the season than any other since he had become involved with baseball thirty years earlier. He had cultivated another winning team, largely from players developed in the Detroit farm system. Leaning back in his office chair with a rare smile spreading across his face, Navin told a reporter midseason, "You know there is a certain thrill and satisfaction in getting what you want, but the satisfaction is greater when you build it yourself—whether it be a home, a garden or a baseball team."

With their boys back in September, Navin and the fans were anxious for the team to consummate their joy. They were so close, up six games. The pennant looked like a certainty, ready to be secured any day. But then the Tigers faltered and dropped three straight to the Athletics. Over in the National League, the Giants—considered such a lock on first place that the commissioner's office worked out the World Series schedule at the Polo Grounds—had a seven-game lead over the Cardinals on September 6. They would capsize, with the Cardinals overtaking them on the penultimate day of the season. Such a fate for the Tigers seemed to their fans cruel and unthinkable—yet entirely possible.

The good people of Detroit had seen their factories close. Their banks fail. Their stocks wither. They had placed their faith in baseball, believing it could lift them from the despair all around them, but now, they feared that baseball, too, would fail them. *Sports Illustrated* writer Kyle Crichton described the solemn scene at Navin Field a half hour before one of the losses to the Athletics: "The crowd was filing to its pews like mourners in a cathedral. They spoke in muted tones, seemed to walk on padded feet and hunched their shoulders in apprehension. They watched infield practice through misty, frightened eyes and the silence was so profound that the crack of a bat sounded like atomic artillery. Down on the field, the Tigers acted like doomed men."

Hank remained the only Tiger still going strong. On Saturday, September 8, he carried the team with his Louisville Slugger, driving in both runs in a 2–1 win. The next day, September 9, he drove in the winning run in the tenth inning. It seemed the Bengals' lone hope for clinching the pennant rested in the strength of Hank's thirty-six-ounce signature bat.

That, of course, intensified the pressure on him to play the next day, Rosh Hashanah. Sunday evening, he attended services at Congregation Shaarey Zedek for the beginning of the New Year, and that night he wrestled with his dilemma. He hardly slept. Navin, Tiger fans and his teammates gratefully accepted his decision to play on Monday—and win the third game in a row with "those two home runs which went whistling out of Navin Field." So, too, did most Jews. "It was a great day for the boys on Chicago Blvd., Rochester Ave., Boston Blvd., and the entire [Jewish] neighborhood bordering on the Shaarey Zedek synagogue," the *Detroit Jewish Chronicle*, Michigan's only Anglo-Jewish newspaper at the time, reported in an article headlined, "'Hank's' Rosh Hashanah: The Epic Story of the Lanky Tiger First Baseman Who Is Hero of the Detroit Baseball Fans and Is Acclaimed by Boys in the Synagogue." "Worshippers on the way to services on Tuesday morning heard the word passed around by our boys on these streets: 'Hank will be in *shul* today [for the second day of Rosh Hashanah].'"

Once again the congregation buzzed when Hank entered through the synagogue's massive bronze doors. This time, it wasn't in speculation of what he would do but in admiration of what he had done. He was Joshua, returning home victorious, walking down the aisle to take his seat. The excitement bubbled into applause. The faithful cheered him not for his religious conviction but for who he was, a Jew, one who had joined them, affirming them in their place. They loved him for who he was and what he had done. Rabbi Abraham Hershman, a bookish man with a thin beard, had been *davening* (reciting prayers), when Hank walked in. He had to ask for quiet to continue.

The *Detroit Jewish Chronicle*'s account of Hank's Rosh Hashanah began,

"There are 75,000 Jews in Detroit—but 74,999 were of no consequence on Rosh Hashanah. Only one Jewish lad mattered to Detroit on that day—Henry 'Hank' Greenberg, the lanky Tiger first baseman. It is no exaggeration to say that many Jews forgot their approach to God—because baseball ruled as king—and that as far as the non-Jewish community was concerned, Greenberg was the only Jew alive." Despite its seeming accusation that Greenberg distracted Jews from their faith, the article lauded him. The abundant national attention focused upon his Holy Day dilemma had cast him as the singular representative of the Jews that day. On the first day of year 5695, Hank Greenberg was America's Jew. And widely revered as such.

While some had criticized his decision to place baseball before religion, the majority had embraced his actions. Not only did he have the blessing of the city's chief authority on Orthodox Jewish law, Rabbi Joseph Thumim, Hank had won the respect of other second-generation Jewish-Americans in the Thirties searching for the way to balance their religious heritage with their place in the new world. "The Jews are completely confused in the second generation," Rabbi Michael Paley explained. "They don't know if they should just assimilate because this is the last place they have to go or stay apart and build their own society as they had done in Poland. That is the clash of identity that sets the groundwork for him [Greenberg]."

Greenberg showed them that assimilation didn't mean selling out. A Jew could fully immerse himself in American life—he could play the national pastime like Hank—and he could be true to his tradition—he had the *choice* not to play, and he could worship in *shul* with his people. By attending religious services in the morning and playing baseball in the afternoon, he struck the perfect balance for the Jewish-American. "His decision not to choose between American and Jewish alternatives, but instead to embrace both has inspired American Jews ever since," historian Jerry Auerbach (and Hank's second cousin) writes. "He affirmed his commitment as a player on the American team without diminishing his identity as a Jew. It was, by any measure, an iconic moment in American Jewish history."

When Hank left Shaarey Zedek to play Tuesday afternoon's game, the children again raced after him. They cheered him as he left, the hero departing once again for the fields where he performed his feats of glory.

The attention and applause—so out of place during solemn services—embarrassed Hank. "He resented being given so much attention while in *shul* for Holy Day services," the *Detroit Jewish Chronicle* noted. Just as he wanted to be a ballplayer rather than a Jewish ballplayer on the diamond, he wanted to be simply a Jew in the synagogue, not the ball-playing Jew. But, as he was coming to understand, his dual identities were inseparable, for better or worse.*

On the strength of Greenberg's two home runs the previous day, Mickey Cochrane moved Hank into the cleanup spot for Tuesday's game. When Hank came to bat, Ty Tyson, the voice of the Tigers on WWJ, referencing the popular song, "Bang, bang, bang, go the British," declared that from now on at Navin Field, it would be "Bang, bang, bang, go the Yiddish." But Tuesday's game proved anticlimactic. Hank went oh-for-three in an eleven-inning loss.

The Tigers' lead over the Yankees dipped to three and a half games, but on Friday, September 14, Hank came to bat in the ninth inning with the Tigers trailing by a run. "Pickle one!" his personal fan Sammy Kaufman yelled from his usher post. That's what Hank did, sending a solo shot over the fence to save the game. The Tigers won it in the twelfth and kept winning.

By Wednesday, September 19, the Tigers had won six straight and increased their lead over the Yankees to seven and a half games. They had not technically clinched the pennant, but it was nearly assured. Hank's

---

* Hank Greenberg used to tell the story that the congregation applauded for him when he entered Shaarey Zedek for Yom Kippur services, but I believe his memory betrayed him. The first recorded account of Hank's version is in Lawrence Ritter's *The Glory of Their Times*, published nearly thirty years after the fact. Greenberg repeated the story in a television interview in 1984, fifty years after the event, and in his autobiography, which he recorded from memory in the year before his death in 1986. His autobiography is not reliable, riddled as it is with errors, particularly surrounding dates, with some events placed in the wrong year. Judy Cantor, who attended the Yom Kippur services at Shaarey Zedek in 1934 and is now the congregation's archivist, told me, "They did not applaud." I am inclined to think Greenberg is right in remembering the applause—an event of that significance seems likely to remain with someone—but mistaken in his recollection of the date. I think the *Detroit Jewish Chronicle* account, published three days after the fact, which reported, "Hank was met by a cheering group as he came and left services on that day," is the most likely to be accurate.

decision whether or not to play that day, Yom Kippur, was different from his decision nine days earlier on Rosh Hashanah. The circumstances had changed. With the pennant race virtually over, the consequences of his decision were more personal than universal. If the team lost without him, he wouldn't be depriving the team and community first place.

So, on Yom Kippur, "the Greatest Jewish Baseball Player of All Time" honored his family, friends and faith by spending the day at Shaarey Zedek. He had attended Kol Nidre services the evening before at Temple Beth El, most likely with his friends Sidney and Harold Allen, who were members there. Hank later gave two reasons for not playing on Yom Kippur. First, it is the Day of Atonement. "You're supposed to put everything aside and atone for the sins of the year," he said. This was important to him as a young man. Second, though perhaps the more compelling of his reasons, was "respect for my parents. This is what they believed in, so naturally I, out of respect to them, go along with not playing on Yom Kippur."

The Tigers lost to the Yankees that day, but they still held a six and a half game lead. Five days later, they secured the pennant and their place in the 1934 World Series. The city threw them a parade. Now that their boys had topped the American League, Detroit fans could not wait for them to do what their beloved Bengals of the previous generation could not: win a World Series. "Delirious Detroit, the ancient city of Cadillac, awaited the start of the World Series with all the accumulated excitement of a million kids who have been promised the first circus parade that has struck town in twenty-five years," *The Sporting News* editor Taylor Spink wrote.

Hank improved tremendously his sophomore season. He played 153 games, every game but one. He batted .339, a jump of 38 points from his rookie year. He drove in 139 runs, scored 118 and broke Moose Alexander's team home run record by slugging twenty-six. He led the major leagues in doubles (63), only four shy of the MLB record. He also improved his fielding percentage slightly while handling 25 percent more chances. Strikeouts continued to plague the free-swinging slugger. He whiffed 93 times, or about once every six at-bats.

Overall, Greenberg had a terrific season, but it was ten days in September that shaped his legend. Edgar A. Guest, the people's poet, celebrated the drama of Greenberg's High Holy Days in his verse "Speaking of Greenberg" that ran in the *Detroit Free Press* on October 4, the day after the World Series started. The Detroit resident knew something about immigration. Born in England, Guest had moved to the United States with his family as a ten-year-old boy and faced the pressures of assimilation himself, though not as a Jew.

He wrote:

The Irish didn't like it when they heard of Greenberg's fame
For they thought a good first baseman should possess an Irish name;
And the Murphys and Mulrooneys said they never dreamed they'd see
A Jewish boy from Bronxville out where Casey used to be.
In the early days of April not a Dugan tipped his hat
Or prayed to see a "double" when Hank Greenberg came to bat.

In July the Irish wondered where he'd ever learned to play.
"He makes me think of Casey!" Old Man Murphy dared to say;
And with fifty-seven doubles and a score of homers made
The respect they had for Greenberg was being openly displayed.
But on the Jewish New Year when Hank Greenberg came to bat
And made two home runs off pitcher Rhodes—they cheered like
mad for that.

Came Yom Kippur—holy fast day worldwide over to the Jew—
And Hank Greenberg to his teaching and the old tradition true
Spent the day among his people and he didn't come to play.
Said Murphy to Mulrooney, "We shall lose the game today!
We shall miss him on the infield and shall miss him at the bat,
But he's true to his religion—and I honor him for that!"

Edgar Guest's poem, which circulated widely, immortalized Greenberg alongside Casey in baseball lore. More significantly, the poem demonstrated that the Jewish ballplayer had become a fixture in the national landscape. Here was a Jew who had become a Jewish hero as a ballplayer and an American hero as a Jew to "the old tradition true." "It was the single biggest thing in sports history to the Jewish community to that time," recalled Marty Glickman, the Jewish sprinter who got bumped from the '36 U.S. Olympic team.

Novelist Leslie Epstein was so taken by Guest's poem that in his novel *San Remo Drive* he has the father recite the verse in a familiar ritual to comfort his sons after a traumatic family fight. In life as in art, the story of Greenberg's observance of the High Holy Days in 1934 has been told over and over like another Bible story. Children learn about Abraham, Jacob, David and Hank. "Every Jewish boy growing up around that time knew that story," said Auerbach, the historian.

Harold Kempner, who left Lithuania in 1925 and settled in Detroit, believed Greenberg was an important symbol of assimilation. Each year, he told his children, Aviva and Jonathan, how Hank had sat out Yom Kippur. "I thought Hank Greenberg was part of the Kol Nidre liturgy," said Aviva Kempner, who directed the documentary *The Life and Times of Hank Greenberg*.

The newspapers in Detroit and across the country praised Hank for his observance. "Besides showing himself to be a diamond star of the first-star magnitude, Greenberg revealed that he was also a good Jew when he stayed out of the lineup Yom Kippur," the *Detroit News* declared. Bill Bryson noted in *Baseball Magazine*: "He had led his ancestral race into a new promised land, the field where they have been comparative strangers." Bud Shaver, the *Detroit Times* sports editor: "He feels and acknowledges his responsibility as a representative of the Jews in the field of a great national sport and the Jewish people could have no finer representative."

Hank read the newspapers. He no doubt felt the pressure that came with all of the commentary on his status, such as that from *Detroit Free Press* editor Malcolm Bingay: "The Jewish people are to be congratulated that Greenberg is such a splendid type of their people. He is in position to do untold good in breaking down the mean and vicious prejudices against an ancient and honorable people." Hank was no longer being asked to carry his team; he was being prevailed upon to carry his people.

That sort of pressure had ruined the major league career of John McGraw's "Great Jewish Hope," Andy Cohen. The Giant second baseman's hot start in 1928 ignited an outpouring of adulation. "Everywhere Cohen played, they feted him with special 'days' and demanded his appearance at their synagogues and organizations, seizing the moment to identify themselves with a young Jewish man making good in a very visible American way," historian Peter Ellis writes. Jewish charities requested his support. Manufacturers asked that he endorse their products. Admirers camped outside his house just to get a look at him. The stress caused him to lose a pound a day. By the end of the season, Cohen had cooled, and the following year he played inconsistently. "Cohen's role as a national symbol for people eager to assert their own claims of Jewish pride and American possibility became a personal burden for the young ballplayer," Levine writes.

Cohen played thirteen more seasons of professional ball, but never made it back to the major leagues. In 1934, he was playing for the Minneapolis Millers in the American Association and Greenberg, who had rooted for Cohen as a Giant fan himself back in the Bronx, could empathize. "Cohen was the victim of circumstances," Hank told the *Detroit Jewish Chronicle*. "Too much was expected of him after all the deliberate effort to build him up for the New York fans. . . . I am on friendly terms with all the players and simply ignore the nasty remarks from the stands, whether they pertain to my race or anything else."

That wasn't completely accurate. The remarks did sting Hank, who still had a thin skin. "Every ballpark I went to, there'd be someone who spent the whole afternoon calling me names," Hank later admitted. He compared them to people who got their jollies at the zoo poking sticks into the animals' cages. "If you're having a good day, you don't give a damn, but if you're having a bad day, why, pretty soon it gets you hot under the collar. It's hard not to be sensitive."

And he was not on good terms with all of the players. Earl Whitehill still didn't like him, the bench jockeys rode him mercilessly, and he had an ongoing feud with the Senators' Heinie Manush. Hank was in for a rude reckoning with the St. Louis Cardinals in the World Series. Would the same fate that had befallen Cohen topple Hank? Or would the "Jewish Babe Ruth" be able to weather the pressure of expectations that mounted with his rising popularity? On the eve of the World Series, he felt the weight of that pressure. "I was so nervous I couldn't eat," he said.

The thirty-first edition of the World Series opened at Michigan and Trumbull on October 3, a cool Wednesday afternoon, with Navin Field dressed up in red, white and blue bunting, and 42,505 spectators—mostly delirious Detroiters—filling the grandstand and new bleacher seats. Henry Ford chomped on peanuts in his box by the home team dugout along with his son Edsel and the popular humorist Will Rogers. On September 17, two days before Yom Kippur, Henry Ford had attended what was believed to be his first baseball game. He watched the Tigers blank the Yankees 3–0. He also saw a profit opportunity in Detroit's hysteria over the Bengals. In August, the Ford Motor Company had hired Mickey Cochrane to present seven weekly radio broadcasts on the major league pennant races over twenty-two CBS stations. The popularity of those first commercially sponsored network broadcasts prompted Ford to pay $100,000 for the exclusive rights to sponsor the World Series over the NBC and CBS radio networks, the first time that Major League Baseball had sold broadcasting rights to the Fall Classic. Commissioner Kenesaw Landis earmarked $42,000 of that money to supplement the players' shares, upping each winner's take by $1,000 and each loser's by $600. That was big money during the Depression, when a loaf of bread cost a nickel and a quart of milk a dime, and an added incentive. It also set the precedent for assigning radio and television revenues to the players' pool.

Ty Tyson settled into his perch high behind home plate to describe the action to those eager fans clustered around radio sets in offices and schools and street corners around the region. He almost hadn't made it there. Initially, Landis had ruled that Tyson could not man the microphone for the World Series broadcasts, lest the popular voice of the Tigers appear "too partial." Tyson, a Tyrone, Pennsylvania, native, had become dear to many Detroiters since he had begun narrating the Tiger games seven years earlier. His reedy voice had become a welcome fixture of their living rooms. Landis had underestimated Tyson's popularity. More than half a million fans wrote the commissioner to protest his ruling. He reversed his decision, and Tyson greeted his listening audience for the start of the Series.

In the other electronic medium of the day, the newsreels showed the Tigers playing catch in front of their dugout. The voice-over noted "Henry Greenberg with that mitt as big as a hot water bottle." That season Hank had jerry-rigged his first baseman's mitt with bicycle tape between the thumb and fingers to form a webbing that extended three inches above the mitt's edge. His modification made it easier to field ground balls and scoop throws than with a traditional mitt, which was flat as a pancake and dexterous as an iron skillet. His Rawlings became an object of fascination, likened to a "miniature lacrosse stick" by the *New York Sun* and called "as voluminous as a whale's pillow slip" by the *New York Post*. Other teams didn't like it, but nothing in the rulebook rendered Hank's adaptation illegal.

Hank also used a crude version of today's Stickum. He chewed licorice and spat the sticky substance into the palm of his mitt to help him grip throws. He worked a piece of licorice on one side of his mouth and gum on the other. When an umpire asked him what he was chewing, he pulled out the gum to show him. The *New York Sun* reported on the eve of the Series, "He is ready to do it again—with the licorice shifted out of bounds in favor of gum whenever it becomes necessary."

The newsreels also captured the Tigers' opponents horsing around in front of their dugout. Hank wished the Cardinals had not overtaken the Giants. The Polo Grounds would have made it convenient for more family and friends from the old neighborhood to watch him play. He also would have relished the chance to show the Giants what they had missed—*Still think I'm "too big and awkward"?!* And that left field fence, only 279 feet down the line, "You could bunt 'em into that Polo Grounds stand," his teammates told him. He took some consolation in the fact that the new wooden bleacher seats Navin had added in left field shortened the fence by twenty feet, from 339 to 319 down the line. He still had to clear the extra twenty vertical feet of the left field screen, but Navin Field now had the fourth shortest left field wall in the majors.*

Instead of the Giants, the Tigers faced the St. Louis Cardinals (who would later become known as the Gashouse Gang),† a ragtag bunch of

---

* Behind the Polo Grounds, Yankee Stadium (301 feet) and Fenway (312)

† According to John Heidenry, author of *The Gashouse Gang*, there is no reference in newspapers from 1934 to the Cardinals as "The Gashouse Gang." The team was tagged with the nickname retroactively, and it stuck. Various theories of its origins abound, with at least two crediting Leo Durocher. Though no definite explanations have emerged, there is agreement that the nickname indicates a slovenly group of social undesirables.

unshaven men in dirty uniforms that "thought they could beat anybody—and they could." They were mostly a group of working-class Southerners with colorful nicknames powered by Ducky Medwick, Ripper Collins, Spud Davis, Pepper Martin, Dizzy Dean along with his brother Daffy and managed by the thirty-five-year-old Fordham Flash, Frankie Frisch, who had put on a show for Hank Greenberg at his first major league game a decade earlier. Jay Hanna "Dizzy" Dean, who had won thirty games en route to being named the National League's Most Valuable Player, admitted his only worry was how to pitch to Greenberg.

While Hank took his cuts for the photographers and newsreel cameras before the game, Dizzy walked by and nudged him aside to take his own cuts and steal the show. Hank, already on edge before his first World Series game, seethed at being shown up.

Hank felt the jitters on the field with all of the reporters and cameras milling about and the fans filling the stadium. Someone told him not to be nervous. "That's like telling somebody not to be sick," Hank snapped. "How in the hell can you help it? It just comes."

When the game began, the Tigers—even the unflappable Gehringer—played nervous, booting five chances and letting the Cardinals grab an early lead with three unearned runs. Or, as Joe Williams put it in the *World-Telegram*, "In the early phases of the game, the Tiger infield functioned with all the grace and smoothness of an antiquated beer truck." Hank had committed one of the Tiger errors, bobbling a ball in the third inning that allowed a Cardinal run to score. Dizzy Dean had yelled from the dugout, "Hey, Moe!* C'mon in the clubhouse and get your meal money. You're the best player we got."

Hank came to bat in the third with the Tigers trailing 3–1. In his first World Series at-bat, he had grounded out with a man on base to end the inning. He admitted he had been scared to face Dean even before he came to bat. Now, Hank walked to the plate with Gehringer on second and Cochrane on third with two outs. A base hit would tie the game. Greenberg dug in and studied Dean on the mound. The right-hander who had led the National League in strikeouts for the third straight year set with his

---

* A variation of Moses, used in a derogatory way.

back bowed, making him look like he had slept on his stomach in a hammock.

"Don't waste your fastball," yelled Leo Durocher from his position at short. Known as "the Lip" and one of the team's leading bench jockeys along with Dizzy and Frisch, Durocher had mocked the Tigers mercilessly for their errors. He, too, was a noted anti-Semite.* Now, with Greenberg at the plate and runners in scoring position, the Lip yelled to Dean on the mound, "Throw the son of a bitch a ham sandwich. He won't touch it."

Dean got two strikes on Greenberg. Hank flailed at the next pitch and missed, contorting himself off balance. His strikeout killed the rally.

In the sixth, Hank managed his first World Series hit, a single to center. Rounding first, he saw the center fielder misplay the ball, and he humped into second. He scored on Goslin's base hit to left, but by then the Cardinals led 8–2.

In the eighth, Dean again faced Greenberg but let the ball get up on him. Frankie Frisch walked to the mound from second base. "Damn it, Jerome, quit fooling around or I'll yank your butt out of there," the Cardinals' player-manager told Dizzy. "Keep the ball down."

"Oh, Frankie," Dean replied. "You ain't a-gonna take out ol' Diz. All these good folks would think you was crazy. I'm just a-figurin' that Moe can't hit my high hard one."

But Dean didn't keep the ball down, and he found out what Greenberg could do with it. Hank unleashed that powerful swing and, as the newsreel described it, "walloped that apple into the left field bleachers for a home run."

The 17,000 fans in left field went crazy along with the rest of the Navin Field faithful. Meanwhile, fifteen miles away, a nine-year-old boy listened to Ty Tyson's call of Greenberg's home run in the auditorium of James Garfield Elementary, Wyandotte, Michigan, along with several other lucky students chosen to provide updates to their classmates. Harvey Frank, the boy who gave his parents nightly reports on Greenberg, returned to his fifth-grade classroom at the end of the inning. While he wrote the score on

---

* When Durocher later managed the Cubs, he frequently called out to Ken Holtzman, one of his pitchers, "Hey, Jew," or "C'mon, kike." He also referred to Holtzman as "a gutless Jew" in front of his teammates.

the board, he said, "Greenberg hit a home run." The other students regarded their Jewish classmate, and he felt a special pride swell within him. "Because he was a hero, I was a little bit of a hero, too," Harvey said.

With Hank trotting around the bases, Dizzy shouted to Frisch, "Don't get excited, Frank, 'cause it won't happen again. 'Sides, you're right. Moe can hit the dog shit out of a high fast one."*

Hank's home run made it 8–3, and that's how the game ended. Afterward, Dizzy complained to the gaggle of reporters in the Cardinals' clubhouse that he hadn't had his best stuff that day. "Greenberg hit a ball that I couldn't get where I wanted it," Dizzy told them. "I was trying to keep my curveball outside on him, and I got it inside. Anybody could have hit that ball for a home run. Our clubhouse boy could have done it. I still don't think he's bad to pitch to."

The next day, Schoolboy Rowe retired twenty-two consecutive batters, a performance unequaled until Don Larsen's perfect game in 1956, but Cardinals pitcher Wild Bill Hallahan pitched equally effectively, limiting the Tigers to one run. With the Tigers losing 2–1 in the bottom of the ninth, the 43,451 fans shoehorned into Navin Field feared their Bengals might drop the first two games before heading to St. Louis for the next three. But Pete Fox singled to right, Rowe moved him to second with a sacrifice bunt, and Gee Walker—pinch-hitting for center fielder Jo-Jo White—drove Fox home with a single to tie the game and force extra innings. In the twelfth, Gehringer walked and so did Greenberg, who'd gone hitless on the day. Hank had a chance to tie the game with an extra-base hit in the bottom of the third when he came to bat with the Cardinals leading 2–0, runners on first and third and two outs. Instead, he struck out to squash the rally. Goslin's twelfth-inning single brought home Gehringer to win the game 3–2 and even the Series.

The teams took the night train to St. Louis for the next three games at Sportsman's Park. Hank batted in the third inning of Game Three with runners on second and third, this time with only one out. With the Tigers down 2–0, Greenberg again had the chance to tie the game with a base hit.

---

* This story has been told in variation about Dean facing other batters. Whether or not it's true, it captures the essence of his swaggering personality.

He faced Paul Dean, nicknamed Daffy. Though not his older brother's equal in talent, Dean had thrown a no-hitter late in the season. Daffy relied on his fastball to get two strikes on Hank. Then Greenberg swung madly at a bad pitch and struck out, once again stranding the runners. He had batted eight times in the Series with teammates on base and failed to advance a single runner. He had struck out four times with men in scoring position. The pressure seemed to have subdued him.

In the ninth, with the Cardinals up 4–0, Hank came to bat hitless on the day, with Jo-Jo White on first and two out. This time, Greenberg connected on a Daffy pitch, good for a triple that scored White. But it was too little, too late for the Tigers, who lost 4–1. After the game, Dizzy Dean continued to target Hank with his criticism. "Now, boys," he told the reporters in the Cardinals' clubhouse. "Don't let this get out, but you know that ball Greenberg hit in the ninth? Well, Paul just laid it in there for him. Felt sorry for the poor guy, striking out all the time!"

Cochrane chewed out his players before Game Four on Saturday, October 6, and pointedly dropped Hank from the cleanup spot to sixth in the batting order. The team responded, drubbing the Cardinals 10–4 to even the Series at two games apiece. Hank led the effort, going four-for-five with two doubles, one of which just missed being a home run, and three RBI. He even stole home on a passed ball. The game's most memorable play came in the fourth inning when Dizzy Dean spontaneously inserted himself as a pinch runner. He took off running for second on a ground ball but never slid. Throwing to first to complete a double play, Billy Rogell beaned Dean in the forehead. Dizzy staggered, then collapsed. His teammates carried him off the field, and he went to the hospital for X-rays.[*]

Dizzy didn't miss his start for Game Five on Sunday. But this time, Tommy Bridges, the Tigers' curveball maestro, bested him 3–1. Greenberg scored the first run of the game after walking in the second inning. In the fourth, he batted with runners on first and third and the chance to add to the Tigers' 1–0 lead, but he struck out on four pitches. He did drive in a run in the sixth on a sacrifice fly to right field that proved to be the game

---

[*] Legend has it that the *St. Louis Post-Dispatch* headline the next day declared, "X-Rays of Dean's Head Show Nothing," but the actual headline in the October 7 edition read, "X-Ray Photograph of Head Shows No Lasting Injury."

winner. The teams headed back to Detroit, where the Tigers felt certain they would finish off the Cardinals, especially after beating Dizzy Dean. "This isn't over yet," Cochrane warned his players. "We got to keep bearing down." Hundreds of fans greeted the Tigers at Fort Street Union Station. They, too, were eager to celebrate Detroit's first world championship.

The largest crowd of the Series, some 44,551 spectators, pressed into Navin Field, filling all of the seats and standing wherever they could glimpse the field. But Daffy Dean put the champagne on hold, outdueling School-boy Rowe. The Cardinals continued the verbal barrage against Greenberg, yelling things so nasty they made Frank Frisch, the veteran player-manager, blush. "The things they said to him were something awful," Frisch said. "All during the Series there were four fellows on our bench that you wouldn't think would ever say a word to anybody, but they kept after Greenberg until the poor guy was nearly crazy."

Hank batted in the sixth with Goslin on first and Gehringer on third, two outs and the Tigers behind 3–1. Hank had struck out looking in the first and popped out to the shortstop in the fourth. This time, he managed to block out the nastiness and smack a Daffy Dean pitch into left field for a single that scored Gehringer and closed the margin to 3–2. He batted in the eighth, again with Goslin at first and Gehringer at third and two outs, this time the Tigers down 4–3. It seemed every time he came to bat this Series was in a pressure situation with the chance for him to shine or stink. A base hit here would at least tie the game. Something in the gap would put the Tigers ahead, perhaps even seal the Series. He had come through for the team forty times that season. He figured Dean would throw him a fast-ball. Sure enough, Daffy hummed a fastball right in Hank's sweet spot.

But Hank stood motionless for a called strike. With all of the stars aligned for him to succeed, he froze. He eventually hit a foul pop fly caught by first baseman Ripper Collins that killed the rally. Yet again. That missed opportunity, perhaps more than any other of the Series, haunted Hank. "I often wondered what would've happened if I'd jumped on that fastball," he said more than forty years later.

The Tigers ultimately lost 4–3, but the pivotal play occurred in the sixth inning. Before Greenberg batted, Goose Goslin bunted to move Geh-ringer to second and Cochrane to third. Bill DeLancey, the Cardinals' catcher, fielded the ball and threw to third. Cochrane slid and thought he had beaten the tag. So did the 44,000-plus fans in Navin Field. Photographs later reinforced the notion. But umpire Brick Owens disagreed and called the Tigers' player-manager out. Had Owens ruled him safe, Cochrane would have scored on Rogell's fly ball to tie the game and Greenberg's hit would have pushed the Tigers ahead. Clark Griffith, the Senators' owner and president, accused the umpire of stealing the Series from the Tigers.

After the loss, Tiger owner Frank Navin was despondent about the call. Cleveland Indians' general manager Billy Evans tried to cheer him up. "Never mind, Frank," Evans said. "By getting beat today you get a seventh game and that'll mean $50,000 to you anyway."

"To hell with the $50,000," Navin snapped. "I'd give the $50,000 and five times that to have won today. I've been waiting thirty-five years to see Detroit win a world championship here, and when we've got one in our grip, some guy blows it for us."

They played Game Seven the following afternoon, Tuesday, October 9. Henry Ford returned to his box seats, this time with his wife at his side. During infield practice, Dizzy Dean wandered over to the Tigers' dugout. Seeing Greenberg, he said, "Hello, Mose. What makes you so white? Boy, you're a-shakin' like a leaf. I get it; you done hear that Old Diz was goin' to pitch. Well, you're right. It'll all be over in a few minutes. Old Diz is goin' to pitch, and he's goin' to pin your ears back."

The game was scoreless after two innings, still anybody's to claim. But Tigers' rookie submarine pitcher Elden Auker loaded the bases in the third. With a full count and the runners going on the pitch, Frisch lined a ball over Greenberg's head. The ball looked like it was hit harder than it was. Hank jumped a fraction of a second too soon. The ball ricocheted off the extra webbing of his glove into right field. All three runners scored. Frisch ended up on second. Cochrane replaced Auker with Rowe, but the onslaught continued through two more pitchers, and the Cardinals racked up seven runs before the inning ended. "The people were so disappointed," Auker said. "They knew right then it was over."

All that excitement and promise screwed to a fever pitch gave way to disappointment and frustration when Ducky Medwick tripled in the sixth inning and slid hard into Tigers' third baseman Marv Owen. Medwick had gashed Cochrane's thigh with his spikes sliding into home in the first game. The ordinarily easygoing Owen snapped at Medwick, and the fans booed. Medwick eventually scored, putting the Cardinals up 8–0 and further inciting the crowd. When he took his place in left field for the bottom of the sixth, the fans unleashed their frustration on him with oranges, bottles, hard-boiled eggs, apple cores, half-eaten sandwiches—whatever they could find. "If somebody had an old Ford, they would've thrown that out at him," Rogell said. Ty Tyson pleaded over the public address system for the fans to end the bombardment. After three delays in twenty minutes, Landis summoned Medwick to his box and ejected him, a first in World Series history. "We want to go on with this game," the commissioner said. "And it wouldn't look so good if a World Series game had to be forfeited. So get it over with."

It was. Dizzy had tamed the Tiger bats, especially Greenberg's Louisville Slugger. Hank managed a single to lead off the fifth inning, but Dizzy struck him out the other three times he faced him. In his final trip to the plate of the Series, Hank batted with Rogell on first, Goslin on second and one out. Another chance to drive in a run. But by then, he was defeated, too. Dean laughed at him when he missed one of his curves. Blinded by his humiliation, Hank swung wildly at a fastball a foot over his head, his ninth strikeout of the Series—the image that would stick in the minds of many looking for someone to blame for the Tigers' defeat.

Dizzy Dean scattered six hits in an 11–0 rout that broke the hearts of the hometown crowd. Greenberg had batted .321 in his first World Series and driven in seven runs in seven games, but the man who had come through in the clutch so many times for the Tigers that season had failed to do so when it mattered most. The press hammered him for that. He took the criticism hard.

That didn't eliminate the accolades, though. Greenberg was cheered as the featured guest at banquets, such as the "Father & Son Night" attended by 1,000 fathers and sons at Brookline's Brotherhood Temple Ohabei Shalom on December 27. The United States Maccabi Association asked him to be its baseball adviser. That winter he spoke throughout New England to promote the Jewish Olympic Games scheduled for the following spring in

Palestine. Along the way, he overshadowed his speaking companions, Giants quarterback Harry Newman, Olympic skating champion Irving Jaffee and former welterweight champ Benny Leonard.

Hank returned to the Bronx a bigger hero than ever. "He was given the biggest reception and ovation by the Jews in the Bronx that New York had ever seen," the *Detroit Jewish Chronicle* reported. "Hank Greenberg owned the town. Jewish matrons saw to it that their offspring were on the sandlots playing baseball as soon as they came home from school. Every kid in the borough who is able to hold a bat in his hand is an embryo 'Bruggy' Greenberg."

He had begun to change the way Jews thought about baseball and the way baseball fans—Americans—thought about Jews.

CHAPTER SIX

MVP

The cruelties of Game Seven seemed destined to replay themselves in an exhibition game the week before the Tigers opened the 1935 season. Hank batted in the bottom of the eighth with a runner on second, the score tied and two out. Here he was with the chance to win the ball game once again, or at least put his team ahead, like he had been so many times during the World Series six months prior. Hank had struck out twice already in his previous two at-bats. He was determined not to do so again, just as he was determined not to repeat his World Series failures. It had been a long winter, brooding on those failures, particularly the nine strikeouts.

The crowd in the Charleston, South Carolina, stadium razzed him when he approached the batter's box. On the basis of his improvement during the '34 regular season, Hank had asked for—and received, without the usual dithering from Navin—double his salary from last year, a $5,000 raise. The fans let him know they expected more of him than a pair of strikeouts. Hank responded by saluting Tigers' first base coach Cy Perkins with his hand held high in the air. The *Detroit Times'* Bud Shaver interpreted his gesture, "Hank was telling the world in baseball sign language that the game was as good as over and that Greenberg's big bat would decide it."

Instead, he struck out. To kill the rally. Yet again.

Hank stalked back to the dugout fuming with humiliation.

This was October 1934 all over again. He had thought too much about what was at stake, tried too hard, messed up his timing—and come up short.

When he batted again in the thirteenth with the game tied, two Tigers on base and one out, the moment was ripe to foreshadow the upcoming season. The crowd harassed him more lustily, venting their frustration. *This guy's the high-paid star, yet he strikes out three times in a row? He makes a show like he's going to win it but whiffs instead? Ha!* "Sit down!" They jeered him. "Who's next?"

Hank, still angry, saluted again. This time the gesture was more, *Kiss my ass* than, *Watch this*. He doffed his cap.

And dug in, knowing he had heaped extra pressure on himself. "He couldn't afford to fail because he had dramatized himself too much," Shaver put it. "He was in deep."

Hank had set lofty goals for himself that season. He was intent upon improving over his breakout season. He wanted to hit 40 home runs. He wanted to boost his RBI production from last year's 139. And, though it took hubris to aim for, he wanted to make himself into the best player in the league. He knew he wouldn't do that by choking in the clutch.

He readied for the pitch—when a plaintive voice from the stands chided derisively, "Oy, yoy! Oy, yoy!"

Hank stiffened. His knuckles whitened. *Bastard.*

He willed his rage into determination and blasted a single to win the ball game.

Something else happened before the Tigers headed north. Before an exhibition game against the Brooklyn Dodgers, Hank sized up the opposition: first baseman Sam Leslie, who had batted .332 and driven in 102 runs the previous season; third baseman Joe Stripp, who had batted .315; shortstop Lonny Frey, who had scored 77 runs and punched 24 doubles; outfielder Buzz Boyle, who had batted .305, scored 88 runs and hit 10 triples. Hank realized these were good ballplayers, but none of them had his talent. He was no longer trying to make the team or win a starting spot. He had established himself as one of the game's top players. That epiphany engendered confidence. For the first time as a major league ballplayer, he believed in himself.

Hank would not be satisfied with the season unless he reached the goals he set for himself and the team won the World Series. His competitive nature wouldn't let him be content with second place. He wanted to show the critics and himself that he had the fortitude to win it all.

So, too, Frank Navin. The Tigers' owner had come close to satisfying his ambition but had fallen short. The stress had taken a further toll on his health, yet he thought this year's team was every bit as good as last year's. The Tigers had led the league in batting average (.300), runs scored (957), doubles (349) and stolen bases (125). They returned all of their starters, with some of the younger players like center fielder Jo-Jo White, third basemen Marv Owen and Greenberg likely to be improved with experience. Their pitching also looked strong. Schoolboy, with his 16-game winning streak, had gone 24–8; Tommy Bridges, with his domineering curveball, had won 22 games; Elden Auker had won 15 games; and Alvin "General" Crowder, a late-season addition, had gone 5–1. The staff had led the league with twelve shutouts. Frank Navin had every reason to believe that this year's team had what it took to fulfill his dream.

But the Tigers stumbled out of the gate. After a 9–2 spanking by the Indians, they had won only two of eleven games and sat like a rock in last place. A month later, after a 3–1 loss in New York, the Tigers were in sixth place with a 17–16 record. Despite his teammates' stumbles, Hank had been steady. The following day, May 28, he went four-for-five, smashing a double and two home runs while knocking in four runs, giving him 11 homers and 41 RBI on the season. "This year Detroit started badly," F. C. Lane noted in *Baseball Magazine*. "Schoolboy Rowe was inconsistent. Nothing seemed to go right. Mickey Cochrane began to wonder. But through it all, Greenberg stood like a tower of strength, poling out long hits, driving home runs. His example was infectious."

Hank had batted sixth most of last season; Cochrane appointed him the Tigers' cleanup hitter for '35. With Jo-Jo White, Cochrane and Gehringer batting before him, Greenberg frequently came to the plate with men on base. His role, as he saw it, was to convert those runners into runs. "It becomes my simple duty to advance them, and, if possible, to drive some of them home," Hank said.

Greenberg, with his powerful shoulders, arms and wrists, had a strong swing. His height gave him leverage. He swung his thirty-six-ounce Louisville Slugger hard at each ball, and, of course, many of those hard-hit balls cleared the fence, but he did not swing for the fences. "If I were on a second division team, where there was little at stake, I might be tempted to develop a stance and swing that would yield a maximum crop of homers," he said. "But in the cleanup position of a team that is fighting for the pennant, my role is to drive in runs, and to do it by any kind of hitting, not exclusively of the home run pattern."

Like many hitters of the day, Hank's swing would give today's batting instructors conniptions. His was anything but fluid and compact. He stood with his hands pushed back, his left arm almost straight. When the ball arrived, he pivoted with his left knee turning inward, drooped his hands belt-high, then reached back to his shoulder, took a big step with his left foot that slid his weight forward and into the lunge of his bat, which he slashed through the strike zone in an uppercut. He threw his entire body into the swing. When he missed, he often stumbled off balance. But when he connected, the ball exploded off his bat. What he lacked in grace, he made up for with extraordinary hand-eye coordination and strength.

Cochrane had convinced Hank to widen his stance for better stability, and Hank had learned to adjust his feet to the varying deliveries of different pitchers. He also benefited from talks in the dugout with Harry Heilmann, who often sat there with Hank before games. Heilmann, a Hall of Fame right-handed hitter who won four American League batting championships during the Twenties with the Tigers, corrected one of Hank's flaws with a terse observation, "Stop moving your head so much." That helped Hank with his balance and timing, allowing him to hit the ball more squarely.

Hank repeated his practice of showing up early at the park to work on his hitting and fielding. He studied other first basemen, like the Senators' Joe Kuhel and the Browns' Jack Burns, to glean tricks for manning that post. He took extra fungoes and throws to work on his hands and footwork. That greatly improved his ability to handle foul pop-ups and stab ground balls to his right. He unveiled a new mitt in '35, with the webbing enlarged over his already-embellished model the previous year. "Last year Hank had a glove which looked like a mattress for a Singer midget," Shaver wrote in the *Times*. "This year he has a bigger one. It is a half-inch larger in diameter, and it looks somewhat like a lobster trap. It has a thumb as long as Jimmy Durante's schnozzle." Hank still had a maddening habit of relying solely on his oversized glove. "He believes in never using two hands where you can use one and tries one hand often when two are absolutely necessary," one Detroit sportswriter sniped.

Hank continued to improve as a hitter, learning to hit the curve. This had several advantages. Not only did it make him harder to fool, it opened up the field. In his first two seasons, he was strictly a pull hitter, so the outfielders shifted, with the right fielder coming nearly to dead center. Learning to hit low curves to the opposite field, Greenberg forced the fielders to be more honest, opening up space for his drives to fall between the gaps. He was also becoming more disciplined, picking his pitches. He realized pitchers had been getting him out by setting him up with the high inside fastball followed by a curve tailing away. He still swung at some bad pitches and let good ones go by, but he showed more patience in his selection.

Heilmann tagged Hank with the fault of being a guess hitter. "The result is that quite often when Greenberg has decided that the pitcher will waste a ball, he finds it cutting the plate, and when his mind is made up that the pitcher will lay the next ball in, he swings on a ball that the pitcher intends to waste," Heilmann said.

Greenberg defended his practice. "I try to guess what the pitcher will give me most of the time," he said. "It is my firm belief that the great majority of ballplayers do the same thing. If I'm right, I am quite successful." But he did admit, "If I guess wrong, I sometimes look pretty bad."

He had been guessing right more often. The home runs and RBI began to rack up. Hank hit his second grand slam of the season on Sunday, June 23, at Navin Field. The temporary bleachers constructed for the '34 World Series had been removed, returning the left field fence to 339 feet, but the screen had also been taken down, which meant that many of the balls Greenberg had hit in '34 that struck the screen and ended up doubles now sailed cleanly over the fence for home runs. His home run that Sunday was his nineteenth of the season, tops in the majors. More important to Greenberg and his team, the four runs it drove in gave him 75 RBI in the Tigers' first fifty-nine games. Though the Tigers lost that day to the Senators, dropping Detroit to fourth place, fourteen of his home runs had resulted in wins.

Yet some people still refused to give Hank the credit he was due. A common gripe among fans at Navin Field, especially after one of Greenberg's spectacular strikeouts with men on base, persisted, "Greenberg never hits when we need it." The evidence proved otherwise, but the sentiment no doubt resulted from the World Series hangover. On Friday, June 28, Hank slugged three home runs in a doubleheader sweep in St. Louis. The day before, he had learned that despite leading the majors in home runs and RBI and batting .313, he had not been named to the American League All-Star squad for the third annual Midsummer Classic. The American League managers had selected Lou Gehrig as the team's first baseman and Jimmie Foxx, another first baseman, to play third base.

After the doubleheader, Hank smoked a cigar in the lobby of the Tigers' hotel. Charles Ward, sports editor of the *Detroit Free Press*, broached the subject of the All-Star selection. "How many RBI have I got?" Hank asked.

"Eighty-four," Ward said.

"Wrong," Hank said. "The number is eighty-five."

He took several puffs off his cigar. "How many does Gehrig have?"

Ward shook his head.

"You don't know, eh? Well, he'll be batting for quite a while before he gets up to eighty-five."

Gehrig in fact had driven in only 39 runs to Greenberg's eighty-five. He had hit only nine home runs. Foxx had 18 homers and 66 RBI. Even when Hank outperformed his rival, Gehrig remained superior in others' eyes. The practice then was to base selections on the previous season's results, but Hank still wondered what he needed to do to prove himself.

He graciously told the reporters, "They probably want experienced men." Double X had driven in 462 total runs the previous three seasons, and Gehrig had averaged 157 RBI the previous eight. Gehrig had won the Triple Crown in 1934; Foxx had won it in 1933. Others openly questioned the managers' picks. Hank smoldered over the snub. He took out his frustration on opponents. In the ten days between the time he found out he wasn't selected and the date the All-Star Game was played in Cleveland, Hank clubbed 6 home runs and pushed 25 runs across the plate.

Hank's fans wrote letters to protest the slight. Many of them were Jews who couldn't help but wonder if Hank had been left off the team for anti-Semitic reasons, either explicit or implicit. Sportswriters opined on the faulty selection. But that didn't change the lineup. All that changed was Hank's tear inspired the Tigers to win thirteen of fourteen games, moving them up to second place, only one game behind the Yankees.

By then, Hank had set a record for most RBI by the All-Star break (110). He led the AL in RBI, homers and was batting .317, which gave him a shot at the coveted Triple Crown. Other than Gehrig and Foxx, only two other AL players (Ty Cobb in 1909 and Nap Lajoie in 1901) had achieved that feat.

Hank was also in position to equal Babe Ruth's single-season home run record of 60, set in 1927. Frank Navin sent a letter and clipping from the *Christian Science Monitor* headlined, GREENBERG IS ONLY ONE HOMER BEHIND BABE RUTH'S PACE, to Hank at the New Yorker Hotel, most likely to inspire him. Other sportswriters caught on to the story. His home runs became "bulletin matter" in their papers and overshadowed the final scores. In Detroit and wherever Hank played, "there is a tenseness in the stands whenever Hank stalks to the plate," *The Sporting News* reported, with fans eager to see him move another home run closer to Ruth's record. The sportswriters started asking "the current home run sensation of the majors" whether he thought he could break the record. Hank admired Ruth, considered him the greatest player of all time, but the focus on his march to break the Babe's record annoyed Hank. He was not out to hit home runs or break home run records. "Many friendly people have asked me if I were trying to equal Babe Ruth's best record," he said diplomatically to a reporter. "I wish they would wait until I have a season, if I ever do, when I'm a good deal closer to Ruth's figures than I am likely to be this year. Perhaps if I saw a chance to equal his record, I might start cutting up at the ball the way he used to do and settle down to the deliberate attempt to make home runs. But, frankly, I have little hope in that direction. I have a nearer objective, to be with a winning ball club and to help them win. And the way to win ball games, as all the world knows, is to score more runs than the other fellow. The good batter, then, is the man who comes through in the pinch."

He also showed a precocious understanding of the way players were regarded in his comments to an Associated Press reporter. "If I set a new mark this year and then drop back to thirty-five or forty next season, the fans will be saying: 'That guy Greenberg isn't as good as he was a year ago.' They'll be counting me out, and I'll be rated as a has-been in my fourth year in the majors."

The attention promptly snipped his home run production. Hank hit only two home runs in his next nineteen games. But he continued to drive in runs and find ways to help his team win. On July 24 in the Bronx, Greenberg smacked his twenty-ninth double of the season, General Crowder shut out the Yankees and the Tigers swiped first place from their New York rivals.

There were other significant events happening that year: Amelia Earhart became the first person to fly solo from Hawaii to California, FBI agents killed Ma Barker in a shoot-out, a New Jersey jury convicted Bruno Hauptmann of the kidnap and murder of Charles Lindbergh Jr. and members of the American Federation of Labor organized the United Auto Workers union in Detroit. The Cincinnati Reds hosted the first nighttime baseball game, playing under the lights at Crosley Field on May 24, 1935. The next day, Babe Ruth hit three home runs—the last three of his career—for the Boston Braves; he retired six days later.

There were a couple subtle signs of economic recovery. The GNP grew 8.1 percent and unemployment dipped to 20.1 percent. Owners of major league baseball teams reported their first net profit in four years.

In March, Adolf Hitler began to rearm Germany and imposed military conscription, a blatant violation of the Versailles Treaty. He had seized absolute power of Germany the previous August upon the death of German President Paul von Hindenburg, declaring himself Fuhrer. Before the 1935 baseball season ended, the Fuhrer would enact the Nuremberg Laws, which stripped German Jews of their citizenship—making them subjects of the Third Reich—and forbid Jews from marrying or having sexual relations with Aryans under "The Law for the Protection of German Blood and German Honor."

In January 1935, Benno Levi and his two siblings were the first Jewish refugee children to arrive in Detroit. The Levi children would see their parents again, when they came over in 1938, but all of the aunts and uncles and cousins they had left behind were murdered in the concentration camps. Benno and his younger brother Ernest settled with the Rosenberg family in the Dexter section downtown, where nearly half of Detroit's Jews lived. Eleven-year-old Benno did not speak a word of English, nor had he ever heard of baseball in Alsfeld, his hometown north of Frankfurt. He and his brother enrolled at Roosevelt Elementary and quickly became acclimated to their new country. "Within three months, I was speaking English fluently and avidly following the Tigers and Hank Greenberg," Levi said. "Everybody followed Greenberg, even the old Jewish ladies. When Hank was up, they would be spellbound. Israel didn't exist then. Hank Greenberg did. He was the equivalent to the state of Israel."

That was how a German refugee became an American—you learned English and rooted for Greenberg. There were other prominent Jews in America at the time. Louis Brandeis had been appointed to the United States Supreme Court twenty years earlier, but until then he had been equivocal about his Jewishness, and, besides, what kid down at the park fantasizes about himself as a Supreme Court Justice? Albert Einstein had recently arrived at Princeton, but he had not yet achieved his folk hero status celebrated in life-size posters on college dorm walls. Boxers like Benny Leonard, Max Baer and Barney Ross had captured world titles, but their profession was sullied by links to organized crime. Albert Kahn, who lived in Detroit and was regarded as the world's foremost architect, was also an Uncle Tom, working for Henry Ford and designing the Detroit Athletic Club, which barred Jews from membership. Hollywood personalities such as Al Jolson and Irving Berlin had questionable moral standards for their personal lives. Other stars like Lauren Bacall had changed their names, assimilating by concealing their Jewish identity. And then there was Hank Greenberg, America's best-known Jew who embraced his identity, was a model citizen, stood tall and handsome as any of Hollywood's leading men and was able to clobber a baseball like Babe Ruth. "Greenberg is the first Jewish-American who truly becomes a popular hero," historian William Simons says.

"Greenberg provided Jewish-Americans of the Thirties with a standard bearer to offset popular portrayals of Jews as weaklings, victims and greedy shylocks," Simons writes. "Greenberg was an especially potent symbol to second-generation Jewish-Americans, the children of East European immigrants. They wanted acceptance, and Greenberg became their role model."

To some, he was even bigger. "I don't think anybody can imagine the terrific importance of Hank Greenberg to the whole Jewish community then," said Bert Gordon, son of a rabbi and an ardent baseball fan who grew up in Detroit during Greenberg's prime. "He was a god. He was the epitome of all the things we looked up to and wanted to do."

Hank Greenberg captured the imagination of the generation nationwide. He faced the same prejudice as other American Jews, suffered the same indignities, harbored the same fears, but didn't back down. In him, they could recognize their suffering and find hope. "For American Jews during the 1930s," as Edward S. Shapiro put it, "Greenberg's struggle against anti-Semitism was their struggle, and his victory over hatred and injustice was theirs also."

Hank had a constituency of fans wherever he played. He heard the Jews of St. Louis cheer for him in Sportsman's Park, the Jews of Chicago laud him at Comiskey, Jews of Boston applaud his home runs at Fenway and so on around the league. His fans were loudest at Yankee Stadium, where, in addition to his family and friends, a man named Moe Greengrass, frequently seated in a box near the visitors' dugout, gave bagels loaded with lox to Greenberg after games. As Benno Levi said, "Our life was baseball, and baseball was Hank Greenberg."

Baseball had become their national pastime, too. The *Detroit Jewish Chronicle* noted in its annual year-end review: "By their achievements during 5695, Jewish athletes have wiped out the illusion that the Jew is inherently incapable of success in sports or that the Jewish people frown on participation in athletics." Ten Jews had begun the season on major league baseball teams, more than ever before, though only five were regulars. The *Chronicle* singled out among them and cited as one of the primary reasons for changing these perceptions, "the climb of Henry Greenberg to baseball stardom."

The Sporting News ran an article in September headlined, "Oi, Oi, Oh, Boy! Hail That Long-Sought Hebrew Star: Hank Greenberg, Greatest

Jewish Player, Touted as A.L.'s Most Valuable." In it, Fred Lieb admitted the shortcoming of his theory that Jews would not make good ballplayers. "This theory may once have had something to it, but in the past few years it has been knocked into a cocked hat by the big bat of Hefty Hank Greenberg."

The Jewish community threw its arms around Hank. Boys wanted to be him. Mothers wanted their daughters to marry him. And men elevated their status with his company. He moved easily among them, somewhat abashed by the adulation, but comfortable with the familiarity, like being back in his Jewish neighborhood in the Bronx.

One day in 1935, Max Lapides heard Hank was coming to dinner that evening at the Aronsson home on Webb Avenue. The seven-year-old worshipped Hank, read everything he could about him, knew all of his statistics. He had watched him dozens of times at Navin Field with his father. When his mother bought him a sweatshirt, Max immediately took a black crayon and drew the number five on its back. The Aronssons had invited the neighborhood boys over to meet Hank briefly, but Max, confined to bed with a cast on his broken leg, couldn't go. He was crushed.

At the Aronsson home, Hank shook hands with the neighborhood boys and signed their balls. Someone told him about Max, lying alone in his bed five doors down. Hank asked where he could buy a baseball. They directed him to the candy store on the corner. He walked there, then over to the Lapides house.

Max's father entered his son's darkened bedroom. "Max, there's someone here to see you."

Max looked up. There, ducking through the doorway, was Hank Greenberg. "Here's your hero, your god, your icon, walking into your bedroom when you thought the world was very dark and you were unhappy," Lapides said later. "I thought I'd gone to heaven."

Hank sat on the edge of Max's bed and chatted with him for half an hour. He gave Max the autographed baseball. He signed Max's cast. Spying Max's favorite book, *Safe!* by Harold Sherman, on the nightstand, he autographed that, too. He left Max with the memory of a lifetime.

The celebrity mantle still chafed Hank's shoulders. A private man, he was not always at ease with the expectations cast upon him by the spotlight.

As a rookie, when he first saw kids lined up for him outside Navin Field, he didn't know why they were there.

"They want autographs," his friend Harold Allen told him.

"I won't give them any autograph," Hank said.

"Oh yes, you will," Harold said.

At times he still didn't like having to feign a cheerful attitude for autograph seekers, but Hank was learning to handle his popularity more gracefully. He answered his fan mail personally, spending many hours on the road penning replies on hotel stationery.

One morning in mid-July, Hank was eating breakfast in Philadelphia with Shaver, the *Detroit Times* sports editor, and opening his mail. He showed Shaver a letter written in pencil on blue-lined tablet paper by a thirteen-year-old Jewish girl. She told Hank that Max Baer, who had lost the heavyweight championship to Jimmy Braddock the month before, had disappointed her bitterly. She had transferred her faith to Hank. "She begged him not to fail her or his people," Shaver related. "There are thousands of little boys and girls like her."

Shaver passed the letter back to Hank. "You have an immense responsibility," he said.

Hank folded the letter and tucked it into his pocket. "Yes, I have," he said.

A local sandlot team won four championships with a boy named Joe Roginski as its mascot. Alex Okray, the Tigers' superstitious clubhouse manager, hired the thirteen-year-old boy as a batboy to bring the team some of his luck. Afraid that he wouldn't be accepted for being Polish and wanting to fit in, Roginski changed his name to Roggin, thinking it sounded Irish. Greenberg looked after him like a younger brother, much as he had done with Sammy Kaufman and Whitey Collins. He accepted invitations to eat at the Roginski home, downing a bowl of *czarnina*, duck blood soup, while neighborhood kids lined up outside to meet him.

That summer, Roggin became Hank's "good luck charm." Superstitious himself, Greenberg played catch before games with the young batboy. After he hit one of his home runs, he wanted Roggin to be the first to greet him at home plate, where he often ruffled the boy's hair.

After games, when he wasn't eating dinner at someone's house, Hank ate at various restaurants around town. Fans stopped by his table to say hello or ask for autographs. When he ate at Boesky's deli, which had a classy restaurant opposite its counter, boys from the Dexter section who heard Hank was there stood outside the window simply to get a glimpse of him. He occasionally dined at Franklin Hills Country Club, where he was less likely to be bothered. His favorite restaurant was the eponymous Joe Muer's, a fine seafood restaurant on Gratiot Avenue. Joe was a large, friendly German who tucked Hank in a corner table where he wasn't disturbed. But that summer, when Hank walked in after hitting a home run earlier in the afternoon's game, the patrons stood up and gave him a standing ovation. "It was embarrassing and very heady stuff for a kid who was only twenty-four years old," Hank wrote. "I hope I didn't let it go to my head. I tried not to, but it was still very gratifying to have people acknowledge you, not only at the ballpark but around town."

Mickey Cochrane's intensity continued to fire the team in his second year. Friday, August 23, the day after the Tigers blew an 8–4 lead, giving up six runs in the eighth to the Red Sox, Black Mike ushered the media out of the clubhouse, closed the doors and lit into his team. "They say the paint on the wall was inclined to curl up and crackle as Mike burned home his shots about Tigers tossing away ball games," the papers reported. It didn't matter to Cochrane that the Tigers remained in first place, seven games ahead of the Yankees. He hated to see his players squander a lead. Bottom line, he hated to lose. And he let them know it. Greenberg had gone two-for-five on the day, slugging his thirty-third homer of the season and driving in four runs, but, when he emerged from the clubhouse to warm up with Roggin, he looked like he had been scolded.

Inspired, the Tigers won that afternoon's game and thirteen of the next fifteen games to build a ten-game cushion in first place. But then they lost two of their next three, their lead slipped to seven and a half games and Cochrane lost his temper again, this time in a Washington hotel room in front of reporters. Upset that his players hadn't seemed to care about losing that afternoon's game to the Senators 6–0, the team's player-manager "kicked savagely at the bed clothes and punched pillows viciously."

"This isn't any cinch," Cochrane ranted. "You can't quit in this racket until the pennant is a mathematical certainty." Cochrane slugged the pillows. "If we blow a ten-game lead at this stage of the race, I'll look swell, won't I? And there are people who think I have a swell job. Give me $100,000 and twenty-five acres, and I'd walk out of here tomorrow!"

Assistant coach Del Baker encouraged Mickey to get some sleep.

The Tigers lost another game to the Senators before heading to New York for a five-game series that gave the second-place Yankees the chance to claw their way back into contention. Hank had not performed well there but this time "I made up my mind to conquer the jinx." The team arrived after midnight and he was tired in the first game on Thursday, yet still went two-for-five with a triple and two RBI in a Tiger win. That night, he went to bed earlier, determined to get a good night's sleep. Instead, he tossed and turned fitfully. Hank arrived at the park exhausted. But Friday the 13th proved to be a lucky day. He had three hits, including his forty-fifth double of the season and his thirty-fifth home run, a poke into the left field corner. His .346 average topped the American League. Hank finally had a big day at Yankee Stadium for his family to cheer. The Tigers won 13–5, and Hank said, "I enjoyed the biggest thrill of my career [to date] that afternoon."

The Tigers headed to Boston with a comfortable nine-and-a-half-game lead. Detroit fans were behind their boys, though this year another pennant would not create the hysteria it did last year. They wanted to celebrate a world championship. So, too, did Frank Navin, who was enjoying the season but would not be content until the team he had built won it all.

Despite his newfound confidence from spring training, Hank still hated to lose and feared the humiliation of failure. He resented a player like his teammate Charlie Gehringer, for whom everything seemed to come so easily and naturally. Hank was constantly afraid of screwing up and looking bad. "It was sheer terror going to the ballpark," he said.

His worst fears were realized the last two weeks of the season, when the summer seemed to lengthen interminably and Hank's thirty-six-ounce bat grew heavier. He crashed into the first slump of his major league career. Over eleven games, he managed only eight hits in forty-eight at-bats, and his average dropped eleven points. The batting title was lost along with his chance to win the Triple Crown. During that stretch, he had only one home run and four RBI, but he still led the league in both categories going into the final day of the season, a doubleheader in Chicago.

Sunday, September 29, was also Rosh Hashanah. With the pennant secured, Hank could have sat without hurting his team. But with the home run title on the line—he had 36 homers to Jimmie Foxx's thirty-four—Hank played. Last year's precedent—with its successful two-homer outcome—no doubt influenced his decision. This time, the press hardly noticed.

Hank swung hard without result. He struck out three times and went oh-for-seven on the day. Even in his final at-bat when the catcher let him know the pitcher planned to groove him something to hit, Hank only managed a weak pop-up. He did finish with 170 RBI. While he had not bested Ruth's single-season home run record nor reached his goal of forty, his RBI total matched Ruth's from 1921. No AL player other than Lou Gehrig had knocked in that many runs since they started keeping track of the stat in 1921. It also set a mark for most RBI by a right-handed batter in the American League.* Most important to Hank, those 170 RBI helped his team win the pennant.

Meanwhile, in a game against the Washington Senators, Jimmie Foxx hit two home runs in Shibe Park to tie Hank with thirty-six on the season. The Senator catcher hadn't wanted a Jew to win the batting title, so he had let Foxx know what pitches were coming. Afterward, the catcher bragged that he had kept Greenberg from winning the home run title. When Henry Coppola, the Senators' pitcher who took the loss, found out his catcher had betrayed him, he punched him in the nose. But the damage was already done: Greenberg had to share the home run title.

Despite the Senator catcher's malevolence, Hank had a terrific season, improving his offensive totals in every category—hits, runs, triples, homers, RBI—except average, which dipped to .328, still very good, and doubles, which fell from sixty-three to forty-six (again, not bad) because more of his long drives in Navin Field sailed for home runs. He also improved his fielding percentage by another two points on more chances and reduced his error

---

* Recent research by SABR member Herm Krabbenhoft reveals that errors in the daily record awarded Greenberg two RBI in 1935 that he did not earn. That makes his season total 168, tying him with Jimmy Foxx's 1932 RBI production for the most by a right-handed AL hitter (though the accuracy of Foxx's total hasn't been similarly scrutinized).

total to thirteen (from sixteen in 1934). Gehringer, the Tigers' brilliant second baseman, deserved some credit there—he cheated toward Greenberg and handled balls hit between them. *Baseball Magazine* put Hank on the cover of its October issue and began the accompanying profile entitled "Baseball's New Sensation" with the simple declaration: "Greenberg, of Detroit, is the outstanding player of the year." The Baseball Writers' Association of America agreed. The eight-member committee unanimously voted Hank the American League's Most Valuable Player, only the third time a player had been the first choice of all the members.* Greenberg, "That Long-Sought Hebrew Star," was the first Jew to win the award.[†]

Despite Mickey Cochrane's tirades and ass-chewings, the Tigers had gone into a tailspin along with Hank and lost nine of their last thirteen games. They headed into the World Series with a negative momentum and their star, the league's Most Valuable Player, in a slump. Meanwhile, the Chicago Cubs, their opponents, had racked up a 21-game winning streak in September. "They were hotter than a gang of bank robbers with the FBI closing in, and the sportswriting fraternity—outside of Detroit—said their momentum couldn't help but carry them to fresh World Series triumphs," Lieb wrote.

Detroit had never won a major championship in a professional sport, and, after coming so close the year before, the fans did not want to be denied again. The first fan took his place in line for tickets two weeks before they went on sale. Once the ticket windows opened, those who hadn't waited in line paid scalpers $25 for $6.50 box seats. The superintendent of schools instructed teachers they could allow the children to listen to Ty Tyson's radio broadcasts of the games, temporarily putting baseball before reading, writing and arithmetic. The press was so carried away with the upcoming Series, it ran a photo of Hank getting a haircut and manicure at the Wolverine Hotel "in preparation of the opener."

Hank eagerly awaited the chance to rewrite the headlines from last

---

* Giant pitcher Carl Hubbell in 1933 and Yankee slugger Babe Ruth in 1923 were the others.
[†] Indian third baseman Al Rosen (AL-1953), Dodger ace Sandy Koufax (NL-1963) and Brewer outfielder Ryan Braun (NL-2011) are the only other three Jews to win the award.

year. Yet he again felt the shudder of postseason nerves. The World Series amplified his daily fear of humiliation. In addition to facing a hot ball club with strong pitching from Lon Warneke, a 20-game winner nicknamed "The Arkansas Hummingbird," he had another issue to contend with this year: Yom Kippur fell on October 7, the same day that Game Six was scheduled to be played, should the Series go that far. Fans petitioned the commissioner with letters and telegrams to change the date, but Judge Landis, no sentimentalist over diversity, refused. Once again, Tiger fans anxiously awaited Hank's decision. He had played on a Holy Day last year and this, but that was Rosh Hashanah; he had sat out Yom Kippur his first two seasons. Those were not important games; this was the World Series. He felt the pressure both ways once again. The press wanted to know what he would do. He remained tight-lipped.

This time, though, his parents understood the situation differently. They had seen what Hank could do on the ball field and come to understand his importance to the team. They also realized what their son meant to the Jews. When David and Sarah Greenberg arrived in Detroit for the opening of the World Series, the reporters asked them, Will Hank play?

"If you really want to know what I think, it's that Henry has been worrying about having to play on the holy day and that is what has caused his recent batting slump," Mr. Greenberg said. "We are Orthodox Jews and while not fanatical or going to the synagogue every day, we always observe the two great holidays, the two days of New Year and Yom Kippur. The boy has been to everybody including Mr. Navin and while they tell him they can't make him play, they explain they have no substitute for him. After all, he belongs to the public and not just to himself."

So he'll play? "We've raised our children to be Orthodox, and I don't want him to play," Mrs. Greenberg said. "But he will anyway. That was for him to decide."

There, the press had its answer—though the Series could be decided before a sixth game was necessary, and other factors could still influence Hank's decision.

Frost etched the outfield grass at Navin Field on the morning of Wednesday, October 2, but by game time the warm autumn sun against the sharp blue sky bathed the field in perfect baseball conditions. The largest crowd to ever watch a baseball game in Detroit, 47,391 fans, squeezed into the bleachers and grandstand. Babe Ruth, recently retired, was among them. So, too, was Henry Ford with his son Edsel. Anticipation hung thick in the air.

If Hank found the Cardinals cruel in the 1934 World Series, he was in for a lesson in true cruelty this year. The Cubs lived up to their reputation as the nastiest bench jockeys in the major leagues. They peppered all of the Tigers with their abuse, but Hank, closest to their dugout and the main threat, became a big, lone target. "The word is that they were tipped off by the Cardinals to ride Hank," the *World-Telegram* reported. They jumped on him right away, hurling all kind of invective their imaginations could conjure. "I learned that the Cubs were a bunch of tough SOBs," Hank wrote. "Charlie Root, Larry French, four or five other guys, they started riding me, calling me Jew this and Jew that."

Augie Galan, the Cubs' leadoff batter, slapped a hit over Schoolboy Rowe's head for a double. The next batter, Billy Herman, the Cubs' best player, chopped a short ball to the right of the mound. Rowe picked it up, but his throw drew Hank down the line, toward the approaching runner. Herman shoved Greenberg and knocked off his oversized mitt. It flew into the field, and the ball rolled up the right field line. Hank chased the ball. Herman stayed at first, but Galan scored to give the Cubs an early 1–0 lead. Hank retrieved his mitt from the infield dirt and shook his left wrist, which was bent on the impact with Herman. The play rattled him.

Hank led off the second inning. The 47,391 fans gave him a "tremendous ovation." But the Cubs were not so kind. "Throw him a pork chop," the shortstop Billy Jurges yelled to Lon Warneke on the mound. "He can't hit it." Hank dribbled a ground ball to the left side, and Stan Hack, the Cubs' third baseman, threw him out. The Cubs continued their verbal rampage against Greenberg. It got so bad that George Moriarty, the home plate umpire, stopped the game in the second inning and told Cubs' manager Charlie Grimm that they had to tone it down or he would clear the bench. The Cubs swore back at Moriarty. They even shouted "Christ Killer" at Jewish umpire Dolly Stark.

Their abuse continued throughout the game. At one point, Greenberg complained about it to Moriarty. In the spring training exhibition game, Hank had been able to overcome his anger, but not in the World Series. He walked in the fourth inning and swung at the first pitch in the sixth, hitting a high fly that Hack caught behind third base. Hank fumbled a ground ball in the top of the eighth, allowing the batter to reach. In the bottom of the eighth, Hank batted with two outs, Gehringer on first and the Tigers down 2–0. Here was his first chance of the Series with a runner on base. He let Warneke's first two pitches pass for balls. He fouled off the next one. Then he hit a ground ball to Hack at third, who threw him out to end the inning.

It turned out the Cubs' run in the first inning was all they needed. The Arkansas Hummingbird shut down the Tigers on four hits to win the first game 3–0. Hank was frustrated with his performance and for allowing the Cubs' abuse to upset him. "I was a sucker to let them get my goat," he said.

Several Tiger fans, fearing Greenberg would repeat his failure in last year's Series to advance runners, wrote a letter to Mickey Cochrane that criticized the manager for not having Gee Walker bat cleanup instead of sitting him on the bench. "What do you think Walker would be hitting if he were batting number four? Here is a guess that the boy would be doing his stuff and be right there where Hank is, perhaps knocking runs in when they are really needed. Somehow Hank seems to knock in runs just in the games that the Tigers lead by a large margin, but in a close game that could be won by one or two runs, Walker has been the boy to knock him in."

Unmoved, Cochrane left Walker on the bench and Greenberg batting fourth for the second game on Thursday, a cold and windy afternoon. In the press box high behind home plate, Ty Tyson turned the collar of his coat up against the chill and delivered his play-by-play in visible wisps of breath. When the band played "The Star-Spangled Banner," Hank, out at first base, was the only Tiger not to face the flagpole in center field. After the abuse he took from the Cubs the day before, he was afraid that if he turned his back on their bench, they would throw something at him.

The Tigers pounced on Cubs' starter Charlie Root right away with three hits. The home team led 2–0 with Gehringer on first and no outs when Hank approached the plate. He dug in, his left foot even with the plate. After a ball and a strike, Root delivered a fastball where Hank liked it. He cocked his hands, took a long stride, opened his shoulders and lunged with his arms fully extended. He connected solidly. Root swiveled his head to watch the ball sail into the left field bleachers.

The crowd of nearly 47,000 Tiger fans, who had nothing to cheer the day before, went wild while Hank trotted around the bases. "Crazed for a World's championship, the crowd went mad in the first inning when the Tigers scored four runs, climaxed by Greenberg's home run with Gehringer on base," one newspaper reported. "Waving blankets in the air, dancing on the seats, punching one another in jubilant ecstasy, Detroiters of all ages and both sexes put on a five-minute celebration that left everybody hoarse, happy—and warm again." On deck, Goose Goslin congratulated Hank at the plate. Roggin was there, too, and Hank shook his hand. His teammates waited at the dugout steps with hands outstretched. They thumped his back, and one took off Hank's hat and tousled his hair. "In the dugout, the Tigers danced with each other, shouting and screaming. Hank was almost mobbed by his playful mates."

Greenberg's home run eliminated Root. He had pitched to four batters and left the game down 4–0. Hank faced Roy Henshaw in the third inning with Gehringer on first, but grounded into a double play. The Tigers chased Henshaw with a rally in the fourth that put them up 7–0 when Hank batted with runners on first and third and two outs. He hit the first pitch back to the new pitcher, Fabian Kowalik, who threw him out once again to end the inning and squelch the rally. He seemed upset in the field the next inning, mishandling a ground ball for an error, making a bad throw to second that spoiled the chance for a double play and dropping a throw at first for another error. The Cubs razzed him mercilessly.

In the seventh, Kowalik threw an inside pitch that struck Greenberg sharply on the left wrist. Hank rubbed his wrist but didn't want to come out of the game. Goslin flied out, and right fielder Pete Fox batted with Gehringer on second and Greenberg on first. With two outs, no one was holding Hank on the bag, so he grabbed a big lead. On the pitch, he took several strides toward second and paused. When Fox smashed the ball through the pitcher's box, Greenberg dashed around second and kept running. Gehringer scored standing up. Hank hesitated a moment coming into third, slowed and checked over his left shoulder for the ball being relayed into second. He didn't see third base coach Del Baker waving him on. Rounding the bag, Hank decided he could score and spurted for home, fast as his flat feet could lug his big frame. Chicago catcher Gabby Hartnett flipped his mask to the side in preparation for the play at the plate. Gehringer yelled at Hank to slide. Billy Herman's relay throw came in perfectly, about three feet up the third base line. Hartnett dropped his left knee to block the plate. Hank slid with his left foot forward, his right arm back. His left hand stretched toward home.

The ball arrived a nanosecond before Hank crashed into the linebacker-sized Hartnett, a violent chest-to-chest collision. Standing behind the catcher, Ernie Quigley, the home plate umpire, looked to make sure Hartnett hadn't dropped the ball, then emphatically swept his right arm up to call Hank out. The crowd instantly moaned and booed. Hartnett stood up and walked slowly up the third-base line. Hank stood, cradling his left wrist in his lap. Billy Rogell snapped at Quigley, then pounded his bat into the grass in frustration. Hank followed the ump behind the plate, like a child asking for a second chance. Baker raced in to confront Quigley on his call. Hank gave up, hung his head dejectedly and walked toward the dugout. Roggin handed him his mitt, but Hank did not put it on right away. He eventually slipped on his mitt and took his place at first but was lucky not to have to field any throws over the final two innings, because he would not have been able to catch them. His left wrist throbbed. He had jammed it in the collision with Hartnett.

When Pete Fox caught a fly ball for the final out, the Tigers' 8–3 win evened the Series. The crowd cheered and the town went wild. One newspaper described the scene: "When the radio carried the news of the game's end, downtown Detroit staged another carnival of rejoicing. Confetti rolls streamed from thousands of office windows upon pushing, cheering throngs to the streets. Boats and factory whistles shrilled and bellowed. A carillon of bells played—of all things!—'Nearer, My God to Thee.' And thousands of voices joined in one long, joyous shout."

On the train ride to Chicago for the next three games, Hank had plenty to think about. He was pleased with his home run, of course, and happy that the Tigers had evened the Series, but he had only one hit in two games and already had failed three times with runners on base. X-rays after the game had not revealed any broken bones in his wrist, but the pain was excruciating. The entire ride to Chicago, he alternated his hand between buckets of extremely hot water and ice.

The next morning, his wrist had swollen to twice its normal size. Hank still hoped he might be able to play that afternoon. He suited up and was the first player on the field for practice. Later, he sat on the rubbing table while Tiger trainer Denny Carroll massaged his wrist with a chunk of ice. Hank winced. Mickey Cochrane shook his head. "Mickey, I want to get in there this afternoon," Hank said. Tears filled his eyes. "You know what this means to me. It's what I've played for all year, and I want to get in there and do my part."

"Hank, you just can't do it," Cochrane said. "You can't take any chances with that hand in the shape it's in."

Hank needed help putting on his warm-up jacket. He sat glumly in the corner of the dugout with his left wrist bandaged while Marv Owen took his spot at first and Flea Clifton played third, according to Frank Navin's orders. Schoolboy Rowe had volunteered to fill in, and Cochrane had thought about playing first himself and letting his backup, Ray Hayworth, catch, but Navin had insisted. "If we lose the Series, it will be on my head," Navin said. One sportswriter called Hank the "most disconsolate figure in Chicago." Owen went oh-for-five at the plate, but he made fifteen putouts without an error, and the Tigers won 6–5 in eleven innings. The Cubs continued to harass Greenberg on the bench.

The two teams split the weekend games: The Tigers won 2–1 on Saturday, and Warneke beat Rowe again on Sunday. The Tigers led three games to two with the chance to win it all the next day back in Detroit. Hank wanted desperately to play, even though it was Yom Kippur. William E. Keane, M.D., the team physician, examined Hank's wrist on the train ride back to Detroit and said it looked better. "The swelling has gone down, and he has a fairly strong grip now," Dr. Keane said. "There should be further improvement between now and game time." Hank promised reporters he would be ready to play.

Hank reported to the clubhouse early on the Day of Atonement for a session with the trainer. Carroll rubbed his magic grease, a brown liniment with a powerful odor, into Hank's wrist, then swaddled it in tape. Hank picked up his Louisville Slugger and took a few practice swings, grimacing with each. He stuffed his bandaged wrist into his mitt and asked Joe Roggin to throw him a ball. When the ball smacked his mitt, Hank nearly dropped to his knees in pain. He would have to observe Game Six and Yom Kippur from the dugout.

Another record crowd, some 48,420 fans this time, swarmed into Navin Field to be there for the chance to see their Tigers finally win a World Series. The Tigers put up their curveball wonder, Tommy Bridges, against the Cubs' left-handed knuckleballer, Larry French. The two teams traded runs, and the score was knotted 3–3 going into the ninth. Stan Hack, the Cubs' third baseman, led off with a triple over Gee Walker's head in center field that hushed the crowd. Bridges bore down. He fanned Jurges on three pitches, all curves. He induced the next batter, French, to hit a weak grounder back to the box that Bridges tossed to Owen for the second out. That put the crowd into near hysterics. Two outs, runner at third, game tied in the ninth. Bridges got ahead of the next batter, Augie Galan, with two strikes, then threw a curve that sailed wide. Cochrane dived and blocked the wild pitch with his chest. He scrambled to collect the ball to keep Hack from scoring. Walter O. Briggs Sr., Tiger co-owner, called it "the most important play of the Series." Galan lofted a fly ball to Goslin in left for the third out, and the Tigers had the chance to win the game in their half of the ninth.

Which is exactly what they did. With two outs, Cochrane on second, Hank on the bench and Goose Goslin batting in the cleanup spot, the Flying Goose blooped a single to short right field that scored Cochrane and gave Detroit its coveted championship. Fans poured onto the field and hoisted Goslin onto their shoulders. Frank Navin forgot his stoicism. "It's wonderful!" he shouted. "I've waited thirty years for this day!" Later that night, he told friends, "I've lived most of my life to see this happen. I can now die in peace."

Detroit's streets filled with revelers dancing, banging dishpans and stopping streetcars. Confetti and ticker tape streamed out of office windows. Fans shouted themselves silly at Navin Field for forty-five minutes before Cochrane returned to the field and thanked them over a hastily installed microphone. "This is the greatest day of my life," he said, choking back tears.

It was the greatest day of all of their lives, everyone there in Detroit, everyone who had suffered through the hard times with factories closing and banks failing and the Tigers losing in seven games. But now, with Cochrane crossing the plate, all was right again. The victory healed all wounds, repaired friendships, restored brotherhood. For that day, at least, if you happened to be in Detroit, where the Tigers were world champions, your city was the greatest of all time, along with all of the people in it, and you knew how sweet life could taste.

They partied late into the night in Detroit, and so did the players who came into the clubhouse whooping and hugging. "With blood-curdling yells that rocked the rafters, the victorious Tigers charged into their dressing room . . . to cut loose in a wild, hilarious celebration. . . all yelling, swearing and sweating," the *Chicago Tribune* reported.

All except one Tiger with a bandaged wrist. He felt more out of place than perhaps ever before in his life. He had led this team to the Promised Land but had not been able to enjoy the romp in it. Thrust in the midst of the "greatest celebration ever seen in baseball" on the Day of Atonement, he was delighted his team had won but deeply disappointed that his injury had reduced him to a mere spectator.

Two days after the World Series ended, Hank's wrist still hurt. He had another round of X-rays taken, with his wrist in a different position, and they revealed "several minor cracks"—he had indeed broken three small bones in his collision with Hartnett. Dr. Keane placed Hank's wrist in a plaster cast for five weeks and thought it would heal completely. Hank did not like having to wear the cast, but he liked Frank Navin's attitude toward him less. "Mr. Navin was very cavalier about the injury," he wrote about his meeting with Navin after the X-rays. "His attitude annoyed me. When I left his office, I made up my mind that he would pay the price in spring training when he wanted me on the ball field. I was going to remember the way he belittled my broken wrist and, when it came time to talk contract, things would be different."

Hank headed home to New York to visit his parents; he planned to spend the winter in Florida, relaxing on the beach. He returned to Detroit in November, sooner than he had expected, for Frank Navin's funeral.

On November 13, the sixty-four-year-old Navin was riding his favorite horse at the Detroit Hunt Club on Belle Isle, when he suffered a heart attack. He was rushed to the hospital but pronounced dend an hour later. He had lived to realize his dream of winning a World Series but died too soon to have fully enjoyed it.

CHAPTER SEVEN

---∞---

*183**

Walter O. Briggs Sr. was in his office when he heard the news on the radio. He immediately calculated the book value of his partner's shares, wrote a check—for approximately one million dollars—and dispatched his right-hand man and CFO Harry Sisson to deliver payment to Grace Navin at the hospital.

"You have ninety days," Sisson said. "Why rush?"

"Harry, I've waited all my life to own this team," Briggs said. "What if he's not dead? I'm not going to take any chances."

Briggs enjoyed baseball but did not have Frank Navin's mind for the game. He was a businessman. The son of a railroad foreman, he had started with nothing and built the Briggs Manufacturing Company into the largest auto-body manufacturing company in America. He was a big man around town whose chauffeured car often received a police motorcycle escort. He had never been to spring training or closer to the team than his stadium box. Soon as he owned the Tigers outright, he began a $500,000 renovation of Navin Field, adding a second deck of permanent seats. Many of the players did not realize that Briggs had been Navin's silent partner. They did not know what it would be like to work for him, but they would soon learn Walter O. Briggs was used to getting his way.

Ten days after Navin's funeral, Briggs summoned Mickey Cochrane to his winter home in Miami Beach and appointed him vice president in addition to his player-manager duties. Two days after that, the new VP told the papers that if Hank Greenberg didn't sign his contract they had Rudy York to play first. York was a big, strong-hitting first baseman who had only six major league at-bats but had made a good impression in Beaumont. Cochrane's comments rubbed Hank wrong. He was still smarting from Navin's cavalier attitude toward his injured wrist. That did not set the scene for smooth contract negotiations.

Before the 1935 season, Navin had offered Hank a two-year contract for $25,000, but Hank was smarter than that. He knew if he had a better year in 1935, he would be able to ask for more in the second year. His MVP season put him in that position. During 1935, Greenberg had also calculated that runs batted in was the most valuable statistic in winning ball games for his team and in arguing his value to the club at contract time. His 170 RBI in 1935—an astonishing fifty-one more than the second-place finisher (Gehrig), a record-setting margin—gave him considerable leverage. He believed he deserved to be the highest-paid player in baseball and asked for $35,000.* "I've only got so long in baseball, and I've got to get all I can out of those years," he said.

The Tigers did not share Greenberg's opinion of his assessed value. While Briggs could spend generously to acquire talent—for example, the $100,000 he put out for Mickey Cochrane in 1934 and another $75,000 he spent to purchase the hard-hitting Al Simmons before the 1936 season— he was notoriously cheap with his workers' wages. During the darkest days of the Depression, he had paid assembly line workers at Briggs Manufacturing as little as ten cents an hour. Greenberg was up against tight pockets. Briggs noted that the team had a replacement for Greenberg, Rudy York, and that the Tigers won the World Series "without the services of Greenberg." Cochrane wrote Briggs in December suggesting he give Greenberg $15,000 or $16,000 "tops." Much more than that, Cochrane wrote, would make it "very difficult to keep the other members of the team in line." The highest-paid Tiger was Charlie Gehringer, whom Briggs paid $25,000 for the 1936 season. In January, secretary-treasurer Charles Navin sent Hank a contract for $22,500, calling it "a very nice increase over the salary you received last year and I think you should be perfectly satisfied with same."

---

* At the time, Gehrig was the highest-paid player with a $31,000 salary for 1936, though Greenberg thought it was $32,500.

Hank wasn't. He met with Briggs in Miami Beach on February 7, but the meeting seemed to antagonize both rather than move them toward agreement. Hank wrote Navin afterward, "I placed myself in an embarrassing position and above all failed to make any impression." Hank appealed to Cochrane, the person who, as manager and teammate, best knew his value to the team. But Cochrane was not an ally. He was management. He forwarded all of Hank's correspondence to Briggs. Cochrane also seemed to hold a grudge against Hank. Some thought he resented Hank for demanding more money than he earned, but that wasn't the case. Briggs paid Cochrane $45,000 in 1936 for his duties as player, manager and vice president. In response to Hank's appeal, Cochrane admonished him to accept the club's offer and urged him not to "jeopardize your position" or make "a serious mistake." He also reminded Hank, "This is not a one man team." Cochrane sent a copy of his letter to Briggs with a note, "My reply may wake him up, if not there is no need worrying about him."

Hank trusted his friends—men like Sidney Allen and Louis Blumberg, successful businessmen who had helped him with his investments and advised him on his contract negotiations—more than he trusted Cochrane. He stuck to his demand for $35,000. Greenberg was not the only player who didn't sign his contract. In mid-February, there were more than fifty ballplayers asking for more money than their clubs had offered, including the Cubs' Augie Galan, the White Sox's Luke Appling, the Cardinals' Dean brothers, and the batting champions of each league, Washington's Buddy Myer and Pittsburgh's Arky Vaughan. Hank, the biggest name on the list, wanted to get his situation resolved in time to report to spring training on March 1.

That date came and went without either side budging. So did March 8, the day that the second wave of players reported, and Hank became an official holdout, only the second in Tiger history, putting him in company with Ty Cobb. The Tigers seemed to be losing patience. Navin wrote Cochrane, "If you give in to him now, he is going to have a whip-hand over the club, not only for this year but future years. You might as well get tough right now as at any time." Hank seemed to suspect the worst of the Catholic contingent—Briggs and Cochrane—negotiating with him. "There seems to be, in the background of his mind, the thought of discrimination," Sam Greene observed in the *Detroit News*.

Navin sent back the still unsigned contract to Greenberg in the Bronx with the threat that if he didn't sign it by March 11, the club would reduce the amount by "at least $2,500." Greenberg told reporters he was going to stay home with his parents until he got a "decent offer." He said he would go to work with his father, if he had to, but what he really wanted to do was play baseball. "Man, I'd like to be with the boys down there in Lakeland," he said.

As the stalemate dragged on through March, the public seemed to lose patience, too. Some thought Hank was asking for too much too soon in his career, that he didn't deserve to earn more than proven veterans like Jimmie Foxx and Lou Gehrig. Others balked during those Depression days at the huge sum—the press reported he was demanding $40,000. The fact that Hank did not show any concern for the factory worker earning five dollars a day—who would ultimately pay his inflated salary—prompted one writer to pen, "Since virtually every ballplayer is assured of escaping the bread lines no matter with whom or for what figure he signs, I'm not exactly concerned about his financial agreements with his employers." One Detroit paper ran an editorial "Hank is Losing Friends," saying, "His salary demands at this stage of his career are a little out of line with precedents established back in the time when baseball generally was a bigger industry than it is today." And "because he was a bust in one World Series and unable to appear in another, some of the fans would like more definite assurance that he can bring all his powers into play when the going is rough and the stakes are high." Iffy the Dopester, Malcom Bingay's alter ego at the *Detroit Free Press*, chastised Greenberg: "You owe a lot to yourself, Hank, but you also owe something to your teammates and, above all, to the baseball public which really pays your dough." The criticism stung Hank. His popularity in Detroit sagged.

Perhaps the same leather-lungs who yelled nasty ethnic slurs at Navin Field took pen in hand to let their venom flow. Oliver Labadie, a resort owner in New Hudson, Michigan, was one. "No wonder Hitler drove the Jews out of Germany," Labadie wrote Cochrane in March. "Keep them out of baseball. They will ruin it."

Others backed Hank in letters to the editor and the club: "Hank is a loyal Tiger and deserves our support," and "He is worth the price." One letter to Briggs from Antoinette Kelly, a Tiger fan who had attended many games in the past, said, "I won't put my foot in your ballpark this summer unless Greenberg gets what he wants." Regarding the idea of Rudy York replacing the Tigers' MVP, Iffy did observe that it was "as though Hank were just like a Ford part that could be tossed out and replaced by buying another just like him at any corner drugstore." Hank's backers accused Briggs of being cheap. More than anything else, everyone agreed the Tigers needed Hank and he needed the Tigers; they just wanted the two sides to agree so they could focus on winning their third consecutive pennant.

Hank had swum when he was in Florida that winter, played his usual regimen of handball in New York and been working out with kids and semipro pitchers at Crotona Park, though he admitted that wasn't the same as hitting big league pitching. Yet as April 14, Opening Day, approached, Hank's teammates worried that once he finally did sign—and they believed he would eventually—he would not have time to get in shape. When word came in late March that Hank was headed down to Lakeland to work out a deal, Goose Goslin said what many of them thought, "He should have been down here before. It's all right for a ballplayer to hold out, but he can't be unreasonable and forget he has some obligations to other players, too."

When Hank arrived in Lakeland on March 26, Briggs summoned him to his room along with Cochrane. They dickered for three hours. Hank did not want to negotiate. He wanted to impress the point that he thought he was worth what he was asking. He was not going to ask for an inflated price only to come down to a compromise price, which was actually what he wanted. Nor did he want the club to start with a lower amount than it was willing to pay. So, seeing he was not going to get $35,000, Hank finally agreed to the $25,000* Briggs was offering. They invited the reporters in, smiled for the photographers and called it a night. Hank was in uniform the next day, but all was not healed and forgotten. Money would prove to be the undoing of Hank's relationship with Briggs.

Now twenty-five years old, Hank had outgrown his teenage social awkwardness. He was tall, athletic, charming, intelligent, on his way to becoming

---

* That's the equivalent of $495,091 in 2012.

wealthy and the handsomest man in baseball. He wore his hair longer than most men of his day and sported clothes more stylish. He rated among America's most eligible bachelors. Vera Brown, the *Detroit Times* columnist, declared Greenberg better-looking than Basil Rathbone, the suave South African actor. Girls melted for Hank the way their daughters would for Elvis. The Associated Press photographers liked to photograph him on the beach with good-looking young women in bathing suits. When the post-debbies attended a game at Navin Field, one asked Cochrane, "Who's the tall one?" then flirted with Hank when the manager called him over. Many female fans went to the ballpark not to watch baseball but to ogle Hank the hunk. They waited for him outside the park after ball games. They signed their names on the white top of his silver convertible. They called his hotel room. This was heady stuff for the young man who had blossomed from the ugly teenage duckling freckled with acne.

Dorothy Tingdahl was a fourteen-year-old girl with a "colossal crush" on Hank. Her mother, a well-known singer in Detroit, invited Hank to dinner and told him how her "baby" adored him. Hank arrived with a teddy bear for Dorothy. When he saw her in a black dress, blonde curls piled on top of her head and done up in makeup, he said, "Some baby."

But he was gentle with the love-struck young girls. He told sixteen-year-old Margie Aronsson, whose father, Maury, often invited him to dinner, he would wait for her. Thirteen-year-old Harriet Greenberg (no relation) memorized everything there was to know about Hank, down to his license plate number (U99). In 1936, a leap year when Jewish females were allowed to propose marriage, she did so to Hank in a letter. He wrote back, graciously saying he was not quite ready to marry. Not long afterward, Harriet met Hank when he was a guest speaker to the Congregation Shaarey Zedek youth group, and she repeated her proposal. He looked at her, his eyes twinkling, and said, "I accept."

Hank did tell the newspapers in 1936 that he would like to be "happily married." One *Detroit News* account in January 1936 had twenty-five-year-old Miss Helen Young, "a striking blonde, tall and slender with gray-green eyes," denying that she was engaged to Greenberg. Her mother, however, told the papers that the large diamond ring Helen wore was from Hank. Walter Winchell, the society columnist, reported the couple was engaged. Their relationship had first come to light when Miss Young accompanied Hank to the All-Star Game in Cleveland the previous July.

Hank's parents were not pleased. Helen was not Jewish. "This is terrible," Mrs. Greenberg told Harold Allen, Hank's older friend, one night at dinner when Hank's parents were in Detroit. Allen tried to mollify them. "Don't worry," he said. "It will pass."

When it didn't, Harold told Hank, "You're doing this against your folks and everything. We're through."

Harold refused to take Hank's calls and did not speak to him for almost a month, until the day Hank called to tell him he and Helen had broken up.

"Hank, you're a young guy," Harold told him. "There are a lot of nice girls. Don't disappoint anybody. Stay on the right track."

Hank had no more formal engagements with gentile ladies in Detroit after that, though he did enjoy the company of women. Harold Allen got another phone call from Hank late one night. "I'm in trouble," Hank said. He had clumsily broken a woman's arm in bed.

Allen arrived at the Leland Hotel with Herman Galante, another friend. Allen called his personal physician and made arrangements for the woman to have her arm set. They snuck her out the back way and through the alley to the hospital. Galante gave her some money. They told her not to say anything. She didn't.

"I never considered myself a ladies' man or a *bon vivant*, but on the other hand, I had a natural appetite," Hank said. Still, he was careful not to let his appetite interfere with a baseball game, especially on Saturday night with a doubleheader the next day. "No woman in the world made it worth an oh-for-eight day," he later told his son Steve.

Hank's wrist had worried him over the winter. When the cast came off, it felt weak and hurt occasionally. He did some conditioning exercises to strengthen it. The wrist felt better when he finally arrived at spring training. He declared it completely healed to the reporters, but questions lingered.

On Tuesday, April 14, the defending champion Tigers won their opener for the first time in six years with a 3–0 victory in Cleveland. Greenberg knocked in two runs. Boxing champ Joe Louis, who had played sandlot baseball growing up in Detroit, threw out the first pitch to comedian Jack Benny, who dropped the ball. The flag stood at half-mast in memory of Frank Navin.

Two days later, the Tigers lost their home opener in Briggs' enlarged stadium, though Hank was two-for-three with a triple and another RBI. Saturday, April 18, the Michigan governor declared a statewide "Day of Champions" in honor of the Tigers as well as the Red Wings, who had won their first Stanley Cup; the Lions, who had won their first NFL championship; and individuals like Louis who had Michigan roots. Winning had become a balm for the city's wounds. "Detroit is proud of its heroes who changed the city into a winning one that leads the nation in recovery as well as sports," one editorial chimed. Hank signed autographs at the banquet that evening and drank in the accolades.

Judging by Hank's hot start, his late signing did not seem to have impaired his fitness, and his wrist appeared healed. He hit safely in ten of the first eleven games with six doubles, two triples, one home run and 15 RBI for a .372 average. Meanwhile, Rudy York, his threatened replacement, had fallen apart when Hank signed, messing up three plays in the field that day in Florida. Fielding would continue to be York's nemesis. He was back in the minors for the season. Meanwhile, Hank felt poised for another strong season.

Commissioner Landis, responding to criticism about Greenberg's enlarged mitt and discussions about the same at the winter baseball meetings, issued a ruling that limited the size of mitts and prohibited artificial enhancements. But glove manufacturers had taken note. By the Forties, they would be turning out larger, friendlier versions of first baseman's mitts with the league's imprimatur, and Greenberg would be credited with sparking one of the game's most significant equipment revolutions.

On Wednesday, April 29, the Tigers played the Senators on a beautiful afternoon in Washington. Jake Powell, the Senators' speedy center fielder, led off the bottom half of the sixth inning. He hit a routine grounder to Marv Owen at third. Owen's throw to first sailed wide to the home plate side and pulled Hank off the bag with Powell bearing down on him.

Jake Powell was one of baseball's bad boys—a fighter, gambler and carouser. A hard competitor whom the *Washington Post*'s Shirley Povich called "ruthless on the baselines," Powell earned a reputation for slamming into first basemen like Zeke Bonura and Joe Kuhel. Powell was also a bigot. Two years later, he would say on a live radio interview with Chicago's WGN that he kept in shape during the off-season as a Dayton, Ohio, police officer (which he wasn't) by cracking "niggers over the head with a police club." While Powell barreled toward him, Hank tried to field Owen's throw.

Powell crashed into Greenberg's outstretched arm and knocked off his mitt. Hank went down. The ball rolled in the dirt. Hank's face turned white with pain. His teammates rushed over. He walked off the field with his head down and into the clubhouse, where the physician who examined him did not think he had broken his wrist. But it continued to swell on the train ride back to Detroit. There, X-rays revealed that Hank had indeed fractured two bones, including the scaphoid, which he had broken in the World Series.*

With his wrist in a plaster cast almost up to his elbow and his arm in a sling, Hank vowed to get back in the lineup. "I'm going to get back in there sometime in June or the first part of July," he told the *Detroit Times* on May 4. "See if I don't!"

He continued his daily solo workouts at Navin Field, only now, instead of batting practice and fielding with a glove, he threw a ball against the outfield wall and caught it with his bare hand. He also ran laps in a rubber suit with temperatures in the high eighties. He wanted to be in shape when his wrist was ready to let him play again. *Detroit News* photographer William Keunzel was surprised to see Greenberg working so hard. "I've been shooting pictures of athletes in all sports for more than thirty years, but I've never seen a more conscientious, more serious, more hardworking person than this Greenberg—unless it was Ty Cobb," Keunzel said. Cobb frequently worked out alone at the park, but Keunzel couldn't remember him working out when he was on the "hospital list."

Yet it was tough for Hank to remain upbeat. He didn't feel like a ballplayer playing one-handed catch with a wall. On a Saturday afternoon in

---

* Greenberg believed that Powell could have avoided the collision. Powell never apologized to him.

late May, Hank watched his younger brother Joe play a game for the Charleston Senators in Akron, Ohio. Hank had arranged a tryout for Joe with the Tigers that spring, and the club had assigned the twenty-year-old third baseman to its Class C organization. When five boys between the ages of eight and thirteen approached Hank in the stands and asked for autographs, he barked at them to leave him alone. He also brushed off the Akron Yankees' business manager Gene Martin, who wanted to introduce Hank to the crowd. The weeks on the sidelines were taking their toll on him.

Hank passed his time working out, coaching first base, sitting in Edsel Ford's box in civilian clothes, watching sandlot games on Belle Isle and having his wrist examined by Detroit bone specialist Frederick Kidner, M.D. The radius bone healed within a month, but the scaphoid bone, which had been rebroken, was taking longer. When Kidner examined Hank in late June, he recommended the cast stay on for another month. Hank resisted. He thought massage and motion would allow his wrist to heal faster. The doctor told Tiger secretary-treasurer Charles Navin that if the bone didn't set properly, Hank's baseball career would be over.

The following day, June 27, the club drafted a letter in Hank's name, saying, "I consider that I can be of no value to the Detroit Baseball Company as a player during the balance of the 1936 season" and asking to be placed on the voluntary retired list. That would finish Greenberg for the season and relieve Briggs of his obligation to pay him. But the club must have held out hope that Hank could return because it never asked him to sign the letter. No one even showed it to him.

Hank submitted to the cast, which he kept on another three weeks, then traded it for a splint. He reported to Kidner's office daily for treatments with a physiotherapist to restore strength, improve circulation and stimulate new bone growth in the fracture. The doctor thought Hank might have use of his wrist again by August 20. But on August 13, Kidner reexamined Hank and recommended he rest his wrist for the winter and not play ball again until the spring. Hank, who had been impatient to get back into the lineup, tried swinging a bat, but, unable to grip it properly, sprained his left elbow. He was done for the season.

Hank left Detroit to spend some time with his parents at their home on the Jersey shore. He played handball and ate Friday night dinners with his family while the Tigers suffered. The day after Hank was injured, Cochrane had obtained Jack Burns from the St. Louis Browns, a twenty-nine-year-old backup with a .279 lifetime batting average. Hank's replacement at first base had fielded adequately, but he produced far less with his bat. Burns would not be a threat to Hank's job, but Rudy York might be. Cochrane had been scheming to try Hank in the outfield when he returned to make room for York at first base, but that experiment would have to wait.

When Hank left in August, the Tigers were in fourth place, fifteen games back. The strain had taken its toll on Cochrane well before that. He'd had his finger smashed, taken a foul tip off the foot and suffered troubles with his eyes and stomach. He couldn't sleep. As demonstrated by his tirades the previous summer, Black Mike's temperament couldn't tolerate losing. In Philadelphia on June 4, Cochrane hit a bases-loaded, inside-the-park home run in the third inning to cap a ten-run rally, then collapsed. He had suffered a nervous breakdown. After ten days in the hospital, he flew to a friend's ranch in Wyoming, where his doctor advised him to ride, shoot and forget baseball. Tiger coach Del Baker took over the reins for two months.

While Mickey convalesced in Wyoming and Hank played handball on the Jersey shore, the Tigers continued to slip farther behind the Yankees.

Twelve-year-old Gerald Utley stood before his father with a question. Living in Cabarrus County, North Carolina, Gerald had adopted the Tigers as his team and Greenberg as his man. His family was not Jewish, but, like many boys around the country, he had been drawn to a winner and its big star. Some of the other boys from his town ridiculed Gerald for rooting for a Jew. One of them had said he was glad Greenberg broke his wrist. "Dad," Gerald said. "Why don't people like Greenberg?"

Mr. Utley looked up from his newspaper and studied his boy. How much of the world's dark side could a twelve-year-old bear? After a moment, he said, "There's nothing wrong with Jewish people. Jesus was a Jew."

Not all Americans shared his open-mindedness. In March, Adolf Hitler had appointed the American Fritz Julius Kuhn in charge of the German American Bund, which promoted Nazi Germany and its ideals, including ethnic cleansing. Other organized anti-Semitic efforts included the Silver

Shirts, Friends of Democracy and the National Union for Social Justice, groups that "seemed to compete for the specific purpose of denigrating Jews."

Sunday afternoons, Jewish children had to be quiet while their parents listened to the radio priest, Father Charles Coughlin. "You couldn't talk in our house," remembers Max Lapides, who grew up in Detroit. "Everybody listened to him. It was a matter of staying current with what was going on in the world." Father Coughlin's views appalled his Jewish audience but found sympathetic ears among many of his ten million listeners. The following Mondays in Germany, the Nazis cheered newspaper reports of his speeches.

In the fall of 1936, Father Coughlin ended his ten-year radio broadcast run and transferred his energies to the National Union for Social Justice, which he had founded two years earlier. The organization was the action arm of his ideology, engaging the political machinery instead of simply utilizing the airwaves. He claimed five million members nationwide who subscribed to his beliefs, which intended to throw "the moneychangers out of the temple." That summer, he raged before 120,000 paying supporters in Chicago against President Roosevelt, whom he branded a "liar and betrayer."

Some workingmen took matters into their own hands. These white male Protestants donned black robes and hoods, swore themselves to secrecy and took an oath to the "native-born white people of America," declaring "we regard as enemies to ourselves and our country all aliens, Negroes, Jews and cults and creeds believing in racial equality or owing allegiance to any foreign potentates [e.g., Roman Catholics]." Thus the Black Legion, a sinister clandestine version of the Ku Klux Klan, set to work placing its members in positions of civic and political influence to carry out its agenda. The black-robed brethren violently dispatched opponents and suspected betrayers in ways that "made the Ku Klux Klan look like a cream puff," *Time* magazine reported.

Some of the Black Legion's activities specifically targeted Jews. One member admitted a plot to poison Jews by injecting typhoid germs into milk delivered to Detroit's heavily populated Jewish neighborhoods. An investigator uncovered a plan to release cyanide gas in local synagogues during Hanukkah in 1935.

The Black Legion had anywhere from 20,000 to 100,000 members throughout Michigan, Ohio, Indiana and Illinois, with about a third of its loyalty in Detroit. The group was suspected of killing at least two auto union activists, though the murders were officially classified unsolved. It supposedly controlled the Packard and Hudson automobile plants and harbored Detroit's chief of police among its ranks. That could explain why the brotherhood got away with hundreds of beatings and murders in the Thirties.

The Black Legion may have continued its silent reign of terror indefinitely if not for the murder of Charley Poole, a twenty-two-year-old Catholic falsely accused of beating his pregnant Protestant wife. The front page news of his murder and the confession of his killer, a Detroit city employee, rocked the community. The story exposed the previously unknown Black Legion and the summer-long investigation dominated national headlines. The exposure and September conviction for murder of eleven Legionnaires broke the organization, though it also stoked fears of how far fascism could spread in the United States.*

In light of this tsunami of anti-Semitism flooding American soil, a broad movement developed to boycott the 1936 Olympic Games in Berlin, where Hitler intended to showcase Aryan superiority. Led by Jewish, Catholic and labor organizations and supported by the *New York Times*, the boycott movement sought to protest the Fuhrer's oppression of Jews and political dissenters. Forty-three percent of Americans supported the boycott, according to a Gallup Poll. But Avery Brundage, president of the American Olympic Committee, criticized the "misguided Jews" behind the boycott, convinced the AOC board that German Jewish athletes were not mistreated, and secured American participation in what became known as the "Nazi Olympics."

Curiously, amidst the swirling anti-Semitism, Hank took a job during the off-season with the Ford Motor Company. Henry Ford, the "arch

---

* The clandestine organization inspired the movie *The Black Legion*, starring Humphrey Bogart as a factory mechanic who first joins, then stands up to the legion.

anti-Semite of America," did not hate all Jews. When he liked an individual Jew, he would say to Harry Bennett, who was closer to him than his own son Edsel, "He's mixed, he's not at all Jewish."

Henry liked Hank. Perhaps this is why Greenberg agreed to work for the company, because Ford liked him. So did Bennett, Hank's supervisor. Bennett was attracted to great athletes. He had employed other Tiger players like Jo-Jo White, Fatty Fothergill and Mickey Cochrane. It was Bennett's Wyoming ranch that Cochrane used after his breakdown. The affection may have blinded Hank to the reality of their prejudice. Hank had heard the ethnic slurs on the field, but at other times people treated him well because he was a star ballplayer. "I don't think Hank realized how horrible anti-Semitism sometimes was because even Jew-haters wanted to shake his hand," his second wife, Mary Jo, said.

In November, Hank was shaking hands with Ford dealers checking out the new V-8s at the Detroit Coliseum. The *Detroit News* reported that he worked in the company's sales department. Other than the fact that Hank was a Jew working for Ford, that would not have been unusual because many of the celebrities the company hired were put in public relations roles. Hank, however, later listed on his military forms that he worked in the personnel department, Harry Bennett's security domain, as a "special investigator." He reported that he earned $5,000 to "investigate subversive activities of individuals against the Company."

This could have been as simple as Hank keeping his ears open out in the community for any derogatory comments he heard about Ford or his company and reporting those to Bennett, in effect making Greenberg a spy. Or it could have been more involved, with Greenberg actively seeking information about certain individuals, most likely union supporters.

The timing is also curious, since Hank's two employers, Walter O. Briggs and Henry Ford, had recently had a falling-out. Briggs had refused to deal with Harry Bennett and insisted upon doing business only with Ford's number two man, Charles Sorensen. "Either you go out that door," Briggs boomed at Bennett. "Or I'm going to throw you out that [seventh floor] window!"

Bennett left and gave Briggs's contract to another company. Briggs's ego and temper had alienated the world's largest auto manufacturer. One can only speculate whether Briggs was one of those individuals considered subversive by the Company that Hank investigated.*

Mid-October, Hank sat in his physician's office for another treatment on his wrist and read the news that Lou Gehrig had won the American League's Most Valuable Player award for 1936. "Last year I was on the top of the heap, and now I have to worry about making the ball team," he said ruefully.

Despite the fact that the New York physician pronounced Hank's wrist sound, Walter O. Briggs was not convinced that Hank could come back after his extended layoff. "The word was passed around freely that things would never be the same for him, that he had been away too long to recover his timing, that his wrist was chronically weak, that his power was gone," Ed Fitzgerald wrote in *Sport* magazine.

Briggs offered Greenberg a provisional contract for spring training, agreeing to pay $1,000 in exchange for him demonstrating his wrist was sound and that he was still capable of playing ball at his previous level. Only then would Mr. Briggs be willing to pay Greenberg his $25,000 for the 1937 season. Hank signed without a fight. "I was full of confidence and feeling that I would have no difficulty regaining my batting eye," Hank wrote.

In January, he headed to Florida to get started on the task of winning back his job. Mickey Cochrane had made a comment before he left that upset Hank. Cochrane, one of the doubters about Hank being able to return at 100 percent, suggested that he would move Greenberg to right field to make room for the promising Rudy York or another young prospect Cecil Dunn, who had hit seven home runs in two games the previous season. "Get yourself a pair of sunglasses," the manager had told Greenberg.

Hank was not going to leave his fate to chance, but was going to do what he knew how to do best, outwork the others. The photographers posed

---

* Ford Motor Company records show that it employed Greenberg during November and December 1936. Hank stated his employment lasted through February, until he reported to spring training. His reason for leaving: to "resume old position," in other words, first base for the Detroit Tigers.

him on the sand poised to throw a coconut left-handed and flexing his reconditioned arm. Hank liked to relax on the beach, and he had discovered the nightlife in Detroit, where he liked to dance at the Grosse Pointe Yacht Club, but he was all business in his rehabilitation that winter. The newspapers reported that he had become a "voluntary exile from the night clubs" with the belief that "early to bed and early to rise makes the left wrist healthy and wise."

"I want to give everything I have to make up for last year's layoff," he said.

He reported to Lakeland two weeks early, hiring Florida Negro pitcher Eagle Eye Newton to throw him a couple hours of daily batting practice while the ground crew took turns shagging balls. Hank started slow once the Tigers began playing exhibition games, but he erased doubts on April 7 in a game against the Senators. Walter Briggs "laughed heartily" while he watched Hank go four-for-five, including two home runs. He was delighted to see his first baseman back in MVP form. After the game, Briggs voided Hank's provisional agreement and signed him to a regular contract for the season at the rate they had agreed to in 1936, $25,000.

Hank didn't shine on Opening Day in Detroit. He was oh-for-three, made an error and got caught stealing. But after that, he took off like he had never been out of the lineup. In the next eleven games, he batted .364 with 16 hits, including three doubles, a triple and three home runs. He had scored 12 runs and batted in sixteen. The Tigers were tied with the Yankees for first place, and the season's prospects looked bright.

Less than three weeks later, the team's fortunes reversed. In the fifth inning on May 25 at Yankee Stadium, Bump Hadley, a stocky right-hander, let fly a high, inside fastball that Mickey Cochrane wasn't able to duck. The ball drilled him in the right temple with a "moist, sickening sound."* Cochrane crumpled unconscious. His eyes rolled up in their sockets. Hadley mopped the motionless Cochrane's brow. Thoughts of Ray Chapman, the Cleveland shortstop who died of a fractured skull after a beaning only seventeen years earlier, flashed though many spectators' minds.

---

* Batting helmets did not come into use until 1941 and did not become mandatory until 1956.

Four teammates carried Cochrane gingerly on a stretcher into the clubhouse. An ambulance rushed him to St. Elizabeth's Hospital, where X-rays revealed he had a triple fracture of the skull, a cracked right sinus and a concussion. For three days, Cochrane teetered between life and death. After two weeks, he was able to return to Detroit, where he spent another six weeks at Henry Ford Hospital listening to Tiger ball games on a bedside radio.

The club put Cochrane on the inactive list. Del Baker once again filled in as the Tigers' skipper, and Rudy York, the young slugger, replaced Cochrane behind the plate. York hit well (he would bat .307 with 35 homers and 103 RBI), which benefited Greenberg. With York batting behind him, Hank saw more good pitches from pitchers who didn't want to walk him. But York proved to be a liability behind the plate, so Baker was as likely to play him at third and put the rookie Birdie Tebbetts at catcher. Tebbetts, who graduated from Providence College with a philosophy major, had a weaker bat but surer hands than York.

Hank reached out to Tebbetts—as he would do repeatedly over the years with rookies and new teammates—and invited him to dinner at the upscale London Chop House on Congress Street. He recalled his own social awkwardness as a young player in new situations—being confused by rural slang in the clubhouse, such as references to a guy who was "horny as a hound dog in heat," and mortified as a dinner guest in the home of the team physician when a chicken bone dropped off his plate onto the hardwood floor. Hank also remembered being shunned by the veteran players. So he reached out to new players like Tebbetts and York, who was an illiterate Southern bumpkin. Hank brought York to a clothing store to buy him some decent clothes and taught him how to knot a tie. Hank was still one of the younger members of the team, but he was moving beyond his one-dimensional role as a player on the Detroit team.

The day after Mickey Cochrane got beaned, members of the fledgling United Auto Workers distributed union literature outside the Ford Motor Company's Rouge plant. In January that year, 2,000 UAW members had walked off their jobs at Briggs Manufacturing to protest the layoff of 200 workers. In less than two weeks, Briggs had given them their jobs back. Henry Ford, who had claimed unions were run by Jewish financiers, continued to resist labor's efforts to organize in his factories. Harry Bennett, head of Ford's security, had hired men to break up such activities.* On the afternoon of May 26, Bennett unleashed his thugs on three UAW leaders. They threw one, Robert Kanter, over the rail of the overpass to a lower level ten feet below. They rolled another, Walter Reuther, down the stairs. They beat the daylights out of another, Richard Frankensteen, who later said, "My head was like a piece of raw beef steak."

Bennett, who raised lions and tigers at his home outside Ann Arbor as a hobby, immediately denied involvement by his men and blamed the violence on plant workers arriving for their shift. Photographs snapped by newspapermen on hand proved otherwise. The outcry over Ford's "Gestapo tactics" employed in the "Battle of the Overpass" turned public opinion against the company and bolstered union membership. By July, the UAW had 200,000 members in Detroit and 370,000 nationwide.

Such was the atmosphere of labor relations as the Depression dragged on. The City of Champions' recovery was not complete. In blue-collar Detroit, there was antipathy against management and its strong-arm tactics. Yet, with workers fighting for their jobs, there was not much sympathy for ballplayers like Greenberg making big money and wanting more.

By June, Hank's hot start had him in the running again as a Triple Crown candidate. After forty-one games, he led the league in home runs (13), RBI (52) and was batting .376, among the best. His charge at Babe Ruth's single-season home run record in 1935 had drawn comparisons to the Bambino in a singular talent category, but now Hank was rating comparisons to Lou Gehrig in career terms. Gehrig stood at the head of the era's great first basemen, including Jimmie Foxx, Bill Terry, Hal Trosky and Zeke Bonura. Hank was establishing himself as a player meriting serious consideration for the title of the best first baseman in baseball. Greenberg had already outdone Gehrig in individual categories—doubles, triples, home runs, total bases and RBI—in different seasons. On pace to drive in 194 runs, Hank

---

* Bennett's goons included Joe Laman, a convicted kidnapper; Charles Goodman, who had been arrested twenty-one times on various charges; boxer Sam Taylor, who had been expelled from the Moulders Union for embezzlement; Angelo Caruso, a former gangster; and ex-pitcher Eddie Cicotte, one of the eight Black Sox banned from baseball.

would not only surpass Gehrig's AL season record of 184, he would exceed the Chicago Cubs' Hack Wilson's all-time mark of 190 RBI.*

Greenberg had silenced the naysayers who thought he was finished and impressed the sportswriters. The *Free Press'* Charles Ward had invoked the adage the previous spring, "They never come back in sport," but by June he admitted, "Henry Greenberg is a better ballplayer this year than he was in 1935. He is hitting the ball harder, and he is hitting to all fields." Moreover, Hank thought he would get even better as the season progressed and he got another look at the pitchers.

This year, when it came time to select the All-Stars, there was no way Greenberg could be ignored. He was in the midst of his third sensational year. By the break, he was batting .340, led the league in RBI (73), had hit 18 home runs and had a stellar OPS† of 1.150.

Hank passed the night in a hot and stuffy compartment on the train ride from Detroit to Washington, where the fifth annual Midsummer Classic was played at Griffith Stadium. President Roosevelt threw out the ceremonial first pitch. American League manager Joe McCarthy started five of his own Yankee players, including Gehrig at first, even though Greenberg's numbers overshadowed Gehrig's, other than Lou's .370 batting average. Hank spent the game on the bench—"All I did was sign autographs for a day and a half"—and took an even hotter train ride back to Detroit. The snub was almost worse than when he had been left off the team two years earlier.

Mickey Cochrane returned to manage on July 27 for a critical series against the Yankees, who led the Tigers by six games. He still suffered splitting headaches, dizzy spells, insomnia, anxiety and fatigue. He had known when he lay in the St. Elizabeth's hospital bed that he would not play again. He had snapped off the bedside radio in frustration many times, unable to bear listening to the Tigers lose. He ached to spur them back to first place. The series against the Yankees seemed the time to take charge. But the

---

* In 1999, Major League Baseball corrected a mistake found in the records of Wilson's 1930 season and added an RBI to his total, making the single-season record 191.
† On-base plus Slugging Percentage, a statistic not tracked in the Thirties but mentioned here to put his accomplishments in context.

team failed to respond, dropping two of three games in New York, and falling seven games back.

The Tigers never got any closer through the final two months of the season, and Cochrane abandoned his managing effort on September 9. Coaches Del Baker and Cy Perkins finished the year at the helm. The Triple Crown had slipped out of Greenberg's reach, but he continued to knock in runs at a record pace. His obsession with driving in runs, what he considered the most critical contribution a batter could make to the team (and, of course, his strongest negotiating chip at contract time), began to define him. "Just get the runner to third," he told Gehringer, who batted ahead of him. "I'll drive him in."

"I suppose if I hit a double with a man on first, you'd probably trip him if he tried to go past third base," Gehringer joked.

Hank couldn't laugh about missed RBI chances. Jo-Jo White had tried to steal home when Hank was at bat because he knew it would upset him to lose the RBI opportunity. White was tagged out. Hank towered over his prone teammate and growled, "The next time you do that, I'm going to hit you right on the head with the bat."

In 1937, Hank's drive to knock in runs consumed him. "I was primarily concerned with and concentrated on driving in runs," Hank wrote. "I had always had my eyes set on beating Gehrig's American League record. With this in mind, I was concentrating with men on base even more than I normally did because I was within reach of breaking the record, and this was one record that I wanted to establish, as it looked like it was going to stand for a long time."

By September 6, Rosh Hashanah, Hank had driven in 147 runs. With thirty games to play, he needed 37 more RBI to surpass Gehrig's record. To date, he had averaged 1.19 RBI per game. That pace would put him in a virtual tie with Gehrig. The Tigers were eleven games back of the Yankees, way out of contention, but Hank played both games of the Rosh Hashanah doubleheader and knocked in four runs. No one seemed to notice that he had played on the Jewish New Year.

Nine days later, Hank had reached 160 RBI, but he sat out the Yom Kippur game, the only game he missed all year. Once again, he observed the Day of Atonement by not playing. This time, there was no pennant race, no World Series, no poetic tribute. His decision did not have consequences for the team—Goose Goslin filled in at first and the Tigers won—but it may have cost him individual glory.

With three games to go, Hank had notched 175 RBI, which seemed to put him too far behind to reach Gehrig's 184. But he slugged two homers and a double, good for six RBI, and suddenly, he was back in the hunt. In the penultimate game of the 1937 season, Saturday, October 2, at Navin Field, Hank came to bat with the bases loaded. He had already driven in 181 runs. The outfield shifted to the left, leaving right field open. Hank blooped a ball down the right field line. On his way to first, he envisioned the bases clearing, drawing him even with Gehrig's 184 mark. Instead, the ball dropped foul by inches. He returned to the plate and lofted a long fly that scored one run, putting him at 182 with one game to play.

In that game, he faced Cleveland's Johnny Allen, a hard-throwing right-hander who had won 15 games in a row and was trying to tie the record held by Schoolboy Rowe and company in his final start of the season. Usually in the last game of the season between two teams not in contention, a team starts a young pitcher to give him the experience and take a look at him. But Hank would get no easy chances that day.

In the first inning, Hank batted with a man on second and one out. He singled to left, driving in his 183rd run of the season. *This is going to be great*, he thought. *It's going to be a high-scoring game. I'm going to break Gehrig's record.* But Allen was throwing well. In his next three at-bats, Hank walked once and failed to get a hit. He finished the year one RBI shy of Gehrig's mark. Had Jo-Jo White not tried to steal home, or that foul ball had landed six inches to the left, or he had played on Yom Kippur, he likely would have equaled or bettered his rival. But that wasn't how the story ended. He fell one short. Next to missing the conclusion of the 1935 World Series, that was probably the greatest disappointment of his career.

In fact, research by Society for American Baseball Research member Herm Krabbenhoft revealed in 2011 that Greenberg *had* driven in 184 runs in 1937. A clerical error failed to credit Hank with an RBI in the second game of the June 20 doubleheader against the Athletics. Krabbenhoft discovered that during the Tigers' five-run rally in the sixth inning, Hank drove in Flea Clifton from third on a fielder's choice that became an error, allowing Hank to reach. The RBI made it into two box scores but was not recorded in the official daily log. Had it been properly recorded, Hank would have finished the 1937 season with the satisfaction of knowing he had tied Gehrig for the American League record.*

Nevertheless, 1937 had been a good year. Greenberg had made a remarkable comeback. In nearly every offensive category, he improved upon his numbers from 1935, his MVP year. He batted .337 (compared to .328 in 1935), hit 49 doubles (46 in '35) and 14 triples. He scored 137 runs (121 in '35) and had 397 total bases (389). His 40 home runs (36) were second in the American League only to Joe DiMaggio's forty-six. His fielding was again a solid .992 percent. But Hank measured the season in a single number, 183. That, for Greenberg, demonstrated his value to the team and how close he had come to proving himself the league's best first baseman.

---

* Elias Sports Bureau, Major League Baseball's official record keeper, is reviewing Krabbenhoft's research and the situation. Retrosheet, considered by most baseball scholars to be the definitive source, has accepted the 184 RBI total. Coincidentally, Krabbenhoft subsequently discovered that Lou Gehrig was also shortchanged an RBI in the official record for 1931, so Gehrig's correct total for his record-setting season should be 185, keeping him one RBI ahead of Greenberg.

CHAPTER EIGHT

The Golden Mark

The Tigers opened the 1938 season in Chicago on Tuesday, April 19. Mickey Cochrane was back to manage but not play. Rudy York took his spot behind the plate. Dixie Walker played center field. Cochrane had obtained Walker, pitcher Vern Kennedy and utility infielder Tony Piet from the White Sox in exchange for the steady third baseman Marv Owen, outfielder Gee Walker (no relation to Dixie) and reserve catcher Mike Tresh. Cochrane's desire for Kennedy, a 21-game winner in 1936, had driven the trade, but Detroit fans howled over the loss of the popular Gee Walker. The deal tilted in the White Sox's favor on Opening Day 4–3, even though Hank Greenberg slugged his first home run of the season.

Three days later, 54,500 fans, the most ever to see a baseball game in Detroit, showed up to watch the Tigers play their first game in the newly renovated and renamed Briggs Stadium with its forest of dark green wooden seats. Walter O. Briggs had spent over a million dollars the past two years to add a second deck around the entire stadium, increasing capacity to accommodate 56,000 paying customers and making it second only to Yankee Stadium in size. "Briggs Stadium was more a monument to its namesake's ego than to his greed," Richard Bak noted in *Cobb Would've Caught It.*

Greenberg hit a triple, but the Tigers again lost 4–3, this time to Cleveland.

Despite those early extra-base hits, Hank started slow. When the team arrived in Boston for a series starting May 3, he was batting a meager .234

after thirteen games. He asked Red Sox owner Tom Yawkey and manager Joe Cronin for permission to take extra batting practice at Fenway in the mornings. His ninety-minute workouts helped. He went seven-for-thirteen, including two doubles and two homers, in the three Boston games.

Hank continued the practice in other parks on the road, arriving early for extra batting and fielding work with several guys he recruited to pitch and shag balls. At Shibe Park in Philadelphia, he had been taking his cuts for half an hour when a groundskeeper told him he had to leave. Hank and the others started to collect the bats and balls when an older man called to him from the grandstand. Hank walked over to the gentleman. "I very much admire what you are doing, young man," he said. "You tell that ground-skeeper to assist you in every way possible. Tell him that those are John Shibe's instructions." Hank had no more trouble in Philadelphia. In all of the American League, only the Yankees barred him from taking the field early.

The Yankees were not about to cut the star of their archrival any slack. The Tigers were to the Yankees then what the Red Sox are to them today. "We hated the Yankees, and they hated us," Birdie Tebbetts said.

The New York club often called up a minor league player specifically to harass Greenberg from the bench. If he got ejected for his verbal abuse, the team didn't suffer. In one game, when a particularly vicious comment about Hank's Jewishness flew from the Yankee bench, Hank stomped over to the dugout and challenged the entire team to fight. No one stirred, though a couple of guys did say, "Sorry."

Yankee pitchers often threw at Hank. In a game after Hank had hit a home run, the pitcher threw a ball *behind* Hank's head. Greenberg ducked but almost not in time. The ball brushed his cap. Having seen what happened to Cochrane, he suffered a sudden flash of terror thinking how close the pitch had come to ending his career. That quickly gave way to fury. He stepped toward the mound, ready to fight, but was stopped before he could put the pitcher in the dirt. Hank was prepared to protect himself with his fists when necessary. "I used to look around and see which ballplayers I'd have to fight some day, which bastards made one remark too many," he said.

Otherwise, Hank liked playing in New York. Though he was still often snakebitten in Yankee Stadium, the trip back home allowed him to see his family and enjoy his mother's cooking. He bragged to his teammates about her dishes and often brought one of them along for a meal.

His parents, too, had adjusted to the attention their son the famous ballplayer brought to them. They let the press inside their home to interview and photograph them. Mr. Greenberg even had fun with his role. While he waited for Hank outside Yankee Stadium, kids recognized him as Hank's father and approached him for an autograph. He signed his name in Hebrew. The boys walked away perplexed.

One day, when Hank left Yankee Stadium, he met an eleven-year-old boy waiting for him. The boy, who lived on the south side of Crotona Park, worshiped Greenberg. Hank looked at him and said, "Son, see that field over there?" He pointed to Macombs Dam Park across the street. "Spend your time there, and don't bother with autographs."

The boy, Sam Tolkoff, took Hank's advice. He went on to star for James Monroe High, Hank's old school, earned a scholarship to Long Island University and returned to coach at Monroe for many years.

That spring, *Snow White and the Seven Dwarfs*, the biggest-grossing film of the decade, played in Detroit cinemas, and nine-year-old Shirley Temple danced her way through *Little Miss Broadway*. The popular radio show, *The Lone Ranger*, broadcast from the Detroit studios of WXYZ, rode again into its sixth season. Tommy Dorsey's band played the Fox Theatre. Americans danced to the "Beer Barrel Polka." But all was not cheery in the Motor City. Auto production fell 48 percent from 1937 to 1938. By March, almost half of the city's workforce—310,000 of 760,000 workers—was unemployed. The Fair Labor Standards Act established a minimum wage of twenty-five cents an hour and limited the workweek to forty-four hours.

In Europe, Adolf Hitler created the *Oberkommando der Wehrmacht* (High Command of the Armed Forces), which gave him direct control of the military. He sent German troops into Austria to annex the country. Word of abuses trickled overseas. Jews in America heard that the Germans were robbing, beating and killing Jews in Europe. They heard Jews in Germany were starving because non-Jewish shopkeepers refused to sell them food. In response, Detroit rabbis called for a day of mourning on May 10 to condemn the mistreatment. They urged merchants to close shops from four to six in the afternoon. In the synagogues, cantors read lamentations and rabbis preached hope.

The Tigers were out East, wrapping up their road trip. They lost the final game in Washington, which put them in fifth place, 8–12. Greenberg hit his seventh home run of the season but also committed two errors. At home in Briggs Stadium, the Bengals continued to lose more games than they won. But on May 25, they turned in a strong performance, beating the Yankees 7–3 on the strength of Greenberg and York, who each hit a pair of home runs. Hank added a double and single to his four-for-four performance. Of his 35 hits to date, he had six doubles, two triples and 11 home runs. Though his .305 batting average was still ten points below where he expected it, he was pleased to be averaging 2.2 bases per hit. He saw his value to the team not in singles but in extra-base hits. "The fellows who drive in the runs don't do it with a lot of one-base hits," he said.

Hank had benefited from third base coach Del Baker tipping him off on pitches. Baker was one of the best in the game at reading pitchers for indicators and at stealing signs. "All right, Hank, you can do it," Baker would yell from the coach's box—and Hank knew a fastball was on the way. "Come on, Hank," meant curve. Greenberg called himself "the best hitter in the world" when he knew what pitch was coming.

The story went around about a game the previous season when Hankus Pankus had looked to Baker for a sign about the upcoming pitch, but, not getting one, had let a perfect pitch go by for a third strike. Back in the dugout, he demanded of Baker, "Why aren't you calling them?"

Baker said he hadn't been able to pick up any telltale sign.

"Well, guess one for me then," Hank supposedly said.

His teammates laughed.

Yet it annoyed Hank when Baker took credit for Hank's success. "At one point it seemed as though if he called a pitch correctly and I hit a home run, he thought it was *his* home run," Hank said. "Baker was a real good sign stealer, no question about it, but there's a big difference between *knowing* what's coming and *hitting* it."

Hank was sensitive to what the criticism implied: that he couldn't hit without Baker letting him know what was coming. He resented references to the coach as his "batting eye." Before the 1938 season started, he had sworn off Baker's signs. "Henry Greenberg announces that he will no longer play Charlie McCarthy to Del Baker's Edgar Bergen," Harry Salsinger put it in the *Detroit News*.

On a muggy night, June 22, 80,000 spectators crowded Yankee Stadium, not for a baseball game, but for a heavyweight title fight, what ringside broadcaster Clem McCarthy termed for the NBC radio audience of over 70 million, "the greatest fight of our generation." The bout between heavyweight champion Joe Louis and German challenger Max Schmeling was loaded with political symbolism. Two years earlier, Schmeling had been the first fighter to knock down Louis, and the first fighter to beat him. The Nazi weekly journal *Das Schwarze Korps* proclaimed: "Schmeling's victory was not only sport. It was a question of prestige for our race." Hitler had welcomed the German fighter home with a reception at the Reich Chancellery, where they watched a film of the match. In 1938, a month after Hitler announced his intentions to crush Czechoslovakia, the rematch assumed much larger proportions. Louis defended not just his title but the ideals of freedom and democracy against the Nazi-endorsed Schmeling.*

Louis, aware of the expectations he bore, set upon his opponent immediately. He pinned Schmeling against the ropes and battered him with punches. Louis knocked down the German with a left-right combination. Schmeling got up. Louis knocked him down again with a sharp right to the chin. It was over in two minutes, four seconds. Schmeling couldn't go on, and the referee raised Louis's arm as the victor. The free world rejoiced.

Jews also had a special reason to cheer Louis. "For the innumerable Jews whose most searing memory of childhood was being beaten and taunted as 'Christ Killers,' Joe Louis—the African American scorned and ridiculed by the Nazis who had humiliated Max Schmeling—was *their* avenger," historians Stephen Norwood and Harold Brackman write in the essay "Going to Bat for Jackie."

---

* Despite being feted by the Fuhrer, Schmeling was not a Nazi sympathizer nor anti-Semitic. He had a Jewish manager, whom he refused to fire despite pressure from Hitler. After *Kristallnacht*, Schmeling hid two teenage sons of a Jewish friend in his apartment and helped smuggle them to safety outside the country.

Hank's batting had been inconsistent in 1938. That upset him. Though he was tied with Jimmie Foxx for the league lead in home runs (22), his batting average had dipped to .285. In late June, he had managed only five hits in nine games, though all five were homers. He spent hours studying his swing in front of a full-length mirror to see if he could detect what was wrong. He worried that his eyes were failing him. He lay awake at night, thoughts of his slump robbing him of sleep.

Despite his subpar batting average, Hank was selected to represent the American League in the 1938 All-Star Game to be played July 6 in Cincinnati. Gehrig and Foxx were also named to the team. Four days before the sixth annual Midsummer Classic, Hank begged off. He said his wrist hurt and that he was going to have it X-rayed and his eyes checked. Yankee manager Joe McCarthy said that was too bad, that he had planned to start Hank at first and Foxx at third. That would have been historic because so far, Gehrig, ever the iron horse, had been the only one to play first base for the American League in the five previous All-Star Games. McCarthy added Johnny Murphy, one of his Yankee pitchers, to fill Hank's roster spot. Hank was miffed that when he asked to be excused, no one insisted that he play. "If I had been told that the league was depending on me, I would have forgotten personal wishes and gone to Cincinnati," he said. "It was even more clear that I was not needed when I saw the substitute picked in my place."

Other players on the team grumbled about Hank "ducking" the game, which was unheard of then, not the common practice it is today. "If Greenberg's wrist is bothering him so much that he can't play in the All-Star Game," they wanted to know, "how's it come that he was able to play two games on Sunday and two more on Monday?"

X-rays showed Hank's wrist was "perfect." So were his eyes. He was relieved to know that and figured it would give him more confidence at the plate. In truth, he had skipped the All-Star Game because he was still angry that McCarthy had kept him on the bench for the last one. He did not want to repeat that experience. So he had petulantly refused to go.

He listened to the game on the radio with friends at the Franklin Hills Country Club. Foxx started at first, and the Senators' Buddy Lewis played third. Early on, McCarthy took out Lewis, moved Foxx to third and inserted Gehrig at first. The American League lost 4–1.

Hank spent the balance of the three-day break taking batting practice. He paid semipro pitchers ten to twenty dollars—a handsome wage in those days—to pitch to him all day. His investment paid off. He caught fire after the All-Star break. Through the rest of July, he batted .382. Most significantly, over half of his hits (fifteen of twenty-nine) were home runs. From July 24–30, he hit nine home runs in seven days. On July 30, Hank and teammate Harry Eisenstat, a fellow Jew, had an especially big day.

Eisenstat, a left-handed pitcher from Brooklyn, had debuted with the Dodgers in 1935 on Rosh Hashanah. The year after Greenberg had made headlines with his decision to play on the Jewish New Year, Eisenstat had consulted his rabbi, who told him it was okay for him to take the field. Called upon in relief, Eisenstat gave up a grand slam on his first pitch.

Eisenstat became a free agent after the 1937 season because Brooklyn had farmed him out three times. Greenberg encouraged Eisenstat to sign with the Tigers, who needed left-handed pitching, for the 1938 season. In Detroit, Hank took Harry under his wing. He showed him around town and introduced Harry to his friends. He taught him how to dress like a big leaguer. He taught him how to talk to sportswriters. He taught him how to handle the anti-Semitism. "Never use the fact that you are Jewish as an excuse," Hank said. "It should be more of an incentive to be successful." Eisenstat also learned from Hank what it took to be successful. On days Harry wasn't pitching, Hank recruited him to throw batting practice and mimic the way opposing pitchers threw. For instance, if they were about to face the Yankees, Hank asked Harry to throw the ball inside on his fists the way Red Ruffing did.

In the Tigers' twin bill on Saturday, July 30, against the Philadelphia Athletics, Eisenstat came in down 6–5 and pitched the last two innings to pick up the win on the strength of Hank's eighth-inning three-run homer. In the second game, Eisenstat pitched four shutout innings of relief for another win, this time thanks to Greenberg's two-out, two-run homer, again in the bottom of the eighth. The 24,700 fans at Briggs Stadium had delighted in the home team's comebacks, from a five-run deficit in the first game and from seven runs in the second. The wins extended the Tigers' winning streak to eight games and lifted them into fourth place. In the clubhouse afterward, the two heroes posed for newspaper photographers, smiles on their faces, Hank's arm draped around Harry's shoulder. Mickey

Cochrane told them, "Fellas, lock yourselves in your rooms tonight because the Jews in Detroit are going to go crazy."

That evening, the two ate dinner at the Franklin Hills Country Club. When they walked into the dining room, the members of the Jewish club cheered them heartily. Not only had it been the most exciting day in the Tiger season, the two had performed the greatest display of offensive and defensive prowess by a pair of Jews on a baseball diamond ever witnessed in America.

While Hank and Harry dined at the Franklin Hills Country Club, Henry Ford celebrated his seventy-fifth birthday across town with 1,500 well-wishers. The German consuls from Detroit and Cleveland bestowed upon Ford the Grand Cross of the Supreme Order of the German Eagle, an award created by Hitler as the highest honor to be given non-Germans. Ford was the first American to receive it. Hitler's personal congratulations were read along with the presentation of the Grand Cross. Newspapers across the country ran photographs of Ford smiling while the German consul from Cleveland pinned the medal on his chest. The *Detroit News* caption above the photo read "Hitler Sends Ford a Birthday Gift."

Ford's acceptance of the medal angered many Americans. In his boss' defense, Harry Bennett explained that the gesture was more indicative of Ford's ignorance than his prejudice. "Mr. Ford just stubbornly refused to believe the stories of Nazi violence and brutality, and put it all down to propaganda," Bennett wrote in his memoir *Ford: We Never Called Him Henry*.

The comedian Eddie Cantor questioned Ford's Americanism and Christianity. He called Ford "a damned fool for permitting the world's greatest gangster to give him this citation. Doesn't he realize that the German papers, reporting the citation, said all Americans were behind Nazism? Whose side is Mr. Ford on?"

The Jewish War Veterans called upon Ford, "in the name of humanity and Americanism," to "repudiate" the German decoration. The organization characterized his acceptance of the award as "an endorsement of the cruel, barbarous, inhuman actions and policies of the Nazi regime" and of the German American Bund with its "subversive un-American activities and other anti-democratic groups subsidized here by Nazi funds." In protest, the Jewish War Veterans sent Ford a telegram refusing the Ford Motor

Company's offer to furnish seventy-five cars decorated with the Star of David to the organization during its upcoming annual convention in Detroit.

Others discouraged the purchase of Ford automobiles. Company officials were convinced that there was "an active and effective boycott against us," but Henry Ford also refused to believe that was happening.

In November, after the horrors of *Kristallnacht* and the partition of Czechoslovakia, Detroit Rabbi Leo Franklin convinced Ford to explain himself. A statement drafted by Franklin and approved by Ford said: "My acceptance of a medal from the German people does not, as some people seem to think, involve any sympathy on my part with Nazism. Those who have known me for many years realize that anything that breeds hate is repulsive to me."

That rang false with those who had known him for many years and read his screeds against Jews in the previous decade. They were not appeased. In response, Secretary of the Interior Harold Ickes said that anyone like Ford and Charles Lindbergh, who received a similar medal, "automatically forswears his American birthright." "How can any American accept a decoration at the hand of a brutal dictator who, with that same hand, is robbing and torturing thousands of fellow human beings?" Ickes asked in a speech to the Cleveland Zionist Society.

Father Charles Coughlin, on the other hand, upped his attacks after *Kristallnacht*. In one of his radio addresses he claimed Josef Stalin and Nicolai Lenin were Jews (they weren't), that all but three members of the Soviet communist party's control commission were Jewish and those three were married to Jewish wives (not true, either statement) and that the Russian Revolution had basically been a Jewish coup (um, not so). Despite Father Coughlin's efforts to revive his flagging popularity, his comments were "transformed into ridicule and scorn in circles which have become aware of the false premises upon which his speech was based," according to the *Detroit Jewish Chronicle*.

Hank's home run output in July rekindled talk that he would break Babe Ruth's single-season mark of sixty set eleven years earlier. At the time, the baseball world figured one of the current players would hit sixty-one. Hack Wilson had hit fifty-six in 1930 and Jimmie Foxx fifty-eight in 1932. When

Hank hit four consecutive home runs late in July—a pair in his final two at-bats and another pair the next day in his first two at-bats—the press picked Hankus Pankus as the man to best the Babe. Hank had thirty-three already, seven games ahead of Ruth's 1927 pace. The press had hyped him three years earlier when he had 30 home runs on August 3, but then he had hit only six more home runs in the final two months. This time seemed different. Hank was a more seasoned hitter. He knew which pitches he could drive and which he couldn't. He had learned to wait for a ball he could pull over the fence. He knew the pitchers better. By the end of July, he had already hit 37 homers—more than he had hit all of 1935—which put him seventeen days ahead of Ruth. What's more, Hank had hit two home runs in a game four times in July. Most significantly, with the Tigers all but out of the race, fourteen games back, Hank's four consecutive homers had inspired him to swing for the record. "From then on I just aimed for the fences," he said. If he was going to break "The Golden Mark," as Ruth's record was known then, this seemed to be his year to do it.

Hank still considered the RBI a more telling and valuable statistic. "I'd trade my chances for a home run record to get the runs-driven-in record," he told reporters that summer. "Last year I only missed Lou Gehrig's American League mark by a run. I'd like to beat Hack Wilson's 190."

Yet to fans and the American public in general, the home run was the glory shot, the stroke of true importance, the celebrity calling card. Babe Ruth reigned supreme in that realm, having established the home run as a fan favorite and thus revolutionizing the game, both in how it was played and how it was viewed. The Babe had elevated the home run to an act of monumental importance. So, as Hank approached Babe's mark, his celebrity grew. He knew he could secure his place in history with the record.

Hank's home runs were more long, hard drives than towering shots, but many of them traveled quite a distance. He set the long-distance mark for half of the American League parks. He was the first one to launch a home run into the center field bleachers in Comiskey Park. He was the only one to park a drive in Yankee Stadium's center field bleachers—not even Ruth had done that. He was the first to clear Cleveland's brick wall in center. And he hit one ball out of Fenway that was estimated at 500 feet. Many of his homers were an event in themselves.

As July turned to August, the story followed Hank wherever he went. The Detroit newspapers posted thermometers with 60 at the top showing how far he had risen toward the total. They ran comparisons of the dates of Ruth's homers in 1927 and Greenberg's in 1938. In every town the Tigers played, the newspapers wrote tallies of Hank's accounts. Fans showed up to see if he could keep up the pace. He had captured the nation's imagination, a welcome diversion from the headlines about hard times at home and violent tensions abroad.

Greenberg's pursuit of baseball's biggest record at the time stirred special interest among Jews. On the streets and in the shops of the Dexter section, people who knew nothing else about baseball asked one another, *"Vos hot Greenberg geton haynt?"* (What did Greenberg do today?) Jewish boys like ten-year-old Max Lapides and thirteen-year-old Harvey Frank clipped every article about Greenberg from the papers and pasted them in treasured scrapbooks.

The mainstream press looked upon Greenberg favorably, which cast all American Jews in a good light. One writer, the *New York Daily Mirror*'s Dan Parker, thought Greenberg would break Ruth's record *because* he was Jewish. "Greenberg has a magnificent physique, a keen batting eye and the fine coordination between eye and muscle that are prerequisites of a home-run specialist," Parker wrote in a 1938 column. "But none of these attributes is half as important to Hank's baseball career as the good old Jewish qualities of thoroughness and perseverance that Greenberg had instilled in him by his parents long before he ever handled a baseball."

This sort of praise bolstered Hank's image among fellow Jews. "This was a time when Jewish Americans of the second generation were extremely concerned with what the Gentiles said about us," historian William Simons said. "The fact he garnered positive responses from Gentiles was seen as overwhelmingly positive among Jews."

The Jewish press proudly touted Greenberg's accomplishments. "The stock question, when things happen in the world, is whether it is good for the Jews or bad," a *Detroit Jewish Chronicle* editorial began. "It has been good for the Jews on the baseball diamond. Hank Greenberg and Harry Eisenstat have contributed to good will—and as long as one hits and the other pitches well, they will remain ambassadors in the movement for better understanding." *B'Nai B'rith Magazine* profiled the "Mighty Slugger" who "stands as a model for all baseball players." The *American Hebrew* called him "The Jewish Babe Ruth" and said, "Whether Henry Greenberg equals or breaks the record, he has conclusively proved himself to be the number one Jewish ballplayer of all time." A Jewish periodical in Boston felt it necessary to define a home run for its readers, and Simon A. Feate in his August 2 "Review of the Jewish Week" syndicated feature explained, "The home run is to baseball what a grand slam in no trumps is to bridge." In other words, they were saying, even if you don't understand baseball, you must know that here is a Jew doing something extraordinary that's good for all of us. "We all felt pride," said Bert Gordon, the rabbi's son. "It was the same pride we felt when the Americans landed on the moon. That was one of your guys doing something exceptional."

The Boston publication put it thus, "We've had pogroms before; we have had wars before; we have had trouble with Arabs before. But never before have we had a Jewish home-run king. . . . A genuine baseball fan just can't be an anti-Semite. The name of Greenberg was shouted out in Fenway Park last week in eight different languages and in twenty-one different dialects. Greenberg is another form of good-will emissary for the Jewish people."

In a dark time, Hank was certainly giving the Jewish community something to cheer, but he was doing something even more significant: In an age when Jews were considered weak, unathletic and impotent, Greenberg stood as a mighty figure and, in his image as a home run slugger, a symbol of power. He changed the way Jews thought about themselves. And the way others thought about them. "All of a sudden, big, tall Hank Greenberg comes along," Rabbi Michael Paley, the baseball scholar, said. "He could hit the ball a mile. That image of the Jew was transformational. It wasn't only transformational for the Jews, looking at Hank Greenberg and seeing themselves—it was amazing for Jews thinking what other people think of us. I did not grow up feeling vulnerable, the pipsqueak getting sand kicked in our faces, because they didn't see us that way anymore; they saw us as Americans."

Hank became the face—and muscles—of Judaism in America. He single-handedly changed the way Gentiles viewed Jews. "That's one of the great achievements in American history," Rabbi Paley said. "Hank

Greenberg came along when most non-Jews were coming into awareness of Jews pouring into the country. Their American-born children were starting to grow up and come into the workforce. All of a sudden, Hank Greenberg articulates, 'I'm an American Jew.' 'Oh, we didn't know,' they say. 'We thought Jews were the Pharisees from the New Testament.' He says, 'No, this is what we look like.' It's not as great a historical achievement as Jackie Robinson, but it's a pretty damn good achievement."

Greenberg, all six-foot, four-inches of his muscular frame, shattered stereotypes with his very presence on the field. "Hank Greenberg was what *they* all said we could never be," noted civil liberties lawyer Alan Dershowitz said. "He defied Hitler's stereotype. For that very reason, I think he may have been the single most important Jew to live in the 1930s."

By 1938, the twenty-seven-year-old Greenberg had matured into a deeper understanding of world events and his place among them. He had begun to read more of the newspapers than the sports pages. He understood the significance of what he was doing. "Being Jewish did carry with it a special responsibility," Hank wrote. "After all, I was representing a couple of million Jews among a hundred million Gentiles, and I was always in the spotlight. I was there every day, and if I had a bad day, every son of a bitch was calling me names so that I had to make good. I just had to show them that a Jew could play ball. I came to feel that if I, as a Jew, hit a home run, I was hitting one against Hitler."

Mickey Cochrane had never fully recovered from his nervous breakdown in 1936 and his beaning in 1937. He remained fidgety and high-strung. He was not the same leader from the bench; he wanted to be directing the action from the field. It bothered him that his big preseason trade hadn't worked out. Vern Kennedy had won his first nine games but then seemed unable to win any more. Cochrane had to bench Dixie Walker. Marv Owen's departure had left a hole at third base. Some fans never forgave Mickey for trading the popular Gee Walker. Cochrane paced the dugout in a rage during losses, second-guessing his teammates. He impulsively fined players for their mistakes. He argued with Walter O. Briggs's son Spike, the team treasurer. On August 6, the Tigers lost to the Red Sox, 14–8, their fourth loss in a row, and dropped to 47–51, seventeen games back.

Briggs called Cochrane into his office afterward. The two exchanged words. Cochrane departed without a job.

Briggs paid Cochrane for the balance of the season but wiggled out of his commitment to pay the final season of his contract. The owner issued a statement: "It seems apparent to both of us that for the good of the club and in justice to the sporting fans, a change should be made." Detroit fans grieved the loss of their beloved manager. Baseball men criticized Briggs for his midseason firing of the man who had brought two pennants to Detroit in his first two years, who had scored the winning run in the '35 World Series, who had come back from his deathbed to manage again. They called Briggs's action "brutal" and "tactless" and charged that the owner "needlessly humiliated" one of the game's finest men.

Mickey took it hard. He eventually found work as a manufacturer's rep, selling steel, wire and rubber goods to Detroit companies, and bought a ranch in Wyoming. He managed the Great Lakes Naval Training Center team from 1942 to 1944, served briefly as Connie Mack's general manager in 1950 and scouted some later for the Yankees, but after the Tigers let him go, he had lost his purpose in baseball. "He never got over being let out as manager by Mr. Briggs," Greenberg said when Cochrane died in 1962. "He never got over the hurt. And this wasn't getting hit on the head by Bump Hadley. Mike's hurt was in the heart, not the head."

Once again, Del Baker took over as manager. Baker had been a backup catcher himself with the Tigers when Hughie Jennings managed the club. Baker later guided the Beaumont team to the Dixie Series and gained a reputation for developing young talent. His protégés included Schoolboy Rowe, Pete Fox, Luke Hamlin, Jo-Jo White and, of course, Greenberg. Baker was stern but fair with the players. Frank Navin had admired him as a tactician. "Baker studies the game like a chess player," Navin said. "He never makes a move without a deliberate purpose."

Hank hadn't hit a home run in August, but he homered in Baker's first game at the helm. Then he lapsed into another lull without a home run for nine games. He went hitless—oh-for-sixteen—during one four-game stretch. As the drought wore on, he worried that American League secretary Henry Edwards had jinxed him. On August 7, Edwards had sent Hank a copy of all of his home runs that season along with a list of all of Ruth's homers; that marked the day Hank stopped hitting.

Perhaps the pressure would undo him the way it had three years earlier. "It's been a strain ever since they started touting me to knock 61 homers," Hank admitted. "Every time I come to bat, I'm trying for one. The fans want them. The result is my batting average has slipped."

Then he clobbered three homers on August 19 in a doubleheader against the St. Louis Browns, including a grand slam in the first game. That gave him 41 taters, the most he had ever hit in one season, and put him eight days ahead of Ruth's pace. He had forty-five games left to hit twenty more.

With every home run he hit, Hank received a card in the mail. The envelopes, addressed simply to "Briggs Stadium—Det.," each had a silhouette drawing of No. 5 completing his swing with a ball showing the number of the homer he had just hit. Inside was a stick figure cartoon and a short note. They came from an art student at Wayne State College named Marjorie Nash. She had started sending the cards in 1935. She also sent ballplayers and movie stars of the day—Jimmy Stewart, Barbara Stanwyck, Clark Gable, Bette Davis, Fred MacMurray, etc.—skillfully-rendered pencil sketches that they returned autographed. She received her first signed portrait from Greenberg in September 1935, noting in her diary, "Hank sent my picture back autographed. He also sent me a card. He's a swell guy!"

Hank was Marjorie's favorite subject. She kept a scrapbook filled with clippings and photos of him from Detroit's three daily newspapers. She spent afternoons drawing sketches of him. She tracked his home runs in her diary. She sent him Christmas cards and small gifts she had made for him. She attended Tiger games whenever she could and snapped photos of Hank. By 1938, the twenty-one-year-old had developed a major league crush on the Tigers' handsome No. 5.

Hank saved the cards. He had shown several to a reporter, and the *Detroit News* printed ten of them with a couple of her envelopes in its Sunday, August 7, edition. That led to an article and photo in the *Detroit Times* a week later. Her cards became a footnote to each of Hank's homers the final seven weeks of the season.

For every home run Hank hit that season, he also received a case of Wheaties. He was featured on the Wheaties box that year, which was as much of a status symbol then as it is now. He had first appeared on the box in 1936 and would be featured again in 1939, 1940 and 1947. General Mills, makers of the "Breakfast of Champions," hosted a "Home Run Hank" movie party in September 1938. Customers who bought two boxes of Wheaties received tickets to the movie released to theatres October 1. Despite the free cases of cereal, Hank preferred fruit for breakfast. He shared his bonus Wheaties with his teammates. "I pass 'em around among the boys on the team who can't hit," he said.

A two-panel billboard outside Briggs Stadium featured a likeness of Hank with his arms around a boy and girl and the caption, "Hank Greenberg says: 'We *all* like Wheaties, the best breakfast food in the land!'" His good looks and national celebrity status also had him pitching Grunow radio sets and Raleigh cigarettes (which he smoked himself). He received royalties from the sale of bats and gloves with his signature. The Curtiss Candy Company, makers of the Baby Ruth bar, had plans to bring out a Hankus Pankus candy bar if he broke the single-season home run record.

Eating his breakfast of prunes at the New Yorker Hotel on the last day of August, Hank assessed his chances to become the new home run king. He had hit 45 homers to date with thirty-six games left to hit fifteen to tie, sixteen to pass Ruth. But September was the cruelest month for a hitter. Fatigue from the long season set in. Pitchers gained an advantage with shadows falling earlier over the infield, making it difficult for hitters to pick up the ball. The weather turned colder and the winds picked up, both working against hitters. Rainouts cancelled at-bat opportunities. Taking all of this into account, Hank said tentatively, "I'd say I'm about a ten-to-one shot to break Babe's mark."

He had thought seriously about his chances, analyzing them with his keen mind the way he did pitchers. He knew that of the Tigers' thirty-six remaining games, five were in Cleveland, three in New York—stadiums where the long left field fences made it difficult for him to hit home runs— "which gives me twenty-eight games in parks where I know I can drive them for four bases," he said. "My best bet, of course, is out in Detroit, where we've got twenty-four games left. Two apiece are left in Chicago and St. Louis."

He liked Briggs Stadium best. The new upper deck in center field created a dark background that made it easier for him to follow the ball. The left field fence 340 feet away was within reach. And the double decks often blocked the wind from slowing low line drives. With Hank batting in that friendly environment for two-thirds of the remaining games, his odds seemed better to his fans.

He was still ahead of Ruth's pace—the Babe hadn't hit his 45th home run until September 6—but Hank knew that Ruth had done the unthinkable in his record-setting season, clobbering 17 round-trippers in the final month of the season. That itself was a record until last year, when Rudy York, Hank's hard-hitting teammate, slugged 18 homers in August. Hank idolized Ruth, whom he considered the greatest ballplayer of all-time. He got upset with a writer who wrote an article in September, "Hank Greenberg Another Babe Ruth," that said he was certain to break the single-season home run record. Hank didn't like the pressure that label hung on him. He objected even more strenuously to the comparison. "I told him [the writer] that I'd never be a second Babe and that no ballplayer ever would be even close to the old master," Hank wrote in a *Collier's* article. His march toward the Babe's "Golden Mark" deepened his admiration for Ruth.

The photographers crowded on the field when Hank batted, at the edge of his peripheral vision, their noisy cameras snapping away. He didn't want to complain about the attention—that he liked—but they were a distraction, almost more challenging than the opposing pitchers. And that distraction mounted the closer he got to Ruth. "I dread to think what I'm going to have to face every time I go to bat the rest of the way out," Hank said.

Hank did homer August 31 in Yankee Stadium, but then stalled again. He didn't smack No. 47 until September 9 in Cleveland. So much for his predictions. It looked like maybe the chase was over, that his power would evaporate the way it had in late 1935. Babe Ruth thought Greenberg had fallen victim to the pressure. "The strain is too great," Ruth said. "The boys are forever reminded about that record, and it is bound to tell on them. It's telling on Greenberg now. I don't think he'll be able to make it."

Greenberg paced the dugout during batting practice, insisting to anyone who would listen that he wasn't worrying about the record. His teammates knew otherwise and figured it was keeping him awake at nights. "I knew he was under a lot of pressure, and he was nervous about it," Charlie Gehringer said.

His teammates were pulling for him. "We all wanted him to break it because he was our Hank, a teammate and a friend," Elden Auker, the submarine pitcher, wrote in his memoir. "We also wanted Hank to beat the record because we knew how hard it had been for him to become a great player. It didn't come as naturally to him as to most of the other stars. He had those big, flat feet and was a little clumsy, a bit awkward. He had to work and work—nobody worked harder at becoming a better baseball player than Hank Greenberg."

Even opponents rooted for the likable Greenberg. Lou Gehrig said he thought Hank could do it. His manager, Joe McCarthy, said, "I hope he does it." Yankee catcher Bill Dickey even tipped off Hank on pitches.

But not everyone wanted to see Hank break the record. "I'm pretty well convinced that Walter Briggs was rooting against me," he said years later. "If I'd broken the record, he would have had to give me a big raise—maybe $10,000."

Babe Ruth had only been retired three years. His legend had not yet swelled to its modern-day proportions. In 1938, it was still growing, but he had already become bigger than life and was widely loved. Fans didn't want to see him dethroned. Nor did the Babe, then a coach with Brooklyn, want to see Hank replace his name in the record books. "He should break it—in that park," Ruth said, as though dismissing the significance of Greenberg's accomplishment because of the nearness of the left field wall in Briggs Stadium while seeming to forget the convenience of Yankee Stadium's 314-foot right field wall.* "The big fellow [Ruth] is a child at heart, and he undoubtedly would reveal the pathos of a small boy about to lose a prized possession, because if there is any segment of his career as a player of which he is proud, it's his home-run record," Joe Williams wrote in the *World-Telegram*.

Then there were those who specifically did not want a Jew to better the popular Babe. Just as years later some Americans objected to the idea of a black man, Hank Aaron, besting the Babe's 714 mark, there were bigots in the Thirties who didn't want Greenberg to break sixty. "For the many

---

* Ruth did have a point, though. Greenberg hit 39 home runs in Briggs Stadium in 1938; Ruth hit 28 at Yankee Stadium in 1927.

anti-Semites in the stands, the press box and between the foul lines, it was inconceivable, and unseemly, that a Jew should break the Babe's record," one writer observed.

"I remember sitting in the stands with my dad and hearing these horrible insults people shouted at him [Greenberg] and wondered how people could be that way, Tiger fans even," Max Lapides recalled. "We just sat there and hoped that Greenberg would hit a home run and shut them up."

Along with Marjorie's envelopes that arrived with each home run, Hank also received hate mail littered with ugly sentiments. Some included death threats. In light of the times, the danger may have been real, with Nazi sympathizers about as happy for Greenberg as the Ku Klux Klan was later for Aaron.

Marjorie Nash wrote in her diary on September 11: "Hank hit No. 48 and No. 49!" He reached 50 the next day. In Europe, Hitler bullied England and France to force Czechoslovakia to cede the Sudetenland to Germany while President Roosevelt declared it would be "100 percent wrong" for the United States to join a "stop-Hitler bloc" and that the country would remain neutral even if Germany resorted to military action. On Saturday, September 17, two days after British Prime Minister Neville Chamberlain met with Hitler in Berchtesgaden, 19,200 fans showed up at Briggs Stadium mostly to see if Greenberg would move closer to Ruth's record. He did not disappoint them, going four-for-four in a win over the Yankees and slugging two taters to reach fifty-three.

The Greenbergs in the Bronx followed Hank closely that month and celebrated his success. "Every home run was New Year's Eve in our family," Joe Greenberg said. His mother promised to make Hank sixty-one baseball-shaped gefilte fish patties if he broke the record.

September had another factor conspiring against Hank: darkness. Games rained out earlier in the season caused doubleheaders to bunch up at the end—in the final seven weeks, the Tigers played eleven twin bills, but with the sun setting earlier and no lights in the stadiums, five games were called on account of darkness sometime after the fifth inning. That cost Greenberg valuable at-bats. All told, that season Hank probably lost 20 at-bats to rain or darkness, which translated into at least two homers, given his season average of a home run every 9.6 at-bats.

Hank was also losing chances to hit the long ball when pitchers walked him, or, worse, threw at him. He was the most formidable hitter in the Detroit lineup, and pitchers were willing to put him on base and face York behind him, rather than risk giving up a home run. Sometimes they walked him intentionally. Other times, they pitched too carefully to him, which gave him a base on balls. And sometimes the walks were accidental, the result of those young pitchers, nervous to be in the big leagues and anxious about pitching to the mighty Greenberg, unable to put the ball over the plate. For whatever the reason, he walked more that season than ever in his career, some 119 times, which made him the most walked batter in the AL along with Jimmie Foxx. The closer Hank got to Ruth's record, the more he walked. In September, pitchers walked Greenberg in 20.4 percent of his at-bats compared to just 15.9 percent of his at-bats the rest of the season. He had three games with three walks in the final month.*

Pitchers also threw at him more often, perhaps out of frustration or to push him off the plate, not let him dig in properly, or out of wildness. He had the bruises on his arms and hips to show for it. "They're dusting me off a bit, too," he said in late August. "I've been hit by pitched balls twice in the last couple of games."

The paucity of parkable pitches frustrated Hank. He had only 556 at-bats in 681 plate appearances, his lowest ratio of at-bats to plate appearances in his career, until his final season.†

Some thought that pitchers were throwing at and around Greenberg because he was Jewish. "There was a lot of anti-Semitism in baseball at the time," said Benno Levi, the German boy who had quickly assimilated by becoming a Greenberg fan and followed Hank's '38 campaign religiously.

When you're a minority in America, you filter any slight or rejection or denial through the possibility it originated in prejudice. Obviously, there often exist legitimate reasons for the slight, rejection or denial, but there's also

---

* "By comparison, he had no three-walk games in 1937, when he drove in 183 runs; one in 1935, when he won his first MVP award; and three in 1940, his second MVP year," Howard Megdal wrote in the *New York Times*.

† Greenberg did actually get some bonus at-bats in the season because the team played 155 games, the extra a makeup with the St. Louis Browns from a tie game called after nine innings. He went oh-for-four in the original game and oh-for-three in the makeup.

the possibility—a nagging suspicion—that bigotry may be the underlying cause. Blacks have certainly experienced that. Native Americans. Gays and lesbians. And perhaps no group more than Jews in the late Thirties. Amidst the climate of hate and fear, one couldn't help but wonder if what happened to Greenberg resulted from natural causes or originated in prejudice.

For the rest of his life, Hank dismissed the notion that anti-Semitism conspired against his pursuit as "pure baloney." Like he told Eisenstat, he did not believe in using the fact he was Jewish as an excuse. Yet he had to wonder. Pitchers walked Jimmie Foxx less in 1932 when he hit 58 home runs than they walked Greenberg in 1938, and Foxx's base on balls percentage did not rise significantly in September the way Hank's did.* On the other hand, pitchers walked Foxx the same number of times as Greenberg (119) in 1938, when Foxx was voted the Most Valuable Player, leading the league in average (.349) and RBI (175) in addition to slugging 50 home runs. The statistics could be argued either way.

Hank's teammates were divided in their opinions. "I don't think they wanted him to beat Ruth's record because of the fact that he was a Jew," Rogell said.

"I can't buy that," Eisenstat said. "There's no way just because he's Jewish. I think people would've liked to see him break the record."

They are probably both right. Some wanted to see Hank get the record and were even willing to help him—witness Dickey tipping him off on pitches. Others, like those who yelled venom at him from the dugouts, did not want to see him better Ruth and certainly did not want to be the pitcher on the mound who contributed to his success. In a late September game, one pitcher walked by Hank and told him, "You're not going to get any home runs off me, you Jew son of a bitch."

The Tigers had languished in the second division most of the season. There was no pennant fever to stimulate Detroit fans this season, but Hank's home run surge gave them something to root for. The city tingled with excitement the closer he got. Ty Tyson's voice seemed to grow stronger with each Greenberg at-bat while everyone hushed to hear what Hank would do.

---

* It went up to 17.1 percent in September from his season average of 16.6 percent.

Hank hit two more home runs in the second game of a doubleheader, one shortened to seven innings, on September 23. That put him at fifty-six with nine games to play. It also marked the tenth time that season he had hit two home runs in a game, an American League record.

He hit two more, again in the second game of a doubleheader shortened to seven innings. His first four-bagger, though, carried an asterisk. In the opening frame, Hank lined the first pitch over second base for what looked like a routine single, but the ball bounced past the center fielder. It rolled all the way to the wall, to the right of the flagpole, and Hank charged around the bases. When he came to third, the ball was not yet to the relay man, so he rounded the base and headed home. Baker, coaching third, would have had "to tackle me to keep me from trying for an inside-the-park homer," Hank wrote. The ball arrived about the same time Hank started his slide. The catcher, Sam Harshany, was certain he had him. Photos show the play was close and that the umpire's view was partially obscured. Hank admitted he was "out by a mile," but the ump, Ed Rommel,* perhaps caught up in the excitement of the moment, called Hank safe. Despite Harshany's and his manager's protests, the call stood. Up in the press box, one writer quipped, "Rommel, at least, deserves an assist." Hank had gotten a gift in No. 57.

His record for hitting two home runs in each of eleven games still stands.† He now had 58 home runs on the season with five games left to play: two in Detroit and three in Cleveland. Sam Greene in the *Detroit News* wrote, "It seems inevitable that Greenberg will crack the record before sundown Sunday." For the first time all season, Hank felt confident he would reach—and likely pass—sixty. When he crossed the plate after hitting his 58th home run, he suddenly thought, *I can do it.*

That night, though, he chatted in his hotel room with *Detroit Times* writer Bob Murphy about the near misses of the season. The way Hank saw it, he should have already reached sixty. "It would be great to have all the home runs you lose through breaks of the game or sensational catches," he said, decked out in his red pajamas. "I can think of four robberies of me this

---

* Not Hank's friend, Bill McGowan, as Greenberg wrote in his autobiography.
† The Chicago Cubs' Sammy Sosa tied Greenberg's record sixty years later in the Steroids Era.

season." There was a shot in Yankee Stadium that hit the left-center field fence 430 feet away. Another one in Cleveland when the Indians' center fielder seemed to run forever to snag a drive. Another day he hit two long balls at Shibe Park that a stiff wind pushed back. Any one of those could prove the difference between him and Ruth.

On Wednesday, September 28, Hank read the headline in the *Detroit Times*: "The World Talks War—Detroit Talks Greenberg and His Home Runs." He saw the photo of himself following through on his swing against the backdrop of soldiers, bombers and tanks. That morning, in the lobby of the Leland Hotel, a young woman approached him and held out a card with a silhouette of No. 5 drawn on it. He smiled and said, "So you are Marjorie!"

She had written him, asking if she could show him her scrapbook. He had written back immediately and invited her to visit. They went up to his room on the twelfth floor. They chatted about his fan mail. He showed her some photos of himself and autographed three for her. He also autographed a ball. He pointed out the bowl of fruit the hotel manager had sent up after Hank hit his two home runs the day before. He invited her and a friend to that afternoon's game against the St. Louis Browns. An hour passed. He walked her to the elevator. Marjorie wrote nine pages in her diary about their first meeting.

That afternoon, with Marjorie watching from a box seat among the players' wives, Hank failed to get a hit, let alone a home run. He hit one pitch solidly, a booming shot over the grandstand, but it hooked foul. The Browns' pitcher was a young left-hander who couldn't find the plate. "The harder he tried, the wilder he got," Hank said. He walked Hank twice. In the sixth inning, Hank walked on four pitches. He remained at the plate a moment, hoping the ump might change his mind. "It was one of the few times a batter would have welcomed a mistake by the umpire," the *Detroit News* reported. Another at-bat, with the count 3-0, Hank swung at what would have been ball four to keep from walking again. He eventually struck out. George McQuinn, the Browns' first baseman and one of the players who wanted to see Greenberg beat Ruth's record, dropped one of his foul balls to give Hank another chance. All Hank could do was nod to Marjorie when she waved her scorecard at him.

That evening, Hank had dinner with Maury Aronsson and his family at their home on Chicago Boulevard.* The talk—as it was at nearly every dinner table in Detroit that evening—centered around Hank's chances. He said if he didn't get one the next day, he didn't think he would be able to break the record. It was too hard to hit home runs in Cleveland, where the Tigers would play their final three games.

Hank faced Bobo Newsom, the Browns' ace, a pitcher with a tricky slider and excellent control whom Greenberg had trouble hitting. Newsom was going for his twentieth win of the season that afternoon. "There was blood in his eye and steel in his arm," Hank said. Newsom pitched Hank carefully, keeping the ball away from him so it was difficult to pull. Hank managed a single, nothing more. Newsom lost his bid to win twenty in a 6–2 loss.

The Tigers took the train to Cleveland for the final three games of the season. Hank's friends Harold Allen and Lou Blumberg made the trip with the team. Allen had called the William Morris Agency and arranged a five-week tour for Hank that would pay him $3,000 if he tied or bettered Ruth's mark. Hank liked the money but not the idea of hitting the banquet circuit. That took a lot out of him. He preferred to spend his off time on a Florida beach and in New York, playing handball, eating at fine restaurants and hitting the nightspots. "Maybe I'm making too much of a fuss of this thing," he told Harold.

Hank still needed two homers to catch Ruth. The Indians played their home games at League Park, except for Sundays and holidays. Hank figured since he was getting pitched outside, he might be able to knock a couple of opposite-field shots into the short (290-foot) right field porch. But Cleveland management wanted to capitalize on the interest in Greenberg's quest, so it rescheduled Friday afternoon's game at League Park to a Sunday doubleheader in the much larger Municipal Stadium. On Saturday, October 1, German troops marched into Sudetenland, and Hank faced Denny Galehouse, a control pitcher who seemed to thrive in pressure situations.† "He pitched the greatest game of his life," according to Hank. Galehouse shut out the Tigers on five hits. Hank was oh-for-four with one

---

* The family had moved since the evening three years earlier when Hank had met Max Lapides, the boy with the broken leg.
† Though he is probably best remembered for starting—and losing—the October 4, 1948, playoff game between the Red Sox and the Indians.

strikeout. In the ninth inning, Hank grounded out to second base. He was so frustrated that he kicked the bats off the rack in front of the Tiger dugout.

Hank was pressing, and he knew it. He had only one hit in his last eleven at-bats and remained two home runs shy of the mark. He had one afternoon and two games left to do it. Given his tendency to hit pairs of homers that year, he knew he could still make it. But he also felt the pressure peaking.

Before the first game, Harold Allen could see how anxious Hank was. "Just relax," Harold told him. "You're going to do it."

The doubleheader drew 27,000 fans to Municipal Stadium, with Greenberg the main attraction. The photographers and newsreel cameramen were all over the field, on hand to document the occasion. Before the game, they crowded Hank. "I hope you beat that record today," one of the cameramen prompted Hank. "I'm going to be trying, you can be sure," he said, looking into the camera. But it came off as a rehearsed line. He looked stiff, his eyes uncertain. There was no swagger in his words.

He faced young Bob Feller in the first game. Rapid Robert, with his unpredictable 100-plus mile per hour fastball, made Hank nervous. He had plunked Hank on the foot one time. Hank had also seen the right-handed Feller throw a ball *behind* the left-handed-batting Billy Rogell. The year before, in an April spring exhibition game, Feller had accidentally beaned Giants' center fielder Hank Leiber with a curve that didn't break and landed him in the hospital. Feller was the only pitcher who genuinely frightened Greenberg. "He had such speed and was so wild that everybody was afraid to go up to bat, including me," Hank said. "He had a very deceptive motion. You never knew where the ball was coming from or where it was going. Neither did he."

The nineteen-year-old Feller was on that afternoon, fanning the Tiger batters in succession with his lightning fastball and occasional curve. In the sixth inning, Hank uncorked a shot 450 feet that caromed off the fifteen-foot outfield wall for a double. He also walked once and struck out twice. By the top of the ninth, Feller had struck out sixteen. He tied the major league record by fanning the leadoff batter, Pete Fox. Left fielder Roy Cullenbine reached, which brought Hank to the plate. He was as determined not to let Feller break the strikeout record at his expense as Feller was not to let Hank get any closer to the home run record. Hank launched a long fly ball to center. Indian center fielder Roy Weatherly made a one-handed catch on the run to rob Hank of a hit, possibly a legitimate inside-the-park home run in that enormous park. No matter, Feller struck out Detroit center fielder Chet Laabs—for the fifth time that day—to set the record of most strikeouts in one game: eighteen.

Ironically, Feller didn't win the game. The Tigers touched him for four runs on seven hits and seven walks, and pitcher Harry Eisenstat became the answer to a trivia question, allowing only one run on four hits.

Hank still needed two home runs in the final game. He would have to hit them against Johnny Humphries, the Indians' rookie right-hander, and do it in a hurry because the autumn sun was sinking. "He was almost as fast as Feller," Hank said. "And he seemed even faster because the shadows were starting to crawl across the field." Hank hit one long ball in the final game, a 420-foot poke that in the cavernous Municipal Stadium was only good for a single. He hit two more singles and walked once before the darkness obscured the field. After seven innings, home plate umpire Cal Hubbard* said to him, "I'm sorry, Hank. But this is as far as I can go."

"That's all right," Hank said. "This is as far as I can go, too."

And that was it. The season was over.

Don Shapiro had listened to the games at home on the radio. The fourteen-year-old Tiger fanatic took it hard. "He failed that day," Shapiro said more than sixty years later, by then a distinguished oral surgeon. He, too, had kept a scrapbook with the daily clippings of Greenberg's progress. "And that day is as indelibly ingrained as the day Kennedy was shot. It seems almost an inappropriate comparison but nevertheless, these are two of the most important dates of my life." Having hoped so hard and come so close, he found the disappointment hard to swallow.

Hank, too, was disappointed, but on the train ride back to Detroit, he told Harold Allen and Lou Blumberg, "Fifty-eight. That's not a bad year." They toasted his season with champagne.

In fact, Hank had enjoyed an amazing year. He had raised his average to .315, right where he thought it belonged; knocked in 146 runs, second

---

* Not Greenberg's friend George Moriarty as Hank wrote in his autobiography.

only to Foxx in the majors; led the majors in runs scored (144); and had the highest OPS of his career: 1.122. In the field, he led the league in putouts and assists.

Hank had not bettered Ruth and he had not stopped Hitler, but he had single-handedly succeeded in changing the way Americans saw Jews. He had given his co-religionists a retort to every charge of weakness or timidity or ineptness. A single word that could stand up to any form of prejudice: Greenberg.

CHAPTER NINE

Shadow Boxing with Fly Balls

The morning of November 10, 1938, Americans awoke to the news of Europe's latest persecution that became known as *Kristallnacht*. In retaliation for a seventeen-year-old boy shooting a Nazi diplomat in Paris—"I did it because I loved my parents [who had been expelled from Germany along with some 12,000 other Polish Jews] and the Jewish people who have suffered so unjustly"—the Nazis and their followers attacked the Jews among them. Through the night of November 9, they broke shop windows (hence the "night of broken glass"), plundered and set fire to an estimated 7,500 Jewish businesses in Germany and Austria. They torched 267 synagogues. They beat the Jews. They carted thousands to concentration camps. They killed another ninety-one. In Vienna, they so terrorized the Jews that twenty-two took their own lives rather than endure the Nazi torture. No Jew in Europe seemed safe.

American Jews worried about their relatives overseas. They had nowhere to go. Poland had granted refuge to only a third of the Jews expelled from Germany. America was likewise unwilling to grant them safe harbor. Secretary of the Interior Harold Ickes had suggested that the United States shelter Jews in the Alaska territory, but the White House did not endorse the idea. President Roosevelt wanted to limit the number of settlers to 10,000, with no more than ten percent of them Jews. Most Americans were sympathetic to the idea of granting Jews refuge, but Father Coughlin led a demonstration in New York where his supporters shouted, "Send Jews back where they came from in leaky boats."

Otherwise, life in the United States went on with a chilling normalcy. Hank took up hunting that winter and shot his first quail on an expedition in Virginia. January found him working on his tan in Florida. Despite speculation Hank would hold out again, he met with Walter Briggs at his Miami Beach home on February 9 and signed his contract for the upcoming season without much hassle, both sides agreeing his 58 homers warranted a $5,000 raise that made him the highest-paid player in Tiger history. When Hank told Briggs he wanted $35,000, Briggs whistled. "You know, that's a helluva lot of money," Briggs told Hank. "When I was your age, I was making only twenty-two dollars a week."

"And that is probably what I'll be making when I'm yours," Hank said. "That's why I need to get the money now."

Question was, when he joined the Tigers for spring training in Lakeland, how could he follow up his past two spectacular seasons, his 183 RBI in 1937 and 58 homers in 1938? He wondered if maybe he had succeeded too quickly, after only five full seasons, and worried that he had already peaked. He viewed 1938 as a fluke season and did not think he would ever surpass Ruth's single-season home run record. "I'll probably never break it," he told a reporter. "I was fortunate to get within two of it. The way I figure it, I'm a regular forty-homer hitter. Nine more came my way because I was especially hot during streaks. The other nine because I knew I could stand up and sock away without hurting the team's chances."

Hank decided in 1939 that he would swing at more pitches, focus on getting on base rather than extra-base hits. But that experiment failed. In spring training exhibitions, he had trouble getting hits of any sort. On the way north to Detroit, he confided in Harry Salsinger, "You know, I'm probably wrong about going after base hits only." He decided to go back to what he knew best, swinging hard.

Hank socked his first home run in only the second game of the season, a fourteenth-inning walk-off shot high into the Briggs Stadium upper-deck pavilion. But it quickly became clear that 1939 would not be a repeat of his previous two seasons. At the end of April, he was batting a phenomenal .429 with 10 RBI but only three home runs.

The Tigers had finished fourth in 1938, though they had gone 37–19 under Del Baker the final two months of the season, an impressive .660

winning clip. That seemed to portend good results for the 1939 campaign, but the Tigers were a mere shadow of the championship team of four years previous. Only six members of the '35 World Series winners remained: Schoolboy Rowe, Tommy Bridges, Charlie Gehringer, Billy Rogell, Pete Fox and Greenberg. By the end of April, on the eve of a home series with the first-place Yankees, the Tigers were only 6–5 and had dropped to fourth place, albeit only a half game behind New York.

The morning of May 2, seventeen-year-old Fred Rice boarded the Trumbull streetcar the way he did every Tiger game day, paid his six cents fare and got off at Briggs Stadium. He joined the group of twenty-five to thirty kids on Michigan Avenue standing outside the big steel door. About 11:00 a.m., the door rolled up and the head usher Chic, a friendly potbellied fellow, looked over the group and picked a dozen boys to assist the uniformed ushers. The boys ran ahead of the paid ushers to wipe off the wooden seats with a rag for penny tips from ticket holders. Fred had been doing that the past seven years. His father was an out-of-work cabinetmaker who ended up selling neckties door to door for a quarter apiece. Fred gave all of the tips he made ushering and the money he made selling newspapers to his mother. Spotting the familiar face among the boys assembled on Michigan Avenue, Chic smiled at him and said, "Come on, Freddy."

Over the years, Fred had gotten to know the ballplayers. He often stood in the hallway and watched them walk by to the clubhouse. Greenberg, Gehringer and the others, even the visiting players, said hello. When Fred was smaller, Lou Gehrig would pat him on the head. "Hi, kid. How you doing?"

That day, May 2, Fred was stationed behind the visitors' dugout on the first-base side. He watched the Yankees take infield practice and thought something didn't look right with Gehrig at first. Lou scooped a ground ball and threw it to Bill Dickey, but his throw bounced weakly in front of the catcher. Gehrig walked off the field and passed in front of Fred. The boy waved and said, "Hi, Lou." Gehrig looked up, smiled his sad smile at Fred and ducked into the dugout.

Fred did not realize it immediately, but that was the last time Lou Gehrig appeared on the field as a ballplayer.

When the starting lineups were announced, for the first time in 2,130 games, Gehrig's name wasn't included. A murmur passed through the crowd. The streak was over. Two years and a month later, the Iron Horse was dead.

The Tigers lost that game 22–2. (That's not a typo.) They lost seven in a row and dropped like a brick to last place. During that stretch, Hank went eight-for-thirty-eight, a .210 pace, the first of many slumps that season. Bengal fans, unhappy with their team, booed the boys, especially Greenberg. Jack Zeller, who had taken over as general manager when Briggs fired Cochrane, was desperate to make a move to resuscitate the team.

Zeller was a jack of all trades. He had been a semipro pitcher, manager, minor league club owner, lieutenant in the Great War, government auditor, oil man, baseball scout and minor league chain director. He was a large man, tall and pudgy, with a thorough understanding of baseball's inner workings. He was a shrewd operator who maneuvered things to his advantage.

At Sportsman's Park when Detroit played St. Louis, Zeller spent two days negotiating a trade for the Browns' ace, Bobo Newsom. Zeller completed the ten-player deal, which sent six Tigers—including pitcher Vern Kennedy—to the Browns for Newsom and three backups. That day, May 13, Newsom, in his last game with St. Louis, beat Kennedy 5–3.

Bobo, also known as Buck, who had finally gotten his twentieth win in his final start the previous season, was a character. He once had two strikes on Greenberg when he ran off the mound and into the dugout, plunged his hands into a pail of water, rinsed his face and toweled off. Greenberg waited at the plate, mystified. Newsom ran back, took the sign from the catcher and fired strike three. Zeller hoped Newsom could bolster Detroit's sagging pitching corps.

Nearly a month later at home, on Sunday, June 11, Newsom beat the Senators—his fourth win for the Bengals against two defeats—but Detroit had still lost more games than it had won. Hank was batting .321 with 15 home runs and 48 RBI but he had been hearing more boos at Briggs Stadium. After his past two spectacular seasons—three counting his MVP year in 1935—the fans had come to expect more of him. Even he had revised his opinion of his hitting, calling himself a .340 hitter, but the *Detroit News* declared: "his self-estimate appears much too low" and predicted he would one day hit better than .400 "if he forgets home runs" and concentrated on base hits.

The boo birds jumped on him when he missed or—worse to their minds—let pitches go by for called third strikes. "We have never known another player who had as many strikes called on him as Greenberg, and the explanation is that Greenberg is a guess hitter," Salsinger wrote, flogging the old complaint. "He has tried to discard the guessing habit and swing at any hittable pitch, but he hasn't succeeded. On the day that Greenberg can break himself of the guessing habit, his average will soar, his strikeout total will shrink and he'll beat the world driving in runs."

After the June game, Hank and Charlie Gehringer boarded a train for Cooperstown, New York, for the official dedication of the National Baseball Hall of Fame, which had picked its inaugural class of Ty Cobb, Walter Johnson, Christy Mathewson, Babe Ruth and Honus Wagner three years earlier. Historians then believed that a West Point military student named Abner Doubleday had invented baseball on Cooperstown fields one June day in 1839,* and Major League Baseball was celebrating its one hundredth anniversary. Players wore centennial patches on their left shoulders all season, and Cooperstown hosted an exhibition of current and retired legends on June 12.

A large crowd turned out to see the stars arrive at the small town's train station, which hadn't been used for so long they had to trim the knee-high weeds on the railroad tracks leading to it. Hank turned down an offer for a car ride to the hotel and walked, followed by a group of awed children. An estimated ten thousand fans showed up that afternoon at Doubleday Field. Hank singled and scored a run in a sixth-inning rally, but his team, which included Dizzy Dean, Johnny Vander Meer, Eddie Collins and Mel Ott, lost to Honus Wagner's squad of Gehringer, Arky Vaughan, Ducky Medwick, Lefty Grove and Babe Ruth. The outcome was not as significant as the experience of being included in the festivities with legends like Ruth and Wagner, as well as others on hand: Tris Speaker, George Sisler, Connie

---

* For a more accurate accounting of the game's origins, see MLB official historian John Thorn's *Baseball in the Garden of Eden: The Secret History of the Early Game.*

Mack, Cy Young, Grover Cleveland Alexander and Walter Johnson. Hank was awed by their presence. What a thrill it would be, he dared let himself think, to one day be enshrined forever with them in the Hall of Fame.

To honor baseball's centennial, the United States Post Office issued commemorative stamps and envelopes in Cooperstown. Hank sent Marjorie Nash a card in one of the envelopes marked "first day of issue." She wrote in her diary, "Wasn't that nice of him? Golly. He's always doing something nice for me." She continued to send him her special envelopes with the stick figure drawings inside after each home run he hit. She stopped by his hotel occasionally to say hello. He invited her and her friend, if she was with one, to have a meal with him. He also gave her tickets to games. The previous Christmas, he sent her three "exquisite bottles of French perfume" and a lapel watch inscribed "To Marge from Hank." Marjorie casually dated other men, and Hank saw other women—rumors swirled about his involvement with various starlets and socialites—but it seemed clear he had a special fan in Miss Nash, the art student.

The Chicago White Sox, led by manager Jimmy Dykes, were notorious for their bench jockeying. Dykes was an early edition Archie Bunker, in appearance and attitude. "Hey, Hank," Dykes used to shout at Greenberg. "How are you playing with three Catholics and one Hebe?" During a doubleheader at Briggs Stadium on July 1, Dykes lit into Greenberg with criticism about him skipping last year's All-Star Game. Someone—maybe Dykes—shouted at Hank when he was running down the first base line, "You big, yellow Jew bastard!"

The Chicago bench continued to harass Greenberg throughout the afternoon while he was in the field. When Joe Kuhel, a skinny guy with jug ears, reached first base in the sixth inning of the second game, Hank heard the White Sox bench yell for Kuhel to spike Greenberg. Kuhel took a large lead, certain to draw a throw. When it came, he slid hard into Hank and spiked him in the foot. Hank punched Kuhel in the face. The players spilled out of both dugouts, but umpire Ed Rommel squeezed between Greenberg and Kuhel before either could throw any more punches. He ejected Hank and shepherded the players back to their positions and dugouts.

The Detroit crowd took up the attack. "Spectators started throwing anything throwable at the Chicago players," the *Detroit News* reported. The players shouted at them. One fan tried to jump the White Sox, but an usher wrestled him back on top of the dugout. Uniformed policemen scurried to the area to restore order. They ejected several spectators. Just when things had calmed down and play resumed, Kuhel scored and the fans renewed their attack. One chucked a bottle at Kuhel. "The policemen again invaded the warring section and once more restored order," according to the *Detroit News*, which deemed the incident a "minor riot."

Still upset afterward, Hank stripped off his jersey, stuffed it in his locker, swapped his spikes for his shower slippers and left without a word. He crossed the hallway to the White Sox clubhouse, walked in and announced, "I want the guy who called me a 'yellow Jew bastard' to get to his feet and say it to my face."

No one moved. Hank walked slowly around the room and looked at each of them. Kuhel. Dykes. The others. Not one of them dared stand up. Hank walked out, paused at the door to look back, then left.

"The guy with the big mouth was the luckiest guy in the world, because Greenberg would have killed him," Elden Auker said later.

Before the next day's game, Hank received a telegram from American League president William Harridge fining him fifty dollars for striking Kuhel. Dykes said he thought Greenberg should have been suspended. Harridge also upbraided the White Sox for "unsportsmanlike conduct and use of insulting and abusive language to members of the opposing team." He warned Dykes that he would have any of his players who repeated such insults ejected and suspended. In a sarcastic gesture, Dykes sent all of his reserves out to the bullpen and said, "I guess that Greenberg won't be able to hear what they say out there, and no one will get run out for saying something uncomplimentary about him taking all those called strikes."

Hank hadn't said anything to his teammates about crossing the hall, but word of him challenging the White Sox in their clubhouse spread around the league. Other players took note. They respected Hank for standing up for himself. Years later, players like the Yankees' Tommy Henrich and the Red Sox's Ted Williams repeated the story in admiration of Greenberg. "You know who stood up?" Williams liked to say as the punch line. "Nobody."

Yankee Stadium hosted the 1939 All-Star Game on July 11. The Yankees had won their third consecutive World Series the previous October, so Joe McCarthy again named the starters from the squad picked by the American League's eight managers. They had selected Hank for the team, based more on the previous year's performance than his hitting in the first half of 1939. He had slugged 16 home runs compared to 26 by the same date in 1938, though he had punched 27 doubles, three times as many as he had at the same point the previous summer. He also had knocked in ten more runs (61). He entered the All-Star Game in another slump, hitless in his previous three games. His average had slipped to .286. McCarthy named six of his players as starters and added Gehrig to the team in a sympathetic gesture—the ailing first baseman was in no condition to play. McCarthy started Greenberg at first base. Hank played the entire game, went one-for-three and scored a run in the AL's 3–1 victory.

Greenberg also made history in the seventh Midsummer Classic. Along with Giants' catcher Harry Danning and Phillies' outfielder Morrie Arnovich, he was one of three Jews on the two squads, the most ever to appear at the All-Star Game to that point.

A boy with cerebral palsy sold pencils outside the Leland Hotel where Hank lived. His face twisted, he spoke almost unintelligibly. Many people, feeling uncomfortable in his presence, passed by him hurriedly. Not Hank. He stopped to talk. He invited him inside for dinner. "Hank was always doing things for the kid," his friend Lou Blumberg said. "It was as if he saw something in him, something that might have been if he hadn't had such a bad break in life."

Another time, at Briggs Stadium, a group of children from the United Hebrew schools attended a game. When Hank took his spot in the field, one of the boys yelled to him in Yiddish as a joke that he was hungry. Hank turned around, called to a peanut vendor to give the boy a box of peanuts and charge it to him.

One of the clubhouse boys traveling east with the Tigers told Hank his dream had been to visit New York. When they arrived, Hank first bought him a new suit, hat and shoes, then took him on a tour that included the

Empire State Building, the Chrysler Building, the Statue of Liberty and a sightseeing cruise around Manhattan Island. Another Tiger employee had asked Hank's advice about getting a deal on a wristwatch his daughter wanted for a graduation present that the man couldn't afford. He thought maybe one of Hank's jeweler friends could sell him one at cost. Hank bought the desired watch at a Fifth Avenue shop, delivered it to the man and told him, "I got it from a pal of mine in the jewelry business, and he refused to let me pay."

Around the league, batboys and visiting clubhouse attendants respected Greenberg as one of baseball's biggest tippers. At Briggs Stadium, Hank knew the ticket takers by name and would ask them how their families were doing. If he heard one of their children was sick, he did what he could to help. He also looked after the ground crew who did so much for him, throwing a party for them at the end of the season.

On the field, though, he played with the intensity of Ty Cobb. In addition to sliding hard into bases, Hank had developed an arsenal of tricks to intimidate the opposing pitcher. While other players swung an extra bat on deck, Hank swung three. He cut a menacing figure hefting three bats. That reminded pitchers of the damage his strength could do. In the batter's box, he took his time getting set, holding up his hand while he dug a hole with his right foot. It was part of his battle with the pitcher, letting him know he was there and intended to be in control. That was before batters stepped out of the box after every pitch to adjust their batting gloves, and his practice annoyed his opponents. "Every pitcher hated it, but Feller was one of the few who would do anything about it," Indians shortstop Lou Boudreau said. "When Greenberg finally would be ready to hit, Feller would throw his fastball up and in, and Greenberg would go down. Once, I remember, he knocked Greenberg down twice in a row, and I'm sure that both of those pitches were not accidental."

But Hank continued to take his time. When he was set, he glared the pitcher in the eyes. They often couldn't hold his gaze and glanced at the grass or scuffed the mound with their spikes or turned away. He knew then he owned the pitcher.

On Wednesday, August 2, in New York, Hank dug in against Spud Chandler, the Yankee pitcher, with Earl Averill on first and one out in the top of the ninth inning. Hank threw his entire frame into his swing. His Louisville Slugger resonated with a sharp crack, and the ball sailed high and deep toward the farthest reaches of Yankee Stadium. Joe DiMaggio, New York's twenty-four-year-old center fielder, was playing almost halfway between the infield and the fence, shaded to right field, since Chandler was pitching Greenberg away. Soon as Hank swung, DiMaggio turned and sprinted toward the wall.

Hank knew he had gotten all of the pitch and figured the ball would hit the wall if it didn't clear it. He raced around first intent on a triple, maybe even an inside-the-park home run. He saw DiMaggio giving chase but did not expect him to catch up to the ball. No one in the stadium did. "It looked as if he was giving the old college try and intended merely to get as close as he could to the ball to take it off the fence on the rebound," Greenberg said later.

DiMaggio kept sprinting back into the monuments—the ball sailed to the right of Miller Huggins's statue, headed for the 461 feet sign. Three times he took his eye off the ball to see how close he was to the wall. Hank was almost to second base—that's how much hang time his shot had—when DiMaggio, after sprinting one hundred feet and with his back to the plate, spied a flash of white—the ball's reflection—on the inside of his sunglasses and thrust his glove over his right shoulder blindly to spear the ball five feet from the fence.

The catch stunned the crowd. After a split-second of disbelief, when it sunk in what an amazing feat they had just observed, the Yankee fans threw up a terrific cheer. The Detroit players rose off the bench, bowed and doffed their caps in homage. Home plate umpire Bill McGowan called DiMaggio's grab "the most remarkable and almost miraculous catch I ever saw." Hank was shocked to see the ball disappear into the Yankee Clipper's glove. It was the greatest catch he had ever witnessed. He stopped on second, put his hands on his hips and muttered, "Just what does a fellow have to do to get a hit in this league?"

The writers in the press box stumbled over themselves to describe the play. The *World-Telegram's* beat writer declared it "undoubtedly the greatest catch in the history of Yankee Stadium." Jack Smith of the *New York Daily News* called it "one of the gol' darndest catches seen in the 100-year history of baseball." Others who later saw Willie Mays's catch of Vic Wertz's drive in the 1954 World Series considered DiMaggio's catch better. DiMaggio said years later it was the best he ever made in his career.

It was fitting that the play forever linked these two players. As the premier ballplayers of their respective ethnic backgrounds in a decade when the press amplified ancestral connections and second-generation immigrants ached to assimilate, they both stood as ethnic standard bearers. DiMaggio was as important to the Italian-Americans and as large a source of pride to them as Greenberg was to Jewish-Americans. "DiMaggio gave Italian-Americans a hero to blunt stereotypes concerning Italian buffoons, gangsters, and fascists," historian William Simons writes in his essay "Comparative Ethnicity: Joe DiMaggio and Hank Greenberg." He made fans of those who cared nothing about baseball but were eager to cheer one of their own, and, like Greenberg, DiMaggio achieved a universal hero status that transcended his ethnic community.

The current world crisis, with Hitler on the march and Mussolini exporting fascism, placed additional pressure on Greenberg and DiMaggio to succeed and lift their respective communities' hopes above their fears and anxieties. Both Greenberg and DiMaggio rose to the occasion.

Hank reached a low point in his career on August 13. Stuck in another slump, the day before, he had gone one-for-five. He had only six hits in the last ten games, a feeble .158 pace. He was exhausted physically and mentally. The daily chorus of boos disturbed him. He had hit 20 home runs, excellent for an ordinary player but below what was expected of him. Del Baker benched his first baseman. That was the first time in his career since his rookie year that Greenberg had not started a game because of his poor showing. Hank was so discouraged he wanted to pack up his Zephyr coupe and head home.

He had to watch Rudy York play his position. York had lived up to his promise with his powerful bat. He had slugged those record-setting 18 home runs during August 1937. He had been selected to the All-Star team in 1938. That year he had pounded 33 home runs and knocked in 127 runs. Baker had occasionally inserted him in the cleanup spot, ahead of Hank. Sportswriter John Lardner claimed York had a better swing than DiMaggio and pulled the ball better than Foxx. "In the opinion of many experts,"

Lardner observed, York "can outhit even Greenberg." He was batting .332 in 1939, thirty points better than Hank.

Part Cherokee, York had grown up dirt poor in rural Georgia. He had quit school in the third grade to work in the town mill. He liked to smoke in bed, often after drinking too much, and more than once his cigarette started a hotel fire after he fell asleep. The joke was that he led the league in home runs and burned mattresses.

But York's biggest liability was his fielding. The Tigers had tried him at third base, in the outfield and behind the plate. At each spot, he failed in innovative ways. Outfield flies proved particularly troublesome. "The only way Rudy could avoid being conked on the skull was to outguess the ball—and the ball often anticipated his next move," Lardner wrote.

The only place York seemed to escape hurting himself or the team was at first base. York didn't have the defensive skills to oust Greenberg from that spot, but he could end up doing so by default since there was nowhere else to hide him. Baker called upon Hank only twice during that week to pinch-hit. He fidgeted restlessly on the pine, watching York play errorless ball at first and continue to hit with authority, including three doubles and a homer in the week.

Baker gave Hank another chance at first, shifting York to catcher for the Saturday, August 19 game. In the third inning, Hank struck out with the bases loaded. The table was set for him again the next inning, and this time he delivered a grand slam. He homered and tripled the next day, but was back on the bench for the next two games. While taking batting practice on an off day, he had wrenched a muscle in his lower back. It hurt to swing. He returned to the lineup later in the week, on August 26, but further aggravated the muscle hitting a fly to right field in the second inning and had to come out of the game. He saw a doctor who took X-rays and administered deep muscle heat treatment. Unsympathetic fans complained that he was quitting on the team, thinking only of himself and unwilling to play through the routine aches and pains a ballplayer suffers over a long season.

Hank was only twenty-eight years old, but his body was starting to show the strain from a decade of professional baseball. In addition to his back, his flat feet troubled him. After games, he had Tiger trainer Denny

Carroll massage them. He had special baseball shoes fitted to ease the pressure. He wore arch supports in his dress shoes. Doubleheaders were killers. He needed a special massage to be able to play the second game. But his feet still hurt him on the field. He sat out another nine games into early September.

On Friday, September 1, Americans heard the news that German troops had invaded Poland. Two days later, France, England, New Zealand and Australia declared war on Germany. Two days after that, the United States announced it would remain neutral in the conflict. Greenberg returned to the Tigers' lineup on September 4 and homered in three consecutive games.

He played on Rosh Hashanah in New York and went hitless in a win over the Yankees. He was back playing every day but sat out on Yom Kippur, when Bobo Newsom beat the Indians. Newsom won twenty games again in 1939—seventeen of them for the Tigers—but he could not save the team. Nor could Hank with 11 home runs in September. They finished 81–73, fifth place, twenty-six and a half games behind the Yankees.

Hank had hit a third of his 33 home runs in September. He finished the season with a .312 batting average, well below where he had expected to be at the start of the year. He hit a respectable 42 doubles and seven triples. He scored 112 runs. He knocked in the same, 112, which would satisfy most players but not Greenberg. That was his lowest total for a complete season until his final year. He led the league in strikeouts (95), fanning once nearly every five at-bats. He also missed seventeen games, mostly due to physical ailments. The league president had fined him after Kuhel had spiked him. And the fans seemed to have turned on him. In many respects, it was his most disappointing season to date.

After the season ended, Hank had dinner with Birdie Tebbetts at the London Chop House before he returned home to the Bronx. Tebbetts had established himself that year as Mickey Cochrane's replacement, pushing Rudy York out of his preferred position. Hank gave Birdie some advice at dinner: "Right before Christmas, they're going to mail you a contract for next season. Don't sign it. Don't mail it back. Put it in your pocket and take the next train to Detroit and negotiate with those guys face-to-face. They'll call you a bum and tell you you're no good, and they'll say your batting average is down, and they'll threaten to bring up some kid from Toledo. But you know better than they do what you've done for the team. You're one of the best, Birdie. Make them come around." That gave the young Tebbetts the boost of confidence he needed to stand up for himself.

Rudy York remained an enigma for the Tigers. They wanted his bat in the lineup, but he had played himself out of contention for a spot in the outfield and at third base. He had insisted before the '39 season that management let him catch, but Tebbetts had outdone him at that spot. The only option seemed first base, where his unpredictable fielding was least likely to hurt the team. That made Greenberg trade bait.

Dealing Greenberg could help the Tigers shore up their infield, where age was catching up with Gehringer at second and Rogell at short. A trade could also bolster the pitching staff. An eighteen-year-old kid from Detroit's Wilbur Wright Prep School, Hal Newhouser, had looked promising when called up in September, and Tommy Bridges had gone 17–7, but otherwise, Schoolboy Rowe's sore arm looked finished, having lost twelve games and only won ten in his comeback attempt. Jack Zeller had traded Elden Auker to Boston and Harry Eisenstat to Cleveland. Suddenly, Greenberg's value to the team seemed greatest in what he could fetch.

Less than a month after the season ended, Zeller admitted publicly that Hank was "trading material." Clark Griffith, the Washington Senators' owner and president who had wanted to sign Hank back in 1929, offered shortstop Cecil Travis for Greenberg. That would have solved Detroit's problem at short, but Zeller wanted more for Hank. He turned down Griffith. With the winter meetings in Cincinnati during December approaching, rumors had Greenberg going to the Yankees to fill the void left by Gehrig's early retirement. "A Greenberg-to-the-Yankees deal would be the biggest trade since Joe Cronin cost the Boston Red Sox $250,000 in players and cash," *Look* magazine observed. "Greenberg, a former Bronx boy, would attract a large Jewish following to the New York turnstiles and help the Yanks at bat."

Rumors of Hank being traded to the Yankees had surfaced before, but this time they seemed more likely to become reality. Hank did not like the thought of the Tigers turning him out—that's what a trade would seem like—but at the same time, he was no longer happy in Detroit. He didn't understand the way the fans rode him. That hurt. "No human being can take that sort of thing daily—and overcome it," he told the *New York World-Telegram*'s Dan Daniel that winter. "Maybe I am too sensitive. But that's the way I am constituted, and that's the way baseball and the fans in Detroit will have to take me. They can't say that I am not giving 100 percent of Greenberg to the Tigers on and off the field."

Zeller returned from Cincinnati with Greenberg still on his roster. Ed Barrow, the Yankees' president, thought his team had done well enough, winning 106 games and its fourth consecutive World Series, without Gehrig or Greenberg. And the *Detroit News* responded to Hank's comments with an editorial entitled "Sensitive Hank" asking fans to ease up on the Detroit star since he couldn't take it. The fans weren't sympathetic. Harry Salsinger reprinted the comments of one Ray S. Findlay in his column: "If Mr. Greenberg is suffering as he claims from a skin too thin for the criticism of fans, he certainly selected the wrong cure by breaking down and having a good crying spell in the public prints." Ty Cobb didn't let the boos thwart his great career, Findlay wrote. Greenberg should be grateful for his generous salary and other benefits: "A prepaid trip around the country and paid endorsements should also go a long way toward easing the pains of a sensitive soul."

There was an unspoken subtext to all this. The *Detroit Jewish Chronicle* speculated that anti-Semitism underscored some of the boos Hank heard. This no doubt contributed to Hank's malaise in Detroit. Cobb did not have to contend with that.

On January 14, Commissioner Judge Landis accused Jack Zeller of violating baseball's rules with "cover-ups," "fake" contract transfers and "gentlemen's agreements" in shuffling players among a dozen minor league clubs. The commissioner turned ninety-one players free from the Tigers and ordered the club to pay fifteen others a total of $47,250 in grievance pay. That cleaned out much of the organization's up-and-coming talent. The most immediate loss was Benny McCoy, seen as Gehringer's replacement at second base, and switch-hitting outfielder Roy Cullenbine, who had been a Tiger batboy in 1930. The Tigers also lost the steady .300-hitting outfielder Wally Moses, whom Zeller had obtained for McCoy and a reserve pitcher in a December trade that Landis nixed.

The blame fell squarely upon Zeller. He accepted responsibility for his shady dealings. "The handling of all minor league affiliations was my job, and Mr. Briggs did not attempt to familiarize himself in any way with those operations," he said.

The Tigers' organization would suffer the consequences for years.

The following week, Zeller phoned Greenberg in New York and asked him to come to Detroit. Hank figured Zeller wanted to discuss his 1940 contract. Even though he had been second in the league in home runs, fourth in RBI and batted a respectable .312, he knew those numbers were down from his two previous seasons, and he expected the team to ask him to take a pay cut. Hank had a good relationship with Zeller, who had been general manager of the Exporters during Hank's days in Beaumont, but he arrived at the Detroit Ball Club's offices on Thursday, January 25, "determined to put up a battle to retain my 1939 salary."

Zeller surprised him. "We want you to play the outfield."

"Why me?" Hank asked. "Why can't York play the outfield?"

He knew the answer to that question, and he knew that it would help the team to have both his and York's bats in the lineup. He also figured it would further help the team for Tebbetts not to have York breathing down his neck at catcher. But Hank had worked hard to mold himself into a fine defensive first baseman. It should be up to York to take the job away from him, not simply have management shift him to the outfield like a piece of furniture. He didn't think he could be a major league outfielder. He remembered how painfully he had failed that day with the Red Bank Towners when the ball bounced off his head. It would be a huge gamble with his career. He had everything to lose in the move. At best, he would embarrass himself; at worst, he would lose his starting position. They argued. Finally, Hank flatly refused.

"All right," Zeller said. "Then you'll have to take a $10,000 cut in salary."

"You're kidding," said Hank, incredulous.

"No," Zeller said. "The only way you can get that money back is to play the outfield."

"Hey, what's going on here?" Hank shouted. "I haven't been cut any $10,000. I'll go see Mr. Briggs."

"Mr. Briggs won't see you. I'm handling the case, and you have your choice of playing the outfield at your 1939 salary or taking a $10,000 cut."

Hank didn't like those terms, but Zeller encouraged him to take a day to think it over. Hank consulted his friends. In talking to them, he saw that maybe the move could extend his career with less bending and wear on his knees. He also realized what a tough spot he was in.

The next day, he went back to Zeller and proposed that he do his best to make himself into an outfielder and that the club not cut his salary. He wanted a $5,000 bonus for giving the outfield a try. If he succeeded and started in the outfield on Opening Day, the club would pay him an additional $10,000. He discussed the idea with Mr. Briggs over the phone as well, and the club agreed. Hank signed his contract that day and told the press, "I have been called an individualist, but manager Del Baker feels the club would be strengthened if I played one of the outfield positions, so I am going to show everyone I am a team player."

Hank still thought the club might trade him, especially if he could not cut it in the outfield. He wasn't sure he could. He confided in young teammate Hal Newhouser, "I can't run. How can I play left field?" And he fretted with the *Washington Post*'s Shirley Povich, "I don't know what they're trying to do to me." But it was not in his character to let himself fail. He reported to spring training a week early to start learning his new position in left field. He spent hours shagging flies, snaring line drives, fielding grounders and taking rebounds off the fence. Trading his large first baseman's mitt with its generous pocket for a flimsy finger glove proved the most difficult transition—he wanted to catch the ball on the fingertips the way he had at first but that didn't work. John Lardner described him "shadow-boxing with fly balls."

Baseball insiders ridiculed the experiment. They figured Greenberg would be back at first base by July 4. They also said the distraction of learning a new position would mess with his hitting. Jimmie Foxx had attempted a similar switch in 1936 but was back at first base the next season. "You can't make the change overnight, and I will be surprised if Greenberg is a complete success," Foxx said. "Anybody can catch a fly ball, of course, but the difficult thing about the job, the secret of it, is in breaking for the ball. By that I mean starting in the right direction the moment the ball is hit. This is a talent or an instinct that takes a long time to develop, and without it you can't hope to be an outfielder. I was confused all the time I was out there, and it was a relief to get back to first base."

Hank's teammates didn't think he would last in left field more than a month. Moving under fly balls, Hank looked nervous and uncertain, almost terrified, like the kid exiled to right field suddenly mortified to see a ball hit his way. "Everybody thought he'd get killed out there," Gehringer said.

Meanwhile, York worked out at first with Hank's mitt. The big kid from Alabama had won the MVP award in the minors with Milwaukee at first base four years earlier. Hank feared that York had stolen his job.

Hank pressed coach Bing Miller to hit him hours of fungoes until Miller's hands were too blistered to raise the bat. Then he had someone else hit him fungoes. Hank had a strong arm, but he had to teach himself to throw overhand, not sidearm like he had done at first. He traveled to other teams' camps to ask veteran fielders how to play the outfield. He asked Joe DiMaggio about fielding base hits. "You can't come in too fast," DiMaggio told him. "You have to try to float in." He also suggested going down on one knee to field ground balls so the ball didn't skip past. By Opening Day, Hank had earned his $10,000 bonus: He started in left field on April 16.

On a cool and overcast day at Briggs Stadium, he went oh-for-four at the plate in a 5–1 loss to the St. Louis Browns, but he had four putouts and an assist. Shortly after, in Cleveland, a fly ball hovered down the left field line. The shortstop and third basemen gave chase. Hank stood and watched. The sun was in his eyes, and he didn't think he had a chance on it. The ball dropped. After the play, Del Baker sent Pete Fox out to replace Hank. Incensed, Hank walked straight into the clubhouse, changed and went back to the hotel, where he phoned Jack Zeller. "Listen, Jack, I don't want to ever be embarrassed again," Hank fumed. "It was a difficult ball for anybody. There was no reason to embarrass me by taking me out of the ball game. If that's going to be the pattern, the hell with it. I'm not going to play the outfield for you. You tell Del Baker he better not pull that trick again."

That phone call was the sort of thing that prompted others to call him "High Henry," but Hank made his point. Baker did not pull his trick again.

When the team returned to Detroit, Hank asked the Tigers' center fielder Barney McCosky for help. McCosky was barely twenty-three years old and had just finished his rookie season, but he was speedy and had played well. He agreed to come out to the park in the mornings to work with Hank. McCosky threw balls against the left field fence, then yelled, "Second base!" or "Third base!" and Hank turned and threw to those bases. They did that for nearly a week until Hank felt confident with his positioning.

But he seemed to be putting all of his attention into his fielding and neglecting his hitting. In the first eight games, Greenberg had not made an error but he had managed only four hits in 32 at-bats, a pathetic .125 start. That frustrated him, of course, but not so much that he forgot to show his gratitude. He called up McCosky on an off day, "Meet me at the Michigan Theater at noon," he said. Hank took the young center fielder to his tailor and told him to make Barney a suit. It was McCosky's first tailor-made suit and easily worth twice what he had ever paid for one. "That's the kind of guy he was," McCosky said.

When the Tigers headed east on a road trip, Hank studied the left field walls and angles of the parks in Washington, Philadelphia, New York and Boston. Balls hit down the line or against the fence bounced differently in each of them. He took extra practice to acquaint himself with each park's idiosyncrasies. Fenway Park, with its tall left field wall, presented a particular challenge. A ball shot back off the lower wooden part but dropped straight down from the upper tin part.

Hank also had to adjust to the new perspective from the opposite side of the field. The ball jumped off the bat differently from that side than it did from his vantage at first. Longer flies hooked or sliced differently. It was like trying to cut his hair in a mirror. Feeling out of place pricked his old fear of humiliating himself. "Hank was tortured by thoughts of the going-over the anvil chorus would give him when he muffed his first fly ball," Stanley Frank noted in a *Saturday Evening Post* profile.

Greenberg committed three errors in the first two weeks and made easy plays look difficult. "When he went for a fly ball, you prayed," said Fred Rice, the Briggs Stadium usher.

At Yankee Stadium, where the afternoon sun glared directly into the left fielder's eyes, Hank initially came in on a routine fly ball, then had to quickly reverse course. He speared the ball while backpedaling but lost his footing and tumbled awkwardly to the grass. After that play, he borrowed Yankee left fielder George Selkirk's sunglasses but "fiddled with them as if they were a new toy" before each inning. Wearing sunglasses became nearly as big an adjustment as his Wilson fielder's glove.

He lacked speed in the outfield. On any ball hit to left-center, he yelled, "Come on, Barney!"

"I'd come over and get it, and he'd look at me and give me the high sign: *all right!*" McCosky said.

Hank's lower back had been sore for the past month. It had not kept him from playing, but he was still batting only .273. Thursday afternoon, May 9, at Fenway, Hank hit what looked like a triple, but as he rounded second, he felt a painful catch in his lower back and stopped short. He had to come out of the game. The pain was so severe it kept him awake that night. He saw Dr. Mitchell at the Henry Ford Hospital the next day. X-rays and Dr. Mitchell's examination uncovered muscle inflammation but ruled out anything wrong with Hank's spine. He was to rest and receive regular treatments. That took him out of the lineup for ten days.

The day Hank was examined at the hospital, Hitler began his serious offensive in Europe; Nazi planes and tanks attacked France, Belgium, Luxembourg and the Netherlands. In April, Germany had invaded Norway and Denmark. Before May ended, Holland and Belgium surrendered. The following month, Italy declared war on France and Britain; Mussolini and Hitler deepened their alliance; and German troops occupied Paris. The soldiers' boots on the cobbles sounded ominous to the Jews of the occupied countries. In April, the Nazis had sealed 230,000 Jews in the Lodz ghetto. Hank read about the unfolding of the war in the newspapers.

By Independence Day in America, Greenberg was still in left field for the Tigers. He was no Tris Speaker and continued to have his awkward moments—he had already made ten errors in only sixty-eight games—but he had improved steadily. Tuck Stainback, a journeyman outfielder who joined the team that summer, showed him how to grip the ball with his fingers close together to get better wrist action and more carry on his throws to the infield. "He wasn't the most graceful outfielder in the game, nor the fastest, but sheer persistence and pride in his work made him a real flyhawk, who guarded his post well and turned in sensational putouts, simply because he never stopped trying, even when catches seemed impossible," *The Sporting News* observed.

Moreover, he had raised his average to .344, had belted 15 home runs, knocked in 69 runs, scored 50 himself and led the majors in doubles with thirty-one. He was selected to represent the American League in left field in the All-Star Game at Sportsman's Park.

His back was not bothering him, but there was another factor he had needed to adjust to in left field: the isolation. At first base, he had kept busy chatting with runners, supporting arguments about the umpire's pitch calls and seeing more action in the field. In the outfield, he was often bored and lonely. "It's like a Broadway traffic cop being transferred out to Staten Island," Hank said. "The afternoon seems like a lifetime. I spend most of my time wondering what I'm going to have for dinner and thinking about my batting average."

The only good thing about being stranded out there was not having to hear the verbal harangue from the visitors' dugout that had been a constant at first base. On the flip side, he stood out as solitary prey for malcontent fans. Salsinger called the infield heckling Hank heard at first base a "mere whisper" by contrast. "Grandstand occupants exercise a certain amount of restraint, but this is entirely missing in the pavilions and bleachers," Salsinger wrote. "The boys in those sections really concentrate on the job of heckling."

In Detroit's final game before the break, played Sunday, July 7, at Briggs Stadium, Hank scored two runs in the Tigers' 5–2 win over the Browns. Schoolboy Rowe flashed shades of his former self, picking up his sixth win of the season against only one loss. York, still at first base and batting .300, had knocked in his fifty-second run of the season, and the Tigers slipped past the Cleveland Indians into first place.

Ted Williams, the American League's starting left fielder, arrived at the St. Louis hotel early for the All-Star Game. The twenty-two-year-old Williams, the 1939 AL Rookie of the Year, was having another terrific season, batting .345, with 25 doubles, 11 homers and 55 RBI. Williams ran into

Hank Greenberg in the lobby. The Kid idolized Greenberg, seven years his senior, and enjoyed the chance to talk batting with him. Williams developed a long-standing admiration for Greenberg.

Five of the world champion Yankees started the game, including two in the outfield, DiMaggio and Charlie Keller. Hank replaced Williams midway through the game. Neither of the two left fielders managed a hit, and the National League blanked the junior circuit stars 4–0.

Bobo Newsom, the Tigers' ace acquired in 1939, did throw three shutout innings. Bobo was a big reason for the Tigers' recent ascent into first place, going 12–1 in the first half of the season. Newsom was a good ole boy from South Carolina who spoke of himself in the third person, as in "Ol' Bobo is on the mound today, and you can put it in the win column." Everybody had their favorite Bobo story. Since the colorful Newsom played for eight teams over twenty years, there were plenty to tell. Greenberg's favorite was about the night Bobo, who also stayed at the Leland Hotel, told Hank that he was going upstairs to get ready for a date. An attractive woman walked into the lobby, looked around and asked Hank if she had seen Newsom, because she was supposed to meet him.

"No," Hank said. "Bobo can have two or three dates in an evening."

Hank ended up taking her to dinner and sleeping with her. The next day at the ballpark, he listened with private glee to Bobo "ranting and raving about this girl who stood him up."

Marjorie Nash, the young woman who sent Hank notes after each home run, had drawn a portrait of Newsom that Bobo autographed and returned. He called to ask her to draw one he could keep. When she told Hank about the phone call, "Hank gave me some sound advice about Buck and his character," she wrote in her diary. "I had already suspected it." She continued to see Hank at games and his hotel. He had given her a portable Victor radio for Christmas. She had sent him a handmade card and some bookmarks she had made. Before an April game, she called to him and waved from her box seat. He removed his cap, tucked his glove under his arm and reached out his hand, but stumbled and nearly toppled into the dugout. "We laughed merrily at his apparent clumsiness," Marjorie wrote.

Marjorie's father, Maurice, a Methodist who worked as a toolmaker in Walter Briggs's manufacturing plant, liked baseball but not Jews. One day

Hank pulled his silver Lincoln Zephyr coupe with the red leather uphol-
stery up to her house on Guilford Avenue in eastern Detroit. Marjorie's
younger brother Ken was so excited to see the Tiger star park in front of
their house that he ran inside and yelled, "Marjorie, Hank Greenberg is
here!" Hank stayed for a while, and Mrs. Nash sent Ken out to play in the
backyard. The next morning, Maurice Nash, who had been at work when
Hank showed up, told Marjorie and her two sisters, "I don't want any of
you to ever, ever bring a Jew into my house again!" Marjorie broke off the
relationship but kept a framed photograph of Hank that he had autographed for her: "My best wishes always."

September 11, 1940, was an unusual day in baseball history: three different
teams held first place all alone in the American League pennant race. The
Indians started the day in the lead but gave way to the Yankees, who beat
them in the first game of a doubleheader. The Indians climbed back on top
when they won the second game, but the Tigers took over first later in the
day when they defeated the Red Sox. The Yankees stumbled while the
Tigers and Indians dueled to the finish.

Four days earlier, Hitler had begun the Blitz, fifty-seven consecutive
nights when German planes bombed London and other cities in England.
Early on, an estimated 2,000 German planes targeted London's East End,
heavily populated by Jews, and almost completely demolished the neighborhood. That same September week, Italian planes bombed homes in Tel
Aviv, killing 112 people, half of them children, and wounding 151. Before
the month was over, Germany, Italy and Japan signed the Tripartite Pact,
establishing the Axis alliance. With war threatening across the Atlantic
and the Pacific, President Roosevelt signed the Selective Training and Service Act on September 16, 1940, initiating the country's first peacetime
draft. The Act required that all American men between the ages of twenty-
one and thirty-five register with local draft boards. The law would have a
tremendous impact on Major League Baseball in general and Hank Greenberg in particular.

Late in August, Tiger pitcher Tommy Bridges, who liked to hunt in the
off-season, discovered that he could read the catcher's signs from the outfield's upper deck with the scope of a new rifle he had bought. The Tigers

positioned someone in the center field bullpen with binoculars to swipe the signs. Another player leaning against the fence relayed the pitch to the batter: If he pulled his right hand down, it meant curve; if he kept his right hand up, fastball. When Yankee manager Joe McCarthy grew suspicious, the Tigers shifted their spy to the upper deck. Some of the Tiger hitters like Gehringer didn't want to know what pitch was coming, but Greenberg did. So did Rudy York.

The two Tiger sluggers started murdering the ball in September. During one seventeen-game stretch, either York or Greenberg hit a home run. Hank batted an eye-popping .458, clobbered five doubles, two triples and 13 homers. He drove in 32 runs and scored thirty. That month, he blasted 15 circuit clouts, the most he had ever hit in September, and jacked up his average eleven points. York hit ten dingers and raised his average five points over the month. The two basically carried the club in September, with Hank doing most of the heavy lifting.

The Indians came to Detroit for a crucial series beginning Friday, September 20, with the two teams tied for first place and only eight games remaining. The Indian players had rebelled earlier in the season. They didn't believe they could win the pennant with manager Oscar Vitt, so they demanded that owner Alva Bradley fire Vitt. Bradley refused, and fans around the league called the Indians "crybabies." When their train arrived in Detroit the day before the crucial series, hundreds of Tiger fans taunted the Indians. They followed them to the Book-Cadillac Hotel and chanted "crybabies" throughout the night. The next day at Briggs Stadium, some fans hung diapers on a laundry line strung up in front of the visitors' dugout. The game had to be stopped several times for the ground crew to pick up garbage Tiger fans tossed at the Indian players.

York and Greenberg's home run streak ended that Friday, but nineteen-year-old Hal Newhouser beat twenty-one-year-old Bob Feller. Rabid Robert was the only pitcher whose pitches Greenberg didn't want tipped to him. "I was afraid of risking the chance of a mistake," Hank said. Feller had already plunked him earlier in the season. "If I hung in there expecting it to break, but it was really a fastball and didn't break, I could get killed." Hank went two-for-four, knocking in a run and scoring the tying tally in the Tigers' 6–5 victory that gave them sole possession of first place.

Schoolboy shut out the Indians the next day with Greenberg driving in his 147th run of the season, but Feller came back on Sunday and beat the Tigers despite Hank's fortieth homer. The Tigers swept a three-game series with the White Sox before heading to Cleveland for the final three games of the season, needing to win just one game to clinch the pennant, their first in five long years.

Baker wasn't sure whom to pitch against Bob Feller. Greenberg suggested Newhouser, but Baker went with Floyd Giebell, a green junkballer who had pitched only once since being called up that month. It seemed Baker was conceding the game to Feller so that he could go with his stronger, better-rested pitchers—Rowe, Bridges or Newsom—in the next two games.

The Cleveland crowd, intent on revenge for the way Detroit fans had treated their players, had thrown fruit and shouted at the Tigers when they arrived at the train station. On Friday, September 27, at Municipal Stadium, they pelted Hank and his teammates with tomatoes, onions, eggs, lemons, oranges and grapefruit when they took the field. Since it was Ladies Day, Greenberg "in a gentlemanly gesture, retrieved some of the produce and handed it back to some of the feminine flingers," the papers reported.

Despite his gentlemanly gesture, when Hank set up to catch a fly ball, the fans hurled tomatoes at him. Umpire Bill Summers announced over the public address microphone that he would rule any Cleveland batter who hit a fly ball out automatically if that happened again.

Meanwhile, Giebell pitched himself in and out of jams without letting a Cleveland runner score. Feller allowed only three hits (including a double by Greenberg), but Rudy York's two-run homer in the top of the fourth was enough for the Tigers to win the game and the pennant. The Tigers carried the unlikely hero Floyd Giebell off the field. They whooped it up in their clubhouse. The news from Europe of Germany, Italy and Japan's new alliance was lost in the din of the celebration. "The Tigers celebrated so lavishly with champagne that they lost the remaining two games of the series," Fred Lieb wrote.

No matter, they were in the World Series for the first time since Frank Navin's death five years earlier. The Tigers had gotten solid pitching from Bobo (21–6) and Schoolboy (16–3); the thirty-seven-year-old Gehringer, whom Lardner called "the gray ghost of the Tiger infield," had batted over .300 for the eighth consecutive season (.313); and Dick Bartell, a.k.a.

"Rowdy Richard," had proven an adequate replacement for Billy Rogell at short. The team had certainly benefited from York's bat in the lineup every day—he hit .316 and finished third best in the league in home runs (33) and second in RBI (134). But Greenberg had driven the train. He led the major leagues in doubles (50), extra base hits (99), total bases (384) and RBI (150). His 41 homers were best in the American League. Granted, he committed more errors than any other outfielder in the major leagues, but he had improved his fielding to the point where he was more of an asset than a liability. *The Sporting News*, baseball's Divine Word, stated simply, "Without him, it is doubtful if the Tigers could have won the flag."*

Hank's contribution went beyond his exploits on the field. Citing Greenberg's willingness to try a new position for the greater good, Mr. Baseball, Dan Daniel, praised Hank as baseball's "Number 1 team player." Columnist Bill Slocum, referencing the same, wrote in late September, "If Detroit wins [the pennant], it will have been more because of the common sense of Greenberg than the power he packs in a ringing bat. For Hank did something that few ballplayers would do. Something that, to my knowledge, no major league player has ever done before quite the same way. He gave up a position in which he was an outstanding star and which he preferred to play for the good of the Detroit team."

The Baseball Writers' Association of America named Greenberg the American League's Most Valuable Player. It was the first time that a player had won the award at two different positions in either league. Greenberg received sixteen first-place votes; Feller rated six. That upset many, who thought Feller had the better season. He pitched a no-hitter on Opening Day and dominated the rest of the way, capturing pitching's Triple Crown with the most wins (27), lowest ERA (2.61) and most strikeouts (261). He also led the league in complete games (31) and shutouts (4). Yet one Detroit writer had not placed Feller in his top ten. When the Cleveland writers at the BBWAA annual winter meeting called him on this, he stood and explained that since Feller had backed the ouster of Indian manager Oscar Vitt, he could not vote for a "mutineer" with a clear conscience.

---

* Greenberg also led the majors in runs created (166), slugging percentage (.670) and OPS (1.103). His at-bats per home run of 14.0 was the best in the American League.

The Sporting News defended the writers' "wise selection." Its editorial noted that "such intangibles as loyalty, disposition and effort counted heavily on Hank's side" and concluded, "Considering all the elements which help to make a player the most valuable to his team, the baseball writers making up the committee did a fine job in naming Greenberg, who deserved the honor bestowed upon him in 1940 even more richly than in 1935, when he won a similar accolade."

Greenberg, of course, had the binoculars to thank. Once he knew what to expect, he seemed invincible at the plate. From September 3, he batted .419. As Stanley Frank put it in the *New York Post*, Greenberg "hit in a sustained fashion seldom equaled and never excelled in baseball history."

Eleven years later, the Giants would clinch the pennant with a home run tipped off by a telescope, and history would weigh that artificial assistance with mixed emotions and opinions. Though the Tigers did not win the 1940 in such dramatic fashion, Greenberg clinched it for them thanks to the advantage of knowing what pitches were coming over the final month. "I think it was picking up those signs that was instrumental in enabling us to win that 1940 pennant," he wrote.

Was it cheating? Del Baker didn't think so. "I didn't hear him talk about it as cheating," Del Baker Jr. said of his father. "In today's world it might be, but then it was A-okay. It wasn't considered cheating."

Ballplayers had been stealing signs since they were first used in the nineteenth century. That became a despised but acceptable practice, so long as opponents didn't cross the line of employing foreign instruments to aid them. "If a player is smart enough to solve the opposing system of signals, he is given due credit," Ty Cobb wrote in the *New York Evening News*. "But the use of field glasses, mirrors and so on, by persons stationed in the bleachers or outside the center field fence . . . is reprehensible and should be so regarded."

That view persisted in baseball through Hank's playing days. "Bootling information to the batter through a hidden observer equipped with field glasses is a dastardly deed," *Herald Tribune* columnist Red Smith wrote in 1950. "But the coach who can stand on the third-base line and, using only his own eyes and intelligence, tap the enemy's line of communication, is justly admired for his acuteness."

Still, most players figured their opponents swiped signals with artificial enhancements. "Every team with a scoreboard in center field has a spy inside at one time or another," wrote Rogers Hornsby, who played from 1915 to 1937. "There's always a hole for the spy to peep through."

Though players and managers opposed the practice when other teams employed it, they were quick to justify their own use of binoculars. "Win any way you can as long as you can get away with it," Giant manager Leo Durocher wrote in 1951.

To Greenberg, stealing signs wasn't cheating because that's the way the game was played. Twenty years later, when he was general manager of the Chicago White Sox, his team was again pilfering signs with binoculars. One of his pitchers, Al Worthington, a devout Christian, told Greenberg the practice violated his religious beliefs. "I can't play for a team that's cheating," Worthington said.

"Baseball is a game where you try to get away with anything you can," Hank told him. "You cut corners when you run the bases. If you trap a ball in the outfield, you swear you caught it. Everybody tries to cheat a little."

Worthington was not convinced. He packed his Bible and went home to Birmingham, Alabama. Greenberg tried unsuccessfully to unload him on another team. "We tried to sell him but the word was out that he was some sort of cuckoo," Hank said.

That's how baseball judged those who weren't willing to bend the rules to win.

The city of Detroit, which had slumped economically after celebrating itself as the City of Champions in 1935, was making a comeback. Many of the factories had switched to armament production around the clock, which boosted employment and gave Detroiters an infusion of new life. They had rallied around their boys, with a record 1,112,693 fans turning up at Briggs Stadium that season. Then the Tigers clinched the pennant, and the people of Detroit could regard themselves as winners again. The World Series programs that sold for twenty-five cents showed a snarling Tiger with long, sharp claws on top of a large baseball globe, illustrating how the team made them feel.

Even though the 90–64–1 Tigers had arrived at the World Series with the lowest winning percentage (.584) of any American League pennant winner, many favored them over the Cincinnati Reds, whom the Yankees had swept the year before. The way they saw it, the Tigers had finished two games ahead of the Yankees, so they should be a better team than Cincinnati. But the Reds had won one hundred games and finished twelve games ahead of their closest rival. They also had slightly stronger pitching, anchored by Paul Derringer and Bucky Walters. Perhaps the biggest wild card would be that the Tigers were not able to put someone in the Crosley Field bleachers to steal pitches—they feared the consequences if he were caught. "They might lynch him," Hank said.

Bobo Newsom faced the Reds' twenty-game winner Paul Derringer in the opener on Wednesday, October 2, in Cincinnati. In his first at-bat, Hank led off the second inning with a single over the third baseman's head. He scored on Pinky Higgins's single, and the Tigers put up five runs to chase Derringer. Hank's parents did not travel to the Series because of the High Holy Days—Rosh Hashanah began at sundown—but a photo in the paper showed them beside a radio when Hank singled: "Papa got so excited, he picked up a bat and thought he was there while Mama began cheering."

Bobo Newsom's father, a sixty-eight-year-old retired farmer, *was* there at Crosley, all the way from Hartsville, South Carolina, to see his son win the game 7–2. "I feel great over this one," Bobo said afterward in the clubhouse, "because my father was out there watching me."

There was less to celebrate the next day, Rosh Hashanah. Hank batted in the first inning with Gehringer on first and McCosky on third. The Tigers already led 1–0. A base hit could blow the game open. Instead, Hank grounded a bad pitch to Reds' third baseman Billy Werber, who turned it into a double play. McCosky scored, but the rally ended. Cincinneti came back to win 5–3. "Hank sure gave me a break," Reds' pitcher Bucky Walters said. "If he had hit one out, that could have been the end of it for us."

Hank did double in the sixth to drive in a run, but it hadn't been enough. The next day back in Detroit, Hank blamed himself for the loss. "I hit a bad ball in the first inning, and it resulted in a double play," he moaned. "If I had been more patient, I might have got hold of one and Walters would have been in deep trouble."

In Game Three, it seemed he would do no better. Hank struck out and grounded into another double play with two runners on. A run scored, but he had again failed to put the pitcher, Jim Turner, into deeper trouble. In his next chance, though, Hank singled off Turner and scored. In the eighth, he hit a leadoff triple and scored. The Tigers won 7–4 to take a two to one lead in the Series.

Cincinnati evened the Series on Saturday, October 5, with a 5–2 win behind the strength of Paul Derringer's pitching. The Tigers got a break when forty-three-year-old catcher Jimmy Wilson started for the injured regular Ernie Lombardi. Wilson gave his signs so low that the Tigers picked them up from the dugout. Once again, Hank had the advantage of knowing what was coming. Hank doubled in a run in the third, but, with Barney McCosky on first with two outs in the seventh and the Tigers trailing 4–2, Hank flied out to left field to end the inning.

Bobo Newsom had not been able to savor his Game One victory with his father. The elder Newsom suffered a heart attack the next day and died in his hotel room. Bobo attended the funeral but was back for his start in Game Five. He dedicated the game to his father. Sunday afternoon, 55,189 fans piled into Briggs Stadium to watch the unusually solemn Bobo shut out the Reds on three hits. Hank did his part with a three-run homer to the left field upper deck. When he took his spot in left field to start the next inning, the fans gave him a hearty ovation, and he tipped his cap. He was three-for-five on the day with four RBI. The Tigers won 8–0 and headed back to Cincinnati up three games to two, confident they would take the Series.

With the chance to win it all, Schoolboy Rowe lasted only five batters, and the Tigers trailed 2–0 after the first inning. They weren't able to come back against Bucky Walters, the National League MVP the previous year with twenty-seven wins. Walters drove in the next two runs himself, one with a solo homer, and the Reds won 4–0 to even the Series once again.

Hank was oh-for-three with a walk and a strikeout. He had whiffed five times in the Series, left four men on base and grounded into two double plays, but just as often, he had come through with runners on base with a sacrifice or a hit. He seemed to have slipped the jinx that plagued him in the clutch his first two World Series. Since getting tipped off on pitches, he had gone four-for-twelve with a double and a home run.

Hank in Cincinnati and his parents back in the Bronx heard more troubling news the day of Game Six: Hitler's troops had invaded Romania. The war had struck closer to home.

For Game Seven, Tuesday, October 8, at Crosley Field, Del Baker sent his ace Bobo Newsom back to the mound after only one full day's rest against Derringer. "The players would have shot Del had he pitched anyone else," Fred Lieb wrote. Newsom pitched well. The Reds spotted him an unearned run in the top of the third when Billy Werber's wild throw allowed Tiger catcher Billy Sullivan to score. With runners at first and third, Hank struck out to end the inning. Newsom took his shutout into the bottom of the seventh Reds; first baseman Frank McCormick led off with a double. Left fielder Jimmy Ripple followed with a drive to right. McCormick paused, uncertain whether right fielder Bruce Campbell would catch the ball. When he saw the ball bounce off the screen, the slow-footed McCormick rumbled toward home. Tiger shortstop Dick Bartell took the relay with his back to home. Bartell had the chance to cut down McCormick at the plate, but he hesitated and held the ball. He didn't think he had a play. Amidst the Cincinnati crowd's excited cheers, he hadn't heard catcher Billy Sullivan and his other teammates call for him to throw home. Cincinnati tied the score 1–1 on the play and Ripple stood on second. The Reds squeezed him across the plate with a bunt and a sacrifice fly. They led 2–1.

Gehringer started off the eighth with a single. Greenberg followed. He had already singled twice himself to lead off the second and sixth innings. But this time, he lined out to the shortstop. York and Campbell could do no better, each flying out, and the Tiger threat was over. The game ended 2–1 with the Reds taking Game Seven and the Series.

It was a tough loss for the Tigers. They had squandered a three to two lead. Disappointment shrouded the train ride home. Hank had batted .357 throughout the Series, second best on the Tigers. He had homered and driven in six runs, which tied him for the team RBI lead with Pinky Higgins. He had come through with men on base. But, he had also faltered with men in scoring position. The alcohol flowed freely between Cincinnati and Detroit. Hank, who was not a heavy drinker himself, welcomed John Barleycorn's comfort. By the time they pulled into Michigan Central Terminal, half of the players had to be helped off the train.

Hundreds of fans surprised the Tiger Special when it pulled into the station shortly before 11:00 p.m. They embraced their Bengals even in defeat. The *Detroit News* reported, "The cheers that rang through the dome of the big concourse sounded like Briggs Stadium after a Greenberg home run."

That was nice, but not enough to wash away the discouragement. "You only remember the ones you lost," Hank said. "You only remember the bad days."

He still hadn't played on a team that won the World Series. With the global situation the way it was, he might never get the chance.

CHAPTER TEN

You're in the Army Now

On Wednesday, October 16, Hank loaded up his Zephyr coupe for the drive home to the Bronx. His brother Joe, who had come to Detroit after his own season in Shreveport ended to watch the World Series, rode shotgun. They left early in the morning and drove about eight hours before they pulled off U.S. 20 in Western New York to find a registration center. October 16 was Registration Day, the date specified by the Selective Training and Service Act when all men between the ages of twenty-one and thirty-five were required to sign up for the draft lottery.

Hank had reached the pinnacle of his career. Twenty-nine years old, he was a two-time MVP, had just played in his third World Series and had the distinction of being the highest-paid player in the national pastime. He was young, healthy and handsome. But with war looming, he was not the master of his own destiny.

Hank and Joe found a schoolhouse in Geneva where the men lined up outside were surprised to see the baseball star join them. On his form, Joe filled in the family's Bronx address: 663 Crotona Park North. That's the address Hank would use on all of his military forms in the future, but that day, he listed the Leland Hotel as his primary residence: 400 Bagley, Detroit, Michigan. His advisers, the Allen brothers and others, had recommended he do so, figuring Hank would not be selected as quickly in Detroit as he would be if he registered in New York. With the United States still uncommitted to the war, he wanted to spend his time gainfully employed as a baseball player.

It turned out that Hank had registered in a precinct with a small number of eligible men. When Secretary of War Henry L. Stimson started pulling blue capsules from a large fishbowl almost two weeks later, Hank wound up with the relatively low number 621. That number from a small pool likely meant he would get called sometime in 1941. Joe, who had registered in the Bronx, more densely populated with men of draftable age, did not get called until two years later.

The Selective Training and Service Act required a year of military service for draftees. Baseball was not enthusiastic about turning over its employees to Uncle Sam. Larry MacPhail, then president of the Brooklyn Dodgers and a World War I veteran, thought players should be able to begin service after the baseball season ended so their hitch wouldn't cut into two seasons.* *The Sporting News* suggested in a May 1941 editorial that ballplayers be assigned duty plying their trade, "slugging the ball for some camp team," where they would be "giving more material aid to the upbuilding of *esprit de corps* than merely shouldering a rifle or squinting behind a machine gun." In other words, before the United States actually entered the war, baseball wanted to limit its financial losses and protect its investments.

As *Time* magazine pointed out, the players were caught in the middle: "Unlike other businessmen, whose earning power increases with age, they had to get theirs while the getting was good. Moreover, as national heroes, they were expected to set a shining patriotic example. A hero could not ask to have his military training deferred."

The solution for baseball players, according to Brigadier General Ames T. Brown, New York's Selective Service director, was to volunteer before the 1941 season began to ensure that they would miss only one season—and not parts or possibly all of two seasons.

With his playing days numbered and the United States still officially neutral on the world conflict, Hank thought missing even one season would cause unnecessary financial losses. After making $50,000 in 1940,† he expected a raise for the coming season, thanks to the MVP honors he earned

---

* Once the U.S. entered the war, MacPhail quit his post as Dodger president in 1942 to join the Army.
† The equivalent of $819,257 in 2012.

in left field. He figured if he missed the 1941 season, he would lose his leverage and have to accept a lower salary for 1942.

Each man who registered for the draft was sent a questionnaire by his local draft board that asked what class he thought he should be in. While vacationing in Hawaii, Hank returned his draft questionnaire. "It is my opinion that my classification should be Class 2 because my years of earning power are limited and one year out of action will reduce my effectiveness considerably," he wrote. "I shall not be able to resume my present capacity after one year's absence." If granted this classification, he would at least be allowed to finish the 1941 season and may be able to avoid military service altogether. The questionnaire responses were supposed to be confidential but, to be safe, Hank included a note asking that his not be given any publicity, perhaps a naïve request given his stature as a national hero.

Class 2 deferments applied to men in civilian activities deemed "necessary to the national health, safety or public interest in the sense of useful or productive work or contributions to employment or well-being of the community or the nation." They were often reserved for those working in vital industries, such as aircraft and other armament plants. Two aspects of the regulation, when interpreted generously, could apply to Hank or any other star ballplayer, if he were a man who "cannot be replaced satisfactorily because of a shortage of persons with his qualifications or skill in a particular activity" and "a material loss of effectiveness in such activity which drafting of such an individual would bring about." The general consensus was that the absence of the 1940 American League MVP in the Tiger lineup would signal "Taps" for the team. Losing Greenberg "would be a dagger thrust into the Tiger heart," the legendary sportswriter Grantland Rice wrote.

In the previous war, Harry Weaver, a pitcher for the Cubs, had asked for exemption because "We have a good chance to win the pennant." That request was denied. Early in 1941, Hugh Mulcahy, the Phillies' ace pitcher,* asked for an occupational deferment. The twenty-seven-year-old bachelor, worried about how he would pay the mortgage on a house he just bought,

---

* A relative term, meaning he was the best of the worst; during four seasons with the cellar dwellers Mulcahy earned the nickname "Losing Pitcher."

claimed his enlistment would place a hardship on his parents. His Massachusetts draft board denied the request, and on March 8 "Losing Pitcher" became Private Mulcahy, the first major league player inducted into the Army since the previous war.

Meanwhile, other ballplayers were turned away from the military because of physical shortcomings. In February, a Superior, Wisconsin, draft board classified Morrie Arnovich, outfielder for the World Champion Cincinnati Reds, 1-B ("qualified only for limited military service") because he lacked one occluding molar. Later that month, Hank's former teammate Beau Bell, currently a Cleveland Indian outfielder, was also placed in Class 1-B because of his varicose veins.

Hank was the highest-profile player to be drafted. Ever since Secretary Stimson had stuck his hand in the fishbowl, the press had mused about Hank's fate and what it would mean for the Tigers in particular and baseball in general to lose its best player to military conscription. When the contents of Hank's questionnaire spilled into print on February 21, the national press jumped on the story. Ben Shepherd, an attorney and chairman of Wayne County Draft Board No. 23, which oversaw Hank's fate, denied that Hank had asked for a deferment. Technically, he was right. Hank had simply answered a question on what he thought was a confidential form, saying he thought his induction should be delayed. But the two other members of the board interpreted Hank's answer on the questionnaire as a request for a deferment and said so to the press, contradicting Shepherd.

The controversy fueled speculation and stirred debate on a hero's obligations. Just as his decision whether or not to play on the High Holy Days in 1934 had aroused national interest in questions about personal faith versus civic duty, Hank's draft status raised even larger questions that struck at the core of America's values and seemed to have worldwide implications. His situation pitted an individual's right to pursue his personal fortune in a capitalist economy against the patriotic duty to serve the common good in a democracy. Hank's status as a national figure—which was heightened by the debate—made his case a touchstone for this discussion. A *Saturday Evening Post* profile that appeared mid-March called him "unquestionably the most controversial figure in the game today," and that was *before* the draft situation flared up. The *Free Press* front page on February 22 ran a banner headline "Britain Moves for War Over Balkans" followed by "Greenberg Asks for Deferment of Draft Call."

The *Free Press* thought it was "sensible" that Hank be allowed to finish the 1941 season before having to serve so that Tiger fans would only miss him for one year. John Considine of the *Washington Post* thought it reasonable that Greenberg only be asked to give up his income for a single season rather than potentially missing two earning years during his prime. A segment of the public agreed. "He's perfectly right in asking deferment because of his limited earning power in baseball," Albert Martino, a Detroit waiter, told the *Free Press*.

Others were not sympathetic to a high-paid ballplayer sipping pineapple juice on a Hawaii beach asking for a delay in fulfilling his military obligation. Scribes and citizens excoriated him for placing his personal interests before the nation's. John Kieran of the *New York Times* argued that ballplayers like Greenberg had an elevated responsibility as "heroes to the boys of the land" not only to serve but to be "lifted above the common citizenry." Common citizens didn't think he was better than they were. "Hank's an American, the same as the rest of us," Detroit constable Edward Hamper told the *Detroit News*. "He should go when called."

Hank's situation divided Tigers management. Del Baker told the press that ballplayers should take their fate into their own hands and volunteer to "get through with their year of service as soon as possible." In response, Jack Zeller said that Walter Briggs had directed company officials to "Keep your hands off all phases of the draft problem."

The press was eager to get Hank's perspective when he returned from Hawaii on February 24. A gang of newspaper reporters scurried on board his liner the *Monterey* when it was still quarantined in Los Angeles. Unaware of all that had been written while he was away, Hank denied that he had asked for a deferment, though he said if called in the middle of the season, he might ask that his induction be delayed until October. Once the *Monterey* had docked, Hank hurried to a telephone to call the Tiger offices and get clarification. Before boarding a flight to New York, he repeated that he had not asked for a deferment. "I do not have any intention, however, of trying to get out of military training," he said pointedly.

When his flight stopped for a brief layover in Chicago, more reporters awaited him. Ever since he had left Honolulu, he had been bombarded by phone calls, radiograms and telegrams from newspapers and press associations asking him to comment on his draft case, but he did not answer them. "The matter is entirely in the hands of the draft board," he told Dale Stafford of the *Detroit Free Press* in Chicago. "Why should I talk about it?" He thought they were making too much of his situation and wished they would leave him alone. Someone asked if he would volunteer, as Baker had suggested. Hank laughed and said, "I'll go when they collar me."

When he landed in New York on a frigid night and another pack of reporters besieged him at LaGuardia with the same questions, his good humor wore off. The *Detroit News* reported: "Growling all over the place, he arrived home last night as sore as an open wound about 1) the statements that he had asked deferred classification in the draft and 2) the publication by a Detroit draft board of the information in his draft questionnaire which he said was supposed to be kept confidential."

"All I know is when my number is called, I'll go, and I'm not asking for a deferment," he said. He kissed his father, who had come to pick him up, pushed his way through the throng of reporters to the car parked outside the terminal and drove home.

Hank had enjoyed a good relationship with the press early in his career with Detroit. Reporters liked that he was thoughtful, conversational and accommodating. But that relationship began to sour when he held out in the spring of 1936. He felt the Detroit news corps had let him down, turning on him instead of supporting him in what he thought was a legitimate demand. He also felt betrayed when two reporters, the *World-Telegram's* Dan Daniel and *Free Press'* Charles Ward, had printed comments he thought were off the record and that had resulted in backlash from readers (his remarks on being unhappy in Detroit and his preseason argument with Jack Zeller about Hank playing the outfield). It got to the point that when one reporter he didn't like greeted him and held out his hand as Greenberg entered the Leland Hotel, Hank refused to shake it. "I don't particularly like you," he said. "I have my reasons and you know what they are. So let's just go our separate ways and you write what you please, and I'll do as I please, and we'll get along better."

The latest hounding rankled him into silence. He stopped answering the phone or door and refused to talk to reporters, though they dogged him on the streets and tried to rouse him at night.

At home, he got the first good news of his return stateside: his contract from the Tigers for the 1941 season. He called Walter Briggs in Miami Beach and, after a long conversation, agreed to the terms of his service: $55,000 for the 1941 season.

Meanwhile, on February 26, Draft Board No. 23 rejected his suggestion he be considered Class 2 and said it would accelerate his induction because of all the attention. This would also allow Hank to get in before the season started and thus out in time for the 1942 season. He reported for spring training on March 9, and the draft board made provisions for him to take his physical examination, foreseen as a routine formality, in Lakeland. The expectation was that upon completion of his physical, he would be classified 1-A and available for immediate induction.

Wanting to avoid drawing any media attention, Hank worked out with the team the morning of March 11; then, after lunch at the hotel, he snuck away for his mandatory physical examination. He was surprised to encounter a young photographer at the doctor's office who asked him to pose for a photo. "No," Hank said.

The photographer clicked one anyway.

"You heel," said Hank, indignant. "I should punch you in the nose."

He didn't, but his threat against the "110-pound" photographer made it into print and tarnished his image.

Dr. Grover C. Freeman, a retired Navy lieutenant commander, examined Hank, finding him in perfect health except for second degree bilateral *pes planus*, or two flat feet. Third degree flat feet with "marked deformity, rigidity or weakness of such degree as to have interfered with the registrant's useful occupation in civilian life" would have rendered him 4-F, or unfit for military service of any type. As it was, Dr. Freeman's diagnosis placed him in class 1-B, meaning he qualified only for limited detail. Hank's flat feet were no surprise—they had troubled him since he was a youth. He had listed them on his questionnaire as a possible impediment. So perhaps it sounded disingenuous when he told reporters at the Tigers' training facility, "I was surprised to learn that he had found flat feet disqualified me for general service. All I can add is that I am ready to report at any time that I am called."

Hank Greenberg, James Monroe High School, Class of '29. He signed his yearbook photo "Hy Greenberg." His senior quote was "Look up the record."

The twenty-one-year-old Greenberg played for the Beaumont Exporters in 1932 and was named Most Valuable Player of the Texas League.

Detroit Tiger scout Jean Dubuc convinced the eighteen-year-old Greenberg (*back row, center*) to play for the East Douglas (Massachusetts) team in the Blackstone Valley League, where Dubuc hoped to shelter him from other scouts. Will "Cannonball" Jackman, a Negro League pitching legend, stands next to Greenberg.

When Hank signed with the Tigers as a nineteen-year-old rookie in 1930, he encountered the psychological warfare that veteran players waged against younger prospects out to take their jobs.

Greenberg with another prodigy from New York City, Lou Gehrig (*left*). He was the reason Hank signed with the Tigers instead of the Yankees. Gehrig became the measure of Greenberg's success throughout his career.

Hank was a keen student of the game, studying pitchers for ways they might tip pitches and seeking any advantage he could find against the opposition.

Hank moved from first base to left field in 1940 and was named the American League's Most Valuable Player that season. He became the first player to win an MVP Award at two different positions.

Hank appeared on the box for Wheaties, "Breakfast of Champions," for five seasons, which was as much of a status symbol then as it is now.

An older, more mature Greenberg after returning from his tour of duty. More than four years of military service changed him.

Hank often posed graciously for photographers, though he developed a mistrust of the press and its motives.

Base hit, Greenberg. Hank had a .313 lifetime batting average. When he retired in 1947, his 331 career home runs ranked fifth on the all-time list.

Hank with his first wife, Caral Gimbel, and her blue-ribbon-winning horse, My Bull. She was an accomplished equestrian; he felt uncomfortable in the saddle.

In the wake of outrage over this photo and the accompanying article that ran in *The Sporting News* on January 1, 1947, Tiger owner Walter O. Briggs Sr. waived Greenberg out of Detroit.

Greenberg played his final season in Pittsburgh, where he hit twenty-five home runs and became the game's first $100,000 player.

Best Wishes from "Hank" Greenberg

Hank's parents initially wanted their son to go to college rather than play professional baseball. His success made fans of them, and they attended his games in New York and Philadelphia.

After his playing days ended, Hank spent ten seasons in the Cleveland Indians' front office. His tenure was marked by successful teams and testy relationships.

Hank signed a new two-year contract with Indian president Ellis Ryan at the winter meetings in New York during December 1951. Before that contract expired, a rift developed between the two, and the board of directors fired Ryan.

As the Indians' general manager, Hank struggled to get along with shortstop-manager Lou Boudreau (*left*) and center fielder Larry Doby (*center*). He fired Boudreau and traded Doby.

Hank with Joe Cronin, the Boston Red Sox's seven-time All-Star shortstop, on the day of their induction into the National Baseball Hall of Fame, July 24, 1956. Hank said that day provided his greatest thrill in baseball.

Hank with his two sons, Steve (*left*), and Glenn. After his divorce from their mother, Caral, in 1959, Hank gained full custody of the boys and their sister, Alva, an unusual situation in that age.

Hank and his older son, Glenn, at a White Sox game. With his buddy Bill Veeck, Greenberg gained controlling interest of the Chicago ballclub in 1959 after a controversial court battle with Chuck Comiskey.

After retiring from baseball, Hank indulged his competitive nature on the tennis court. He won a slew of celebrity tennis titles but was a demanding doubles partner.

Hank and his second wife, Mary Jo Greenberg, at a baseball dinner in the White House, guests of President Richard Nixon.

Hank next to Whitey Ford at an old-timers game, Shea Stadium, June 28, 1975. Greenberg hated playing the exhibitions because he rarely did well in them. Former Yankee catcher Bill Dickey called Hank the worst-looking old-timer he ever saw.

Hank with Mary Jo. He rented a boat to sail off the coast of Los Angeles for her birthday celebration.

Greenberg's statue (by Omri Amray) in Comerica Park stands alongside fellow Tiger greats Ty Cobb, Charlie Gehringer, Willie Horton, Al Kaline, and Hal Newhouser.

HANK GREENBERG

Word of the doctor's finding spread quickly, met with incredulity. *Wait a minute, the guy can run the bases and patrol the outfield, but he's not fit to shoulder a rifle and march in rank?!* Some cried favoritism. Others suspected he had bribed the doctor. This violated the ideals of democracy and the concept of the citizen soldier. George Washington himself, whose military and political leadership had provided the foundation of this nation, had promoted the belief that "every citizen who enjoys the protection of a free government owes . . . his personal service to the defense of it." Yet here was Greenberg seemingly shirking his duty.

Some lost faith in him. "I think he is making a foolish move by destroying our hero illusions," said Mrs. Murray McDougall, a Detroit housewife.

Others lost faith in the system. "When the Army has to let down for a baseball game, there's something wrong in this country," E. Whincup told the *Free Press*.

Even though the draft's intention had been to staff the armed services with the country's most physically fit men and in its first year fifty percent of all draftees failed their examination, the members of Draft Board No. 23 did not want to be perceived as showing favoritism. They sought a second opinion from Detroit physician Benjamin F. Freeman (no relation to Grover, the Lakeland physician). After reading the examining doctor's report, Dr. Freeman recommended that Hank be reclassified 1-A. The Army had inducted other men with second-degree flat feet, he said, implying that Greenberg should not be granted special treatment for any reason. The draft board referred Hank's case to its medical advisory board. Until only days earlier, that board had been at Ford Hospital, which also served as the Detroit Tigers' hospital. It had been shifted—as a routine matter, the draft board asserted—only days earlier to Harper Hospital. The doctors there would determine Hank's draft status on Friday, April 18, the day of Detroit's home opener.

Once again, Greenberg's situation divided public opinion, and the discussion eclipsed the war. Hank was the talk of barbershops, watercoolers and front porches. Mothers thought Hank should serve like their sons. Wives thought he should go like their husbands, who made much less working in factories but still willingly gave up their pay for the cause. Many Tiger fans wrote the team saying they wouldn't pay to see Greenberg play.

They called him a "slacker"* and a "yellow-bellied punk." One fan wrote, "Hello Flat Feet: Are you a Dodger or a Tiger?" Only a few wrote to defend his desire to earn what he could while he could. The *New York Evening Post's* Stanley Frank wrote that the draft board was guilty of a "grave injustice" for portraying Hank as a slacker by saying he had asked for a deferment and as a draft dodger by throwing out his initial examination results.

Hank's mother thought he should serve, too, when his time came. "My boy is just like any other young American," Mrs. Greenberg said. "If he is called, he will answer willingly."

The conversation continued across America. "I don't think he should be given any more freedom than anyone else, and the fact that he is a ballplayer makes him all the more eligible as a soldier," said Pauline Savas, a Detroit waitress. John Warner, an elevator operator at City Hall, disagreed. "I think they ought to stop picking on the poor guy," Warner said. "I carried a pack in the last war, and I'd hate to have to do it again with flat feet."

Other veterans weren't sympathetic. The local Detroit American Legion stated that Hank's deferment "undermines the confidence of the public" in the fairness of the Selective Service Act. "It's too bad that he should claim exemption on the flimsy grounds that he has and it's certainly inexcusable that he should get it. . . . We aren't a bit proud of Hank. He has turned us from boosters to booers."

Others worried about the message that Hank's deferment would send. "If he's good enough to play baseball, he's good enough to march," said Nina Phil, a court recorder and baseball fan. "It's just too bad. So many young boys regarded him as a hero. Now they won't."

The Berkley (Michigan) VFW post drew up a resolution condemning Greenberg's deferment. "What about the effect deferment of Greenberg will have on the youth of the nation?" Ray Blackwell, the post's commander, said. "Plenty of young fellows are facing good pay jobs for the first time since they reached maturity. They cannot claim flat feet. This country has given Greenberg plenty, and he should see his duty."

The *Washington Post* ran an update of Hank's status alongside a photo of Hank at bat. An editor had circled both feet and penned "$25,000" under each.

---

* A particularly charged insult with its origins in the war hysteria of 1917.

The Tigers went through spring training distracted. "The explanation for the lackluster exhibitions is not difficult," Baker said. "Chaotic world conditions are responsible. The type of baseball this spring is a reflection of a confusing present and an uncertain future."

In late January, Romania's ultra-nationalist Iron Guard conducted a gruesome pogrom as part of a military coup. For five days, they raged against Jews "in an orgy of murder which has no parallel in modern times." The Legionnaires waylaid Jews in the streets, trucked them to fields where they sliced off ears and fingers with jeweled earrings and rings, raped young girls and hacked off women's breasts. They smothered the Jews with gasoline, lit them on fire and threw the charred bodies in dumps. In one Bucharest slaughterhouse, the thugs forced a group of Jews to kneel at chopping blocks, then slit their throats and hung their corpses from meat hooks "in a grisly parody of kosher butchering."

"Policemen assigned to guard the Jewish districts ignored the cries for help, and, in many cases, joined forces with the green-shirted Legionnaires," the *Detroit Jewish Chronicle* reported. An estimated 2,000 Jews had been slain and thousands more wounded.

In Detroit that spring, a union strike shut down the Ford Motor Company's Rouge plant. Henry Ford was certain that the Jews were behind the unions and that the strike was a "Jewish plot" against him. Harry Bennett claimed he convinced Ford this wasn't the case, but that did not alleviate Ford's suspicions.

The same ugliness tainted the mail that poured into the Detroit Ball Club's offices at Michigan and Trumbull:

"Hey Kike, For once try to forget the only creed you kikes have: money."

"Any bastard who says money first, my duty later, should be voted the most valuable player in Hitler's league and not the American League."

"If you dare to play baseball this year with your poor flat feet and your big Jewish nose, you will be America's No. 1 slacker."

"No wonder the world folks are more and more against the Jews race and you are [not] aiding to overthrow that opinion by being a slacker."

"Maybe you are like all the rest of Jews here in New York City—you must be a friend of Hitler."

"Don't be a slacker and show your Jew colors. Be a man and take the medicine like the rest of our boys."

Fans warned management of the consequences Hank's action would have for the team: "If you don't tell that big Kike that he is an American and his duty to his country comes before his big salary, the Tigers will get the worst booing around the circuit that any ball club ever received." And "Flat feet don't stop the Gentiles from joining the Army but will stop me from going to the games."

Swallowing the rhetoric of Charles Lindbergh and the like, some accused the Jews of duping America into the conflict unnecessarily. One mother wrote: "Greenberg's race has been one of the chief instigators to have us enter this terrible war." A Mrs. F. Johnson wrote: "It is the Jews that made us get into this war and they are getting out of it while our sons of Christian people fight *their* war."

Other Jews told Hank he put them in a bad spot and encouraged him to do his duty for the country. "Your big desire to make the dough is arousing more anti-Semitism in the country than anything else." And: "It will look bad if you don't go in the Army. The fans will ride you with yellow and slacker everywhere," Abe Cohen wrote along with an attached newspaper clipping about Hank entitled "Fugitive from Uncle Sam."

After dropping the Opening Day game in St. Louis, the Tigers returned for the home opener in Detroit on Friday, April 18. That morning, Hank put on a blue suit and dark tie and reported to Harper Hospital accompanied by his friend Harold Allen. The three doctors of the medical advisory board, including Frederick Kidner, the orthopedic surgeon who had treated Hank's broken wrist, examined him for half an hour. The doctors did not consider his flat feet a handicap; they found him qualified for general military service. Not yet knowing the results, Hank left the hospital "in good spirits" for that afternoon's game at Briggs Stadium. While Hank played left field, batted fourth and went oh-for-three in the Tigers' 4–2 win over the Indians, the members of Draft Board No. 23 released a statement that they had officially classified Greenberg 1-A. He had five days to appeal but didn't. The Associated Press reported, The Tigers "won a ball game today but lost their outstanding star."

On April 23, the board mailed Hank official notice at the Leland Hotel to report to the Detroit Induction Center, 1040 West Fort Street, at 6:30 a.m. on Wednesday, May 7, 1941. It also posted a copy of the induction order on the wall outside of its offices in the Cadillac Square Building. Uncle Sam had bagged his biggest star.

Viola Gifford, a Tiger fan, wrote Mr. Briggs with the suggestion that the team stage a "Hank Greenberg Day" before the team's star left. His son, Spike Briggs, the team's vice president, responded: "It would be impossible for us to have 'Hank Greenberg Day' before he leaves for camp. Hank himself wants to leave quietly without any fanfare."

Hank's teammates did throw him a going-away party at the Franklin Hills Country Club on the eve of his last game. They invited the Yankees, who were in town, and Hank's close friends. Charlie Gehringer presented him with a gold watch—a tradition the Brooklyn Dodgers had started for players departing for the First World War—with all of his teammates' signatures on the case. Del Baker told Greenberg that nobody would be able to take his place. When it was his turn, Hank addressed his teammates: "There's no chance of a reprieve. Even now, I can hardly realize that I'm about to leave baseball. It's a pretty tough thing to give up. It's almost the only thing I've thought about all my life."

He looked at them all looking at him, from Gehringer, who had been there before him, to rookie Ned Harris, who would take his spot in left field. "I've enjoyed every minute of my play with you," he told them. "Some of you I've criticized but never with viciousness or malice. I've been misunderstood when I thought I was being constructive and helpful. I'm sure those things have all been forgotten. In my own heart, I have no ill feeling toward anyone."

He addressed his close friends like Lou Blumberg and the Allen brothers: "I want you people to know that you helped me to build my career and that you deserve much credit for any success I've attained. I don't know how I could have kept on without your encouragement and inspiration." Walter Briggs Sr., who did not get out much now that his polio had confined him to a wheelchair, did not attend but sent a message to be read.

The next day, after Hank took batting practice and returned to the clubhouse, one of the Briggs Stadium attendants gave him a pen and pencil desk set from all of the attendants. "That's one of the greatest presents I ever received," Hank said. "It came from the heart of those fellows."

In his farewell game the next day, Tuesday, May 6, the Tigers played the Yankees. Beforehand, a flock of photographers, reporters and newsreel cameramen crowded around Hank at his locker. He was in a foul temper. He refused to pose for photographs, but that didn't stop the flashbulbs from popping in his face. They wanted to capture his every thought. He didn't want to talk to them.

He did tell Dan Daniel, "Honest, I don't mind going into the Army, but I don't want these newspapermen here to think they are forcing me into it."

He told Rud Rennie, also from the *World-Telegram*, "I don't want the papers to think I'm a good guy, because I'm not. I think the papers are horseshit."

"I'm sore about the way the papers hammered away at me, printing untruths and making a heel out of me," he said. "I'll be glad when this day is over. It will be a relief to get in the Army. This has been an awful strain."

Hank had gotten off to one of his slow starts, hampered even more this season by the distraction of his pending induction, the negative press, pointed barbs from bench jockeys, comments on the street, harassing telephone calls and nasty mail. His heart was not in baseball. He was simply going through the motions. "My spirit for the game has been sapped during the past few weeks and months," he told Bob Murphy of the *Detroit Times*. "I feel I have been given more unjust rap than anyone ever deserved."

Harry Salsinger commented that Hank's batting average had become "the barometer of his confused emotions." In eighteen games, he was hitting only .258. He had five doubles but no home runs. Baker had dropped him in the batting order to fifth behind York.

Despite his stated optimism that he would be back next year, Hank thought May 6 could very well be the last game he ever played. He figured the United States would enter the war eventually and that it was certain to be a lengthy conflict. Who knew how long the Army would require his service?

When he batted for the first time against the Yankees, leading off the second inning, the 7,850 fans who had shown up to say good-bye gave him an ovation. That pleased him. On a 2-0 count, he sent Tiny Bonham's pitch into the upper deck of the left field pavilion. Rounding the bases, he heard the crowd thunder its approval.

The next inning, he came to bat with York on first and one out. He again connected with Bonham's 2-0 pitch and parked it in the upper deck of the left field pavilion. The fans loved it.

In the outfield, Hank started counting up all of his home run clouts in the major leagues. With those last two, he tallied 249. It seemed an even 250 would be a good number to go out with. Then he remembered that he had never hit three home runs in a game, "and I thought it would be great if I really put on a splurge." He had not been swinging for the fences in his first two at-bats, but when he batted in the bottom of the eighth—likely his last at-bat because the Tigers were up 7–4—he sure planned to. The bases were loaded. He could end with 250, his first three-homer game and a grand slam to boot. The situation was ripe.

On the mound, Atley Donald had replaced Bonham. His first three pitches missed. Hank checked the third base coach for the sign. Baker gave him the green light. Everybody in the stadium seemed to want him to hit another. Bill Dickey, the Yankee catcher, told him, "Nothing but fastballs."

Donald's fastball came in over the plate, but Hank was so busy thinking about what he was going to do that he didn't do anything. He took it for a called strike. Three and one. Donald's next pitch was outside, but Hank didn't want to walk, so he swung anyway and missed. Three-two; full count. Donald's last pitch was perfect, a fastball over the plate, right in Hank's wheelhouse. He was so eager to knock it out of the park that he swung early and missed. Strike three.

Still, Hank's three RBI had provided the margin of victory. The Tigers swept the series, won their fifth straight game and slipped into second place. That's where he would leave them.

The next day, the Tigers planned to hoist the pennant flag from the 1940 season. The Detroit mayor had requested that Hank's induction be delayed a day so he could attend the ceremonies. After the game a reporter told Hank that the local draft board had granted the request. Hank hadn't asked for the favor, nor had the club, and he didn't want special treatment.

After all that he had been through the past three months, he also didn't trust the draft board's members. No, Hank said. "I was ordered to report for military service at 6:30 Wednesday morning. I'll be there."

After he had showered, dressed and packed up his corner locker, the newsreel cameras filmed him taking his uniform off a hook and handing it to Del Baker. "Well, Del, this is good-bye," Hank said in a wooden voice. "It was swell to work with ya. It's kinda tough to leave baseball, but when your country calls, there's nothing to do but respond."

"Hank, it's tough to lose ya," Baker said. "Uncle Sam is gettin' a great guy, and I hope ya hurry up and come back to us."

The photographers popped their flashes when Hank stooped for Mrs. Briggs to give him a farewell kiss.

"So long, boys," he said to his teammates. "I'll be back next year."

With that, he walked out of the Tigers' clubhouse, perhaps for the last time.

The next morning, Hank reported to the draft board's headquarters on the second floor of the Cadillac Square Building at 6:25 a.m. Several of the other draftees there asked for his autograph. Wearing a light-colored suit with a dark tie and carrying his belongings in a leather satchel, Hank walked with the other fifty draftees to the induction center at 1040 West Fort Street. People along the way called out, "Good luck, Hank!" Newspaper photographers snapped photos that ran on the evening editions' front pages.

Joe Roggin, the Tiger batboy whose hair Hank tussled after home runs, showed up to say good-bye. Hank posed for a photo with his arm around Roggin's shoulder. When he met the members of the draft board, he willingly posed with the chair, Ben Shepherd, whom he thought had treated him fairly, but he would not pose with the two members he did not like.

In a serious mood, Hank filled out forms, answered questions, provided his fingerprints and submitted to an hour-long physical examination. He passed, his flat feet "satisfactory for Army service," and was assigned serial number 36,114,611. Along with the other men, he raised his right hand and took the oath to "bear true faith and allegiance to the United States of America and to defend them against all their enemies."

The whole time, the newsreel cameras rolled, photographers snapped pictures and Hank signed autographs. A thirteen-piece WPA orchestra played swing music, considered good for morale.

He cooperated but was uncomfortable with all of the attention. "I don't understand it," he said. "You'd think I was an escaped convict, and they finally caught me."

After a lunch break, the new buck private boarded a train with the other new members of the Army for the three-hour ride to Fort Custer, 125 miles west of Detroit. He received a telegram from Edsel and Eleanor Ford: "Best Wishes for new duties." He took a nap, then listened to the end of the Tigers game on a buddy's radio. They raised the 1940 pennant but lost the game 4–2. He chatted baseball with other men who approached and asked for autographs. The press recorded every detail.

Several hundred fans greeted his arrival at the train station and called for him to appear on the train's rear platform. "Shall I make an acceptance speech?" he joked and signed more autographs. Before the day was over, he figured he gave a thousand autographs. When he arrived at Fort Custer, about a third of the 15,000 Fifth Division based at the reception center watched his arrival. He was issued his Army clothes and assigned a bunk in the barracks. At the men's request, he led them across the camp to the mess hall for dinner.

There, the *New York Times* reported he ate "plentifully of pork chops, mashed potatoes, creamed peas, fruit salad and milk." The *Detroit News*, on the other hand, wrote that he "feasted on vegetable soup, baked spare ribs, mashed potatoes, salad and coffee." So, he could have eaten beef ribs, but the accounts gave the impression that he was willing to suspend kosher law as a soldier; he was willing to make sacrifices for his country. "Perhaps the press wanted to emphasize the egalitarianism of the military—anyone could be drafted, everyone had the same opportunities for leadership, and everyone ate the same food regardless of personal wealth or religion," Jacob Baska notes in his paper "I'll Go When They Collar Me."

Thus did the press begin working the transformation of Greenberg from the star athlete into the model citizen-soldier. *Life*, the most popular magazine in the country, ran a three-page spread on Greenberg's induction. The photos showed Hank with his mouth open, a doctor peering down his throat with a flashlight; Hank in his boxers and undershirt, arms raised while a uniformed man wrapped a tape measure around his chest; Hank in uniform with overcoat giving a smart salute. They showed him submitting to the military, documented the metamorphosis of Hankus Pankus, the American League MVP into the Army's No. 36,114,611. The highest-paid player in the national pastime had traded in the luxury lifestyle, the spotlight and cheers for a cot, khakis and twenty-one dollars a month.

On the day of his final game, the *Free Press* opined that Hank had "endeared himself" to the fans of Detroit and stated that he had been "more than a great athletic asset to the City Dynamic. He has been a unique personality: friendly, kindly, considerate, on and off the field of play. . . . You've been an honor to the game, Hank, an honor to your people and to your Country." The following day, a *Detroit Times* editorial declared: "Hank Greenberg will go down in history as one of Detroit's greatest baseball heroes. . . . Greenberg has been a great credit to Detroit, to baseball and to himself by his gentlemanly conduct both on and off the field. The national pastime has known no keener student. The way Hank overcame handicaps to reach stardom attests to this." The paper bid him good-bye and God-speed.

New York Times columnist John Kieran wrote that Hank's induction would wake up some citizens to the seriousness of the United States' defense program and concluded, "He's a stand-up, steadfast gent and in this corner he has a rooter in any game he plays."

Now that Hank had complied, the press dropped its complaints and praised him. An AP story reported that he was studying his soldier's field manual. "I've got to learn the rules of this game," he said. "You wouldn't play baseball without knowing what hits and runs are, would you?"

The press was eager to show how well he had adapted to Army life, molding him into what it wanted to believe about him. "Hank Greenberg has won the admiration of military men and civilians with the splendid attitude he has shown since joining the Army," the *Minneapolis Tribune*'s George Martin gushed in the patriotic tone characteristic of the sports pages those days. "Officers are impressed with the eagerness he is showing in mastering his new duties and to adhering rigidly to all rules and regulations. His fellow buck privates have found him a 'regular guy' in every respect."

He also won the admiration of those serving in public office. Senator Josiah Bailey of North Carolina praised Greenberg for being willing to serve his country, especially when it meant giving up his $55,000 baseball salary for twenty-one dollars a month in Army pay. Sen. Bailey held him up as an example of young men willing to make a "real sacrifice" for their country: "To my mind, he's a bigger hero than when he was knocking home runs."

The Jewish community was also pleased with its Hank, who had already done so much on the baseball diamond to break down stereotypes and ease the integration of Jews into American society. "Now, Hank, wearing the uniform of Uncle Sam's Army, is the symbol of another calling—of the responsibility and loyalty of the youth of the nation towards the country's defense needs," a *Detroit Jewish Chronicle* editorial observed. "He blends with the rest of the young men of our great land to form the major element of importance in a people—not the individual star who is an object of admiration on the arena, but part of the mass substance which is the symbol of strength for the entire people. Henry Greenberg in the U.S. Army uniform is not less important than Hank in the Tiger uniform, but far more important because he is part of the larger element that represents free America fighting for the retention of human liberties." Finally, regarding the controversy that surrounded his draft status, the paper concluded, "Hank emerges as patriotic as any of those who criticized him."

Once again, Hank had taught American Jews another lesson in assimilation, modeling what it meant to be both an American and a Jew. He was blazing the trail and setting an example for others to follow. "That was precisely what American Jews most needed to hear (and still do): to be a good Jew was compatible with being a loyal American," wrote historian Jerry Auerbach. "Hank Greenberg validated their deepest yearning to join the American team."

Hank may have had another reason for not wanting to enter the Army in the spring of 1941: marriage. His parents had long wanted their son, now thirty years old, to get married. "Married to some nice, quiet girl from a nice, quiet family—and if she has only sweetness and modesty and a faculty for making my boy happy, she can come without a dime," David Greenberg said in 1940. Hank had expressed the desire himself.

He may have finally met Miss Right, Miriam Landau of New York. Walter Winchell, the nation's most famous gossip writer, reported the week before Hank's induction that he had proposed to Miss Landau, "a childhood sweetheart." The *Detroit Jewish Chronicle* congratulated the couple on its engagement. Some thought Hank was seeking a last-minute exemption by getting married. When a reporter asked him about his betrothal, Hank snapped indignantly, "That is a personal affair. I won't talk about it."

The two never did marry. Harry Salsinger dismissed Winchell's report as simply the latest example of Greenberg's situation being misreported: "Greenberg has been the subject of more fake rumors and false gossip than any other ballplayer that we can recall offhand."

Michigan Governor Murray Van Wagoner had requested that Hank be given the option of whether to remain at Fort Custer with the 5th Division or be assigned to the 32nd Division at Camp Livingston, Louisiana. Hank asked for "combatant service with the infantry," which meant he would head to Louisiana. He bought a $10,000 Army life insurance policy, about ten times larger than that of the average soldier, and named his parents the beneficiaries. At the same time, he expressed his desire to stay in Michigan. Though the newspapers initially reported that he would report to the Louisiana unit, five days later, Hank was officially assigned to C Company, 2nd Infantry, 5th Division, an antitank unit housed among the clapboard buildings of Fort Custer. He was issued a rifle and a gas mask and settled into Barracks No. 1022.

The press was still tracking his every move. Everywhere he turned, someone wanted an autograph. He hid from them in the woods whenever he could. The day his unit passed through Cincinnati en route to Tennessee for a month of training, a newspaper headline boasted, "Greenberg and Buddies Here." When they marched through Cincinnati's streets, men along the route offered Greenberg steins of beer. All of the fuss annoyed him. "I'll appreciate it very much if the public will just let me get lost in the Army and forget about me," he told the reporters. "All this publicity is doing me more harm than good. I just want to be another one of the boys." They backed off somewhat after that.

Other than letting the press invade Fort Custer, the Army did its part to keep Greenberg's profile low. Officials denied the request for Hank to attend a patriotic celebration in Chicago on May 18, citing his decision not to attend the Tigers' flag-raising ceremony. "At the time of his induction Greenberg made the specific request that he be treated exactly as any other trainee," Major General E. S. Adams wrote. "If the precedent is established of sending Selectee Greenberg to one point, there will doubtless be continued demands for his presence at others, thus interfering with the training which he should receive."

Hank found Army life humbling. His initial duty on maneuvers in Cumberland Springs was water boy, filling canteens. But he was willing to do his part. On one particularly hot day, the soldiers had struggled to install a heavy mortar detachment when the sergeant told them he thought it was too close to the road and had to be moved one hundred feet up a hill. Quickly, Hank, sweaty and tired, replied, "Okay, Sarge." A half dozen other soldiers followed his lead. They dug out the mortar, shoved it up the hill and fitted it to its new position—with Hank doing most of the work.

Another time, his outfit pretended to lay siege to a town, lying on the street corners through the night. They camped in front of a drugstore. The longer they lay on the street corner, the more appealing became the thought of an ice cream soda at 7:00 a.m., when the proprietor opened the doors. But at 5:00 a.m., the order came to clear out. Hank was not at Dorfman Drugs anymore; he was under orders.

That doesn't mean he didn't try to improve his situation. North Carolina's other senator, Robert R. Reynolds, who served on the Committee on Military Affairs, interceded on his behalf with a request to Secretary of War Henry Stimson that Greenberg be transferred to the Morale Branch, where he would be able to "better serve by encouraging our young men of the Army in the field of athletics and clean and wholesome living."* Secretary Stimson denied the request on the grounds that Private Greenberg was not eligible for service in the Morale Branch, which was composed of commissioned officers.

Many of the men in Hank's unit had served fifteen or twenty years without holding a job on the outside. Hank did not find a lot in common

---

* It was a curious request coming from Senator Reynolds, who was not known for showing sympathy toward Jews. Quite the contrary, in fact. He had defended Nazi aggression and collaborated with Gerald L. K. Smith on the *Defender*, an anti-Semitic newspaper.

with the "roughnecks," as he called them. He kept mostly to himself, spend-ing a lot of time reading. He gained some weight but played racquetball sev-eral times a week at the local YMCA to stay fit. He returned to Detroit on the weekends to see his friends, though he did not go to Briggs Stadium, and took a furlough to New York to see his family, stop in at Toots Shor's and attend the Fritzie Zivic vs. Sugar Ray Robinson boxing match.

Other than a couple of speeding tickets, he stayed out of trouble. The first speeding ticket, when he was pulled over for driving 42 miles an hour in a 25 MPH zone off the base at 12:30 on a Wednesday morning, an hour and a half after his superior officer had checked him into bed, created a stir in the press.

In his first six months, his company commander promoted him three times, to first class private, then corporal and finally sergeant, bumping his pay up to sixty dollars a month. He was in charge of a five-man crew and responsible for the care of the Army's 37-millimeter antitank guns along with the truck that hauled it into firing position. Greenberg "is a good sol-dier and has exhibited the qualities of leadership and initiative we need in our noncommissioned officers," Captain Glen A. Sikes said. Hank's char-acter rated "excellent."

Truman Connell, who had played minor league ball and coached the Fort Custer baseball team, tried to recruit the Tigers' slugger, but Hank resisted. He was also cool to the idea of appearing in an amateur game at Briggs Stadium in July. He did not want to spend his free time practicing with the camp team. "No way," he told Connell. "I left a $55,000 contract, $11,000 a month, to sign up for the Army for twenty-one dollars a month, and I'm not going to waste it playing baseball."

He made an exception in August. His friend Abe Bernstein, former capo of the infamous Purple Gang, asked Hank to play in an exhibition between the Fort Custer nine and the home team at Southern Michigan State Prison. Abe said it would benefit his brother Ray, serving a life sentence there, because the warden was a big baseball fan. Ray Bernstein, a smooth talker and flashy dresser, was twenty-eight when he arranged the Collingwood Massacre on Detroit's West Side the afternoon of September 16, 1931. That day, he and two other Purples met three gang members who had double-crossed them and shot the men dead at the Collingwood Apartments. Ray, who had driven the getaway car, and the two gunmen were convicted of first degree murder. Hank agreed to play the prison game as a favor to Abe.

The Army baseball uniform didn't fit him but the prison had one that did, so Hank played first base for the prison team and was easily the crowd favorite, though—perhaps it goes without saying—it was a rough crowd. The ump was a fellow inmate whom the 4,000 or so captive spectators rode mercilessly, "You crook! You thief!" But they cheered mightily for Hank, who, despite not having hit a baseball for three months, had a perfect day with two doubles, a single and a 390-foot home run to lead his side to a 10–2 win. When he tagged the ball over the prison wall, all of the inmates naturally volunteered, "I'll get it!"

The Tigers missed Hank's bat. Without him, they had realized the predictions of their demise. "Just as no man could fill the uniforms of Babe Ruth and Lou Gehrig with the Yankees, so will no player be able to replace Greenberg on the Bengals," Dan Daniel had written. Too true. With Hank at Fort Custer and rookie Ned Harris in left field, it took the Tigers a week to win a game. They didn't spend a day in first place all season. The thirty-eight-year-old Gehringer was a shadow of his former self, batting .220, more than one hundred points below his career average. Dick Bartell was also washed up—the *New York Times* observed his "range as a shortstop is down to the width of a dime"—and the Tigers released him in May. The wheels had come off the pitching staff. Bobo Newsom, whom Walter Briggs had wanted to pay more than Bob Feller so Briggs could boast he had the highest-paid pitcher in the league, was a twenty-game *loser* and posted a 4.61 ERA. Schoolboy Rowe's arm went bad again. And Floyd Giebell, the surprise star of the 1940 pennant-clinching game, flopped. Without Greenberg, attendance dropped almost 40 percent at Briggs Stadium; on the road, the AL defending champs drew 250,000 fewer fans without their MVP.

On July 8, Detroit hosted the All-Star Game, which proved to be baseball's high point in the city that summer. One of the largest crowds to pack Briggs Stadium, "54,674 rabid partisan AL rooters," watched their side, managed by Del Baker, fall behind late in the game. In the bottom of the ninth, with the American League trailing 5–4, Boston's Ted Williams came to bat with two out and two on. Williams, still only twenty-three years old, drilled Claude Passeau's first pitch into the right field upper deck. "It was a homer from the moment it left the bat, and left Detroit as happy as after a World Series victory," Fred Lieb wrote. When Ted saw the ball clear the fence, he skipped happily around the bases. "I think that's the biggest thrill I've ever gotten in baseball," he said years after he had retired.

That summer was the Williams and DiMaggio show. The Splendid Splinter batted .406, the last player to hit over .400, though, of course, no one knew that at the time;* and the Yankee Clipper hit safely in fifty-six consecutive games.† It was a hitter's summer. Had Greenberg, the league's reigning MVP, been there for the duration, he, too, may have turned in an epic season.

Meanwhile, the war spread to Iraq, Syria, Iceland and Estonia. Italy, Romania, Hungary and Finland declared war on the Soviet Union. Hitler invaded Russia. Japan moved its forces into southern Indochina, and the United States tightened its embargo on the Land of the Rising Sun. President Roosevelt froze the American assets of Germany, Italy and Japan. Roosevelt and British Prime Minister Winston Churchill signed the Atlantic Charter, officially declaring their opposition to fascism. And the widespread massacre of Jews began in earnest.

On June 27, government forces in Romania launched the Iasi pogrom, one of the most violent in history, which killed over 13,000 Jews. The Nazi *Einsatzgruppen* (Special Action Groups) put into action Hitler's plan to exterminate Europe's Jews, murdering 7,000 in Lvov, Poland. The ethnic murders continued throughout Poland, Lithuania and the Ukraine. On the last day of July, Nazi Reichsmarschall Hermann Goring authorized the Final Solution.

In August, the United States Congress passed a law that released men over twenty-eight who had been drafted from their military obligation. Hank

---

* Williams would have actually batted .412 by today's standards because he hit six fly balls that were not scored as sacrifice flies but would have been after 1945.

† The streak was actually fifty-seven straight games, if you include the All-Star Game (but no one does). After the Indians stopped DiMaggio's streak on July 17, he hit safely in another sixteen straight games. If it hadn't been for two fine fielding plays by third baseman Ken Keltner, DiMaggio's streak would have been seventy-two games (not counting the All-Star Game).

might request his release in time to rejoin the Tigers for the last month of the season. The press pounced upon him again, lying in wait at the Detroit airport when Hank returned from a weekend in New York. They wanted to know his plans. He was not glad to see them. "I don't care who you are," he brushed off one reporter who introduced himself.

He did apply for his release, but it would not be immediate. There were others ahead of him whose discharges had to be processed first. The newspapers guessed he would be out in January, maybe by Christmas. Hank was not happy with that. He had asked Walter Briggs to expedite his release by filling out a form stating the Tigers' need for his services, which would have sprung him in time to finish the '41 season, but Briggs declined to do so. Perhaps he also thought that Briggs could have intervened to keep him from being drafted in the first place. In late September, after watching Joe Louis defend his heavyweight title against Lou Nova in New York, Hank told the *Washington Times-Herald*'s Vincent X. Flaherty that he would never play ball for the Tigers again. When he did return to baseball, Hank said he wanted to play for the Boston Red Sox, with Jimmie Foxx's pending retirement opening up first base and Fenway Park's short left field wall inviting home runs.

But in November, when Hank rode on a tank through the streets of Detroit as part of the Armistice Day parade, the city's population was happy to see Sergeant Greenberg, and he seemed pleased to see them. All along the route, they called out to him. The thousands of young and old residents lining the streets cheered him as "if he had just hit a game-winning homer." He waved back, smiling.

Shortly before his release, Hank consented to an article in the *Fort Custer News* printed with his name in the form of a letter, Dear Alonzo (Alonzo being the Fort's Ann Landers). In it, he asked for advice in dealing with the press again, whom he despised for the way they had hounded him, misconstrued facts, sensationalized his speeding tickets, etc. He compared them to flies: "You swat at a fly and it comes back to your sweating hand." Hank came off sounding like a whiner, and the newspaper flies were only too happy to point that out.

On December 5, 1941, the Germans abandoned their attack on Moscow, and the United States Army released Hank Greenberg from active duty

at 10:30 a.m. No doubt in a good mood over his emancipation—and probably to appease his critics—Hank indulged the photographers by carrying his
Army locker to the warehouse three times, making his bed twice and repeatedly pretending to draw his final check from the Army (ten dollars back
pay). He shook a few hands, drove back to Detroit in his khaki uniform,
registered at a hotel, changed clothes and spent the evening with friends.
Then he set out for New York to ponder the 1942 baseball season.

He had gotten over his pique with Briggs at least enough to be willing
to return to the Tigers. On the eve of baseball's annual winter meetings, he
was intrigued by talk of Detroit trading Rudy York for a second baseman to
replace Gehringer. That would put Hank back at first base.

He admitted to reporters that the biggest thrill of his honorable dis-
charge was the chance to resume his baseball career. "Now I am able to
become a ballplayer again. Since I've been in the Army there hasn't been a
chance even to think about baseball. All that was either in the past or the
distant future. But now I can go home to New York, wait for spring and
begin training for my old job with the Tigers."

Two days later, the Japanese bombed Pearl Harbor.

————————— ∞ —————————

CHAPTER ELEVEN

War's My Business Now

Everything changed that day. Americans were no longer simply spectators to the War; suddenly, it was game on.

Sunday, December 7, Bob Feller was driving from his family home in Van Meter, Iowa, to negotiate his 1942 contract in Cleveland when he heard the news on the car radio. Feller, like Hank before him, had been the subject of controversy during the 1941 season when he was classified 3-C. His mother had appealed to his local draft board for a deferment because Feller's father was dying of cancer and the pitcher supported the family. The public and press had criticized him for being unpatriotic. His draft board had stated he would face induction before January 1. When Feller heard the radio report about Pearl Harbor, he made up his mind to enlist immediately, which he did that Tuesday.

On December 10 in Chicago, filmed by newsreel cameras and broadcast live over the radio, the twenty-three-year-old Feller raised his right hand, and Lieutenant Commander Gene Tunney, the former world heavyweight boxing champion, swore him into the Navy.

The day Feller enlisted, Hank told reporters in Philadelphia, where he was visiting friends, "I'm going back in. We are in trouble, and there's only one thing to do—return to the service." Rather than wait for the call as a member of the reserves, he went to Washington, D.C., and enlisted in the Army Air Forces. He'd had enough of the infantry. This time, he gave 663 Crotona Park North as his home address. In the blank on his application that asked the length for his tour of duty, he stated, for the "duration."

Hank knew it was going to be a long war and that his decision had probably ended his baseball career. Unlike the twenty-three-year-old Feller, who could afford to miss several seasons and still return to baseball a relatively young man, Hank, three weeks shy of his thirty-first birthday, could not count on coming back. "This doubtless means I am finished with baseball, and it would be silly for me to say I do not leave it without a pang," Hank said. "But all of us are confronted with a terrible task—the defense of our country and the fight of our lives."

Hank had grown up during his first hitch. Until then, baseball had been all he had known since he discovered the game in Crotona Park. His pursuit of excellence on the field had consumed him. In the Army, he had seen the world from a perspective other than that of the privileged life of a professional baseball player. "When I was playing ball, I used to squawk if the hotel mattresses weren't thick enough," he said. "I'm afraid I was a little bit selfish. I got in the more important money pretty rapidly."

A year earlier, Greenberg had reservations about missing the 1941 season. Yet he had answered the call, served his time and could have returned to the Tigers in 1942, at least until he was activated from the reserves. But, after America entered the war, he voluntarily set aside his personal interests to serve the country's greater good. This was different from giving up a big paycheck for a year; he could be sacrificing his career. The move won him widespread admiration, elevated his status from a baseball star to a true American hero and completed his assimilation from immigrant son to complete citizen.

Taylor Spink praised Greenberg in *The Sporting News* for his willingness to protect the ideals of American democracy that had allowed for the son of Romanian immigrants to achieve success. Greenberg had become more than a Hebrew star; he had become a national hero who embodied American ideals. Spink gave credit to Hugh Mulcahy for being the first major league ballplayer drafted while the country was still neutral and to Feller for being the first to enlist after the declaration of war. "But the decision announced last week by Hank Greenberg gave the game and the nation a special thrill," Spink wrote in his editorial. He noted that Hank could have stayed home, said he had already done his bit, but he decided to serve again. "Fans of America, and all baseball, salute him for that decision."

The New York chapter of the Baseball Writers saluted Greenberg with a special award for his "extraordinary service to baseball" at its annual dinner. "Greenberg's prompt reenlistment after Pearl Harbor constitutes a great favor to baseball," Tom Meany explained in his *New York PM* column. "All the pious mouthings of the magnates about building up public morale via baseball fail to fool the public. When the highest-paid ballplayer in America voluntarily joins the armed forces, however, it indicates to the fans that ballplayers are as patriotic as any other profession."

Hank accepted the award graciously, saying he thought Mulcahy deserved similar recognition, then boarded a train for Fort Dix, New Jersey. There, on January 31, he returned to active duty, absent the media circus that had surrounded his first induction. In his routine physical, his flat feet were classified "normal."

A friend of Hank's, Sam Edelman, wrote on his behalf to have Hank promoted to the rank of Captain and assigned as an athletic director in the Air Corps at Bolling Field. Two Brigadier Generals carried the request to the War Department, lobbying for the educational qualifications to be waived for Greenberg. The Adjutant General denied the request on the grounds that it was "contrary to the policies of the Secretary of War." An internal War Department memo noted, "If this commission were granted, it would be a blow to the system of officers training camps. This because of the inevitable publicity that will follow the promotion." Once again, military officials did not want to be accused of showing preferential treatment.

They were, however, quite happy to employ Sergeant Greenberg in their propaganda. Around the country, Americans watched newsreel footage with Hank the leading man in an inspection of female Red Cross ambulance drivers. Enthusiastic voice-over: "The former American League home run champion goes down the lineup." He pauses to adjust one young woman's cap in a gesture more flirtatious than officious. She smiles. "That's the right angle—and the girls pass inspection!" The clip concludes: "Hank takes to his new post with the same spirit that carried him to the top in baseball."

A story circulated Jewish neighborhoods that burnished Hank's legend with its ethnic propaganda: One day a big drunken sergeant is weaving his way among soldiers, saying in a loud voice, "Is there anybody here named Ginsburg or Goldberg? I'll kick the living daylights out of him." A soldier stands up and says, "My name's Greenberg, buddy." The drunk looks him up and down, all six foot four inches and 215 muscular pounds, and replies, "I didn't say Greenberg. I said Ginsberg or Goldberg." Though the incident probably never happened, the story spoke of Hank continuing his mission to transform the way Gentiles regarded Jews even as he served in Uncle Sam's outfit.

Greenberg was assigned to the air corps at MacDill Field in Tampa, Florida. There, he directed the physical training program for the cadets. The ground at the MacDill Base was too sandy for a baseball field, but he worked out daily, running and playing handball—an hour and a half at a time "until I was drenched in sweat and my eyes sank in their sockets." In March, he visited the Tigers in Lakeland, pulled on his No. 5 and practiced with his former teammates. He had been assigned to the Orlando Air Base team for a March 27 game against the Washington Nationals at the request of the Orlando commandant and didn't want to embarrass himself. He hadn't swung a bat since the prison game but knocked three balls over the left-center field fence. He also practiced his base running and fielding. When he left, he took his uniform with him.

Hank played first base in the game at Tinker Field. His former skipper, Bucky Harris, now managing the Nationals, told his pitchers, "They came here to see Hank. Throw him some stuff he can hit."

Harris's pitchers served up some fat pitches, and Hank swatted three hits, but, afterward at dinner with Shirley Povich, one of the sportswriters he counted among his friends, Hank wasn't satisfied. "Hey, you hit the ball pretty good," Shirley said.

"Shit, they're all singles through the infield," Hank said. "That's as hard as I could hit them."

Hank was as fit as he had ever been from the hiking. He had never felt so strong. But, he complained, it was Army muscle, not baseball strength. "To get back to baseball, you have to break these muscle-bound things," he said.

The sportswriters sang his requiem. "Unless the war ends this winter, there is very little chance that Greenberg ever will play league ball again,"

Charles Ward wrote in the *Free Press*. "And there seems less chance that the war will end this winter." Hank was already old. By the time the war finally ended, Ward figured he would be too old to come back. "Greenberg has done many things through sheer determination that other men have found impossible to do. Still it is doubtful if even he could overcome the effects of those years away from the game."

In mid-May, Hank was transferred to the Officers Candidate School of the air corps technical training command in Miami Beach for a twelve-week intensive course. Two months later, Lieutenant Mickey Cochrane, managing a squad of Army-Navy All-Stars requested Hank for his team in an exhibition against the American League All-Stars, who won the Midsummer Classic the previous day. The War Department denied the request—Hank was too busy with his training course to take time out for baseball—and also that for three other players, including Mulcahy.*

After Hank completed his course in Miami Beach the first week of August, he was commissioned a second lieutenant and assigned to the Headquarters Flying Training Command in Fort Worth, Texas. The following week, on a short furlough en route, he dropped in on the Tigers at Briggs Stadium for a workout. The Bengals had suffered without him. His replacement, Ned Harris, batted .271 with nine homers and 45 RBI—vastly inferior to Hank's production—and the team would finish in the second division, thirty games back. He must have felt some longing to see the game going on without him.

In January, Commissioner Landis had asked President Roosevelt if baseball should suspend play in deference to the war effort, the way it had in 1918, but the President had replied famously, "I honestly feel that it would be best for the country to keep baseball going." And so it had without Hank and scores of other players who traded their bats for rifles. In a move deep with symbolism, Hillerich & Bradsby converted its Louisville

---

* Chief Boatswain's Mate Bob Feller lasted only one inning for Cochrane's crew on July 7 in Cleveland, where Joe DiMaggio and Ted Williams powered the AL team to victory. Williams had enlisted as a Navy fighter pilot the month before but was criticized for asking permission to finish the season before reporting to duty. He won the Triple Crown in 1942 with 36 home runs, 137 RBI and a .356 batting average.

bat factory equipment to manufacture more than one million M-1 carbine gun stocks.

Detroit also had adapted to the war. The Tigers' front office, like other major league clubs, set aside ten percent of their salaries to buy war bonds. The clubs also donated receipts from designated games to war-related charities. The Tigers offered a twenty-five-cent war stamp for every foul ball turned in by fans and shipped the balls to troops overseas. As in other cities, Ty Tyson, broadcasting Tiger games on WWJ, and his counterpart on WXYZ, Harry Heilmann, were not allowed to mention weather conditions, even during rainouts, for fear the information could aid enemy bombing raids. The citizens of Detroit participated in blackouts while volunteer air-raid wardens patrolled the streets to make sure all lights were extinguished. Since the day the United States had declared war on Japan, Army guards were stationed at the Ambassador Bridge and the Detroit-Windsor Tunnel, the city's two points of entry from Canada. And "The Star-Spangled Banner," formerly played only on special occasions, became a regular pregame ritual in the major leagues.

The war revitalized the city's economy. In February 1942, Detroit's factories ceased production of passenger cars for commercial sale and converted to the manufacturing of bombers, trucks and other military equipment that transformed the Motor City into the Arsenal of Democracy. Responsible for the bulk of America's war hardware, Detroit became perhaps the most important city in the nation. "Other towns make arms, as other towns make automobiles," a *Forbes* reporter observed in 1942. "But whether we win this war depends in great measure on Detroit."

The federal government pumped $65 million into the manufacture of the Willow Run plant, which began turning out the B-24 Liberator, a four-engine bomber, in May. But the elaborately designed plant—a mile long and a quarter-mile wide, with 100,000 workers manning seventy subassembly lines—never quite lived up to its hyped promise. Walter Briggs benefited, too, supplying the United States armed forces with over a billion dollars' worth of stamped steel and aluminum products, including parts for an amazing new bomber, the B-29 Superfortress. All told, Detroit manufacturing plants were awarded nearly $12 billion in defense contracts during the first two years of the war. That created jobs, which attracted some

350,000 people, many of them Appalachian whites and Southern blacks, to the nation's fourth-largest city.

The influx created volatile racial tensions. Employees at the Packard plant staged a strike to protest the "mixing of white and black workers" on the production floor. On a muggy Sunday evening in June 1943, white sailors skirmished with black youths on the Belle Isle Bridge and outside the Brodhead Naval Armory on Jefferson. Rumors spread through Paradise Valley, a black neighborhood, that whites had thrown a black woman and her baby off the bridge. Other rumors had a black man raping a white woman. Violence erupted downtown. Blacks stoned streetcars and beat white passengers going north on Oakland. Whites stopped streetcars on Woodward and beat blacks. Mobs turned over cars, looted stores and pummeled pedestrians. White police officers stood by while blacks got beaten or beat them themselves. During the riot, police killed seventeen people, all black.

Mayor Edward Jeffries closed bars, and on Monday President Roosevelt sent in 5,000 federal troops who steered the crowds with bayonets. The Tigers canceled their game on Tuesday. They played Wednesday afternoon with 350 helmeted and armed federal troops patrolling the stadium. When order was restored after three days, the dead numbered thirty-four (twenty-five blacks). An estimated 675 people were injured and 1,893 arrested (82 percent of those black).

The three days had once again exposed the ugliness of racial hatred in the city and the systemic failures of addressing it—barely one percent of the city's 3,400-member police force was African-American.

In Fort Worth, Hank was the assistant athletic director, in charge of supervising the base's athletic program. He traveled around the country inspecting training facilities for cadets, bombardiers and gunners. He was promoted to first lieutenant in November and four months later, in light of his "superior" performance, was promoted again to captain. When a reporter asked his thoughts on the upcoming baseball season, Hank said, "I don't have time to follow baseball closely enough to make any predictions. I haven't seen a sports page for a week."

Hank had wanted to be a pilot in the Air Forces, but he was too old.

"I wish that I were young enough to get into our cadet training," he wrote Arnold Edson, a family friend. "That sounds funny, me being only thirty-two and as healthy as anyone in this command. Yet, the age limit is twenty-seven and that's that." He had been taking flying lessons on his own time in the hopes of one day getting his private license and had already logged twenty solo hours.

In 1943, he shared an apartment with the actor William Holden, who had starred in several films, including his breakout role opposite Barbara Stanwyck in *Golden Boy* four years earlier. Holden traveled frequently in his public relations role for the military. Hank returned to their apartment late one night from a two-week trip, not realizing that Holden was there. When he turned the key in the door and flipped on the lights, Hank found Holden sitting in his bed with his revolver trained on the door, ready to pick off an intruder. "Boy, are you lucky," the actor told his roommate. "I was ready to pull the trigger."

Hank's former teammate Birdie Tebbetts passed through Fort Worth that summer for an exhibition game with a service team he managed. Hank enjoyed the chance to catch up with Birdie, Bruce Campbell, a fellow Tiger on the 1940 pennant-winning team, and others he knew from baseball. On an inspection tour out East, he had seen Charlie Gehringer and the two reminisced about "the old days in Detroit." For forty-year-old Charlie, those days were memories, but Hank, thirty-two, still missed the game, and found it uncomfortable to talk about his playing days in the past tense, though it was beginning to look more like that was the case. An article in the Army weekly *Yank* ran that spring under the headline HANK GREENBERG SAYS GOOD-BYE TO BASEBALL with Hank saying, "Another year of this Army life, and I'm resigned to the end of my baseball career."

He did get the chance to play again, if only for a day, in a War Bond game that August. He rejoined Tebbetts and others such as Corporal Enos Slaughter and Lieutenant Johnny Beazley, both formerly of the '42 World Champion Cardinals, on an all-service all-star team that faced players from New York's three teams (Giants, Dodgers and Yankees) at the Polo Grounds. In an old-timers' game beforehand that included Tris Speaker, Honus Wagner, George Sisler, Walter Johnson and Eddie Collins, Babe Ruth thrilled the crowd with a trademark home run into the upper right field stands. Hank started at first base, but he struck out in his first at-bat and was replaced later in the game by Bob Detweiler, a former Brave. The Camp Cumberland All-Stars lost 5–2, but the game was a huge success, with the sellout crowd buying more than $816 million in war bonds for admission. Sergeant Barney Ross, the Jewish ex-boxing champ and one of 300 wounded soldiers on hand, received the largest applause of the day when he limped with the aid of a cane to the microphone and thanked those present "on behalf of my buddies who are here, those who are gone and those who are going."

The war dragged on with battles fought in the Pacific and Atlantic, throughout Europe and in Northern Africa. After sixteen months at Fort Worth, Hank decided he did not want to spend the war inspecting training facilities. He requested duty overseas, closer to the action. On March 1, 1944, Captain Greenberg shipped out to the China-Burma-India theatre with the first group of B-29s employed overseas. Less than three decades since the Wright brothers first mastered thrust and lift, the B-29 Superfortress seemed to defy physics. Ninety-nine feet long, and with a 141-foot wingspan, the Superfortress weighed 120,000 pounds or more when fully loaded and required four 2,200-horsepower engines to become airborne. Once in the air, the Superfortress reached speeds of 350 miles per hour, faster with tailwinds. Most significantly, the B-29 could carry huge bomb loads and travel long distances—able to attack the Japanese islands from points that the B-24 could not. The United States planned to bring down the Japanese on the backs of these planes. After a brief period scouting the area from India, Greenberg's unit set up a base in China's south-central province of Szechuan where they would launch the raids. Hank was the administrative commanding officer of the 58th Bombardment Wing that began bombing the Japanese homeland from the Kwanghan Airfield on June 15.

But all did not go smoothly on that first mission. One B-29 failed to clear the runway and burst into flames. Hank and a chaplain who had just blessed another plane dashed out of the control tower toward the wreck. When they were maybe fifty yards away, the plane's bomb load began exploding and knocked them off their feet. They got up and continued toward the plane. They were surprised to find five crew members alive. The men had managed to climb from the wreckage. While Hank and the chaplain circled the plane to search for other survivors, the plane's bombs began exploding again, followed by its ammunition, pinning them to the ground. When the shelling subsided, they leaped up and ran to safety along with the remaining crew members, who had crawled into a rice paddy beyond the runway. "Some of them were pretty well banged up, but no one was killed," Hank said. He could not hear or talk for several days but was grateful simply to be alive. "That was an occasion, I can assure you, when I didn't wonder whether or not I'd be able to return to baseball."

For Hank, who had never been out of the country, Asia presented its share of culture shock and left him often feeling uncertain. One night when he smoked a cigarette on a street corner in Kunming, hitching a ride back to the base, his imagination ambushed him. "I kept waiting for some Sax Rohmer character to step out and plant a knife in the middle of my back," he later recalled. He noticed one Chinese man studying him intently. Hank puffed nervously on his cigarette. No truck was in sight to take him back to the base. He felt isolated. Frightened. Was this the man ready to plant a knife in him? Hank flicked his cigarette aside. The man quickly grabbed it and left.

When Hank told the story to the *New York Times'* Arthur Daley, he grinned sheepishly. "That's one reason why you can't help but like Hank Greenberg," Daley wrote. "He was a great baseball player, feted and acclaimed, but he still has something of the small boy quality to him, surprised at his success but never quite believing it."

Hank tried his hand at softball with limited success. The tantalizingly slow, arcing pitch bamboozled him at first, frustrating him while entertaining his comrades. He did have a good game at a hospital base in Kunming that summer. When he came to bat, a voice yelled, "Come on, Hank. Hit one into Cherry Street!" Knowing that young man must be from Detroit, Hank wanted to do it for him. "Luckily, I really got hold of one that day and gave it a ride," he said.

He was troubled by bursitis in his right shoulder that spring and summer, receiving two rounds of heat therapy for it. He also suffered an attack of malaria in July that landed him in the hospital for three weeks, though he made a full recovery.

The Kwanghan base had its shortcomings. The remote location made it difficult to supply, particularly with fuel for the planes. All supplies had to be flown in over "The Hump," the eastern part of the Himalayan Mountains. Movies for the staff's entertainment and mail from home were slow to arrive, resulting in what Hank described in a letter to his brother Ben as "a serious morale problem." Hank predicted they would move to a new base in the South Pacific in about four months, but U.S. troops captured Saipan just three weeks later, and the Air Force brass shifted its B-29 base there.

Jack Bell, the *Free Press* war correspondent in India, visited Hank in September. Seated in his office dominated by a large map on the wall, Hank expressed his desire to see more action and his confidence that America would eventually win the war. "We'll have those Japs licked one sweet day," he said. "Nobody over here underestimates them. We know what they can do; but we know what they can't do. They can't build planes and ships as we can, nor can they operate them as well as our boys."

Hank had heard of more troubling things. There was faint talk of the German concentration camps but even louder rumblings of the Japanese atrocities in their P.O.W. camps and their raids. Like so many others during that time, Hank was troubled by man's inhumanity to man, and his faith in organized religion dwindled. He did remain committed to living his life by the dictates of the Ten Commandments.

Hank ended his hitch overseas in India. At a base in Kharapur, he listened to the Armed Forces Radio broadcast of the St. Louis World Series (the Cardinals defeated the Browns four games to two). *You're thirty-three years old*, he thought. *You may never get to play in another one of those.*

Hank returned to the United States on October 28, three days before the first B-29 took off from Saipan for a reconnaissance mission over Tokyo. That month the Superfortresses began their bombing campaign on the Japanese capital. He had been under consideration for promotion to major but that was denied in October, in part because of his request for reassignment from China. He was awarded the Presidential Unit Citation and four bronze battle stars. With the transfer of the B-29s, the Kwanghan Airfield was more or less useless, and he wanted to be closer to the action. But his bout with malaria restricted him from another overseas assignment for six months. Hank was assigned to the Air Technical Service Command's production division based in Manhattan, where he assumed the role of cheerleader. Along with other young officers returned from overseas, he visited war plants that were lagging in production and talked to the workers to boost their motivation. "No, I never talk about baseball," he said. "War's my business now, and so I talk war, stressing the dire need for greater effort."

The production lines, when functioning well, amazed him. "I get such a kick out of seeing all this equipment pouring off the assembly lines," he said. "I'd seen it all before, of course, but I'd never paid any attention to it." His time in the service had opened his eyes to a deeper understanding. It also gave him a broader perspective beyond baseball and his place in the game.

But he had not given up thoughts of returning to baseball, the only profession he had known outside of the military. In fact, he had lain awake many nights during the past three years, tossing and turning on his cot, dreaming of returning to Briggs Stadium and hitting his 250th home run. Of hearing the fans cheer for him again. . . . In early November, he visited friends in Detroit, the first time he had been there in more than a year. The sportswriters, hearing he was in town, sought him out. Although Hank was pushing thirty-four, he was trim and fit. During his service, he had kept his weight steady. Could he play again? He thought he could in the outfield, though admitted it would be a challenge to get his timing back at the plate. "I miss baseball, and maybe that's why I was so happy to get back," he told them. "I think I'll still be of value to the Tigers after the war. I always figured I could play ball until I reached forty."

At the 1944 World Series, baseball insiders had discussed whether or not players returning from duty would be able to play at their former level. The consensus was that those who entered the service under thirty would, but those older wouldn't. Greenberg seemed the exception. Many thought if anyone his age could do it, he could, given how hard he had worked in the past. *Free Press* sports editor Charles Ward, who watched Hank beat a pro squash player in a game at a Detroit gym during his visit, had "no doubt that Hank will be able to make a comeback if the war ends in a year or two. . . . He would need only to sharpen his batting eye to be able to return to his old post."

Hank didn't tell Ward or the other reporters about his physical ailments. In addition to the bursitis in his right shoulder last summer, he had suffered persistent pain in his lower back for the past four years, and it had flared up recently. When he woke in the morning, he felt a sharp pain that subsided into a dull ache throughout the day. He also had occasional pain in his abdomen. The cause was undetermined. He'd had his appendix removed as a child. Military doctors ran tests on his kidneys, but they checked out fine. He might just have to live with the pain. The question was how it might crimp his play if he returned to baseball.

The Tigers, like other teams, had lost a lot of talent to the war. In addition to Greenberg, Birdie Tebbetts, Al Benton, Fred Hutchinson, Ted Gray, Robert Uhl, Roy Clark, Bob Hogue, Harv Riebe, Les Mueller, Bill Hitchcock, Murray Franklin, Lambert Meyer, Walter Evers, John Lipon, Pat Mullin, Barney McCosky, John Mueller, Dick Wakefield, Jimmy Bloodworth, Rip Radcliff, Virgil Trucks, Hal White and Tommy Bridges all wore Uncle Sam's uniform. More than 60 percent of the players from the major leagues' starting lineups on Opening Day 1941 had left baseball for the war effort. The minor leagues had been similarly depleted, leaving a shortage of talent to replace the big leaguers. Some owners, like Sam Breadon of the Browns and Alva Bradley of the Indians, had thought that Major League Baseball would not be able to field teams with adequate talent to complete the 1944 season. They were right and wrong: MLB had completed its season, but the talent was not all adequate. Unimpressed, the fans stayed away *en masse*. One Red Sox–Athletics game at Fenway Park drew only 800 spectators. The teams and fans were desperate for the real players to return.

A large assortment of players classified 4-F—more than a third of all MLB players—had stayed behind. The majority of the Browns' lineup—eighteen players—were deemed somehow physically unfit for military service. Hal Newhouser, the Tigers' young up-and-coming star pitcher, had tried to enlist but was turned away four times because of a faulty heart. Pitcher Dizzy Trout had a hearing impairment, flat feet and poor eyesight. Rudy York's knee injury kept him on first base instead of a military base. A dozen other Tigers kept their jobs for a variety of reasons: heart murmur, ulcers, flat feet, hernia, stomach disorder and age. Despite their ailments, Trout went 27–14 and Newhouser 29–9. Prince Hal, the 1944 AL MVP, led the league in wins and strikeouts (187), and was second in complete games (25), shutouts (6) and ERA (2.22). The Tigers lost the pennant on the last day of the season to the Browns.

In December 1944, War Mobilization Director James F. Byrne asked the Selective Service to begin reexamining professional athletes classified

4-F. Phillies outfielder Ron Northey, who three times previously had been turned away because he couldn't hear in one ear, was deemed fit in January and sent to play baseball at Fort Lewis in Washington State. By the end of 1944, the major leagues had already contributed 470 players to the armed forces. Major League Baseball feared a further depletion of its ranks. It had lost its great defender when Commissioner Landis died in November. Senator Albert B. "Happy" Chandler of Kentucky made a speech defending the 4-Fs playing ball. Not surprisingly, the owners picked the ebullient Chandler to become baseball's new commissioner on April 24, 1945.

The thought of players like Greenberg returning one day raised the question of job availability. Baseball players were about the only tradesmen not protected by the law that said a serviceman must be given his old job back if he applied for it within forty days after being mustered out, though a league rule did provide for him to be paid for at least sixty days at the same rate he was earning when he was inducted. Hank recognized that players weren't the same after missing years to the service, but thought baseball should amend its rules to accommodate them on their return. "Baseball talent's a funny thing," he said. "It runs out on you, whether you're playing or not. I think that the situation is obviously unfair to the returning ballplayer. He should be given the courtesy of being made a free agent, so he can make the best possible deal for himself with some other club."

That wasn't a change the owners were going to make anytime soon. If Greenberg returned, he would have to win back his job with the Tigers.

As much as Hank would have liked to be playing baseball again, he had other priorities at the moment. "The important thing right now—and for some time to come—is the war," he said. "Nothing else matters."

Hank's superiors were pleased with his commitment and performance, which they rated "superior." He seemed ideally suited to head the group of Contractor Employee Morale Officers that visited the war plants. Major A. D. Bowman, chief of the Production Division, wrote in an April memo, "Capt. Greenberg's personal qualifications . . . together with his fine character traits of personal sincerity and attention to duty qualify him peculiarly for his important function." Citing "innumerable letters" of appreciation and commendation from those Hank had visited, Major Bowman asserted, "The success of the Contractor Employee Morale program in the Eastern District thus far has been largely due to the ability and attention Capt.

Greenberg has focused on the program and to his particular qualifications for the assignment."

The quality of play in Major League Baseball seemed destined for further decline in 1945 with elderly and crippled ballplayers populating rosters. Forty-seven-year-old Hod Lisenbee, who hadn't played in nine years, pitched for the Reds, one of many over-the-hill ballplayers. Pete Gray, who'd lost his right arm in a farming accident as a child, played outfield for the Browns. Most of the 4-Fs from 1944 were back, despite War Mobilization Director Byrne's intention of inducting them.

The Tigers had lost outfielder Dick Wakefield to the Navy along with third baseman Pinky Higgins. Pitcher Al Benton returned from the Navy but broke his leg in May. When he came back in July, he was not as effective. Dizzy Trout, troubled by "a misery in his back," also was not as effective as the previous season. General Manager Jack Zeller had traded for shortstop Skeeter Webb in the off-season, whom one writer called a "great shortstop" who couldn't "hit his way out of a paper bag," and shortly after the season began made another deal for outfielder Roy Cullenbine, one of the players Commissioner Landis had set free in 1940. Doc Cramer was forty years old, but played like a young man. Rudy York, still troubled by his knee, was not his old self, but second baseman Eddie Mayo "played better than he knew how." Hal Newhouser was on pace for another MVP season. Somehow, the team held together and on June 8 slipped into first place.

Meanwhile, on April 28, Italian partisans hanged Benito Mussolini. Two days later, Adolf Hitler, hidden in his bunker, shoved a pistol in his mouth and pulled the trigger. On May 7, German troops surrendered to the Allies. With the war in Europe over, the Armed Services no longer needed all of its officers. The Army Air Forces placed Capt. Greenberg on the inactive list, and on June 14, 1945, he walked out of Fort Dix willing—if not ready—to return to the Tigers, who held a slim half-game lead over the Yankees.* He ordered a dozen bats and billed the club.

Hillerich & Bradsby's invoice for the bats confirmed that Greenberg

---

* Interesting to note that in his exit physical, the examining physician once again diagnosed second degree *pes planus*, though noted his flat feet were "nonsymptomatic, nondisabling, no eversion, strong to test." No one seemed to notice.

intended to return to the Tigers. Jack Zeller could hardly contain his enthusiasm. "We haven't had such good news since VE Day," the general manager said.

Steve O'Neill, who had replaced Del Baker as Detroit's manager in 1943, expressed confidence in Greenberg's return. "Hank is a tremendously hard worker and one of the most aggressive and conscientious players I've ever seen," he said. "As you know, he's thirty-four now, but he'll be back in shape in a very short time. With Hank back, he'll take a lot of pressure off of Rudy York."

But Hank knew it wouldn't be easy. He had been away a long time. He had served forty-seven months, longer than any other regular major leaguer not named Hugh Mulcahy. He had not played a major league game since May 6, 1941, more than four years ago. The world had changed since then, and so had he. Much as he wanted to play again, he was not certain he could.

CHAPTER TWELVE

Playing from Memory

After visiting his parents and family in New York, Hank boarded a flight for Detroit the afternoon of June 20, unsure of what awaited him. He did not want to step back into the controversy that had surrounded his induction, yet here he was returning to baseball and a $10,000 monthly salary while many Americans had sons and husbands and brothers still fighting the war in the Pacific. He had wanted to slip back into town quietly, but word of his arrival leaked, and when Hank stepped off the plane at the Detroit airfield, he was surprised to see the group of reporters and fans there to greet him. When he checked into the Leland Hotel, bellhops, telephone girls, lobby sitters and friends welcomed him back. He invited the reporters up to his room, showed them he was in shape—the suit from 1941 he wore still fit him—and said, "It's hard for me to visualize I'm going to play baseball again."

The reporters followed him to the ballpark the next day. No one had come back after an absence as long as Greenberg's. Players like Hank Gowdy, Ty Cobb and Grover Alexander returning from the previous war, which was not nearly as long, had been able to pick up pretty much where they had left off. But Hank had been away from baseball four years, one month, two weeks, one day and counting. The skeptics doubted that Hank would be able to adjust to big league pitching, the years away having dimmed his batting eye and ruined his timing. Age also worked against him. At thirty-four, he had passed his prime, and the conventional wisdom of the day was that athletic skills began to erode at thirty, the time when he had left the game. "Their reflexes, so 'tis said, as well as their arms and legs, have passed their peak," sportswriter Frank Wilgus wrote. "In a game where so much depends on timing, it isn't easy to regain the touch after a prolonged layoff."

On the other hand, Hank had three factors in his favor. For starters, he wouldn't have to face Bob Feller, Sid Hudson and Early Wynn—the war had thinned the ranks of quality pitchers, and while some, like Newhouser, had never left and others had started to return, the level of competition had not resumed its prewar standard. Also, Hank had stayed fit, even if it was Army fitness and not baseball shape. Perhaps more than anything, his "native determination to excel," as the *Detroit News* termed it, which made him the hardest-working player in baseball and had played such a large role in his prewar success, could be the deciding factor in making his comeback possible. "He has that tenacity of purpose, a burning desire to make good at every task to which he might be assigned," Associated Press writer Whitney Martin pointed out.

Hank showed up early on June 21, donned his old No. 5 (which rookie pitcher Bill Pierce had been wearing but gladly returned) and stepped to the plate for a special batting practice session before that afternoon's game. "Ready, Hank?" manager Steve O'Neill called from the mound.

Hank nodded. The photographers dug in. The sportswriters focused. His teammates watched. O'Neill tossed.

Hank slammed the first pitch back up the box.

He crushed the second pitch to left field, only inches shy of clearing the tall screen into the bleachers. "How about that!" said Eddie Mayo, one of Hank's new teammates, in the dugout. "That guy is ready to get in there right now. He really can swing."

Hank took a few more cuts, sending another long drive to left, then trotted around the bases, caught some flies in the outfield and fielded some balls at first base. He had no plans to play the game, but as three o'clock approached, the cries of "We want Greenberg" grew so loud that Hank climbed on top of the dugout to greet the fans. A swell of youths pressed toward him. They thrust out their hands to shake his or just to be able to touch him, old Hankus Pankus, returned from the war to redeem their team, to bring another pennant to Detroit, something they hadn't seen since his last full season, five years earlier.

O'Neill, with his team already in first place, liked the boost Hank gave the Bengals. The skipper figured even a faded Greenberg was better than most of the players currently in the league. Zeller agreed. "If he hits anywhere near his old clip, we're the club to beat for the flag," the general manager said.

Greenberg back in Detroit meant more green to Walter Briggs. He knew the draw Hank would be at home and on the road, not to mention the additional revenue he could bring the club if he helped it win another pennant. Having saved what he would have paid Greenberg the past four years, Briggs was pleased to start signing checks for him again, knowing how the investment would pay off.

Hank was happy to be back on the field. For starters, the war had cost him a fortune. He had lost well over $200,000 in salary the past four seasons. When he left, he had placed his father in charge of his investments. David Greenberg had bought war bonds, which were worth about the same amount when Hank came out as when he went in. He had some other unfinished business. Even though he had hit two home runs in his last game at Briggs Stadium, he was still one shy of 250. He wanted to get there—and beyond. He also stood at 1,299 career hits. He liked the idea of getting to 1,500. Even more than his personal finances and milestones, he wanted to find his place again in baseball, this game he loved. He figured he could be ready in two weeks or so, if he worked hard.

When the team left the next day on a road trip, Hank stayed behind. The Tigers hired Bill Crouch, a Detroit high school teacher who had pitched three years in the National League, as Hank's personal batting practice pitcher. They also hired a young boy to collect the balls Hank hit over the left field fence. Greenberg spent long hours that weekend swinging, fielding and throwing. The sweat soaked his shirt. Blisters swelled on his hands. He wrapped them in athletic tape and kept swinging. The skin peeled off his palms.

He wished he had the luxury of spring training to get himself baseball-ready. Those eight weeks under the Florida sun improved his precision timing by 50 percent, he believed. They also fine-tuned his ears to the sound of the bat meeting the ball, an aid in the field. Having missed that chance, he had to cram his preparation into the middle of the season. "I hope most of the boys will start their comebacks in spring training," he said. "It's tough this way."

Some pitchers like New York's Red Ruffing and Hank's teammate Al Benton had already come back after a hitch in the service, but many baseball insiders, including Hank, thought it was easier for the pitchers to find their old groove than the hitters. "Somehow you don't lose the knack of pitching," he said. "You are stationary on the slab and the ball does start from a dead rest, but the hitter faces a moving target that whistles up at him, high, low, inside and out with varying speeds from a white bullet that sizzles to a tantalizing balloon. If you are a photographer handling fast lenses, you will get an idea of what I mean when I say that if you are just 1/100th of a second off in your precision timing of eyes, wrists, arms, shoulders and legs, the job is ruined."

After ten days, Hank did not feel like his former self. He had strained his arm, and his legs had no spring. He was not certain he had his timing back, but there was only one way to find out. He planned to play in the Tigers' doubleheader on July 1.

The date had been eagerly anticipated. Hillerich & Bradsby ran an advertisement with a reprint of Hank's telegram from June 18 ordering a dozen bats and the text: "There is joy in Detroit today—and everywhere for that matter—because mighty Hank is home from the wars!" The J.L. Hudson Company welcomed him back with an ad which praised Hank's "indomitable will to succeed" that helped him rise in the ranks from private to captain. "All Detroit is Rooting for You and the Tigers—Hit 'em, Hank!"

Hank's return was more than an aging ballplayer's personal quest to regain his former job. It transcended the fans' interest in one of the game's great players, the AL's MVP in his last full season. Hank's comeback was steeped in symbolic significance.

Soon as Hank returned to Detroit, a front page *Detroit Jewish Chronicle* headline read, "Greenberg Lifts Pennant Hopes." That's what Greenberg gave the Jews—hope—a commodity in short supply that past decade. If he could succeed again, prove to be the star he had been, he could once again raise their spirits and rekindle that beacon of hope that Hitler had nearly extinguished.

To all Americans, he represented another sort of hope. They had coped with more than lousy baseball the past few years; they had endured gas rationing, abstained from eating meat, worked extra hours and buried loved ones who had paid the ultimate price of war. Now, they turned to the national pastime for healing. If the players could return, they could restore the game to its previous dignity and glory, and, in so doing, restore a sense of normalcy to the nation, something Americans desperately craved. Hank was the test case.

Those servicemen who once earned their living playing ball looked to Hank to see if they, too, might be able to play again and return to gainful employment. In the days leading to his return, the Associated Press' Whitney Martin had written: "He will be watched as a symbol of hope to all the other ballplayers in the service who fear their absence from the game might impair their effectiveness and money-earning capacity."

The feeling was that if Hank, with his skills, fitness and work ethic, couldn't do it, then nobody could. "We'll all have the answer pretty soon," said Al Simmons, Hank's onetime teammate. The future Hall of Famer had tried making a comeback himself at forty-one after sitting out the 1942 season but abandoned the attempt after forty games. "Hank Greenberg is coming back. If he can't make it, all the rest of them better cash in their GI pay and open a poolroom somewhere."

The other returning players would not have it as tough as Hank, though. He was older and had been gone longer than most. Only about twenty-five of the approximately 500 big leaguers who served spent more than three years away from the game. What's more, while DiMaggio powered the Santa Ana Army Air Base nine, Johnny Mize played the Pacific Islands circuit and Enos Slaughter starred for the 509th Squadron San Antonio base team, Hank had hardly swung a bat since hitting his two homers on May 6, 1941. He had played only a few times: at the Michigan prison, during the spring training exhibition in Orlando, in the War Bond game at the Polo Grounds, plus a handful of softball games in China. Many other ballplayers kept their skills tuned while in the service; not Hank.

With so much riding on his return, all eyes focused on Hank Greenberg July 1, 1945. On that day, Allied troops moved into Berlin, and Greenberg returned to the Tiger lineup. Newspapers from places without MLB teams such as Memphis, Asbury Park, Flint, even Windsor, Ontario, covered his return. The largest and most popular magazines of the day, *Life*, *Time*, *Newsweek*, etc., were there. Newsreel cameras whirled. Everyone awaited the sequel to VE Day.

The largest crowd of the year so far turned out at Briggs Stadium to see Hank's return in the Sunday doubleheader against Connie Mack's Philadelphia Athletics. The 48,811 faithful—which included more than 1,000 servicemen granted free admission—cheered Hank heartily each time he came to bat as the Tigers' cleanup hitter. His hands still blistered, he was determined to do well for them. In his first three at-bats, he flied out twice to the right fielder Hal Peck and popped up to the catcher. His timing had been a bit off, slow in getting his 36-ounce Louisville Slugger around on pitches, but his eye had been good, taking three balls in two of his first at-bats. He walked on four straight pitches in his fourth at-bat in the seventh inning. The home plate umpire, Bill Summers, remarked after the game that he found Hank's ability to pick out the good pitches "nothing short of amazing."

In Hank's absence, Rudy York's "bat has been mute much of the time in the last four years," Harry Salsinger wrote. Hank's presence in the lineup had been expected to give York, batting two spots behind him, a boost. It did just that. York drove in the Tigers' first run with a single. His next time up, after Hank had walked and Doc Cramer singled, York blasted a three-run homer.

With York playing first, Hank was back in left field. Before the game, Connie Mack had shaken Greenberg's hand and wished him luck. Hank asked him for a favor.

"What can I do for you?" Mack asked.

"When your team is at bat, would you mind waving your scorecard to me in left field and direct me where to play for your hitters?" Hank said. "I've never seen any of them before, and it's going to be tough playing position for them."

Mack made no promise, but it turned out he didn't need to. Hank had only one fielding chance, a long fly in the top of the eighth inning that he pulled down in front of the left field fence. But it hurt getting to the ball. In the seventh, Hank had pulled his left hamstring running from first to third on Cramer's single.

Hank borrowed Cramer's 34-ounce bat in the Tigers' half of the eighth.

He hoped the lighter bat would help him get around better on the ball. Once again, the fans cheered him when he stepped to the plate.

Across the state of Michigan, down into Ohio and Indiana, and up into Canada—as far as the WXYZ radio signal carried, baseball fans listened to Harry Heilmann's call of the game. Hank faced Charlie Gassaway, a twenty-six-year-old wartime replacement pitcher. Heilmann let his listeners know that Greenberg watched three straight balls from the lefty Gassaway, then took the fourth pitch for a called strike. On Gassaway's next pitch, Hank whipped around Cramer's 34-ounce bat and got all of it. The fans rose at the familiar crack. "Trouble," Heilmann called. "Trouble!"

The ball landed in the left field pavilion, 370 feet away. The crowd's cheers shook the steel girders of Briggs Stadium, rippled across the field and rumbled down Michigan Avenue. The standing ovation continued while Hank rounded the bases. Harry Heilmann didn't need to say anything more. He dangled the microphone by its cord outside the press box.

"Listen," he finally said quietly, "to the voice of baseball."

Victory had come at a price. Hank had wanted to play both games, but when the second started, he was in the trainer's room, soaking his sore left leg in a whirlpool. His arm had also locked on him several times that afternoon. Yet being back still tasted sweet. The bat had felt so right in his blistered hands when he connected with the ball, and the fans' applause had engulfed him on his trip around the bases. Cramer had shaken his hand when he crossed home plate, "Nice goin', Hank!" His teammates had slapped his back in the dugout. He had dreamed about a moment like this. It delivered a thrill better than any baseball had given him to that point.

With the second game tied at 3–3 after the third inning, Hank put on a dry uniform and returned to the dugout in case O'Neill called on him to pinch-hit. But the Tigers' manager didn't need Hank in Detroit's 5–3 win. The two victories, combined with the Yankees' two losses that day, gave the Tigers a three-and-a-half-game lead, the largest held by an American League club that season. But this was not the same team Hank had left. Only four players—York, Benton, Newhouser and Trout—remained from the crew Hank had played with at the beginning of 1941. The 1945 team was like a late edition. With the exception of the "youthful" Bob Maier at third base, who wouldn't turn thirty until September, the entire starting lineup was over thirty years old. Greenberg in left put the average age of the starting eight position players at thirty-three. With half of the pitching corps over thirty, the Tigers earned their nickname, "Nine Old Men." Doc Cramer, the starting center fielder, turned forty in July, but he wasn't the oldest player on the team. That distinction belonged to backup outfielder Chuck Hostetler, who turned forty-two in September.

The thirty-four-year-old Greenberg had certainly shown in his first game he would help the team's pennant chances if he could stay healthy, but the question remained whether this aged bunch had the stamina to hang onto its lead through the dog days of August and down the home stretch of September.

Hank's body ached but he continued to contribute. On Independence Day, Captain Greenberg had the hometown feeling patriotic when he homered off of another veteran, Red Sox pitcher Boo Ferris. He sat the second game of the doubleheader and the next day to rest his blistered hands and sore legs, but came off the bench in the ninth inning July 5 to hit a two-out single in the rain that drove in the winning run. He was back in the lineup for another doubleheader on Sunday, July 8, against the Yankees. This time, 56,164 fans jammed Briggs Stadium. Hank homered in the first game, doubled and drove in a run in the second game, but had to come out in the fifth inning because his legs hurt. Marching in the Army had not required the quick starts needed in the outfield and on the base paths. Those had given him charley horses in both legs. His tender hands had swollen like a catcher's mitt. "I was all adhesive tape and drugstore smells for a month," he said.

Despite his ailments, he had clubbed three homers in 21 at-bats, compared to York's six in seventy-two games; he was batting .286, second only to Eddie Mayo's .287. Even in the games he couldn't play, he worked out beforehand, stretching on the outfield grass, doing push-ups and leg exercises and shagging fly balls. And the Tigers were drawing record crowds. At least to Walter Briggs's way of thinking, Greenberg was earning his wages as baseball's highest-paid player.

Colonel J. Monroe Johnson, who headed the Office of Defense Transportation, had summoned American League President Will Harridge and

National League President Ford Frick to Washington shortly after the 1945 season began—and before Happy Chandler had been named commissioner—to see what could be done to reduce transportation costs in baseball. The teams had already eliminated trips south for spring training. As their part in the war effort, the league chiefs agreed to cancel the All-Star Game scheduled for July 10, 1945, at Fenway Park. It was the first time since 1933 that the Midsummer Classic was not played.

After the non-All-Star break, the Tigers headed East on a road trip. Detroit fans had welcomed Hank back warmly, but he wasn't sure what to expect in other cities. "There was still a chance of hostile sentiment among those with sons at the front or otherwise bound to Army and Navy orders," the *Detroit News* noted. "Emphasis on Greenberg's salary check exposed him to critical fire that might have been smoldering."

But when the public address announcer at Fenway, the Tigers' first stop, announced, "Greenberg, left field," the Boston crowd applauded. They cheered even louder on his first trip to the plate. That reception continued in New York and Washington, where newspapers in each city carried sympathetic features about his return. Everywhere he went, it seemed, people wished him well, from a traffic cop on the street to a widow in the lobby of his Washington hotel.

In Philadelphia, Hank sat out the first game because of a pulled muscle in his leg, though he did walk in a late pinch-hitting appearance. O'Neill, who had been nothing but supportive and encouraging of Hank, wasn't sure if he would put him in the lineup the following day. Connie Mack, the Athletics' manager and owner, appealed to O'Neill to announce on Saturday that Hank would play in the Sunday doubleheader to boost attendance. O'Neill consented, and nearly 30,000 showed up to welcome Greenberg back. "A roar of applause hailed Greenberg's first turn at the plate," the *Detroit News* reported. While the fighting continued in the Pacific and the United States tested the first atom bomb in the New Mexico desert, fans everywhere embraced Greenberg as a returning hero.

But his legs hurt when he ran, which slowed him down, so he sat out the second game. He had not spent time trying to get his legs back into shape; mostly, he had focused on batting and throwing. He had paid the price, with the blisters and a sore arm, for what he had done. And he was paying the price for what he hadn't with the pulled muscles and cramps. "I believe I drove myself too hard trying to get in shape in a hurry," he said.

His body's failings frustrated him. In Washington, he had hit a couple of balls that would have been doubles or triples before the war, but he was barely able to leg them out for singles. His running had become more plodding. It seemed to take him forever to get out of the batter's box—he lowered his head, bent over and churned his legs to get into gear. That cost him hits. In the outfield, the sore legs reduced his range from little to less. His arm stiffened up—he wasn't able to straighten it and had difficulty making routine throws, let alone long ones. He had to sit out games to nurse his pains. He grew discouraged and thought he was not helping himself or the team.

He considered quitting. Spike Briggs, the owner's son, team vice president and one of Hank's biggest supporters, talked him into sticking with the team.

Manager Steve O'Neill remained patient. His support motivated Hank and the other players. "There was no man on the club who didn't want to win for Steve—a man who never second-guessed a ballplayer and always understood," Hank said.

Hank continued his extra workouts and lucky local kids shagged the balls he hit. One day that summer, the Tigers had invited a fifteen-year-old prospect from Cooley High to work out early, and the kid was on the field when Greenberg showed up for his batting practice. The kid, a huge Tiger fan, was more excited at this chance than for his tryout. But Greenberg, despite his big swing, only hit the ball to the shallow outfield. The kid from Cooley High felt a twinge of disappointment—*this* is Homer Hank? After awhile, Greenberg's hits landed closer to the outfield fence. Then, suddenly, he was blasting the ball into the bleachers and upper deck. The kid wondered, *What's going on here?* Only later, he found out that Hank had started soaking balls in water to hit at the beginning, the heavy balls functioning much like a weighted bat in his warm-up. He then switched to dead balls and finally hit regular balls—those that ended up in the stands.

Incidentally, when the kid graduated from Cooley High two years later, the Tigers offered him $5,000 to sign. He said, "Make it $10,000 or I'm joining the Marines." After four years of Semper Fi, he accepted the Tigers' $5,000, played three years in the organization but never made it back to Briggs Stadium as a player. Instead, he bought the team. His name: Mike Ilitch.

By August, Hank's timing seemed to be coming back. Two days after a U.S. B-29 dropped the first atomic bomb on Hiroshima, Hank collected three hits, including two doubles, in the first game of a twin bill at Briggs Stadium against the Red Sox. That started a fifteen-game hitting streak.

The second game was tied in the tenth inning when Hank batted. He faced Boston's Jim Wilson, a rookie right-hander with a promising future. Wilson delivered, and Greenberg lined a shot back at him. The young pitcher had no time to duck. The ball struck him on the right temple and knocked him to the ground with a fractured skull. Hank was mortified.

Police officers carried the unconscious Wilson off the field on a stretcher, and medics took him to Henry Ford Hospital, where doctors performed surgery to save the injured pitcher. Hank kept vigil outside. "Greenberg wouldn't leave the hospital until he knew that Wilson came out of the operating room alive," Hank's teammate Bob Maier recalled.

On Tuesday evening, August 14, President Harry Truman announced to the nation that Japan had surrendered. The war was over. In downtown Detroit, the bells rang in the Old Mariners' Church on East Jefferson. People spilled into the streets. In the Dexter section, a band played along the boulevard. In Cadillac Square, strangers embraced and kissed. Relief and joy mingled late into the summer night.

The Senators came to town for a four-game series that they won 3–1 to trim the Tigers' lead to a game and a half over Washington. Hank's fifteen-game hitting streak ended on August 20 when he failed to get a hit in both ends of a doubleheader, but the next day, when it was "raining so hard you could hardly see the players through that liquid gray curtain," he doubled in the ninth to drive in the tying run and set up the win. The day after that, he smashed a home run into the left field upper deck at Briggs Stadium and drove in two runs in the Tigers' 4–1 win. Hank had raised his average to .333, but the Senators had trimmed Detroit's lead to half a game by winning both games of a doubleheader.

As summer wore on and the war ended, more players—such as Charlie Keller, Red Ruffing, Spud Chandler, Sam Chapman, Buddy Lewis, Hugh

Mulcahy, Luke Appling, Dutch Meyer—returned to the major leagues. The most unusual was Bert Shepard, a left-handed minor league pitcher prior to the war who lost his right leg after his fighter plane was shot down in Germany. Shepard pitched five and a third innings of relief for the Washington Senators on August 4, 1945, allowing only three hits and one run—the first and only leg amputee to pitch in an MLB game. The return of Cleveland pitcher Bob Feller captured almost as much interest as Greenberg's. Feller, the biggest star to be discharged since Greenberg, was scheduled to pitch his first major league game after almost four years in the Navy on August 24 at Municipal Stadium against the Tigers.

Feller dueled Hal Newhouser. Since joining his hometown club as a fresh-faced eighteen-year-old in 1939, Newhouser, a hard-throwing left-hander, had struggled with his control, but he found his stride during the war years. In 1944, he won 29 games, most in the majors, lost only nine, posted a 2.22 ERA, pitched 25 complete games and led the majors in strikeouts (187). But the skeptics claimed his success resulted from inferior competition. Prior to 1944, Newhouser had never won more than nine games in a season, and had never won more games than he had lost. Newhouser had also gained a reputation for his temper, often as out of control as his pitching. After the manager yanked him, he once shattered a case of Coca-Cola bottles, one by one against the clubhouse wall. Other times, he picked up a bat in the dugout and smashed the lightbulbs on the way to his locker. In light of these tantrums, Dan Daniel dubbed him "Hurricane Hal." But Newhouser had picked up a new pitch, a slider, and, most significantly, improved his control, both of his emotions and his pitches. He had become a pitcher, able to mix his dazzling speed with a sharp curve and change of pace that baffled batters. So, to many, it was not surprising that Prince Hal was having another terrific year—he had won his twentieth game in his previous start.

Feller's teammates gave him a Jeep and his wife a fur coat in a special ceremony before the Friday night game. The stadium was packed with 46,477 fans delighted to see Chief Specialist Feller back with the Tribe, but one person not happy to see him was Hank Greenberg. "He couldn't hit me with an ironing board," Feller said.

The crowd had also cheered heartily for Greenberg, but when he faced

Feller in the first inning with two outs and a man on third, Rapid Robert struck him out. The night game played under the lights, a novelty for Greenberg, made Feller seem even faster. He fanned every starter in the Tiger lineup except catcher Paul Richards, twelve strikeouts total, including Hank twice, and gave up only four hits (none to Hank). In the showdown of the two pitching stars, the best of the prewar era versus the best of wartime baseball, Newhouser pitched well, but not as well as Feller, and lost 4–2. The Tigers clung to a meager half-game lead over the Senators.

Detroit had cheered the end of the war along with the rest of America, but there was no happily-ever-after ending for the Jews. News of Hitler's gas chambers and ovens brought heartbreak and outrage. Pogroms persisted in Poland, where 128 Jews were killed in Lodz during July. And after a brief hiatus when patriotism subdued ethnic division, anti-Semitism resumed in America. Hank heard it in taunts from the stands of "hebe" and "kike." Max Lapides, the boy with the broken leg whom Hank had visited a decade ago, had grown up to attend college. At one game, Max and his father listened to a fan behind them ride Greenberg with nasty ethnic slurs. When Hank homered, Max's father, in a moment completely uncharacteristic of him but no doubt feeling emboldened by Greenberg, stood on his seat, pointed at the bigot behind them and shouted, "You, asshole, you!"

The night of Tuesday, September 4, a group of gentile teenage boys harassed some Jewish boys on Dexter Avenue in Detroit's largest Jewish neighborhood until passersby drove away the bullies. The following night, the bullies returned with reinforcements from the St. Cecilia and Nardin Park gangs, twenty-five to thirty strong, looking for a fight. They beat up several Jewish boys before being chased off by a group of young Jewish men from the Bowl-O-Drome that heard what was happening. The next night, Thursday, September 6, a massive group of approximately 500 Jewish young men turned out along Dexter Avenue to protect their neighborhood. Many of them wanted to seek revenge on the bullies in their own neighborhood, but the others talked them out of it. The police moved in to keep the peace but at least one officer was "said to have made derogatory remarks against Jews," the *Detroit Jewish Chronicle* reported. Rosh Hashanah started at sundown the following evening. The Detroit chief of police dispatched extra officers to guard the city's temples and synagogues. The show of force dissuaded the thugs from returning, but in the wake of the recent atrocities in Europe, the violence put Detroit's Jewish population on edge.

The Tigers were in New York at the time. On September 5, Hank smashed a two-out, 425-foot home run in the ninth inning to help his team beat the Yankees. It was the longest homer hit in Yankee Stadium all season. On Rosh Hashanah, he went three-for-five, scored two runs, drove in five and hit his eleventh home run. But the next day in Boston, he slid into second base and came up lame with a sprained ankle, which swelled up and hurt badly. He missed seven games. When the Tigers went to Washington for a critical five-game series, his ankle was still too swollen for him to be in the lineup. It frustrated him that just when he had started to really contribute, he could no longer help the team. He pinch-hit three times, driving in a run with a double in one appearance, but the Tigers still lost the game. With the Tigers in a tight pennant race, he seemed willing to pinch-hit on Yom Kippur, but rain canceled the game and spared him the decision. The Tigers left Washington clinging to a one-and-a-half-game lead with seven games to play.

Hank returned to the lineup on September 19 in Cleveland, but his ankle still hampered him in the outfield. It further reduced his range and made it difficult for him to set properly to throw. Runners advanced easily on him. He became a liability in the field. Meanwhile, Jim Outlaw had played well as Hank's replacement. Maybe the Tigers didn't need him the way they once had.

That month, rumor had it that Greenberg would retire when the season ended. His body had given him too much trouble. "The Tiger outfielder has not come back as strongly as he expected, and he is toying with the thought of retiring," *The Sporting News* reported on September 13, 1945. "'Baseball, before I joined the Army,' he confided to a friend, 'used to be fun, and now it's work. How those legs ache. I have to force myself all the time.'"

No doubt Hank did think about retiring. The game had become a labor, and it had become clear he was no longer the player he had been before his long furlough in the Army. But there was a twist. *The Sporting News* also reported, "Wedding bells will ring for Hank Greenberg at the end of the season or after the World Series."

Those rumors had circulated before, of course, but this time there was truth to the story that Hank had become seriously involved with a woman.

Caral Gimbel Lasker was the daughter of Bernard Gimbel, chairman of the Gimbel Brothers and Saks Fifth Avenue department stores and the "top merchant in America." A painter of some talent, Caral had dropped out of high school to study art in Paris during the early 1930s and mingled with the great painters living there at the time. "One of society's most brilliant equestriennes," Caral had competed in hunting and jumping events with her mother and twin sister, winning over 500 ribbons since she started riding as a six-year-old.

Hank had met Caral one Sunday afternoon at the Chieftains, her parents' estate in Greenwich. Bernie, a huge sports fan, invited Greenberg to his house in November 1944 after Hank had returned from China. They had lunch with their mutual friend, Louis Marx, a toy manufacturer for Gimbels, and Caral, who happened to be visiting that day. Caral was not a baseball fan, had never heard of Greenberg, but was impressed by his size and good looks. "I thought he was the most gorgeous, handsome, virile man I had ever met, and he had a divine sense of humor," she said later. He saw in her a strong-willed, athletic, cultured and beautiful brunette heiress who was not bashful about her attraction. "She was giving me the old charm," he wrote. She also gave him her phone number. Not long after, he called to invite her to dinner.

They dated that winter and into the baseball season, though they tried to stay out of the public eye because of a small complication: She was still married to Edward Lasker, the son of Albert D. Lasker, once the U.S. Shipping Board chairman. Their nuptials in 1935 had been "one of the most lavish weddings in society." But it hadn't been much of a marriage. Lieutenant Commander Lasker had spent much of it on naval assignment overseas. Caral had married him at twenty even though she didn't love him. "Ed Lasker was crazy about her," said Hope Solinger, Caral's twin sister. "He finally wore her down. I don't know why she married him. I guess she just gave up on saying, 'No.' It was doomed from the beginning." Now Caral thought she had discovered true love with this handsome, virile man. He felt the same about this beautiful, spirited woman.

Hank did not believe Caral would reconcile with her husband, but he had a baseball season to finish before he could talk marriage. The Senators had finished their season a week early—with a win on September 23 to put them at 87–67, only a game behind the Tigers—so Clark Griffith could rent out the stadium to the Redskins football team. The 87–65 Tigers arrived in St. Louis for their final two games needing one victory to claim the pennant.

Rain, which had been falling steadily for nine days in the Midwest, washed out Saturday's game, making Sunday a doubleheader on the final day of the season, September 30. More rain delayed Sunday's start. The ground crew did its best to mop up the water, but the infield dirt was the consistency of grits. With the thermometer at fifty-seven degrees, fog shrouded Sportsman's Park. A mist continued to fall, but the American League didn't want its pennant decided by default—wartime rules stipulated that the final games would not be played if they were rained out, which would make the Tigers the "Umbrella Champions"—so, after nearly an hour delay, the plate umpire, Charley Berry, finally called, "Play ball!"

Hank had his own reasons for taking the field. He wanted the chance to stick it to the Senators. "I hated Washington," he wrote. "They had played a lot of dirty tricks on me over the years, like Jake Powell running into me for no reason at all and breaking my wrist, and that catcher telling Jimmie Foxx the pitches so he could tie me for the league home run title in 1935. And Joe Kuhel, the former White Sox player with whom I once had a fight, was now the Senators' first baseman." Beating St. Louis to take the pennant outright from Washington would be sweet revenge.

Virgil "Fire" Trucks, discharged from the Navy only two days earlier, started for the Tigers against the Browns' Nelson Potter, a screwball pitcher who had shut out the Tigers in Detroit the last time he faced them. Trucks gave up a run in the first, then settled down while the Tigers took a 2–1 lead, but Trucks got into trouble again in the sixth, loading the bases. O'Neill brought in Newhouser, who pitched out of the jam but gave up the tying run in the seventh. The Tigers threatened to take the lead in the top of the eighth. Hank had singled and made it to second with only one out. When Rudy York hit a ground ball, Hank ran to third and took a big turn, perhaps thinking he could score the go-ahead run. But the Browns' second baseman, who had made the force at second, fired to third and trapped Hank off the bag for the third out to kill the rally.

Greenberg the goat. When the Browns' one-armed outfielder Pete Gray scored in the bottom of the eighth to go ahead 3–2, Hank feared that's how he would be remembered for his comeback. *Greenberg? Yeah, he's the guy who blew it when we had the chance to beat the Browns to win the pennant in '45. Got caught off third. Choked in the clutch. Again. The bum.*

Back in the dugout for the top of the ninth, Hank grabbed his Louisville Slugger and sat down next to two rookies, John McHale and Ed Mierkowicz. Greenberg had noticed that Potter stopped his windup at the top of his cap when he threw his screwball but took his hands all the way to the back of his neck for his fastball. "If I get a chance in this inning, I think I've got this pitcher figured out," he told the pair of rookies.

The Tigers would need a rally to get Hank back to the plate. Hub Walker, another one of the team's old men at thirty-nine, led off, pinch-hitting for Newhouser in the number nine spot. He singled. Skeeter Webb bunted Walker to second and wound up safe on first. Eddie Mayo moved the runners to second and third with a sacrifice bunt. Doc Cramer batted while Hank moved to the on-deck circle. He rubbed his bat with a hunk of bone, eager for a chance to redeem himself for his base-running gaffe the previous inning. The Browns decided to walk Cramer to pitch to Greenberg, thinking they might be able to eliminate the slow-footed slugger with a double play. They figured Potter's screwball, which broke in on right-handed batters like Hank, would be more effective against him than against the left-handed Cramer. That was not a move many teams made before Hank joined the Army: walking a forty-year-old with a .275 batting average to get to Greenberg with the bases loaded in the ninth inning. Hank tossed aside the bone and approached the plate. He settled his spikes the best he could in the muck of the batter's box. This was his chance to shine—or secure his status as the goat.

Fewer than 6,000 fans had shown up at Sportsman's Park for Sunday's twin bill. By the ninth inning, the rain had chased many of them away. But Tiger fans back in Michigan were glued to the radio broadcast of the game. Nine-year-old Mickey Briggs, Walter O. Briggs Sr.'s grandson, sat in his living room listening to the play-by-play on the family radio. Hank Greenberg was his favorite player. He had to do something special. *How can we come this close and not win?* Mickey thought, as though the baseball gods were playing a bad trick on him. Across town, two brothers, Carl and Sandy Levin, leaned into their family radio. Harry Heilmann, tucked in a basement studio under the Telenews Theater on Woodward, broadcast the game over the WXYZ airwaves with the wire from St. Louis. "Potter delivers the first pitch." He paused. "Ball one." Heilmann's voice gripped the boys and all of those within range to hear him.

Hank glared out at Potter. "Here's the windup." Hank saw Potter's hands stop at his cap—screwball. "Potter delivers the pitch." Right down the middle. "Greenberg swings." Hank hit the ball like a rocket, a long, low drive down the left field foul line. "Trouble!" Hank knew if it stayed fair, the ball would easily reach the seats. If it stayed fair. He paused down the first-base line. He feared the ball would hook foul. "Trouble, TROUBLE!" The ball cleared the wall about a foot inside the pole. "IT'S A HOME RUN!"

Carl Levin and his brother Sandy screamed in delight. Their father thought the house was on fire. Instead, he found his sons running around wildly in excitement. "Greenberg hit a grand slam!"

Hank rounded the bases in awe. A year ago, he had been in India, wondering when the war would end. Now, the war was over. "And, not only that, but I'd just hit a pennant-winning, grand-slam home run. I wasn't sure whether I was awake or dreaming."

His teammates waited for him at home plate. Red Borom, who had scored from third, kissed him on the cheek. His other teammates hugged him, thumped him on the back and shook his hand. The home run his first game back had given him a thrill, but this was bigger. *Way* bigger.

Al Benton put down the Browns in the ninth to make the 6–3 game official: The Tigers were the 1945 American League champions. Greenberg had punctuated his return with a grand slam to win the pennant! "Never was a title won in more dramatic fashion," the *New York Times* reported.*

The blast gave Hank some personal satisfaction in his grudge against the Washington team, which was about to catch a train to Detroit for a playoff, confident the Browns were about to win. "The best part of that home run was hearing later what the Senator players said: 'Goddamn that dirty Jew bastard—he beat us again!'" Hank wrote in his autobiography.

---

* That was six years before Bobby Thomson would hit his shot heard 'round the world.

"They were calling me all kind of names, and now they had to pack up and go home, while we were going to the World Series."

The Tigers celebrated briefly in the clubhouse around Greenberg, changed uniforms and headed back to the field for the second game of the doubleheader. With the rain falling harder and the outcome irrelevant, the umpires called it after half an inning, allowing the Tigers to begin their celebration in earnest. Walter Briggs phoned the clubhouse and told the players that he wanted them to enjoy themselves on the "Victory Special" back to Detroit. The players happily followed the owner's instructions. The liquor flowed freely in "a wild scene that lasted all night," according to *Free Press* sports editor Lyall Smith.

When their train pulled into the Detroit station, thousands of fans waited to celebrate the pennant with the Tigers, their first in five years, their first since before the war. That pennant, hung on Hank's home run, meant a lot to them. The Tigers had come through again, lifted the city when it had been low. They had done it during the Depression with pennants in 1934 and 1935, when the city's recovery slumped in 1940 and now, with local factories engulfed in labor struggles over conversion to postwar production. "Every time it seems the worst is happening in the country and Detroit, the Tigers come through," Mickey Briggs reflected years later.

Hank's grand slam resonated beyond Detroit. Jews rejoiced that once again the Hebrew star had triumphed. Greenberg had come through in amazing and dramatic fashion. "It was like a major Jewish holiday in our neighborhood to celebrate this incredible historic event that this great Jewish star had won the pennant for the Detroit Tigers," said author Maury Allen, who grew up in Flatbush.

The blow became the *coup de grâce* for Hank's legend. He was everything America imagined in a hero: the immigrant son who worked hard to become the national pastime's most valuable player, the baseball star who set aside his personal interests to serve the nation in its time of war and now the star returned to fulfill his team's dream in storybook fashion, giving Americans who wanted simply to return to normal life hope that anything is possible, that in this postwar era they could dare to dream the impossible dream. Fifty years later, Carl Levin, having grown up and become a U.S. Senator, recited the lead in the next day's newspaper: "'Call him the hero of heroes. Call him the champion of champions. Call him the hero of Bengaltown,'" Senator Levin said. "I almost weep remembering what it meant to us, that home run."

Hank had returned in glorious fashion. Despite his body's failings, he had proven he could still play baseball well. He batted .311, only two points below his career average—and two points better than the AL leader, the Yankees' Snuffy Stirnweiss, though Hank didn't have enough at-bats to qualify for the batting title. Hank punched 20 doubles—not bad for a guy who couldn't run anymore. He knocked in 60 runs and slugged 13 home runs in only 270 at-bats. Curiously, he did not make a single error in the outfield, though if he had been charged for balls he should have reached, that statistic would read differently. Certainly the drop in the level of play— Hank thought the quality had fallen off by 25 percent or so—benefited him. He even said, "If the leagues had continued on a prewar basis, guys like myself couldn't have come back after four years." But that modesty didn't acknowledge that he had stayed fit during the service, worked hard to sharpen his baseball skills, played through niggling injuries and applied his "indomitable will." All of that added up to his successful return. For those looking to him for hope, he delivered.

Hank had shown what one man could do, but his return alone could not restore baseball to the glory it had enjoyed prior to the exodus of the majority of its players and the young ones from the minor leagues who would have replaced them under ordinary circumstances. Both the Tigers and their National League opponent, the Cubs, had fumbled their way to their respective pennants in less than respectable fashion, spurning opportunities to clinch and choking under pressure, the New York Times' John Drebinger noted. The "Nine Old Men" had taken the flag with a .575 winning percentage, the lowest in AL history, lower even than when the Tigers won it in 1940. Yet the Tigers, with the oldest lineup to start a World Series, were still the favorites. Chicago sportswriter Warren Brown complained, "I don't believe either team can win." The Series would provide its share of sloppy play, but it would also serve up a good dose of meaningful moments.

A year earlier, Capt. Greenberg was in India, wearing khaki and thinking he might never play in another World Series. His first three had not been fully satisfying. In 1934, despite putting up decent numbers, he had been criticized for failing to come through in the clutch when the Tigers lost to the Cardinals and Dizzy Dean had mocked him with three strike-outs in Game Seven. The next year, his injured wrist had forced him to the sidelines of the team's victory. In 1940, his last full season, he had endured another disappointing seven-game defeat, this time at the hands of Cincinnati. Now, he had another chance, not only to play, but to set right his World Series record. It would be his last chance.

Wednesday, October 3, felt like the dead of winter: a cold, bleak Detroit day with temperatures in the forties. Newhouser, who had collected his twenty-fifth win of the season in the final game that Hank really won with his bat, was the obvious choice to start for the Tigers. Prince Hal claimed the pitcher's Triple Crown with the most wins, best ERA (1.81) and most strikeouts (212) and repeated as the league's MVP. But in Game One, he pitched more like the skeptics expected, giving up seven runs before O'Neill mercifully pulled him in the third inning. The Tigers managed only six hits off of the Cubs' ace, Hank Borowy. Greenberg had one of those, a single. He also walked, was hit by a pitch and struck out. In their 9–0 loss, "The Tigers were a hapless, bush-league outfit today," the *New York Times'* Arthur Daley assessed. The crowd of 54,637 filed solemnly out of Briggs Stadium.

Nearly the same number returned for Thursday's game, greeted by warmer temps near sixty degrees but not a better start. Stan Hack, the Cubs' fleet-footed third baseman, led off by beating out a ground ball to short. The next batter bunted him to second. Then Peanuts Lowrey singled to left. Greenberg, whose ankle still bothered him, fielded the ball on one hop. Hack flew around third, confident that Hank's tired arm wasn't up to throwing him out. Greenberg knew he needed to make a perfect throw to nail the speedy Hack. He rifled a strike to the catcher, Paul Richards, that beat Hack by three feet. The throw surprised the Cubs, saved a run and turned the momentum in the Tigers' favor.

Fire Trucks pitched well for the Tigers, though the Cubs touched him for a run in the top of the fourth to go up 1–0. By the time Hank batted in the fifth, the Tigers had tied the score. In his first two at-bats, Greenberg had hit a deep fly to center and grounded out to Hack. He faced the Cubs' Hank Wyse, who had won 22 games that year. Tiger pitcher Jim Tobin, who had played in the National League, told Hank he could expect a curve from Wyse. Hank took that to heart. With runners on first and third and two outs, he watched two fastballs that put the count at 1-1. He turned on the next pitch, a high, inside curve, and blasted it nearly 400 feet into the left-center stands. That brought the 53,636 fans to their feet and gave the Tigers a 4–1 lead. "All the happy people stood and roared as though they were his brothers and sisters and children and wives," Al Laney wrote in the *New York Herald Tribune*. The normally reserved Will Harridge, AL president, was so pleased that he nearly fell out of his box reaching to pat Hank on the back when he returned to the dugout.

Trucks, the recently discharged sailor, blanked the Cubs the rest of the way, prompting the reporters who gathered around Greenberg's locker afterward to call the Tiger win the "Army-Navy victory." Hank insisted that Trucks be part of any pictures the photographers snapped. They wanted Hank, the ex-Army man who had hit the game-winning homer, to plant a kiss on Trucks's cheek. "What the hell," Hank said. "Here we're supposed to be hard, rough tough men, and you want me to give the guy a kiss?" Instead, he wrapped Trucks in a bear hug and told him, "You certainly pitched a beautiful game."

Benno Levi, who had become a Greenberg fan in his acclimation as one of the first Jewish-German immigrants to Detroit in 1935, was serving his new country in the Pacific in October 1945. More than a dozen time zones away, he woke himself at 3:00 in the morning each day to listen to the radio broadcasts aboard his ship. He took special delight in the victory spurred by the two vets that day.

Claude Passeau, the right-hander who had given up the walk-off home run to Ted Williams in the 1941 All-Star Game at Briggs Stadium, pitched for the Cubs in Game Three, which started late because of rain. He offered the Tigers no favors. Rudy York managed the lone hit, a harmless single in the second. Hank went oh-for-three. The Tigers suspected Passeau, who had a reputation for doctoring the ball, of scuffing the horsehide with sandpaper hidden in his glove. "He was a great pitcher, but he pulled a snow job on the umpires and us," Eddie Mayo said. The silent bats frustrated the 55,500 Detroit fans. Fred Lieb sympathized with them during the team's 3–0 loss: "It was about as interesting as watching a dear friend being led to the gallows."

The Tigers caught the 4:30 p.m. train to Chicago for the conclusion of the Series, an arrangement made to accommodate the travel restrictions. Jolly Cholly, whose team had lost the '35 Series to the Tigers, felt confident. His pitchers had held the Tigers scoreless in all but one of twenty-seven innings. "This time we're going to win," the Cubs' manager told the fans that met the team's train at the Chicago station. "They can't stop us."*

On a dark and cloudy Saturday afternoon, four Cubs pitchers blanked the Tigers in eight more innings, but the Tigers only needed one inning to win the game. In the fourth, Hank singled to drive in a run and later scored in a four-run rally that held up behind Dizzy Trout's strong performance. The Tigers won 4–1 and again evened the Series.

The 1945 Series presented a dilemma for Chicago Jews such as twelve-year-old Matthew Simon. Should he root for his home team or for his hero Greenberg? His parents had let him watch a season's worth of Sunday games at Wrigley Field in exchange for the promise that he would commit himself to his bar mitzvah training. But when Matthew took the El to Wrigley Field with his father on Sunday, October 7, he felt conflicted.

The sun shone warmly that afternoon for Hal Newhouser to prove he was a champion pitcher. The Tigers had started a rally in the third to go up 1–0 when Greenberg faced Hank Borowy with a runner on first and two outs. He tagged a fly deep to right-center, but Cubs' center fielder Andy Pafko robbed him with a brilliant catch to end the threat. The Cubs evened the score in their half. It was still 1–1 in the sixth when Hank doubled to drive in Cramer from second. Matthew Simon's father felt no inner conflict—he readily cheered for Greenberg. That won over Matthew, who also applauded Hank. When the rally ended, Newhouser had a 5–1 lead. The Tigers made it 6–1 in the next inning after Hank doubled on a blooper over the shortstop and scored. The Cubs managed two runs off Newhouser

---

* That was, of course, before the goat. The story goes that Billy Sianis, a Greek immigrant who owned a Chicago tavern, had bought two $7.20 tickets to Game Four, one for himself and one for his pet goat, Murphy. But Andy Frain, the Wrigley Field usher supervisor, objected to the "smelly goat" and ejected Sianis and Murphy. Offended by the slight—his goat had a ticket!—Sianis fumed, "The Cubs are going to suffer because of what they did to my goat." And so, legend says, began the curse accountable for the longest championship drought in the history of professional sports. Not only have the Cubs not won the World Series since 1908, they haven't even made it back since that year, 1945.

in their half of the seventh. Hank doubled and scored again along with Cramer in the top of the ninth to stretch the lead to 8–3. The Cubs put another run across in the bottom half, but Newhouser hung on to win 8–4.

Hank's first double could have been a triple. In the sixth inning, after smacking the ball to left field, Hank had fallen rounding first base on a slick patch where Mayo had also slipped earlier. Seeing the big guy going down, a fan yelled, "TIM-BER!" The fall aggravated his injured ankle, but he managed to scramble to his feet and limp into second. He had finished the day with three doubles and scored three runs, but Hank wasn't satisfied. He wished one of his drives had carried into the stands. In four World Series, he had never hit more than one home run in any of them. He pledged to hit a home run the next day.

Hank's tumble, along with Mayo's, the misplayed balls, muffed chances and the accumulating errors (six already in the first five games) drew criticism from the press. The sloppy play met the pre-Series expectations. *Baseball Magazine's* Clifford Bloodgood called it, "A comedy of errors—loosely played but good entertainment."

The comedy continued in Game Six, though not everyone would find humor in the errors. Trucks, unable to repeat the magic of his Game Two performance, exited in the fifth after the Cubs took a 4–1 lead. The Tigers got to Cubs' starter Claude Passeau in unusual fashion in the sixth when third baseman Jimmy Outlaw knocked a ball back through the box. Passeau knocked it down with his bare hand, grabbed the ball and threw out Outlaw. He then danced around in pain, holding his middle finger of his pitching hand—the ball had torn off the nail and split the skin. Passeau stayed in the game, but his wounded finger affected his delivery. In the Cubs' half, Hank chased Mickey Livingston's pop-up blowing back toward the infield. He managed to get his glove on it, but couldn't make the catch. The ball fell for a double (the official scorers charitably awarded Livingston a hit rather than charge Greenberg with an error), and Livingston later scored to put the Cubs up 5–1.

Grimm replaced Passeau the next inning after he gave up two singles and walked Greenberg. Hank scored along with Cramer to trim the Cubs' lead to 5–3. It would have been 5–4 if it hadn't been for the Hostetler Flop. Chuck Hostetler, at forty-two the Tigers' fastest runner, had rounded third on Cramer's single, hell-bent on home when his toe caught the turf. He stumbled, lurched forward several strides, windmilling his arms, then belly-flopped in no man's land. Instead of scoring, he was tagged out.

The Tigers rallied in the top of the eighth, pulling to within a run at 7–6. Hank faced the gray-haired left-hander Ray Prim with two outs and nobody on. Greenberg worked the count to 3-2. Then he clubbed the ball. Despite a strong wind blowing in, Hank's clout soared over the left field ivy and tied the game. The Tiger players jumped to their feet, cheered and danced spontaneously. "That's it!" Steve O'Neill yelled from the third base coach's box. "That's the payoff." They were certain victory and the championship was theirs.

Until Hank Borowy came on in relief and closed the door. In the tenth, Hank grounded into an inning-ending double play. Trying to drive the ball to the opposite field, he felt something snap in his right wrist. He didn't mention it to anyone. Dizzy Trout, relieving for the Tigers, shut down the Cubs.

Two innings later, with shadows cramping visibility, Stan Hack batted in the bottom of the twelfth with a runner on first and two outs. He smacked a routine single to left. Hank moved in to field it, wanting to nip the runner at third to finish off the Cubs. He dropped to his right knee to take the ball on the bounce—the way Joe DiMaggio had instructed him—but it struck a sprinkler head and hopped over his left shoulder. He wheeled to chase it to the wall, but the runner scored standing up. The three official scorers, led by Harry Salsinger, held Greenberg responsible for the loss, E7.

While the Wrigley Field crowd whooped and hollered, Hank made the long, lonely walk from left field to the Tigers' clubhouse entrance on the first-base side with his head down, growing angrier by the step. Instead of celebrating a World Series victory—once again the Tigers had squandered a three-two series lead—he lamented an extra-inning loss pinned on him, the bum. He stomped into the clubhouse, and most gave him a wide berth. When a reporter asked, "What happened to you on that play, Hank?" Greenberg snapped, "What happened to *me*? What happened to *you*?! Did you see the game?" Always sensitive to criticism about his limitations in the field, Hank was incensed that the scorers had charged him with an error on a ball he didn't think he had a legitimate chance to field. It had bounced over his shoulder! He never touched it. Still, he was down on himself that he had let it get by.

Hank's teammates agreed that he had been unfairly accused of misplaying the ball. "How in the hell could anyone give an error on such a play?" O'Neill demanded.

The second-guessers extended beyond the Tigers' clubhouse. Members of the press argued over the call back at the Palmer House, their Chicago headquarters for the Series. They finally wore down Salsinger and the other two scorers, who reversed their decision—the first time that had ever happened in the World Series—and gave Hack a double and an RBI. Hank was off the hook but not pleased. He had hit his second home run of the Series, as predicted, but that no longer mattered. They had lost. The scorers wouldn't change that fact.

Hank's nonerror notwithstanding, the sloppy play had worsened in Game Six, which amplified the criticism. "Actually, the game was won and lost a half dozen times by the two clubs on stupid base running, ineffective pitching, unpardonably bad coaching and damaging errors," Shirley Povich wrote in his *Washington Post* column. "Only five errors were charged against the teams, but there were other mishaps."

Both teams took the next day off so the Cubs could sell more tickets for the final game. It worked. Almost 42,000 Cub fans, eager to see their team win its first world championship in thirty-seven years, jammed Wrigley Field on a sunny Wednesday afternoon. But a cloud hung over the Tigers. Ten minutes before the start, Hank pulled O'Neill aside and told him his right wrist hurt. The pain had not subsided overnight like he thought it would. Much as it killed him to do so, Hank told his manager he didn't think he should play. "I can't throw. I can't grip the bat properly, and with all that it means to the rest of the players, I think I should get out of the lineup."

O'Neill expressed his concern that Hank's absence would hurt the team's morale more than his presence could hurt its play.

Recognizing O'Neill's predicament, Hank agreed to play. "I'll go in and try it," he said. "If anything goes wrong, get me out of there."

They did not tell anyone else, and the Cubs did not notice that Hank only made a show of taking batting practice. O'Neill figured he would shift

Jimmy Outlaw to left and put Bob Maier at third if he had to take Greenberg out.

The Tigers immediately jumped on Borowy, who had beaten them twice, with three quick singles. By the time Hank batted with runners on first and second, Grimm had replaced Borowy with Paul Derringer, who had beaten the Tigers in Game Seven in 1940 when he pitched for the Reds. It was an ideal situation to bust the game open. Hank would have loved to swing away. But his lame wrist wouldn't let him. Instead, with the infielders playing the Tigers' power hitter back for a possible double play, he fooled them with a bunt down the line. (He had not bunted all season.) Cubs' first baseman Phil Cavarretta picked up the ball and tagged Hank out, but his sacrifice moved over the runners, who both eventually scored. Before Hal Newhouser even threw a pitch, the Tigers had spotted their starter a 5–0 lead.

Newhouser, taking the mound on only two days' rest, had pulled the cord out of the telephone in his hotel room to make sure no one disturbed his sleep the night before. He struggled a bit, giving up a run on a double, bunt and single in the first, but then settled down.

Hank walked in his next two at-bats. With a runner on second, he struck out in the sixth, but by then the Tigers led 6–2. The Tigers added a run in the seventh and increased their lead in the eighth with another rally. With Mayo on third and a run already in, Hank swung away despite his sore wrist, lining a sacrifice fly to left to make it 9–2. The Cubs nicked Newhouser for another run in their half. In the ninth, O'Neill replaced Greenberg in the field with Ed Mierkowicz. Newhouser fanned his tenth batter of the game. That gave him 22 strikeouts, a Series record.* He closed out the game with a routine ground ball, and the Nine Old Men were the World Champions.

The players tumbled into the clubhouse, popped the champagne, sprayed some on one another but made sure to drink their share. The party continued on the train ride back to Detroit with stops to accommodate fans along the way in Fort Wayne, Indiana; Montpelier, Ohio; and Adrian, Michigan. It was after midnight when the "Tiger Special" pulled into Union Station,

---

* That record stood for eighteen years until the Dodgers' Sandy Koufax whiffed twenty-three in the 1963 World Series.

where a crowd of eight thousand welcomed home the world champions. "The champs were literally swallowed up by the jumping, screaming, yelling fans—including swarms of pretty bobby-soxers," one Detroit paper reported. Hank hopped off the back of the train and walked away from the crowd with his bags. He didn't want to get mobbed.

Hank had only played half the season, but the Tigers voted him a full cut of the World Series shares, a $6,445 bonus for the winners, divvied up from a record total take of $1,493,454. "If it wasn't for him hitting that home run in St. Louis, we wouldn't have been in the World Series," Mierkowicz said. Hank had also been a key factor in the Series. Many heralded Newhouser with his 22 strikeouts and two wins, including Game Seven, as the hero, but the Tiger bats had provided large leads he only needed to defend. Despite being hampered by his sore ankle and injured wrist, Hank had swung the hottest bat, leading the team in doubles (3), homers (2), RBI (7) and runs scored (7—tied with Doc Cramer). He also led the team in OBP (.467), SLG (.696) and OPS (1.162). His .304 batting average was second only to Cramer's. His home run had won Game Two. He drove in the tying run and scored the winning run in Game Four. His double in Game Five drove in a run that gave the Tigers the lead, which they never lost, and he scored three more runs himself. His second homer tied Game Six and sent it into extra innings. His surprise bunt in Game Seven set up runners to score in the Tigers' first inning five-run rally. This Series, he had at last established himself as a true champion. "Greenberg was a colossus straddling the eccentric path along which this series twisted," Joe Trimble wrote in the *New York Daily News*. "His was the dominant figure. Without him, the Tigers could not have won the pennant. Without him, they would have lost the Series."

Walter O. Briggs Sr. had finally made good on the promise he had made the day he bought out Frank Navin's widow to give Detroit the "best team in the finest park in the country." Seated in his wheelchair behind the Tiger dugout, he had basked in the congratulations that afternoon at Wrigley Field once Mayo stepped on the bag for the final out and people began coming up and congratulating him, including manager Steve O'Neill. His investment in Greenberg had paid off—the Tigers led the majors in attendance, attracting more fans than ever in the team's history: 1,280,341.

Briggs threw a large party for the team the following night back in Detroit at the Book-Cadillac Hotel. The city's Chamber of Commerce, so pleased with its boys, hosted the event. Each player received a silver trophy. Governor Harry Kelly sent a telegram with his congratulations. Businesses gave the players certificates for free shirts and other products. Ed Mierko-wicz won a car in the raffle. Some of the veterans resented the late-season call-up winning it since his only appearance had been in left field the inning he replaced Greenberg, but Hank stood up for him. "Hey, he is a rookie, and he can use it more than we can," Hank told the others. "Don't begrudge the kid his luck."

Remembering the pen and pencil desk set that the Briggs Stadium crew had presented him before leaving for his military service in 1941, Hank gave the ground crew a gift. He threw a party for them and their wives at the Ball Park Grill on Michigan Avenue. Although he was not able to attend, he made the arrangements and picked up the tab on the food and beer.

Benno Levi was maybe the only Detroiter not happy with the outcome of the World Series. His ship had landed in Japan, and he did not listen to the last game because he could not find a radio. He had a friendly bet on the Series with one of his shipmates, a buddy from Chicago. The buddy told him the Cubs had won, so Benno paid him five dollars. It wasn't until later that Benno found out he'd been had, but the Tigers' win meant more to him than that fiver.

Hank returned to the Bronx and played in an exhibition game the fol-lowing Sunday in Brooklyn. Some players had supplemented their summer salaries quite handsomely with postseason barnstorming games. That fall, Bob Feller had convinced Commissioner Chandler to waive the ten-game limit so that returning players could work themselves back into shape and recoup wages lost during their military service. Hank had appeared in only two other barnstorming exhibitions, playing first base for the Glendale Farmers a dozen years earlier after his rookie season in a doubleheader against Jimmie Foxx's All-Stars and rejoining his Bay Parkways team for a game against the Brooklyn Bushwicks in 1938. For most of his career, he had earned far more than he spent and didn't need the extra income. He also wanted a break from baseball. But this year, he made an exception and basked in the glory of his return in a game against the Bushwicks at Dexter Park. Greenberg's All-Stars, which included his teammates Eddie Mayo and Doc Cramer, lost the first game of a doubleheader 5–1. They were winning the second game 6–1 when rain cut it short in the third inning. Hank played left field but didn't bat because of his bum wrist. The organizers made a special provision for him to use a "substitute batter," or, as we would call it today, a designated hitter. The fans were happy just to see him on the field.

Hank was the runaway choice among sports editors in the Associated Press poll for the most amazing comeback in sports that year. He had done what no other player had: returned from an extended absence past his prime to play at the highest level. Despite not being the player he once was—he said he was playing from memory—he had performed among the game's best, in large part due to his pride, determination and work ethic. Most significantly, he had delivered in the clutch, slugging the homer in his first game back to shower hope on other returning vets and smacking a handful of game-winning hits, capped by his grand slam to clinch the pennant. He topped that off by leading his team to a dramatic seven-game World Series victory. Next in line was Ben Hogan, who had won four golf tournaments after coming out of the service. Hogan received 30 votes; Hank got 109. His was not only the most amazing comeback of the year, it was one of the greatest comebacks in the annals of sport.

Hank had told Bob Murphy of the *Detroit Times* his retirement plans. "Win, lose or draw, I'm playing one more season of baseball and calling it quits," Hank said. He hadn't said where, exactly, he would play that final season.

As he was honored—and roasted—by the Circus Saints and Sinners at the Waldorf in late October, Hank said, "I have achieved a lot of honors in Detroit, and I haven't got much farther to go in my baseball career. It would be nice to wind up in an atmosphere of home city folks as well as those of Detroit." Reading between the lines, Dan Daniel wrote, "I got the impression that the slugger from the Bronx would welcome a chance to finish his baseball career as a member of the Yankees." The idea was not a novel one, but it renewed discussion about the possibility.

———————

Rumors that Hank was engaged and planned to open an automobile dealership in Brooklyn raised more questions about Hank's future. Did he plan to marry? Would that signal the end of his baseball career? If he did play, would it be with the Tigers or the Yankees? And, given his injured wrist, would he even be able to play? Hank didn't want to discuss these issues with the press, but the next year would bring about many changes in his life.

—————— ∞ ——————

CHAPTER THIRTEEN

Good–bye, Mr. Ball

In November, Hank and Mrs. Caral Lasker headed to Las Vegas, where they stayed at the Hotel El Rancho Vegas. The New York papers reported that "the attractive young horsewoman" was establishing residency in Nevada with "a new life in mind." Hank squired her about the city, but the Las Vegas press left the couple alone—which was the way the publicity-shy Caral and reporter-wary Hank wanted it—until Walter Winchell broadcast their intentions on his Sunday evening ABC radio show. "Attention, *Review-Journal*," Winchell said, calling out the Vegas daily, Mrs. Lasker, née Gimbel, was scheduled to file for divorce on January 7. Soon as the court granted Caral her freedom, Winchell told the nation on December 30, she planned to marry Hank Greenberg. He repeated the juicy bit in his column, syndicated in 2,000 newspapers nationwide. With his microphone and typewriter, he notified 50 million Americans of Hank and Caral's personal plans.

Hank was embarrassed. He had wanted to work out the delicate logistics of his romance quietly. Winchell had ruined that with his blabbing, yet this time the rumors wouldn't be so easy to brush off. Reporters from the *Review-Journal* began hounding the couple. The next night when Hank took Caral out to celebrate New Year's Eve, a reporter accosted them for details. That set off Hank, who, after his induction ordeal, had come to view the press as vultures, out for a story with no regard for the facts or the feelings of those they preyed upon. According to the *Review-Journal*, he "scorched the hide off a press representative and informed the newsman that he resented, with all his resenting ability, any attempt on the part of the press of the nation to invade his private life."

Hank had been willing to pose in a western outfit, complete with cowboy hat, sitting on a fence and stroking the muzzle of his favorite horse at El Rancho, a palomino named Tony, for *Nevada Life* magazine, but he refused to discuss his relationship. Caral retreated to avoid the attention. In court, she charged Edward Lasker, her husband of nearly eleven years, with "extreme cruelty (mental in character)." She and Edward had already executed a property settlement agreement in November. On January 9, the judge granted Caral her divorce. As Vincent X. Flaherty put it in the *Los Angeles Examiner*, that entitled her to "life, liberty, pursuit of happiness and Hank Greenberg."

The couple celebrated their unimpeded future together in Los Angeles, where they stayed at the Los Altos Apartments on Wilshire Avenue. Flaherty, a columnist for the *Examiner* who enjoyed a good relationship with Greenberg, ran into Hank and Caral at a Hollywood club where Desi Arnaz's orchestra was performing. Hank took a break from dancing the samba to stop at Flaherty's table. That evening, he was not shy about confiding his love for Caral. When he left Flaherty, he removed a rose from his lapel and gave it to the reporter. Flaherty predicted the couple would soon wed.

Hank and Caral returned to New York long enough for Hank to work out the details of his 1946 contract over the phone with the Detroit ball club and to pack up his car for spring training. They drove off with plans to elope that only several family members knew. He was thirty-five. She was thirty-one. They were old enough to make such a decision. Besides, Caral had already had her storybook wedding. Perhaps she wanted to avoid the attention of a do-over. They certainly wanted to avoid the tensions a formal wedding would accentuate between their two families. The Greenbergs were Orthodox immigrants who had achieved middle-class status through David Greenberg's frugality and hard work. The Gimbels were secular aristocrats, Jewish in name only. Bernie Gimbel, one of the wealthiest men in the country, was managing the empire his grandfather had founded; his wife, Alva, had also been born to wealth, the daughter of a New York cotton converter. Hank and Caral also wanted to avoid the media circus of a high-profile wedding, though they would not be able to escape the public's fascination with their union.

They drove to Florida with plans to marry in historic St. Augustine only to discover that state law required a five-day wait on marriage licenses. Georgia, they learned, required no such wait. So Hank made a few phone calls, they motored to the resort town of Sea Island and knocked on the door of Edwin C. Dart, a Glynn County justice of the peace, on Monday evening, February 18.

Mr. Dart had no idea who this pretty woman in the dark blue suit, pearl necklace and pearl earrings and this tall, handsome man in a salt and pepper business suit were. The judge asked his wife to pick some flowers for the bride from their garden, performed the ceremony in his living room and bid them farewell with instructions to drive, "very, very slowly" back to Florida. It wasn't until the Darts' phone started ringing later that evening, after Bernie Gimbel issued a press release about his daughter's wedding, that the honorable Dart realized he had just presided over the most sensational event of the season.

The story crackled over the wires and dominated the front page of Detroit's newspapers the next day: HANK GREENBERG WEDS HEIRESS the *Detroit News* shouted to its readers in bold 72-point type. No ballplayer had attracted such attention for saying "I do."* Here was the biggest star of the national pastime coming off a dramatic return from the war and a World Championship—the hero of heroes—marrying the fruit of the American dream, the daughter of America's most successful retailer, a woman both beautiful and rich. Had today's tabloids existed then, they would have run out of ink covering the story. Meanwhile, Hank's wedding shattered the dreams of many Jewish mothers and broke the hearts of teenage girls in Detroit, who wore black bobby socks to mourn the loss of the city's most eligible bachelor.

When Hank arrived in Lakeland with his new bride, he wanted the chance simply to enjoy a brief honeymoon out of the spotlight before he started slugging baseballs again. That's what he told the photographers who

---

* Joe DiMaggio had not yet wed Marilyn Monroe.

spotted the couple on the tennis court. "Hey, we're tired from a long drive," Hank said. "Will you give us a day alone together?"

They clicked away. That ticked off Hank. When the couple finally did agree to be photographed, he was willing to talk baseball but not about his private life. The reporters were impatient with him, thinking their readers had a right to know because he was a public figure. Hank had other ideas about the responsibilities of celebrity.

February 1946 proved to be a good month for Hank financially. Not only had he married into a fortune, he negotiated a creative contract with the Tigers. According to Hank, Walter Briggs had offered him a $20,000 raise. Instead of taking that as part of his regular pay, Hank asked for his base pay to remain the same $55,000 he had collected the year before and for the $20,000 to be deferred until the team traded or released him. The arrangement provided a tax shelter and set aside a nugget for him to collect when his career ended. While deferred payments are common in today's contracts, Hank was the first baseball player to structure his payment this way. George Trautman, who had taken over as the Tigers' general manager when Jack Zeller retired at the end of the 1945 campaign, agreed to the unusual arrangement, basically viewing it as severance pay if the club let Hank go.

Hank's celebrity status beyond strictly baseball circles had exceeded even his prewar level. In March, the Custom Tailors Guild of America named him one of America's Ten Best-Dressed Men, included with Perry Como, Guy Lombardo and Gwynne Vanderbilt II. *Look* magazine featured him on the cover of its April issue for its "1946 World Series Preview," a close-up of Hank from the waist up posed in his batting stance. But Hank Greenberg was not the same man since his last time at spring training five years earlier.

He had grown up. His years in the service during the war had broadened his views beyond the American League circuit and deepened his perspective on world events. "Baseball wasn't that important," he realized. "I had seen a lot of things happen in the world, and I didn't think that baseball was the only thing in my life." What's more, he was no longer a carefree bachelor; he was married, ready to start a family. Baseball, once the passion of his youth, had become a profession.

Physically, it had become a challenge for the thirty-five-year-old. Even with the benefit of spring training, which he had missed in his crash course to return last season, he started slow. After nearly a month of exhibition games, his batting average sagged below .200. "Hank Greenberg, the handsome honeymooner, can blame his batting slump on the fact that love is blind," one writer put it cutely. Francis E. Stann didn't sugarcoat his assessment in the *Washington Star*: "He looks worse than at any time since he came up to the big tent fourteen years ago. It's even money that Greenberg won't finish the season as a regular."

Despite his customary routine of extra practice, Hank struggled not just at the plate but also in the field, where O'Neill had put him back at first base. Hank had been reluctant to return to the infield. Seven years had passed since he played there. Never nimble, he had lost what little quickness he once had. He could no longer count on Gehringer with his incredible range to bail him out on ground balls. But the Tigers had an opening at first after trading Rudy York to the Red Sox, and with Roy Cullenbine in the outfield along with Dick Wakefield and Barney McCosky back from the service, there was not a spot for Hank there. O'Neill said first base would spare Hank from having to run back and forth between the dugout and outfield every inning—he claimed players ran at least a mile a game doing so—but first base, where Hank had to set himself for every pitch and was involved with most plays, was certain to strain his aging legs more. Some thought he was a sucker to go back to first base while others praised him for being willing to accommodate the team's needs. "I had to readjust, and I wasn't as enthusiastic," Hank admitted in his autobiography. "As a result, I don't think I played up to my previous performances at first base."

The baseball season opened on Tuesday, April 16, amidst an atmosphere of great expectations. In addition to Greenberg, Feller and the sprinkling of other players who had returned in 1945, by Opening Day 1946, DiMaggio, Williams and the rest of the stars were back. President Harry Truman threw out the ceremonial first pitch at Griffith Stadium amidst great fanfare before a sellout crowd. Across the country, 236,730 fans passed through the turnstiles at eight American and National League parks, twice as many as the year before and the highest inaugural day attendance in fifteen years.

"People confronted by this awful thing which jarred their minds had to recover," observed John Rossi, author of *A Whole New Game: Off the Field Changes in Baseball 1946–1960*. "One of the ways you recover is to embrace all of those things that were traditional and normal from your past."

At Briggs Stadium, a record Opening Day 52,818 fans, including 700 servicemen let in *gratis*, watched the Tigers play the St. Louis Browns. Mrs. Hank Greenberg, wearing a black fur coat on a chilly day, sat in box seats along the first base side with her brother Bruce Gimbel and his wife. Prior to marrying Hank, Caral had seen only one inning of a rained-out Yankees game. During spring training, she had attended games, though sportswriters had chastised her for appearing bored by reading the *Blood Horse*, the thoroughbred horse scene's *Sporting News*, in her box seat. The photographers clustered around her even though she told them she wanted them to take "twice as many [photos] of Hank and leave me alone." The newspapers had snapped her photo for winning equestrian events but never shown her so much attention as someone's wife. They trained their cameras on "Hank's Heiress Bride" every time Hank batted. "It's all new to me, this being the wife of a ballplayer," she said. "It's all very strange."

The influx of ballplayers exchanging khaki and navy for flannel uniforms jiggered the lineups. Hank was the only vestige of the Nine Old Men in Detroit's starting lineup on Opening Day 1945. Yet he liked the Tigers' chances to repeat with a dozen reinforcements from the military and the best pitching staff in baseball: Hal Newhouser, Dizzy Trout, Fire Trucks and Fred Hutchinson. "I've heard all about the Yankees and the Red Sox," he said. "They will be good, but we will be better."

Hank's comeback in 1945, amazing and admirable as it was, still carried the asterisk of happening against inferior competition. This season, with the regulars back, would be the true test. "Greenberg will be out to demonstrate that ballplayers can come back after being away from the game for four years," Tiger manager Steve O'Neill said in the spring. "And you can bet that he will leave nothing undone to prove his point."

As if Hank hadn't proved himself in 1945, he reiterated the point on Tuesday, April 16. Leading off in the fourth inning, he dug in opposite Nelson Potter, the pitcher he had faced in the bottom of the ninth to close out last season, and promptly drove Potter's second pitch on a line into the left field stands to win the game, 2–1. Opening Day foreshadowed good things for the Tigers, baseball and the country.

The Motor City boomed. Nineteen forty-six marked the Automotive Golden Jubilee and saw a surge in demand for new cars. In 1945, there were 25 million automobiles registered in the United States; that figure leaped to 40 million by the end of the decade. The auto manufacturers worked out their differences with labor—General Motors settled a strike that had lasted four months—opening bountiful factory jobs with generous wages for unskilled workers thanks to union contracts. The booming economy replaced the Depression not just in Detroit but across the nation. Americans had money to spend again, and many spent it at the ballpark. That year, MLB attendance leaped to 18.5 million—a 71 percent gain from the 10.8 million in '45 and the largest jump from one year to the next in baseball history. After following the war in Europe and the Pacific, Americans eagerly turned their attention to peacetime diversions. Walter Briggs benefited from the good times as much as anyone—his boys would draw 1,772,590 fans at home (and another 1,352,218 on the road), surpassing the previous year's high water marks.

After his Opening Day promise, Hank did not prosper. In May, he was twenty for ninety-one, a meager .220 average. He went hitless in nine games. Pitchers he used to own blew the ball by him. He had also lost confidence in the field. Routine ground balls bounced by him. Every day became a struggle. Caral saw how the slump dragged him down. "I couldn't understand it when he did have good days—he had a lot of bad days, very bad days depressed him—and then the days when he really had a splendid game when he hit a home run or two, he wouldn't rejoice," she said. "I don't mean celebrate and have a lot to drink or anything like that, but spiritually he wasn't delighted. He never seemed elated enough. Because I guess he was thinking tomorrow he might go out and get no hits."

Hank was not playing like the game's highest-paid ballplayer. Some teammates, like pitcher Dizzy Trout, who was being paid less than half of what Hank was, resented this. Trout had won 27 games in 1944. His back had hindered his performance since then, but he still thought he should be making more and that Hank, with his inflated salary, was taking money out of his pocket. Ordinarily easygoing, Trout had a sharp tongue when vexed. His frustration collided with Greenberg's in Fenway Park on Sunday, June 9. Trout had given up three runs in the fifth inning. then in the sixth, Boston's leadoff man hit a wind-blown double; the next batter beat out an infield hit; the third batter, catcher Hal Wagner, hit a ground ball to Greenberg at first. The ball took a low hop and skipped past Hank's mitt into right field. Two runs scored. Instead of getting a double play and having one out to go, Trout was suddenly down 5–0 with no outs and a runner on base. He barked at Hank about not being worth his salary. Hank snapped back at him. The argument escalated when the inning ended and the two returned to the dugout. "You should've had that ball," Trout said.

"If you're so good, why don't you play first base yourself?!" Hank retorted.

The six-foot-two, nearly two-hundred-pound pitcher lunged at Hank, who swung back. O'Neill and the players broke up the tussle. The two didn't hurt one another, but the incident showed Hank still vulnerable to his hypersensitivity and quick temper, ever his Achilles' heel.

It didn't help that his body had begun to betray him. His lower back, which had troubled him during his military days, continued to nag him. He spent more time on the trainer's table after games, having his back, legs and feet rubbed down. "I feel I'm on borrowed time," he told a reporter from the *New York Sun*. "I don't have the old beans anymore out there, and I'm not the hitter I used to be."

Worse, the fans had turned on him. They booed him around the league and at Briggs Stadium. Not all of them, but enough to make their dissatisfaction audible. Some, new to town, had not known the pleasure of Greenberg's great days before the war. Others liked him only when he did well. "When you're hitting .350, you're a great guy," Hank explained. "When it's .250, they want no part of you."

Detroit could be brutal on its players. The boo birds had run Rudy York out of town. Now they pounced on Hank's shortcomings. They booed him at the plate. They booed him on the field. They even booed him during infield practice when he let a ball get by him. "They gave me a blast that almost carried me out of the ballpark," he said.

Caral winced with each catcall. Hank told her she shouldn't let it bother her. But it bothered him. He could not hear the cheers for all the jeers. The fun had leaked out of the game, leaving a void filled by frustration and resentment. "The game became drudgery," he wrote. He later admitted that he did not realize that the majority of fans were still rooting for him; he thought they had all turned on him.

Hank figured the fans resented his high salary, especially when he wasn't playing up to it. Beyond that, he thought they held it against him that he consistently sought ways to leverage his position for profit. Throughout the Depression, when others had scrimped and scraped to get by, he had negotiated and even held out for more money. That didn't go over well in a blue-collar town. "Looking back, I think one of the reasons I wasn't very popular is that I was always figuring out how I could better myself financially," Hank wrote.

He also felt the disapproval from organized baseball. In those days of imperial owners, players who did not accept what was given them graciously and gratefully were viewed as uppity. Someone like Greenberg, advocating for his own financial well-being, also strayed into the stereotype others harbored of Jews as greedy. No doubt that inflated and even defined the resentment against Hank. "The clubs didn't like it," he wrote. "Maybe they didn't like Jews coming up with such ideas."

The All-Star Game served up another frustration. The AL managers selected Mickey Vernon as the starter, which wasn't a surprise because the Senators' first baseman was enjoying one of the best seasons of his twenty-one-year career. The surprise came with their selection of Rudy York as his backup. Boston's new first sacker had nearly an identical batting average to Greenberg's: .276 to .275. He had batted in seven more runs but played nine more games. He had hit only ten homers to Hank's twenty-one. Hank, admittedly, was not at his best, but he still thought that his previous year's performance merited him a spot among the league's finest. O'Neill had voted for Greenberg, and Lyall Smith, sports editor of the *Detroit Free Press*, called Hank's omission "the oddity of the 1946 baseball season."

Greenberg felt bad about being left off the team. "Hank had said to me from the moment we were married, 'The one thing I want you to see is the All-Star Game,'" Caral said. "It was an awful blow to him that he wasn't picked. He was crushed."

Hank skipped the Tigers' first game after the All-Star break. The official word was that he had food poisoning. The truth was he meant to hand in his uniform. He had considered doing so weeks ago but backed off from the idea. Now he wanted out.

After some long conversations with Caral, who was pregnant, Hank decided to rejoin the team in Boston on July 12. When the Tigers reached New York, he told Dan Daniel that he planned to finish the season. "I have decided to stay the fifteen rounds," he said.

Hank's decision seemed to boost his batting. He went two-for-four the day he returned and continued at a .392 clip over the next two weeks. But then his bat cooled off. His slump resumed in August. The jeers persisted.

He was ready to quit again. When he received the duplicate copy of his contract, he was surprised to see that it didn't include terms for the payment of his $20,000 if he left before the season ended. He had thought it did. Not so, the general manager told him.

"If you retire now, you won't get that $20,000 bonus," Trautman said.

"Wait a minute, George," Hank said. "You're not giving me any $20,000 bonus. This is money I'm earning right along. I had a $75,000 contract, and I'm just taking payment in a different manner."

No, read the contract, Trautman said. That's the one you signed.

Trautman took the matter to Walter Briggs. "If that's what Hank thinks is right," Briggs said, "let's change the contract to read the way he wants it."

So Trautman changed the contract to include payment of the additional $20,000 even if Hank decided to retire before the season ended. Trautman clarified this arrangement with the league office in a letter dated August 17, 1946. But the discussion about that payment hadn't ended.

After Hank squeezed out only three hits in seven games, O'Neill started Roy Cullenbine in his place, playing first and batting fourth, in a doubleheader on August 23. The Tigers had lost four straight, and O'Neill said he was simply shaking up the lineup. "I'm not benching Hank," he said. "I'm just giving him a rest." O'Neill called on Hank to pinch-hit late in the first game, but Hank failed to get a hit. He looked glum on the bench and didn't like the tag "world's highest-paid benchwarmer" that the AP slapped on him.

But then something happened. The next day, Hank returned to the lineup and knocked in four runs with two singles and his 26th home run of the season to beat the Senators. The day after that, he put the Tigers ahead with a solo homer in the sixth inning, and two innings later drove in the first run of a five-run rally that finished off the Yankees. Two days after that, he hit another home run and drove in three runs to help the Tigers beat the Red Sox. Maybe O'Neill's "rest" had awakened the old Hankus Pankus. Or maybe it was Ted Williams's bat.

Hank and Ted had become friends. They went out to dinner after Hank had helped beat Boston. They loved to talk hitting. Hank considered The Kid to be the greatest hitter in baseball but thought he should swing at more balls with the game on the line. He also thought Ted should work more on his fielding. Williams admired Hank's mind and memory. "Greenberg is one of the best students and keenest observers in baseball," Ted penned in his *Boston Globe* column. "I have yet to meet anyone who has a better or more thorough knowledge of the game than Hank."

At that point, Ted had hit 33 home runs to Hank's twenty-eight and knocked in 111 runs to Hank's eighty-four. But Hank surged in September, bashing 16 home runs and pounding in 39 runs in twenty-seven games. He hit the majority of those with one of Ted's bats. At Fenway, Doc Cramer had pilfered one of the Splendid Splinter's tools and given it to Hank, who used the Louisville Slugger until he broke it on a curveball September 18. Ted wrote in his column that he had given the bat to Hank. At any rate, Hank continued to power the ball at a pace Williams could not match. On the 17th, Hank hit the 300th home run of his career and his thirty-eighth of the season, a three-run drive in a win over Washington that tied him with Ted for the league lead. He was only five RBI behind his friendly rival. A week later, Hank hit three home runs in a September 24 double-header that put him ahead of Williams in homers and tied him for RBI.

His first home run of the day was a solo shot to the Briggs Stadium upper-deck pavilion in the bottom of the ninth with the score tied 3–3 that won the game. His two homers and four RBI in the second game were enough for the Tigers to win their tenth game in a row and clinch second place. The day inspired Bob Murphy to comment in the *Detroit Times*, "Greenberg undoubtedly is one of the greatest clutch players in the business. You can't measure such a player's worth by mere statistics. The fire that enables him to hit his peak when the pressure is fiercest makes him a priceless asset to any club." Hank's strong September pushed the Tigers to win twenty-eight of their last thirty-eight games.

Hank hit his final two home runs of the season, Nos. 43 and 44, on Rosh Hashanah. Thursday afternoon, September 26, bottom of the eighth, score tied 2–2, he settled his spikes into the dirt, raised his bat and looked out at Stanley Ferens. Hank worked the count to 3-2 then hammered Ferens's next pitch into Briggs Stadium's green left field seats. That marked the second time in his career he had hit two home runs on Rosh Hashanah to win the game.

Hank referred to his strong finish as "my annual salary drive." Even though the boos had persisted from some impossible-to-please fans, Hank seemed to be enjoying his success. He had put off thoughts of retirement. "Right now I'm figuring on spring training," he said after his three-dinger day.

At the close of the season, Ted telegrammed Hank asking for his bat back, apparently unaware that Greenberg had cracked it. The Red Sox had long ago sealed first place and awaited the winner of a Dodgers-Cardinals playoff to determine their World Series opponent. Williams also congratulated Hank on beating him for the home run and RBI titles: "Your comeback one of the finest I've ever known. You deserve the best."

For anyone who had thought Hank's successful return in 1945 was a fluke, he erased all doubts with his amazing finish in 1946. There had been disappointments, of course: his slumps, the boos, the way he had to push his ailing body, missing thirteen games, the All-Star slight, struggling at first base (where his 15 errors were the most among AL first basemen) and his batting average had dropped to .277, the first time he had failed to bat over .300 in a complete season. But his 44 home runs on the season marked the fourth time in his career that he had hit forty or more. He led the AL in homers for the fourth time. His 127 RBI were best in the league, also for the fourth time.

To put his 44 home runs in perspective, Williams finished with 38. Next was Charlie Keller with 30. DiMaggio had clouted 25. Ralph Kiner had led the National League with only 23 round-trippers. Rudy York finished with only 17. Among the Tigers, Hank had hit as many home runs as Roy Cullenbine, Dick Wakefield, Eddie Lake, Jimmy Bloodworth and

George Kell *combined*. The way he won his titles, coming on so strong to surpass the much younger Williams in homers and RBI, generated widespread admiration. Dave Egan of the *Record* called Hank "a remarkable person . . . held together by tape and piano wire" deserving of MVP honors.

Those went to Feller, who set the major league record with 348 strikeouts. Yet Grantland Rice found much to praise in Hank's finish: "Only a great competitor could have rallied in this fashion in the sunset of his career. In my opinion, Greenberg's September surge was one of baseball's greatest achievements when you consider all the angles involved—the four years away from action, Greenberg's age, the handicap he faced in moving after such a power hitter as Williams has been."

Greenberg met up with Williams for a three-game exhibition series in Boston while the Red Sox awaited the outcome of the National League playoff. After the second game, which Greenberg helped the All-Stars win with his single and double, Hank gave Ted one of his Louisville Sluggers in exchange for the Williams bat he had broken. Papers across the country ran photos of Hank in his Detroit uniform presenting the bat to Williams in the trainer's room after getting plunked on the elbow. Caral finally had the chance to see her husband play an All-Star Game at Fenway, but it was anticlimactic—Hank played in two of the three games intended to keep the Red Sox fresh for the Series before small crowds averaging fewer than 2,200 fans.

While the Red Sox headed to St. Louis to play the Cardinals, speculation continued about Hank's future. Hank said he would take the off-season to decide, but if he did play again, it would be as an outfielder. "There's one sure thing," he said. "I'm never going to try to play first base again. I know I'm too far gone for that." O'Neill agreed.

The smart money had Hank retiring. Joe Williams gave three reasons: One, Hank didn't need the money. "He's financially fit." Two, physically he wasn't. "He's run out of legs." Three, the boos. "Even the most understanding ballplayer can stand only so much abuse."

With his market savvy, Hank wanted to buy a team in the Pacific Coast League. He didn't think it would be profitable immediately but predicted that the investment would pay off in ten years or so when Major League Baseball was ready to expand to Los Angeles or San Francisco. He had tried to buy the Hollywood Stars that summer, but the team had reorganized instead. Some reports had him making an offer on the New York Giants, but he denied those. Joe Williams predicted the Greenbergs would relocate in California. "I know it interests the missus," he wrote. "And you know how the gals are once they make up their minds for their husbands."

Another report had Hank buying into the Indians with Bill Veeck, who had called Trautman to see if Hank's involvement would violate any rules. Others pegged Hank to close out his career in his hometown with the Yankees. The fact that his wife had roots there and the couple now owned an apartment in Manhattan gave the old idea a fresh twist. "Larry MacPhail [Yankee president], who can use a first baseman, would gladly give him the opportunity to wind up his career in the Bronx," the *New York Journal-American* reported. "That is said to be another Greenberg ambition." Indeed, MacPhail had already tried to pry Greenberg from Detroit, and he had not exhausted his efforts.

The sportswriters began to eulogize Greenberg. "I never met a more affable, sincere or pleasing personality in the game," Joe Williams wrote. "Hankus Pankus has been a credit to the game, and if he does hang up the spikes as an active player, his deeds on the diamond will be lasting in one's memory," Ed Delaney of the *Philadelphia News* chimed in. Red Smith called Hank, "One of the greatest players of our time, one of the most unselfish team men, one of the finest gentlemen." Bill Boeder added in the *World-Telegram*: "One of baseball's true aristocrats as a player and a gentleman."

Back in New York, Hank enjoyed his time with Caral. "I am so deliriously in love, which makes the days pass so quickly that I find time for nothing but dreaming," he wrote his friend Billy Sullivan, a teammate for two seasons in Detroit. By mid-November, Hank had not made up his mind about 1947. "Last season was torturous," he wrote Sullivan. "How I ever got through is inexplicable. The mere thought of going through a similar campaign makes me cringe. . . . What can I do if I don't play? This is a bigger problem than the money, as we can get by for a while."*

So Hank pondered his future, dined with Caral at the Stork Club,

---

* Hank had saved $300,000 of the $447,000 he had made playing ball. Add to that Caral's dowry, and they would be able to "get by."

attended horse shows with her, played Santa for a group of kids at the Children's Center on East 104th Street and awaited the birth of their first child, due in January.

Hank had played a part in Major League Baseball's reformation during the 1946 season. Returning from the service, many players believed they deserved raises that were not forthcoming. That opened the door for the rival Mexican League to raid MLB teams for talent in exchange for fat contracts. Conditions were also ripe for Harvard lawyer Robert Murphy to register the American Baseball Guild as an independent union. On June 7, the union nearly staged its first strike when the Pittsburgh Pirates voted 20–16 not to take the field for that afternoon's game—just four votes short of the two-thirds majority required to strike.

Feeling the threat of a talent exodus and/or a work stoppage, Major League Baseball's power magnates agreed to listen to the players' demands, a historical move. For the first time in baseball's 107 years, players "will have a voice in the mapping of player-owner contracts," the *New York Times* noted. Team representatives, including Hank from the Tigers, met with their respective league presidents on July 29. After a series of meetings over the balance of the summer, the owners agreed to nearly all of the players' demands, including a minimum annual salary of $5,000 (at the time, more than 10 percent of MLB players earned less than that), a pension plan, a maximum salary cut of 25 percent, delayed start of spring training, earlier issuance of contracts to allow more time to negotiate terms and reimbursement of specific expenses for travel, moving and medical treatment. The items might seem trivial by today's standards, but they marked a landmark moment in the evolution of the players' ability to define their working arrangements and determine their compensation. One writer heralded the new agreement as "baseball's Magna Carta."

Dan Daniel had written so often over the years that Hank wanted to finish his playing days as a Yankee that people hardly paid attention anymore. But his article in *The Sporting News* on the first day of 1947, Hank's thirty-sixth birthday, effectively ended Greenberg's career in Detroit.

Under the headline, "Hank Hints He'd Like to End Career as Yankee,"

Daniel wrote he was "in a position" to know that "Greenberg would be more than delighted if the Yankees made a deal for him and he were able to wind up his career in the Bronx." Mr. Baseball also wrote that Greenberg would "definitely" not play first base for the Tigers in 1947 but would be "delighted" to do so for the Yankees, who needed a first baseman. Many questioned how Daniel—"who regularly cooks up sales or proposes harmless trades that seldom come off," according to *New York Daily News* sports editor Jimmy Powers—was "in a position" to know this when he didn't seem to know that Yankee manager Bucky Harris and Larry MacPhail had twice in the past six months tried to pry Hank from the Tigers. Knowing what a great drawing card Greenberg would be in New York, the Yankees had been willing to pay the Tigers as much as $75,000 for him. But at the winter meetings in December, Briggs, who didn't need the cash, had his representatives demand second baseman Snuffy Stirnweiss, the 1945 batting champ, catcher Aaron Robinson and another player in return, an outrageous proposition. "The Detroit club had no intention of letting Greenberg come to New York except in a player deal which would have helped them and hurt us," MacPhail said.

Writing that Greenberg believed he was in large part responsible for the Tigers' record attendance in 1946 though admitting that he "refused to discuss his financial affairs," Daniel also claimed to be "in a position to say that if Hank decides to play again in 1947 he will demand $75,000." Then Mr. Baseball misreported Hank's pay for 1946.

The kicker to Daniel's *Sporting News* article, though, was a large photo of Hank holding up a Yankee jersey and smiling with the caption, "Hank Greenberg admiring Yankee flannels." The photo seemed to grant Daniel the credibility his reporting lacked.

Two of the Detroit dailies rebuked Hank. The *Detroit Times'* Bob Murphy led the attack: "He has insulted Detroit baseball fans by posing in the off-season with a Yankee uniform," Murphy wrote. That "is proof enough for me Greenberg does not want to come back to Detroit as a player. I think the Tigers should respect his wishes." To wit, dump him for this unpardonable breach of loyalty and gross display of ingratitude. "He certainly has asked for it!" Murphy fumed.

Hank was furious. He had not posed with a Yankee uniform in the off-season. The photo had been taken in August 1943, when Hank had come to

New York the day before the War Bond game and needed a uniform to practice in. The Yankees lent him one, and a photographer snapped the photo. But *The Sporting News* had run the three-year-old photo without that explanation, leading everyone who saw it to believe it was a fresh shot. Hank fired a critical telegram to the baseball bible's editor-in-chief, Taylor Spink, who was unapologetic.

Perhaps no one was more furious than Walter O. Briggs Sr. when he picked up that issue of *The Sporting News* and saw the photo of Hank admiring the Yankee pinstripes. *That ungrateful bastard*, he must have thought, *after I gave him his $20,000. After all I've given him. . . .*

Briggs's impulsive temper was legend. One time, at a party to celebrate a record year at Briggs Manufacturing, the general manager who ran the company's plants came over to Briggs after having a couple of drinks, draped his arm around the owner and said, "Well, Walter—"

Briggs cut him off. He insisted on being called "Mr. Briggs"; only his wife and Henry Ford could call him "Walter." "If you ever call me that again," Briggs growled. "I'll fire you on the spot."

The pain medication he took for his polio only quickened his temper. The *Sporting News* photo ignited Briggs's anger toward Greenberg. The owner had a rocky relationship with his star, dating back to their first contract negotiations when Hank held out. He had tried to dump Hank previously, placing him on waivers four times in the last year. The first time, in January 1946, when the White Sox claimed Greenberg, Briggs seemed to have second thoughts about the Tigers having to compete against the two-time MVP and he withdrew the waivers. That must have given other teams pause because no one claimed Hank when Briggs placed him on waivers in July, September and December. He knew that releasing the popular Greenberg would cause repercussions but the outcry over *The Sporting News* article gave him the opportunity to play out his resentment. "We don't deserve that kind of treatment from a player we've been overly generous to," he bellowed to Billy Evans, who had recently taken over for Trautman as the team's general manager. "Get rid of him!"

Saturday, January 18, Hank and Caral, who was due any day, drove to the Chieftains to spend the weekend at her parents' Greenwich estate. Hank heard the news over the radio that the Detroit Tigers had sold him to the Pittsburgh Pirates. All seven of the American League teams had passed on him. "In light of recent happenings, it was felt that a change of scenery might prove highly beneficial to player Henry Greenberg and the Detroit club," Briggs said in a statement, as though the team was doing Hank a favor. Evans also issued a statement: "His going to Pittsburgh will give him a chance to perform in new fields that should be a happy solution to Greenberg's problems."

Greenberg's problems? That blamed Hank, when the Tigers had discarded him like yesterday's rubbish.

Hank was stunned. He had been a member of the Tiger organization since 1930. Played 1,292 games for the team. Led them to four World Series. Won two of them. Given Detroit fans plenty to cheer. Provided dramatic moments of Detroit lore. Won four home run crowns, four RBI titles, two MVP awards. Moved to the outfield and back to first base to fill the team's needs. And this was their thanks?

Being waived out of the league insulted him. The way the Tigers handled the situation worsened it. No phone call. Just a terse telegram from Evans that greeted him when he and Caral returned to the city: "This is to inform you that your contract has been assigned to the Pittsburgh club of the National League. Trust you will find your new connection a most profitable one."

That cut him deep.

Never before had a club released outright the reigning home run champ. The sale became the most dramatic development in the off-season, eclipsing even Jackie Robinson's pending major league debut with the Dodgers. Journalists soon exposed *The Sporting News* photo for what it was, an outdated, recycled image, and blasted Briggs. "It all adds up to a mighty flimsy excuse for the callous canning of one of the greatest sluggers of our time," Jimmy Powers wrote.

A year later, Billy Evans appeared to reveal the true reason for Greenberg's release when he said, "We got rid of a financial headache last winter when we sold Hank to Pittsburgh."

Upon hearing the news of his release, Hank wired the Tigers for the $20,000 due him as stipulated by his 1946 contract. Evans sent him a check for $16,170, after withholding taxes. "I left Detroit with a very harsh, bitter taste in my mouth," Hank wrote. He would return to the city only a handful of times over the next forty years.

The fans, outraged about Greenberg being sold down the Detroit River, had cause to lynch the owner. "For a time this affair threatened to take on the aspects of a hideous crime against civilization," Joe Williams wrote in the *World-Telegram*. "It is undoubtedly a tribute to the tolerance of people that Walter O. Briggs, owner of the Detroit club, plainly a man with a dark heart, was not measured for a tight-fitting hemp collar."

Detroit fans who had embraced and idolized Greenberg took his ouster personally. "It was like your *bubbe* moved to Mississippi," lifetime Tiger fan Bert Gordon said.

"It was a trauma," Gordon's friend and fellow lifetime fan Don Shapiro agreed. "There was a sense of rejection."

Art Neff was eleven years old on January 19 when he read the awful news in the Sunday newspaper. "I still remember the devastation I felt on that morning when I picked up the *Free Press* with the headline 'Greenberg Sold To Pirates,'" Neff said over sixty years later. "The hurt was there for a long time."

Like many of his teammates, Hal Newhouser lost a friend. Some thought Briggs had allowed his pride to hurt the team. "We felt Briggs had made a mistake," Virgil Trucks said. "Greenberg certainly would have helped us." Another player, who wanted to remain anonymous, told Jimmy Powers, "He [Briggs] got mad at Hank and blew up. Now he regrets it, but it is too late."

Hank became a father on January 22 when Caral gave birth to a boy weighing eight and a quarter pounds at Presbyterian Hospital in New York. Caral liked the name Glenn, so they named him Glenn Hank Greenberg and called him "Little Hank." But the swirling rumors and Hank's hurt over his release overshadowed the occasion.

Various reports had Hank buying out his contract from the Pirates so he could sign with the Yankees, the Yankees buying him outright from Pittsburgh, the Pirates selling him to the Giants, Hank purchasing a stake in the Pirates and Hank joining his friend Louis Marx in the toy business.

Hank and the Pirate management took turns denying the various rumors. The papers also reported the Pirates had paid the Tigers somewhere between $25,000 and $50,000 for Hank. Nobody seemed able to discover the correct amount, but it was well over the standard $10,000 waiver price.

There was also conjecture that Hank's fight the previous summer with Dizzy Trout had edged him out the door. After the altercation, O'Neill had reportedly told Hank not to worry about it and hinted that he meant to trade the pitcher. But, the writers pointed out, Trout remained on the Tiger roster and Hank did not.

In fact, Hank had wanted to become the Tigers' general manager. In December, the day George Trautman resigned, Hank sent a letter to Briggs stating his interest in the position. Briggs had not responded. A week after being released, Hank read the letter during a radio interview as evidence that he had wanted to stay in Detroit. Briggs claimed that no letter from Hank dated December 16 had been received by the club. Hank said he must have gotten the date wrong on the radio, that he had written the letter the first week of December and sent it to Briggs's Miami home. Even so, Briggs said, he would not have hired Greenberg: "I desired a man with executive baseball experience, a qualification which Mr. Greenberg obviously does not possess."

That smeared salt on Hank's wounds.

Pittsburgh was as happy to welcome Hank as Detroit was sad to lose him. A new quartet of owners had bought out Barney Dreyfuss's widow the previous August, after her son-in-law had driven the team and its fan base into the ground. The four owners had ambitions to turn around the pathetic Pirates, who had finished seventh, thirty-four games back, and the money to back them. They invested $850,000 into renovating the neglected Forbes Field and another $600,000 into developing a farm system. Greenberg figured prominently in their plans: a marquee player who could generate excitement and put fans in the seats.

It worked—immediately after Pittsburgh purchased Hank, advance ticket sales soared to record levels. General manager Roy Hamey and president Frank McKinney, one of the owners, made generous overtures to Hank. They thought they had terms in place for him to sign at the Pittsburgh baseball writers' dinner on February 9 and booked him a flight for that date. They had even purchased a $100 pen for him to sign with that they planned to auction off afterward for charity.

But instead of boarding his flight that day, Hank called to cancel his appearance. He told McKinney that he meant to retire rather than play another season.

The decision had not come easily. He had been up pacing his Manhattan apartment much of the night. Forbes Field had a much deeper left field than Briggs Stadium. Failure there would spoil his reputation as a power hitter. He also harbored enmity toward the National League, a sentiment natural among American League players—and mutually reciprocated. He dreaded the thought of going from a contender to a doormat. Beyond that, the hurt lingered. The way Briggs had disposed of him soured him on the whole business. "It just took the heart out of me," he wrote. "I became so disillusioned overnight that I made up my mind to quit."

Hank invited reporters to his 66th Street apartment and read a formal announcement about his retirement. He tried to be gracious, but his disappointment was clear when he said, "I love the game and feel there is yet much good baseball in me as a player and executive. But after seventeen years and 1,150 games in a Tiger uniform,* I always expected to finish my career at Detroit. Since it was decided for me this could not be, I do not desire to start anew in a strange environment."

That night at Toots Shor's, he was less diplomatic. When a writer suggested that playing in the senior circuit could be a good thing because Hank wouldn't have to face Bob Feller, Greenberg scoffed. "Why kid me? Going to the National League is like going to the minors."

"You can put it down that Hank is through with baseball," his friend Louis Marx chipped in. But Bob Murphy, one of the writers present, attributed Hank's decision more to "wounded pride."

It may actually have been concern about—rather than scorn for—National League pitchers that gave Hank pause. He didn't know them the way he had come to know the American League pitchers and would have to

---

* Hank actually played 1,292 games for the Tigers, including regular season and World Series games—even more if you count preseason games.

start all over with his study of them, much the way he had with the new crop he faced after returning from the service. National League umpires defined the strike zone differently, calling more low-ball strikes, which would hurt Hank, who was not a low-ball hitter. National League pitchers also threw at batters more frequently. After Hank's comments, they would relish the chance to dust him off the plate. "When he says he wants to retire with a home run title, he has in mind how his reputation would suffer if he had to spend a season swinging against National League pitching," one of his former Tiger teammates said.

But the Pirates had not given up. The week after Hank announced his retirement, John Galbreath arrived in New York with the singular mission of winning over Hank. One of the four new owners, Galbreath had made his fortune in real estate. He also raised and raced thoroughbred horses. A native Kentuckian who now resided in Columbus, Ohio, Galbreath knew how to engineer deals. Refusing to take no for an answer, he spent three days working on Hank.

Galbreath prevailed upon Hank's pride. Pittsburgh fans are expecting you. If you say no to them, your name will be mud. You owe it to them and to yourself. Hank certainly did not savor the thought of becoming Public Enemy Number One in Pittsburgh.

Galbreath also worked on Hank's objections. Left field too deep? No problem, they already had plans to add bullpens that would pull in the fence to nearly the same dimensions as the friendly confines of Briggs Stadium. You have trouble sleeping on trains with those cramped compartments? Okay, we'll fly you on road trips. Now that you're married you don't want a roommate on the road? Fine, you can have your own suite. Money? How does $100,000 sound? You'll be the highest-paid player in the history of the game. Not enough? Your wife can pick out a yearling from my stable of Kentucky Derby hopefuls, take any one she likes.

Galbreath had some help. The day he had arrived, Bing Crosby, another one of the four new owners, called from Hollywood and spent half an hour trying to convince Hank to sign with the team. Crosby followed that with a three-page letter appealing to Hank's love for the game and his chance to lift the Pirates out of the cellar, which no doubt tickled his ego.

Knowing the value that Greenberg would bring to his league, Ford

Frick, the National League president, also got in on the sales job. "The smooth-talking Frick convinced Hank that his circuit could stand up with the best the American League could offer," *The Sporting News* reported. "In fact, didn't the National League now have the world champion Cardinals?"

After three days, it all started to sound pretty good to Hank. Sitting in his apartment during that long winter with the baby crying while other players started to report to spring training, he figured he would be in Florida, too, if the Tigers hadn't released him, looking forward to another season. He realized he still wanted to play the game. That desire was all he had known. What else was he going to do, change diapers all summer?

Okay, he told Galbreath. Make it $100,000,* but I want it structured this way: Forty grand in base pay; then I purchase $75,000 worth of team stock that you buy back at the end of the season for a guaranteed price of $135,000. That netted Hank the $60,000 balance and reduced his tax liability from income to capital gains tax. In return, he promised to hit 25 home runs for the Pirates.

After they came to an agreement in Frick's office in the RCA Building on February 21, Hank played squash at the Lone Star Boat Club. He felt happier than he had expected. The pressure had lifted. He did not have to wonder what he would do for the next year. He felt the old enthusiasm a new season brought. "I was really happy to have decided to play baseball again, even if I wasn't in the condition I had been in four or five years earlier," he wrote. "Baseball was still in my blood."

The next morning, his right arm hurt so badly he could barely straighten it to comb his hair. He thought maybe he had slept on it funny. But the pain persisted. The squash must have mangled it. "Naturally, I didn't want to announce that I had arm problems after the Pirates had agreed to all the requests I made, so I suffered with it and went to spring training," he wrote.

Before he left, Hank paid his idol Babe Ruth a visit in his Riverside Drive apartment. Ruth had recently been released from the hospital after nearly three months, recovering from surgery to remove a malignant tumor from his neck. The surgery made it difficult for him to swallow, which

---

* Equivalent to $1,028,664 in 2012.

trimmed fifty pounds off his once hefty frame. Radiation treatment had thinned his hair.

Ruth had refused interviews and visitors but made an exception for Hank. The frail Babe, still in his pajamas, showed off his trophies and spoke of the glory days. He demonstrated his secret grip on the bat that allowed him to follow through completely with his wrists. Hank drank it all in "like a boy sitting at the feet of the stricken master." He asked for his hero's autograph, and the Babe signed a photo for him.

"I'm glad you finally signed up, Hank," said Babe, sipping a beer— doctor's orders. "A man's got to keep playing if he's fit. Don't quit until every base is uphill."

Eighteen months later, Fred Lieb began one of the most famous obituaries, "Baseball's most renowned of all stars, the inimitable George Herman (Babe) Ruth, the idol of millions, is dead. . . . A shocked nation heard the verdict, 'You're out,' with the sense of personal loss one feels when advised of the passing of one's kin or a dear personal friend." Hank cherished his "unforgettable" memory of that morning with his idol.

A week after agreeing to play for the Pirates, Hank and Caral boarded Galbreath's four-engine B-24 at LaGuardia and flew to Miami. That marked the first time an owner had escorted a player to spring training on his private plane. The owners offered the Greenbergs a luxury suite in Miami's poshest oceanfront hotel, but Hank chose to stay in the same hotel with his new Pirate teammates. That won him points with the rank and file.

The first day of spring training, when the workouts ended and players headed into the clubhouse, Hank called to Ralph Kiner, the twenty-four-year-old who had led the National League in home runs in 1946, his rookie season. "Hey, kid, how would you like to take some extra batting practice?"

Kiner, who grew up in the Los Angeles area, had become a Tiger fan during the 1934 World Series and idolized Greenberg. "Gosh," Kiner said. "Yes."

Hank saw in Kiner an unrefined hitter with sharp eyes, exceptional wrist action and a natural swing in need of some schooling. He found a willing pupil, one who respected Greenberg's intelligence and admired his résumé. Kiner trusted Hank knew what he was talking about.

Hank moved Kiner closer to the plate so he could pull the ball better. That also reduced the strike zone for pitchers. He urged Kiner to spread his feet a bit to balance his stance. He tutored him day after day and passed along his work ethic. Perhaps most significantly, Hank taught him to think rather than simply swing away, especially with two-strike counts.

"Suppose you play 150 games and average four times at bat," Hank said. "That's 600 times at bat, totaling about 2,400 pitches. Suppose 1,000 of those were strikes. Do you think you could hit thirty-five of those strikes out of the park?"

"Sure," Kiner said.

"That's all there is to it," Hank said. "Now, the secret is to make the pitcher throw strikes. If you learn the strike zone, you're automatically going to have 35 home runs a season."

"It was sort of an advanced course in calculus," Kiner said later. "He was the most astute student of hitting I ever knew."

Hank taught Kiner how to study pitchers, how to figure out what they were going to throw. He also taught him how to work pitchers so they would deliver the pitch he wanted. "He told me he'd go up maybe the first time, with nobody on base, and purposely look bad on a curveball," Kiner said. "Then, later in the game, in a situation where it meant something, he'd look for that pitch and usually get it."

Hank took Kiner under his wing. They worked together daily after the official practice sessions had ended and before games once the regular season started. Hank took him out to dinner with Caral and taught him how to dress. "He was the single greatest influence on my baseball career and adult life," said Kiner, who lost his father when he was four years old. "I remember him not as a man who taught me how to play but as a man who showed me how to live."

Much as Kiner trusted Hank, the young man did not absorb his batting curriculum overnight. It took time for him to become comfortable with the adjustments. Time, Hank learned, Kiner might not be able to afford. He struggled early in the season. Manager Billy Herman wanted to send him to the minors. "That was the lowest point of my life," Kiner said. "I knew I was going to go out, and my dream was going to go up in smoke."

But Hank had not lost faith in the kid. He talked to General Manager

Roy Hamey and President Frank McKinney. Before the season had begun, Hank had such confidence in Kiner that he bet McKinney a new suit that the youngster would hit over a 100 RBI (the year before, Kiner had hit eighty-one). He told McKinney he still had confidence in his pupil, to stick with him. He waived his no-roommate clause and offered to bunk with Kiner on the road. "He's young, has a beautiful swing, a great stance and great power," Hank said. "I'm sure he'll put in a good performance."

McKinney agreed. Hank's lessons finally took root. Kiner started hitting at a solid clip, edging over .300 for the first time in his career and sending many long balls over Forbes Field's shortened left field fence, into an area which had been christened Greenberg's Gardens but would become known as Kiner's Korner. "If Hank Greenberg doesn't hit another home run, he'll be worth his salary for what he has done with Ralph Kiner," Hamey said.

Hank, however, was not enjoying similar success. He had planned to play the outfield but when regular first baseman Elbie Fletcher dislocated his ankle in the final exhibition game, Hank volunteered to fill in. He played first for the opener on April 15, and that's where he stayed, weary legs and all. Through the first three weeks of the season, he struck out almost as many times (nine) as he hit safely (ten). He had three home runs, nine RBI and a couple of game-winning hits, but he had also grounded into two double plays and one triple play. He had been hit by two pitches and dusted off more often. His miserable .204 average suggested that the NL pitching exceeded his expectations.

Worse, his right elbow troubled him. Ever since his vigorous game of squash in February, it had hurt. He had sat out several spring training games when a specialist told him to avoid throwing hard. In Boston, the Braves' physician took X-rays that revealed bone chips. Hank left the Pirates to see his doctor in New York, who performed a procedure to work the chips out of the joint. That gave him temporary relief but did not improve his hitting. Surgery to remove the chips was an option. Hank relegated that to a "last resort," since it would cause him to miss at least four weeks.

Greenberg rejoined the team in Pittsburgh shortly before the Dodgers and Jackie Robinson, less than a month into his major league debut, came to town. The week before, the St. Louis Cardinals had planned to strike rather than take the field with a Negro player. Robinson received loads of hate mail and phone calls. Bigots threatened to kill him or to kidnap his infant son, Jackie Jr. After the threats became public on May 9, Philadelphia players aimed bats like rifles at Robinson and pretended to fire at him. Ben Chapman, who had harassed Greenberg and antagonized Yankee Stadium fans with his anti-Semitism, had become the Phillies' manager. He threatened to fine his pitchers fifty dollars if they didn't throw at Robinson when they had two strikes on him and ordered his players to hurl racial taunts at him. Led by Chapman, the Phillies unleashed "a barrage of insults so venomous that Jackie came close to a nervous breakdown."

After Walter Winchell—who was as much social activist as gossip columnist—lambasted Chapman on his radio show, Commissioner Chandler told the Phillies' owner Robert Carpenter to stop the harassment. Okay, Chapman said, but "we will treat Robinson the same as we do Greenberg, Garagiola, Ryan or any other man who is likely to step to the plate and beat us." White fans praised Chapman for his fairness. That same month, an all-white jury in Greenville, South Carolina, had acquitted twenty-eight "confessed lynch murderers" who had tortured a black man to death. Basically, whites could abuse blacks with impunity; it was culturally and legally acceptable.

So Jackie Robinson was feeling especially vulnerable when the Dodgers arrived in Pittsburgh for the three-game series beginning May 15. That afternoon, Hank was disappointed that Herman had told his pitchers to throw at Robinson if the count ran to three-and-oh and disgusted to hear his Southern teammates shouting, "Hey, coal mine!" and "You dumb black son of a bitch. We're going to get you!" He could identify with Jackie and the abuse heaped upon him. Though the color of his skin didn't keep Hank out of hotels and restaurants, he knew how it felt to be the subject of widespread scorn. "I had feelings for him because they had treated me the same way," Hank wrote. "Not as bad, but they made remarks about my being a sheeny and Jew all the time."

In the first game, Robinson bunted and sped for first. Pirate pitcher Ed Bahr fielded the ball but hurried his throw wide of the bag. Hank reached out his mitt and collided with Robinson. The ball eluded Hank. Jackie stumbled and fell. The crowd hushed. Black men were not supposed to crash into white men, especially aging superstars. Many critics of the Robinson experiment awaited just such a moment to touch off a race riot.

Had the collision involved another white man—say, one of Hank's more vocal Southern teammates or one of the Phillies aiming bats—the anticipated riot probably would have occurred. But Hank showed no sign of anger. Jackie bounced up and raced to second.

The next inning, Hank walked. "Hope I didn't hurt you, Jackie," Hank said to the Dodgers' first baseman. "I tried to keep out of your way but it was impossible."

"No, I didn't get hurt," said Jackie, surprised yet pleased by Hank's comment. "I was just knocked off balance and couldn't stay on my feet."

"Listen," Hank said. "I know it's plenty tough. You're a good ballplayer, however, and you'll do all right. Just stay in there and fight back. Always remember to keep your head up."

Hank's comments meant a lot to Jackie, especially coming when they did. "I found out that not all the guys on the other teams are bad heels," he said. "I think Greenberg, for instance, is pulling for me to make good."

When Robinson told others about the incident, he concluded, "Class tells. It sticks out all over Mr. Greenberg."

The moment held lasting significance for Robinson. It also burnished Hank's reputation as a hero for the way he conducted himself. He was a Jew that other Jews happily identified with. In writing about Hank's encounter with Jackie, Milton K. Susman wrote in his *Jewish Criterion* column, "Nothing that Greenberg says or does the rest of his life will make this corner prouder that he is a Jew."

Hank had arrived in Pittsburgh as part of the new optimism sweeping the city. Twenty years since their last pennant, Stormy City fans embraced the new owners' promises to turn around the team. The fans delighted in Bing Crosby's appearance at the home opener and the good luck he seemed to bring the team. Hank, who became fast friends with the Hollywood crooner, even recorded a song with Crosby and Groucho Marx, "Good-bye, Mr. Ball," that celebrated Hank's slugging prowess.

But when the Pirates persisted in their losing ways—June 1 they fell below .500 and never rose above it—and Hank did not resemble the star they had read about who played for Detroit, the optimism faded to pessimism.

Fans continued to show up at the park, not wanting to miss Hank working some of his old magic, but, when he didn't, they let him know their frustrations. Some days, Forbes Field sounded like Briggs Stadium with the boos that filled it.

Hank could not adjust to playing for a losing team. He despaired at the attitude of the other players, some of whom showed up for games inebriated. Losing did not seem to bother them. After games, when they played records in the clubhouse on a phonograph Bing Crosby had given them, an observer could not tell by the atmosphere whether the team had won or lost.

As usual, though, Hank was unhappiest with himself. Pirate trainer Doc Jorgenson had worked out some of the pain in his lower back, but his elbow still bothered him. At times, Hank could shake the chips loose and relieve the pain, but when they lodged in the joint, he couldn't straighten his arm. Over the All-Star break he consulted specialists at Johns Hopkins Hospital about an operation, who told him it could wait. Unable to throw, he stayed on first base. He continued to play all-out—trying to stretch singles into doubles, sliding hard into bases—but without the results of the past. He occasionally quieted what one writer dubbed "the Hank Greenberg Heckling Society," like he did on July 6 with a towering blow out of the park said to equal one of Ruth's parting shots in distance of nearly 500 feet, but he did not satisfy himself. In late July, after going five-for-twenty-seven the past ten games, Greenberg asked Herman to take him out of the lineup "for the good of the team."

Hank tried to break out of his slump with extra batting practice at the park. He also studied the unfamiliar National League pitchers through a new medium in his living room: television. "I'm not too old to try to learn something new," Hank said. "I watch the pitchers and hitters over and over again, studying their styles and mannerisms. Television is a great thing. It brings a classroom right into your home."

Despite his low average, Hank did contribute to the team. He continued to come through in the clutch, advancing runners more often than any other Pirate hitter, including Kiner, who was belting homers at a tremendous clip and crediting Hank. On his way to leading the league in walks, Hank put himself on base and moved runners along with his discipline at the plate.

But he couldn't do what he once had, what he expected of himself, and that discouraged him.

In one game, a batter hit a routine ground ball. Hank bent for it as the pitcher, Jim Bagby, whom Hank had played against in the American League, ran over to cover first. The ball passed through Hank's legs. "You big Jew son of a bitch," Bagby said. "You make enough money to catch that kind of ball."

It was a replay of the incident with Dizzy Trout, who had ridiculed Greenberg for his high salary and lousy play. This time, though, Bagby had insulted him with an ethnic slur, and Hank considered the Georgia-raised pitcher "a dumb son of a bitch."

"I'm going to kill you after the game," Hank retorted.

Bagby waited for Greenberg afterwards in the men's room. He had changed his spikes for tennis shoes. When Hank roared in after him, his spikes slipped on the tile floor. Bagby landed a punch that left Hank with a black eye. Their teammates separated them. This time, Hank's temper had gotten the better of him.

Hank got hot after his late-July rest. In a doubleheader at Forbes Field on August 3, he hit three home runs, including a grand slam and another blast of nearly 500 feet, though the Pirates failed to win either game. Bing Crosby wrote to congratulate him "on the big day you had with the willow." Over the next twenty games, Hank batted .343 and belted eight homers. Then his fortunes reversed, and he collected only ten hits in the final twenty games he played. He also struggled to hit at night. Having spent the majority of his career playing day games, he never adjusted to hitting under the lights, batting only .198 at night.[*]

Meanwhile, his protégé Ralph Kiner shined. He batted .313, a great improvement over his .247 average the previous season. In September, he joined an exclusive club (Babe Ruth, Jimmie Foxx, Hack Wilson and Greenberg) when he hit his fiftieth home run. He finished the season with fifty-one, tied with the Giants' Johnny Mize for best in the major leagues.[†]

---

[*] About a quarter of the games Hank played in 1947 were night games.
[†] Kiner would lead the National League in home runs the next five years for an amazing seven-year reign as the senior circuit's home run king—an unparalleled feat in either league.

Kiner also knocked in 127 runs, so Greenberg won his bet with McKinney, who graciously bought suits for Hank and Ralph.

In addition to mentoring Kiner, Hank had performed other mitzvahs in Pittsburgh. He let teammate Wally Westlake use his extra car to drive his family home to California at the end of the season. He convinced Roy Hamey to give his friend and former teammate Billy Sullivan a job as a third-string catcher, even though the thirty-six-year-old Sullivan hadn't played for four years, so Sullivan could collect on the pension plan that had been enacted since he retired. When Hank won a $200 prize from the *Pittsburgh Sun-Telegraph*, he gave it to the guys who had helped him out with extra batting practice, including one of the groundskeepers who shagged fly balls.

With his career winding down, his New York neighbors hosted "Hank Greenberg Day" at the Polo Grounds between games of a doubleheader on Saturday, August 23. Hank initially resisted the idea but consented on the condition that instead of gifts all money be donated to the Rehabilitation Institute, an organization that helped disabled veterans. Flanked by an American Legion color guard and fifteen of Hank's teammates from his Monroe High baseball team, James Lyons, the Bronx borough president, presented Hank with a $500 check for the charity, a plaque, a portable radio and a wristwatch sent from Bing Crosby. Hank made a short speech at the microphone set up on home plate. "I've never wanted a 'day' in a ballpark," he said. "The only kind of day I ever desired was one with a chance to hit in the winning runs, and fortunately I've had a few of those in my time."

The sportswriters trotted out their tributes. "This wholly admirable character is an object lesson to everyone pursuing a diamond career, a living example of what hard work and intelligent concentration can do," Arthur Daley wrote. "He's been a model for all ballplayers: intelligent, articulate, friendly and dignified."

"Many have worn their honors with grace. But few with such consummate dignity and none with more genuinely unselfish modesty than Hank Greenberg," Red Smith added. "As long as he has been in baseball, players have pointed to Hank Greenberg as the criterion of team loyalty, excellence and hustle."

As the season wound down, the only lingering drama surrounded the questions of whether the Pirates would finish dead last and get the first pick for the upcoming minor league draft and what would happen to Hank. Once again, the rumor mill churned. Hank would play another year for the Pirates. He would retire. He would manage the Pirates. He would buy the Athletics. He would buy a Triple-A team.

With a 61–92 record going into the last game of the season, the Pirates needed a loss to secure last place. They won 7–0, putting them in a tie for seventh with the Phillies. Characteristically, the Pirates lost the coin toss to decide who got the first draft pick.

There were no Rosh Hashanah heroics for Hank this year. He went oh-for-three in a loss to the Phillies. He failed to get a hit in the next two games; then, aching and not hitting, he sat out the Pirates' last seven games. Elbie Fletcher finished the season at first base.

Hank had hit 25 home runs to make good on his promise. That was the fewest he hit in a full season during his career. All of his other offensive numbers dropped to their lowest totals as well, including a discouraging .249 batting average. His best statistic was measured at the gate—the Pirates almost doubled their attendance from the previous year, drawing a record 1,283,531 paying customers. They paid to see Greenberg; they stayed to watch Kiner.

Citing the rise in attendance, Hank's work with Kiner, his tolerance of disgruntled fans, his willingness to play first base and his high moral character, Harry Keck, the *Pittsburgh Sun-Telegraph*'s sports editor, observed: "Hank came in modestly amid the greatest fanfare for any player in the Pirates' history, and he's going out the same way, a man of quality and substance. Even at his great cost and tremendous salary, he was the biggest bargain the Pirates purchased in their profligate spending this year."

Hank announced before the Pirates' final game that he would not be back. He asked for—and was granted—his outright release, making him a free agent. Caral did not like Pittsburgh. She was competing on horseback again, though she never did collect on Galbreath's offer of one of his horses. Hank needed surgery on his elbow. He could not bear playing for a losing team. The game had become manual labor. All signs pointed toward retirement. But the decision was not as easy as it was obvious.

CHAPTER FOURTEEN

Playing Hardball

W hen the Pirates' season ended, Hank headed back to New York
with Ralph Kiner to watch the Yankees play the Dodgers in
the World Series. Walking out of the stadium after one of the games,
Hank met Bill Veeck, who had bought the Indians the previous summer.
Veeck strode alongside Greenberg with his crutches—his leg had been
injured in the war and amputated nine inches below the knee in 1946—
and invited Hank to dinner that evening at Toots Shor's. They closed down
the place at 4:00 a.m. Veeck's energy and knowledge fascinated Hank,
whose intelligence and good nature attracted Veeck. Thus began a beautiful
friendship.

Veeck recognized that Hank had lost some might at the plate but still
had clout at the gate. Veeck, who also ran the Indians, encouraged Greenberg to join his team. Hank was ambivalent about his future. Caral did not
like the idea of him playing another year. He certainly didn't want to repeat
a season like he had endured in Pittsburgh, where he failed to perform to
the level of his salary. He wanted to own a club and run it. Yet he had surgery in December to remove the bone chips from his elbow, what many
took to be a sure sign he planned to play again. Once the cast was removed,
he played tennis, squash and handball to get in shape. In January, Hank
returned to Pittsburgh to attend a dinner honoring Kiner and to cash in his
Pirate stock. That opened the door for him to join another club.

He continued the conversation with Veeck about various possibilities with the Indians. He also talked to the Athletics, who made him an offer to play the outfield and pinch-hit, but he turned it down because the offer didn't include the possibility of him moving into the team's front office. He wanted to catch on somewhere that would indulge his long-term ambitions. Rumor had him talking again to the Giants. Another had him signing with the Dodgers to play first with Jackie Robinson moving to second. Yet another had him returning to the Tigers.

In late February, Veeck finally convinced Hank to sign a one-dollar tryout contract and join the Indians in Tucson for spring training. Hank gave up drinking and smoking, determined to "get into a great physical condition" before making up his mind whether or not to play. His elbow felt good and he appeared in several exhibition games. The thirty-seven-year-old struggled with the thought of no longer playing the game that had been his passion for so long. But by the end of spring training, he had worked out a deal with Veeck to buy nearly a ten percent stake in the club for about $100,000, which would make him the second-largest shareholder. He planned to stay in shape in case injuries forced him into action, though he preferred such an emergency didn't occur. "I don't want to be put in the position of competing with any of the boys on the squad for jobs," he said.

He was almost pressed into duty as soon as Opening Day with both of Cleveland's first basemen ailing, but that didn't happen. Hank's playing days were over.

He had played nine full seasons, plus parts of three more (twelve games in 1936 before breaking his wrist; nineteen games in 1941 before his Army induction; and seventy-eight in 1945 after returning from the service). Given time he missed to aches, slumps and to Harry Davis his rookie year, his 1,394 major league games averaged nine 154-game seasons. During that period, Greenberg posted a .313 career batting average, won four home run titles, four more RBI titles* and led the league in doubles twice. In four World Series, he had a .318 average with five home runs and 22 RBI. His 58 home runs in 1938 tied Jimmie Foxx for most home runs in a single season by a right-handed batter. He is sixth on the all-time list for power

---

* Only Lou Gehrig led the American League in RBI more times (five). Like Greenberg, Babe Ruth and Ted Williams each led the AL in RBI four times.

average,* ahead of Hank Aaron, Willie Mays, Stan Musial, Mickey Mantle and other formidable sluggers. Greenberg and Babe Ruth remain the only players to collect at least 96 extra-base hits in four different seasons. Hank averaged .92 RBI per game, tying him for the most all-time with Lou Gehrig and Sam Thompson. When Hank retired, his 331 career home runs rated fifth-best in baseball history. Given the chance to play the seasons he missed due to over four years of military service, Greenberg would have boosted his career statistics by roughly 50 percent, according to projections by the Society for American Baseball Research, ranking him 26th all-time for home runs (502), 11th for RBI (1,869) and tied for 54th for runs scored (1,554).† Baseball historian Bill James thinks Greenberg could have reached 600 home runs, especially if he had batted against replacement pitchers during the war years. Not bad for the gangly kid from Crotona Park.

Veeck gave Hank the title of vice president even though the team already had a vice president, Harry Grabiner, who had run the White Sox. Hank's role was not clearly defined, though Veeck wanted him to do some coaching. He thought Hank might be able to work the same magic he had with Ralph Kiner on the Indians' Pat Seerey, "who goes to mental battle every time at bat." The twenty-five-year-old Seerey had slugged 26 home runs in 1946 but also led the league in strikeouts. In 1947, he batted .171 and managed only 11 dingers. Hank recognized in Seerey the same tendency he had of being "strikeout conscious"—afraid to swing at a pitch that might be a ball and afraid not to swing because it might be a strike. He also discovered a hitch in the young right-handed hitter's swing. But he did not find in Seerey a pupil as willing as Kiner. Frustrated by the adjustments Greenberg suggested, Seerey told him, "I have to go back to my natural style." That decision resulted in only one home run and a trade to the White Sox in early June.

Caral was pregnant again. She and Little Hank joined Greenberg in Cleveland at the start of the season. Hank hadn't seen his son for eight weeks. When Caral approached her due date, Hank returned to New York with her and waited four weeks in their Park Avenue apartment, but the

---

* The sum of home run average and batting average.
† Through the 2012 season.

baby didn't arrive. The day after he went back to Cleveland, September 8, Caral gave birth to their second son, a nine-and-a-half-pound boy they named Stephen. Hank was away most of the next months. When he returned home for a day in December, he noted, "I still haven't gotten around to recognizing my two sons, and I am sure they will probably be very frightened when next they see me."

The Indian stock deal fell through when one of Veeck's friends changed his mind about selling, but Hank agreed to serve as Veeck's assistant to learn the business. Together, they worked the banquet circuit around Ohio, promoting the Indians. Hank also traveled the minor league circuit, studying Cleveland's farm system.

The son of the Cubs' president, Veeck had grown up at Wrigley Field, where he had sold peanuts, done odd jobs and acquired his baseball acumen. He taught Hank about baseball as show business. Before the final home game, when Veeck promised to donate gate receipts to the Community Chest and a large crowd turned out, he convinced Hank to put on a slugging exhibition beforehand with Bill pitching. Veeck dished up baseballs that he had secretly saturated in the steam room, then iced in a freezer. Hank could not pound the frozen balls out of the infield. When he discovered what Veeck had done, Hank was miffed but a little wiser in the way the showman approached the game as entertainment.

Aided by the largest stadium in the league, Veeck capitalized on the Cleveland fans' hunger for a winner—the city had not won a baseball pennant since 1920—to set a major league attendance record. In a city of 900,000 people, he attracted 2,620,627 fans. "I think that Veeck's genius of drawing more than two and a half million fans to Cleveland in 1948, a town that typically drew less than a million, was as big an accomplishment in its own way as Ted Williams hitting .406," Hank observed.

Veeck had put together a solid team, including Larry Doby, who broke the AL color barrier, and Satchel Paige, at forty-two the game's oldest rookie. Under the guidance of shortstop-manager Lou Boudreau, the Indians beat the Red Sox in a one-game playoff to clinch the pennant. Perhaps Hank's most significant responsibility during the season was organizing the ensuing celebration at the Kenmore Hotel. "There was plenty of laughing and drinking, and a little fighting as well, before the party ended,"

Hank wrote. "On the train back to Cleveland the next day, the party resumed. The players ruined the club car and damages assessed to the team were $6,500."

Everyone could laugh it off when the Indians defeated the Boston Braves in the World Series.

Hank did commit a PR gaffe as a rookie executive. A Binghamton, New York, man had requested autographed baseballs from all of the major league teams for Bobby Amidon, a twelve-year-old boy who had his leg amputated that summer. All of the teams complied, except the Indians and the Browns. Instead of a ball, Hank sent a letter explaining that the management was too busy with important duties to be mailing baseballs and suggesting the man purchase one at the ballpark. Charley Peet, *Binghamton Press* sports editor, wrote, "Immediately this thought enters our mind: Wonder if Bill Veeck, who, like Bobby, had to have a leg amputated, knows anything about this?"

The move seemed out of character for Hank, who as a player often went out of his way to give autographs. On several occasions, he delivered signed baseballs to the homes of boys who had requested them. Perhaps he thought his obligations to the fans changed with his switch of roles. One baseball official reportedly remarked, "If Greenberg wants to be a successful front office man, he'd better smarten up."

In 1949, Veeck placed Hank in charge of the Cleveland farm system, sixteen teams with 400 players. Hank applied himself as completely to his front office job as he had to his job on the diamond. The previous year, he had discovered the teams operating as isolated units. He decided to revamp the system based on the Dodgers' model which consolidated the teams during spring training. He converted an abandoned Air Force base in Marietta, Florida, into the organization's central training facility. He grouped players across levels by position to work with the appropriate specialty coaches. The managers of the various clubs, accustomed to running their own show, initially resisted but eventually conceded to Hank's authority. At the end of the season, thirteen of the sixteen teams made the playoffs, the highest percentage of any farm system and a testament to the success of Hank's idea.

Hank moved his family to Cleveland, where they lived in a rented house. He and Caral played tennis. She brought one of her favorite horses along and rode almost daily. She also attended the Indians' home games. The boys kept growing.

Early in the season, Hank, Veeck and almost a dozen Indian ballplayers played themselves in a movie about a boy from a broken home saved from juvenile delinquency by his job as the team's batboy. *The Kid from Cleveland* opened in September and flopped. Veeck panned the movie: "I never allow my kids to mention or see that abortion."

He had another reason to regret the film. The work had been tough on the players, requiring them to be on the set at League Park from 9:00 a.m. until lunchtime with only a couple of hours off before night games. Worse, it had proven a distraction. Lou Boudreau considered the movie a "major factor in our downfall" that season, when the club finished third without spending a single day in first place. "There's no doubt it had a negative effect on the whole team," the Indians' player-manager wrote in his autobiography. "Though Veeck never admitted it, I've got to believe he was sorry he let us go ahead with it, but by then it was too late to back out."

Hank had a small speaking part in the film. He appeared stiff and self-conscious. He recited his lines as though demonstrating to a teacher that he had memorized his assignment. He also spoke with a slight smirk, like it was a joke to be making a movie. His matinee idol good looks belied the fact he was not a natural on the silver screen.

The disappointments of the 1949 season included Bill Veeck's divorce, which taxed his enthusiasm. Needing cash to pay the settlement with his ex-wife and set up a trust fund for his three children, he sold the team after the season to a Cleveland syndicate headed by forty-five-year-old insurance executive Ellis Ryan. First thing Ryan did was hire Hank as general manager "to bring championship baseball back to Cleveland." Hank felt sorry to see Veeck go but excited by the prospect of running a ball club, long his aspiration—and one quickly realized. Only two years after retiring from the field, Greenberg had become a rising star in baseball's executive ranks.

In his new role, Hank wanted to improve labor relations. He resolved not to criticize players publicly to gain leverage during contract negotiations, a tactic he thought management employed unfairly during his playing days. He wanted to pay players well enough to be satisfied but not more than they were worth. If they were disgruntled, he would trade them. "As a player, I felt there was a line—call it coldness—between the playing field and the front office," he said. "I want to eliminate that line if I possibly can. . . . I'm going to try to encourage the players to drop into the front office, say hello and consider us their friends."

Ah, easier said than done. Negotiating from the other side of the desk had not eliminated Hank's competitiveness. He thought Veeck had been overly generous with players, exaggerating their sense of worth. Hank sent out contracts he thought more in line with each player's value. That included a $20,000 wage reduction for Bob Feller and immediately put the new general manager at odds with several employees. Hank also dumped three players with high salaries, including the popular Satchel Paige. He seemed to forget his resolve not to criticize players during contract negotiations when he cited catcher Jim Hegan's .224 batting average as justification for a pay cut. Although Hegan was regarded as the best defensive catcher in the league and "among the really indispensable Indians," according to one writer. "'It isn't about the money,' Greenberg rationalizes strangely. 'We just want Jim to realize he should be a better hitter.'"

Indians' ace Bob Lemon thought his 22 wins in 1949 warranted far more than Greenberg offered. Each time Hank tried and failed to come to terms with Lemon, the general manager seemed to lose face. The situation put Hank and Ellis Ryan, the new owner and president, in a tough spot. "They are both extremely anxious to avoid public feeling that they are being niggardly with a man who is perhaps the most valuable player in the league, yet they fear for the future," the *Cleveland Press* observed. "If they give in to Lemon this time and he has another good season, they wonder where the ceiling will be."

Hank finally signed Lemon, but the early difficulties had invited criticism. The worst came at the end of spring training. Greenberg had observed that Ken Keltner, a seven-time All-Star and the Tribe's regular third baseman for twelve seasons, had slipped the previous year. He viewed the thirty-three-year-old Keltner as an aging and undisciplined player. Boudreau, who had played alongside Keltner for more than a decade and thought he should be in the Hall of Fame, played his pal regularly in an effort to win over Greenberg, but after Keltner struggled to field two bunts and a slow roller in a game less than a week before the opener, Hank told Boudreau to cut him. The move proved highly unpopular in Cleveland, where Keltner, the man who had stopped DiMaggio's 56-game hitting streak and clinched the '48 pennant with his three-run homer in the playoff with Boston, was a fan favorite.

Keltner's replacement complicated matters. Hank promoted a promising twenty-six-year-old named Al Rosen, who happened to be Jewish. The working-class Cleveland public and conservative press did not like the idea of a Jew replacing a Catholic at the hot corner and said so. The *Akron Beacon Journal*'s Jim Schlemmer made slurs about Hank being Jewish. On Opening Day, when the public address man announced Rosen at third base, many of the 65,744 Cleveland faithful shouted, "We want Keltner!" They targeted Rosen with their unhappiness but saved their derision for Greenberg.

Though time would prove Greenberg right in this instance—Keltner retired after the Red Sox cut him two months later and Rosen led the league in home runs—he complained about the way the press treated him over the decision and others he made. "The newspaper people started picking on me," he wrote. "Every time the writers had an opportunity to jab me or the club in the press, they did so."

In June, Greenberg made one of the worst trades of his career, sending Mickey Vernon to the Senators for Dick Weik. Ever hear of Dick Weik? Of course not. A right-handed pitcher with a befuddling lack of control, he had won five games and lost seventeen in two and a half years with the Senators. Vernon played nine more years, an All-Star selection five of those, and led the league in doubles twice and batting once. Weik won one game for the Indians in only eleven appearances. One Cleveland writer asserted the Vernon trade cost the Indians at least one pennant. Perhaps Greenberg had been upset at Vernon for sending back his contract unsigned even though Greenberg had offered a modest pay increase. Vernon was thirty-two when Greenberg traded him, but hindsight—ever the measure of such decisions—proved Hank should not have let him go for so little.

Before the season, Hank had boldly—and naively—predicted the Indians would win the pennant. That put extra and unnecessary pressure on the team, which was hampered by injuries to several key players, including Larry Doby, Luke Easter, Dale Mitchell, Al Rosen and Ray Boone. They also suffered several monumental collapses at critical moments. In late August, the Tribe headed to Boston only two games out of first place. Feller squandered a 7–0 lead in the first game that the Red Sox won 11–9. The next day, the Indians gave Lemon a 10–0 advantage but ended up losing 15–14. When the Indians dropped four in a row to the lowly Browns in September, Hank called it a "disgrace." "We don't even seem to be hustling," he complained to the press.

Cleveland finished a disappointing fourth in Hank's debut season as general manager. That sealed Boudreau's fate. The tension between the two preceded Hank joining the team. At a Cleveland baseball writers' dinner honoring Boudreau in February 1948, Hank had been gracious with his remarks about the Indians' player-manager, but the guessing game surrounding Hank's future had taken the spotlight off the evening's honoree. The uneasiness intensified during spring training with talk of Hank coaching, which would have undermined Boudreau's authority. It worsened when Veeck invited Hank to join his morning-after debriefing sessions with the manager. Boudreau resented being second-guessed by Hank without justification. "I confess Greenberg was not one of my favorite people," Boudreau wrote. "I felt he didn't have any regard for my managerial ability."

Veeck, who had inherited Boudreau as a manager when he bought the team, had tried to unload him after the 1948 season in a trade with the Browns, but the public outcry—some 4,000 letters of protest to the Cleveland offices—had stopped him. That's when he said, "Sometimes the best trades are the ones you don't make." Even though Boudreau's performance on the field had fallen off—he had benched himself for part of the season when he batted .269 (well below his career .295 average)—Boudreau remained so entrenched in the hearts of Cleveland fans that they didn't think Hank could fire him. After the "disgraceful" sweep by the Browns, Dan Daniel had observed, "Local baseball writers and conceivably most of the fans here, hold Boudreau blameless." When Greenberg called a press conference in November, many sportswriters thought he would announce an extension for Boudreau. He surprised them by introducing Al Lopez, who had successfully managed the Indianapolis club in the American Association, as the Tribe's new skipper.

Greenberg had not informed Boudreau of his decision. He left that task to Ellis Ryan. Hank wrote that he had talked to Boudreau about being a bench manager, but Boudreau denied such a conversation took place. At any rate, the popular player-manager's dismissal ignited another round of outrage from Cleveland fans. Hank's reaction didn't help. "General manager Hank Greenberg, a good country slugger in his day but not yet a good public relations man, tried to pour soothing oil on the fans' hurt, but nearly drowned himself in it," *Time* magazine noted. "After acknowledging that Boudreau was 'probably the most popular player in Cleveland history,' Greenberg bubbled on that, in sacking him, the new management was just trying to 'do what was right for the fans.' Boudreau fans considered that Greenberg had done them dirt."

Yet the backlash drew out Greenberg supporters, fans who commended him for his intelligence and courage in making a change. Writers beyond the Forest City supported Greenberg's managerial switch. "Despite the sentiment of the Cleveland populace, baseball folk will tell you that Greenberg made a wise move," Bob Cooke of the *Herald Tribune* wrote. Boudreau, for all of his good looks and popularity, had only won one pennant—and needed a playoff to do it—in nine years despite having the best team on paper several seasons.

Replacing Boudreau with Lopez put pressure on Hank and the new manager to justify the change. Lopez had logged 1,950 games as a big league catcher (more than anyone else at the time), including the 1947 season in Cleveland. He was a likable guy respected by the writers. He had managed successfully in the minors but was still unproven in the major leagues. His first three seasons, the Indians did well, winning 60 percent of their games, but the Yankee dynasty, which won five straight World Series from 1949–1953, bumped them to second place in '51, '52 and '53.

Hank and team president Ellis Ryan had become friends. They socialized together and played gin rummy on flights. Ellis extended Hank's contract after the 1951 season for a reported $60,000 annually. Hank ran the baseball operations though Ellis sometimes disagreed with him. Shy and nervous, Ryan seemed unable to exert the authority he wanted to wield within the ball club. Ryan's major decision, to purchase the Indianapolis club of the American Association—a decision Hank had opposed—exposed the rift. The minor league club lost money, and after the Indians finished second again in 1952, the stockholders demanded that "something be done."

That could mean Hank's job. He had antagonized some of the directors with his "iron confidence in his own judgment and automatic determination to stand by it" and his "complete disdain for compromise" as the *Cleveland Press*' Ed McAuley put it. For his part, Hank didn't like having to answer to Ryan and other stockholders with no baseball experience who thought they knew better how to run the club. They had called him to task for uttering rash statements, like saying he hated the Yankees, that hurt the team by making enemies. "I've told Hank already that I have money invested in this team, and I can't afford to be wiped out," one director said. "He's got to try and get along with people."

In the end, the other directors voted Ryan out of office, Greenberg remained general manager and the new president, minority stockholder Mike Wilson, a sixty-five-year-old insurance executive with little baseball knowledge and no experience running a sports franchise, said he would let Hank oversee operations.

Another threat arrived that summer in a typewritten letter postmarked Youngstown, Ohio: "To Al Lopez and Hank Greenberg: If the Cleveland Indians even so far as try to win the American League pennant, I will endanger your lives as well as the ballplayers. So think it over." It was signed "A fan," though it did not specify whose. Hank figured the letter was written by some "crank" and did not pose any real danger to anyone. Lopez had received several other threatening letters but was not worried by them. They did notify the police, who turned the matter over to the Federal Bureau of Investigation. The FBI determined that the letter was typed on a Remington and the return address was that of a Woolworth 5¢ and 10¢ store, which did not have a typewriter on the premises. J. Edgar's boys did not discover who wrote the letter.

At the time Greenberg received the letter, the Indians were tied for first. They stayed in contention with the Yankees and climbed back into a tie with a week to go in the season, but then collapsed, losing five of their last six games. It was a disappointing ending, especially for Hank, since four of the last losses were dealt by Detroit. Lopez had threatened to quit near the end, frustrated by Hank's meddling. But the board of directors urged him to stay, offering him a two-year contract. Wilson also gave Hank another two-year deal. Lopez signed on condition Hank would let him handle the field duties. They pinned their hopes on next year.

Al Rosen gave them reason to. The third baseman Hank had promoted to replace Ken Keltner four years earlier had a terrific season, leading the league in runs, homers, RBI, total bases and slugging percentage and winning the AL Most Valuable Player award. Rosen's rookie year, Hank had taken him to dinner, the way he had so many other young ballplayers. Rosen was in awe. Growing up in Miami's Little Havana neighborhood, he had two heroes, Greenberg and Gehrig. But Greenberg had the edge, being a Jew Rosen could emulate. The summer Hank chased Babe, Rosen was an impressionable fourteen-year-old who noted each home run with an astute awareness of what Greenberg's quest meant to baseball history and cultural status.

Observant and quick-tempered, Rosen had felt the sting of anti-Semitism in the minors. He knew Hank had faced worse and thrived. Greenberg was everything Rosen aspired to. So Rosen listened intently when Hank told him to ignore the bigots and play to the best of his ability.

Rosen led the league in home runs his rookie year, but believed he could be better. That fall, he barnstormed with Ralph Kiner, who told him how Greenberg had helped him with his hitting and encouraged Rosen to ask his general manager for advice. Rosen, "an intent-faced perfectionist forever nagging at himself to improve," did the following spring. Flattered, Hank worked with Rosen before the team's regularly scheduled practice in Tucson. He moved Rosen closer to the plate to be able to reach the outside changeups that had been giving him trouble. Like Kiner, Rosen proved an apt pupil who benefited from Hank's mentoring.

But the honeymoon had ended. The pressure Greenberg put on Rosen had become more of a distraction than a motivation. In 1953, Rosen batted .336, losing the batting title to Mickey Vernon's .337. One more hit that season would have secured for Rosen the Triple Crown and, very likely, a spot in the Hall of Fame. But Hank got in the way. "At that point, I wasn't thinking about the batting championship," Rosen said. "I was thinking about Greenberg up in the front office."

When the season ended, Hank called Rosen into his office at the stadium to discuss his 1954 contract. After his big year, Rosen expected a handsome raise. Instead, Hank opened the left-hand drawer of his desk and pulled out a green book with his statistics. "You just completed your fourth year," Hank said. "Let's see what I did in my fourth year."

Rosen hit three more home runs. Otherwise, Hank edged him in every department. Al batted .336; Hank batted .337. Al scored 115 runs; Hank scored 137. Al hit 27 doubles; Hank hit 49. Al knocked in 145 runs; Hank knocked in 183. Al recorded 367 total bases; Hank recorded 397. Even though he had come this close to winning the Triple Crown, Rosen started feeling like he'd had a bad year. "He reduced me to ashes," he said. "It was absolutely devastating."

Instead of getting the $55,000 he had hoped for, Rosen signed for $37,500 plus a $5,000 bonus. Hank had played hardball and won. That was Hank's way. He had always negotiated in his own interest. Now the general manager, he negotiated on the team's behalf at the players' expense. Rosen resented him for it.

Cleveland, which by 1950 had become the seventh largest city in the United States with a population of 914,808, had built itself into a manufacturing magnet with its convenient location on the southern shore of Lake Erie. It had not established itself as a bastion of tolerance. Just as the townsfolk and press had criticized Hank for replacing a Catholic (Keltner) with a Jew (Rosen), they also complained about him replacing another "nice Catholic boy," Bob Kennedy, with a Negro, Harry Simpson, in the outfield. Sixteen percent of Cleveland's population was African-American, but the majority did not want to see blacks taking jobs from whites, not in the factories and not on the ball field. Veeck had opened the door by integrating the American League with Larry Doby, and Hank continued the practice of signing capable black players. At a time when other teams still resisted integration* or only signed a token Negro or two, Hank had no quota. Some blamed that policy for the Indians' failure to topple the Yankees. "We have five of them," they said. "That's three too many." They wrote letters of protest to

---

* Five years after Robinson broke the color barrier, only five of sixteen teams had added a Negro player (Minnie Miñoso played for the White Sox in 1951, but he was a dark-skinned Hispanic, not an African-American).

Greenberg, but he noted, "The only time the fans complain is when the Negroes aren't delivering."

Cleveland also had a large number of African-American players in its farm system. Hank fingered Dave Hoskins, a right-handed curveball specialist who could also play the outfield, as the best candidate to integrate the Texas League, where Hank had played with Beaumont. He encouraged Hoskins to join the Dallas Eagles, Cleveland's affiliate, in 1952. The only African-American in the league, Hoskins drew record crowds and endured threats. But he blazed the trail, and Hank promoted him to the Indians the following season. "His determination in the front office to promote desegregation was undoubtedly influenced by the anti-Semitism he experienced in baseball," Stephen Norwood and Harold Brackman note in their essay "Going to Bat for Jackie."

On a road trip with the team late in 1955, Hank discovered that the Lord Baltimore Hotel (in Baltimore, of course) did not allow the team's five African-American players to stay there. The players had to find host families who would put them up. The same thing happened to them in St. Louis and Washington. Rankled by this injustice in the days when Martin Luther King Jr. drove the Montgomery bus boycott, Hank instructed Cleveland's traveling secretary Spud Goldstein to find hotels that would accommodate the entire team in 1956, no exceptions.

Hank also desegregated the player accommodations in Tucson, where the Indians trained. And he wrote a directive to Cleveland's farm clubs not to play in towns who subjected African-American players to Jim Crow laws. In the *Cleveland Call & Post*, an African-American newspaper, Sheep Jackson declared Hank "a friend to the race."

When Jackie Robinson retired after the 1956 season, Hank wrote him a letter to express his "admiration for the exemplary manner in which you have conducted yourself—both on and off the field." He continued, "You have been a credit to baseball and an inspiration to thousands of other youngsters."

For all of Hank's broad-mindedness and compassion in race relations, he did not let that soften his negotiations with players. In 1952, after Doby had "slumped" to .295 from .326 the year before and his RBI total dropped from 102 to 69, Hank sent him a contract for $19,000—a $6,000 pay cut.

Doby thought it was a joke, but Greenberg assured him he was serious and that Doby would not be welcome at spring training until he signed. Doby signed, led the league in homers in 1952, knocked in 104 runs and asked for the salary Hank paid him in 1951. Hank balked. Doby, he noted, had only batted .276, another drop. This time, the African-American press took Hank to task. "After Hank, who got all he could get when he played for Detroit and Pittsburgh, agreed to pay Bob Feller, a nine-game winner in 1952, $40,000, he should have jumped at the chance of getting Doby for $25,000," Doc Young wrote in *Jet* magazine. "Even Al Capone would have drooled over that kind of steal."

Greenberg admired Doby's talents but didn't like his personality. He found the star center fielder "belligerent" and "grouchy." Perhaps not surprisingly, Hank traded him after an All-Star 1955 season to the White Sox for Jim Busby, a center fielder nowhere near Doby's peer, and an over-the-hill Chico Carrasquel—another trade that failed to go over well with the public or on the field.

Although Hank played rough with individual players during contract negotiations, he did look out for their collective interests. In 1952, Commissioner Chandler appointed Hank and John Galbreath, who had become the majority owner of the Pirates, to negotiate an upgrade for the pension fund with Ralph Kiner, the NL player rep, Allie Reynolds, the AL player rep, and their lawyer, J. Norman Lewis. The owners had initially refused to meet with an attorney representing the players. Thanks to Hank, whom Kiner credited for brokering the deal and selling it to the owners, the players walked away with 60 percent of radio and television revenue from World Series and All-Star Games in addition to 60 percent of net gate receipts from All-Star Games. That became the foundation for the most generous pension plan in sports at the time.

Though the press dwelled on his mistakes, Greenberg the GM made some good moves. Many jumped on Hank for letting the rookie Minnie Miñoso go—especially after the speedy Cuban led the league in triples twice, stolen bases three times and was an All-Star the next four years with the White Sox—but the Miñoso trade netted Lou Brissie, who filled Cleveland's immediate need for a left-handed relief pitcher. In 1953, Hank signed Roger Maris out of high school, convincing him to turn down a college football scholarship for a better financial future in baseball. In 1954, Hank promoted Al Smith, an African-American outfielder, from the Cleveland farm system; Smith scored 101 runs and became an All-Star the following season. In 1955, Hank traded for Gene Woodling, who batted .321 with 78 RBI as a thirty-four-year-old left fielder in 1957. On June 1, 1954, Hank pulled off one of his better deals, acquiring hard-hitting Vic Wertz in exchange for young relief pitcher Bob Chakales, who had a better nickname, "The Golden Greek," than fastball. Wertz, previously an outfielder, filled the hole at first base and proved the missing link needed to finally unseat the Yankees.

The 1954 Indians won a league record 111 games* behind the mighty pitching of Bob Lemon (23 wins), Early Wynn (23), Mike Garcia (19), Art Houtteman (15) and thirty-five-year-old Bob Feller, who went 13–3 by learning to throw more breaking balls after his blazing fastball cooled off. Hal Newhouser, whom Hank had talked out of retirement, was strong in relief, going 7–2 with a 2.51 ERA. Rosen, Doby and second baseman Bobby Avila led the offensive attack. The veterans were pushed from below by seven products from Cleveland's farm system that Hank had helped develop. The Tribe's phenomenal 1954 season quieted Hank's critics.

Until the Giants swept the Indians in the World Series. And the grousing started all over again.

Hank and Caral sold the Manhattan apartment and bought a spacious house at 16470 South Park Boulevard in Shaker Heights with a tennis court and swimming pool on two wooded acres. Hank hit tennis balls high in the air for his boys to catch and gave them rides on his back in the pool. Alva, a little girl named after her maternal grandmother, arrived in 1952. Caral rode less and immersed herself in Cleveland society. She volunteered for the American Heart Society's fund-raiser, joined the hunt club, bought season tickets to the symphony and became a member of the junior council of

---

* The 2001 Seattle Mariners won 116 games, and the 1998 New York Yankees won 114—both during 162-game seasons—but 111 was the most in the American League when the Indians won that many in 1954. Their .721 winning percentage remains the best among American League teams all-time. The MLB best is the 1906 Chicago Cubs, who won 116 games.

the Museum of Art. She entertained guests like her twin sister Hope, who visited annually, and new friends from the art museum. A housekeeper, Gertrude Garland, helped with the children.

The Greenbergs did not immerse themselves in Cleveland's Jewish community. They did not join the Jewish country club or attend synagogue. Hank had become disillusioned with organized religion, and Caral had never participated in it. They did not even discuss religious training for their children; Friday night was no different from any other at their house. Hank supported Jewish causes and defended Israel but celebrated Christmas with his family.

Hank tried riding Caral's horses but trembled astride them. She enjoyed socializing with Hank's baseball pals like Ted Williams but was not a wife who read the box scores. Weekends, she attended the symphony and local horse shows; he went to the ballpark. Hank and Caral took trips together during the off-season, Europe one year, Christmas in Cuba the next, yet they drifted into separate lives.

Their strong personalities clashed. The sediment of bitterness hardened. Hank criticized Caral for sleeping in. None of the other ballplayers' wives he knew slept as late as she did.

"I'm not going to get into a competition with other ballplayers' wives," she snapped back. "Why don't you marry one of those?"

Caral petitioned for divorce in February 1955. She claimed Hank "had been guilty of gross neglect of duty and extreme cruelty." She requested that Hank be restrained from fleeing with the children and from making any financial transactions regarding their property and/or investments. He denied Caral's charges of neglect and cruelty. On the contrary, he swore "that at all times he has been a good and faithful husband and a good and affectionate father." He claimed Caral had threatened to take the children to New York and would do so unless restrained. If they divorced, he wanted custody of the children: Little Hank, eight; Steve, six; and Alva, two.

Separate restraining orders prohibited either one from taking the children out of the county. They both stayed in their Shaker Heights home. When the divorce proceedings became public in early May, the Indians were in first place. Hank said he was "terribly distressed" and "I hoped and tried to avoid it. My primary and only concern now is what's best for the children."

He and Caral bickered throughout the 1955 season. Hank was more optimistic about the Indians; he figured they were certain to repeat. They held first place as late as September 14, but the general manager watched helplessly from the box seats while they collapsed again, losing six of their last nine games, and the Yankees reclaimed the AL flag.

In the Cleveland press, Hank's job was never secure. Reports had Hank on his way out—one of them had him headed to Pittsburgh to become general manager. With the Indians still in first place, Mike Wilson squashed those rumors when he renewed Hank's contract. "This also is our vote of confidence for the splendid job which Greenberg has done for us," the team president said.

In October, Hank realized his dream to buy a California baseball team. Or at least he thought he had. He reached a verbal agreement with the owners of the San Francisco Seals to take over the team's $200,000 debt. He planned to serve as the team's president and remain the Indians' general manager, an arrangement that would benefit both clubs by pooling player talent. This was the first step toward Hank's long-term goal of bringing a major league franchise to California. He intended to start by reviving baseball interest in the Bay Area, then finding somebody—perhaps the city, maybe the county—to build a 45,000-seat baseball stadium. But when the Pacific Coast League directors did not approve the ownership transfer as quickly as promised, Hank backed out of the deal in frustration.

Four months later, he did finally become owner of a major league club when he joined Cleveland industrialist Bill Daley and St. Paul oil magnate Ignatius O'Shaughnessy in purchasing the Indians for nearly four million dollars. Hank remained general manager and became a member of the board. Mike Wilson stayed on as president.

That month, February, Hank also reconciled with Caral. She withdrew her suit for divorce almost a full year after filing it. But a rift had opened that would never quite close.

On January 25, 1956, a reporter called Hank at his stadium office with the news that the members of the Baseball Writers' Association of America had voted him into the National Baseball Hall of Fame. *All my hard work paid off,* Hank thought. He would have something to show his boys, Little Hank and Steve, who had never seen him play. He choked up thinking of his parents, wishing his mother were still around to hear the news* and knowing that his father would be proud.

Seventeen years earlier when he was still a young man and had played that exhibition game in Cooperstown, he had dared to dream of one day being enshrined with baseball's immortals. On July 24, 1956, that dream came true when he and Joe Cronin, the Boston Red Sox's seven-time All-Star shortstop, were inducted into the Hall of Fame. Caral was there with the children. So were his brothers, Ben and Joe, and his sister, Lillian. "I've had many thrills in baseball," Hank said in his induction speech to the crowd gathered on Cooperstown's Main Street. "This, though, is the greatest. Today I have the same butterflies in my stomach that I used to have when I came to the plate with the bases full with Grove or Gomez or Ruffing pitching."

Meanwhile, Bill Veeck had remarried and returned to baseball, buying the St. Louis Browns in July 1951. (That's where he secured his reputation as a Barnum & Bailey promoter when he hired the midget Eddie Gaedel to pinch-hit.) He and Hank continued their friendship, even as rivals. Veeck kept trying to slough players from his last place team onto Hank's pennant contender. When Hank was in Europe with Caral, Veeck tracked him down at his Rome hotel to propose a swap. Another time, Veeck had called Hank repeatedly in his effort to unload first baseman Bill Arft. Hank replied with a telex at the end of the day saying, "Keep your Arft Arft Arft Arft Arft. Keep your dog in St. Louis."

"We left the office laughing because we knew how frustrated Bill had to be trying to reach me and getting nothing but barking," Hank said.

Hank's loyalty showed in the way he dealt for friends and former teammates during his days at Cleveland's helm. When Rudy York's wife called to tell Hank that Rudy was drinking too much during his idle time, Hank found a place for him to manage in the Cleveland farm system. He brought

---

* Sarah Greenberg died of a heart attack during an operation to remove gallstones in 1951.

former Tiger teammates Jo-Jo White and Birdie Tebbetts into the system's coaching ranks. He gave his brother Joe and his friend Billy Sullivan jobs as scouts. He hired Al Benton and Newhouser to pitch. He also traded for his pal Kiner at the end of his career to pinch-hit and mentor young ballplayers. Hank tried to trade for Ted Williams before the 1951 season in a long session with Tom Yawkey at Toots Shor's but was unwilling to give up the top pitchers Yawkey demanded.

The friction persisted in his relationship with Al Rosen. Hank envied Rosen's popularity among the fans and press. When the Oakwood Country Club, Cleveland's prestigious Jewish establishment, admitted Rosen, Hank asked, "How can you get into Oakwood and I can't?" Could be that Rosen volunteered for the United Jewish Appeal, the Jewish Welfare Federation and the Cleveland Jewish Community Center; Hank did not. Rosen won the MVP in 1954 but after an off year in 1955—batting only .244 though he did hit 21 homers and drive in 81 runs—Hank slashed his salary by 20 percent. Meanwhile, he paid Kiner $40,000 to bat .243, hit 18 home runs and 54 RBI.* Rosen's production dropped the next year, in part due to a whiplash from a car accident and a knee injury on the field. When asked at a luncheon of the journalism fraternity Sigma Delta Chi about Rosen's status for 1957, Hank let honesty trump tact. He said Rosen had reached "the mental state where he can't play in Cleveland any longer." He added injury to insult by cutting his contract offer to $27,500, the same amount he had paid Rosen his rookie year. Offended, Rosen asked for $50,000.

Stalled and not wanting to deal directly with Rosen, Hank called in Veeck, who had sold his interest in the Browns and ran a public relations firm, to assist with negotiations. Unable to persuade Rosen over the phone, Veeck drove to his Shaker Heights home and offered $40,000. Rosen warmed to that amount but Hank didn't. Rosen said he would rather retire than play on Hank's terms.

Al Lopez, who had quit the Indians after the '56 season and now managed the Chicago White Sox, wanted Rosen to play for him. He called Hank and asked permission to talk to Rosen. Hank said no. "If he doesn't

---

* To be fair, Kiner had voluntarily taken a $25,000 pay cut—the maximum allowed—to play for the Indians, but Hank still signed him for more than he was worth relative to what he paid the other players that year.

play for me, he doesn't play for anybody," he told Lopez. That ended Rosen's career.

Greenberg did not emerge from the Rosen fiasco smelling too sweetly. Even Hank's friend, *New York Times* columnist Arthur Daley, observed afterward, "He [Hank] has an unhappy knack of destroying his appeal because he hasn't the foggiest notion of what public relations mean. He constantly says or does the wrong thing, and thereby alienates the intense and mercurial Cleveland fans."

After the 1956 campaign, when the Indians finished second again, nine games behind the Yankees, the *Cleveland News* cried, BREAK UP THE INDIANS. "You'd think we had ended up in last place and needed to refurbish the entire team," Hank later wrote. "It was always the same, always looking to find fault with the management, find fault with what the general manager was doing. Under those circumstances it was difficult to have a winning team on the field."

In 1957, the Indians didn't have a winning team. They turned in their poorest showing since Hank became general manager, finishing 76–77, in sixth place, twenty-one and a half games behind the Yankees. Attendance, which had been falling steadily since the Indians' '54 pennant season, sank to 722,256.* Only two teams in Major League Baseball drew fewer fans. The Tribe stood to lose money for the first time in Hank's eight years at the helm. Herb Score had missed most of the season after nearly being decapitated by a line drive and Bob Lemon had sat out the last two months because of shoulder trouble, but fans still blamed Hank. The year before, after attendance had dropped below the one million mark for the first time in the postwar era, Joe Williams had opined: "A baseball operation that loses 362,000 cash customers in one season is a sad reflection on the way a general manager runs the store." That opinion had become more widespread throughout Cleveland. At the insistence of several directors, Hank reluctantly fired manager Kerby Farrell on the last day of the season and replaced him with ex-Pirate manager Bobby Bragan. That exposed Hank to bear the brunt of the lingering blame.

Some was legitimate; he did have shortcomings as a general manager.

---

* From 865,467 in '56, and 1,221,780 in '55.

When Lou Brissie virtually begged Hank to trade him rather than send him to the minors, Hank turned him down coldly. He let players he cut loose, like Brissie in '54 and Dale Mitchell in '56, hear the news from outsiders rather than tell them himself. He had blanched at the $10,000 bonus promised rookie free agent Luis Aparicio, offered him $5,000 and offended the future Hall of Fame shortstop into signing with the White Sox for $6,000. In these ways, Hank had failed his own intentions when he had taken the job. Ever competitive, smart and hardworking, he had striven to assemble a winning club with a strong farm system to replace aging veterans, but he had also remained thin-skinned, stubborn and undiplomatic.

The press had excoriated him for his mistakes and his prickly manner. Whitey Lewis, the *Cleveland Press* sports editor, had been especially hard on Greenberg, constantly second-guessing and criticizing him. Hank suspected Lewis had ambitions for his job. He fired back, lambasting Lewis at a luncheon with the newspaper writers before the 1956 season for "irresponsible" stories that the Cleveland ball club meant to part ways with Feller, even though Lewis hadn't talked to Hank, Lopez or Feller about the matter.

But the damage had been done by Lewis and company. Their constant criticism had turned the fans against Hank. They blamed him for everything from the team's losses to not being able to get a decent seat at the stadium. To their thinking, the only cure for the club's ills was to sack Hank. The team's directors feared that the fans would boycott until they excised the problem. Hank saw it coming, but he still presented his case at the board's annual meeting on October 16. During his eight years running the club, the team had won more games (with a .600 winning percentage) and made more money than any team in the league other than the Yankees. Indians stock had risen from $100 per share to $1,500 per share during Hank's tenure. The discussion lasted almost two and a half hours. But he could see his fellow directors had already made up their minds. He abstained from the vote. When the tally showed a 10–2 decision to terminate his contract, he slumped in his seat, "like a guy sitting in the electric chair."

Hank smiled gamely when the directors filed out of the meeting. They rode the elevator to Bill Daley's offices on the 23rd floor of the Terminal Tower and entered a conference room where the press eagerly awaited word of the meeting's outcome. Spying two of his leading detractors among the assembled, Hank said with bitter sarcasm, "I'm glad to see my friends here. I was afraid you might not come."

Daley, the board chairman, delivered the news but could not give a reason for Hank's dismissal. When pressed for one, team president Mike Wilson explained, "The fans insisted on it."

Speaking into a cluster of microphones, Hank said he was "keenly disappointed" by the decision. He choked up. "While I have gained many honors in baseball, I feel my work here has been my greatest achievement."

On his way out, he passed Whitey Lewis. "Congratulations," Hank said. "You won."

Outside of Cleveland, the press criticized the "weak-spined board" for firing Hank without "legitimate justification" by its own admission. Jimmy Cannon berated the directors' "cowardice" and "stupidity." Bernard Kahn, sports editor of the *Daytona Beach Evening News*, called out the elephant in the living room: "They fired Hank because the Cleveland sportswriting militia—perhaps the most vicious in the country—kept sniping at Hank's heels and encouraged the more rabid fans to fang him."

Hank's release became baseball's loss. *The Sporting News* commented that he was "the type of thoughtful, energetic leader which the pastime cannot well spare." For instance, thinking games lasted too long (over two hours when his Tigers had finished many of theirs in 1:30 or 1:45), he had used a Jeep to hustle relief pitchers in from the bullpen, and even offered the players a one hundred dollar bonus for every game they won in less than two hours. He advocated for a baseball draft like the NFL's, where the worst teams would have first pick of the best amateur talent to equalize the league. He also proposed that second division teams be exempt from the trading deadline to bolster sagging fan interest late in the season. He pushed for the American League to expand to ten teams. He spoke out against the fallacy of the reserve clause. He was one of the first to champion interleague play to give fans the chance to see the stars of the other circuit. He was "outstanding as a general manager and progressive as a baseball executive, perhaps even ahead of his time," Don Wolfe, *Toledo Blade* sports editor, wrote. Time would prove Wolfe right.

No matter how energetic and progressive he was, the fact remained when the calendar flipped to 1958 and Hank turned forty-seven, he was out of a job, adrift for the first time in his life. With the Dodgers and Giants moving west and the league broadening its horizons, Hank had worked behind the scenes in an effort to move the Cleveland franchise to Minneapolis, figuring that the burgeoning Twin Cities would generate more fans than the shrinking Cleveland market. Hal Lebovitz of the *Cleveland News* had found out, and his story incited the Cleveland fans' rancor. *He wants to steal our team!* The issue divided the Cleveland stockholders, who ultimately voted against the move. The unpopularity of Hank's plotting had been yet another reason the fans had called for his ouster.

In the spring, Hank and Caral traveled to the Orient for two months. Hank marveled at the way Japan had rebuilt itself after the war. He attended a baseball game in Tokyo, impressed by the pitching but underwhelmed by the hitters' lack of power. He thought more Japanese players could be playing in the United States and offered to serve as a liaison, but that proved to be another idea ahead of its time. He seemed to enjoy his time with Caral. When they returned and the kids headed to summer camp, he looked forward to relaxing at their Shaker Heights home, playing tennis and dining alfresco with Caral. "Our family is in great shape," he wrote his friend Billy Sullivan.

But it wasn't. Seven months later, on January 2, 1959, the day after Hank's forty-eighth birthday, the two argued mightily. Caral claimed Hank threatened to hurt her. They separated. Almost two weeks later, she again filed for divorce. This time, she sought a "quickie divorce" in Alabama. Divorce had become a lucrative cottage industry for the state. In 1960, Alabama granted 17,328 divorces compared to 9,274 in Nevada. Quick and easy, it could even be done by mail. Tina Onassis, Lady Iris Mountbatten and *What's My Line?* host John Daly had all availed themselves of the convenient process. So, too, did Caral on January 14, 1959, filing in Cullman County and swearing she was "a bona fide resident citizen of Alabama."

She again alleged cruelty. Hank denied it. The truth? Caral was having an affair. One that lasted about a year. Hank used that as leverage to demand and win full custody of the children. But he remained bitter toward Caral for her betrayal.*

At the close of the 1958 season, when the Indians finished fourth and attendance continued to drop, Hank and two other stockholders, the Baxter brothers, Charles and Andrew, tried to wrest control of the club by demanding the dismissal of the team's brass, except for Hank's replacement, general manager Frank Lane, whom they claimed was "working under the same handicaps that prevented Hank Greenberg from having the complete authority his position called for." The directors did not comply. Instead, Bill Daley bought Hank and the Baxters out for $800,000—a $700,000 profit on their investment two years earlier. That freed Hank to become involved with another club.

He sold the house in Shaker Heights and rented an apartment in Manhattan, near Caral, so the children could be close to their mother. He left Cleveland wounded. Thirty years later, he still hadn't gone back to visit. "The only way I'd come back to Cleveland is if the plane goes down while I'm passing over the city on my way to New York," he said.

Meanwhile, in 1959 Bill Veeck invited Hank to join him in his bid to purchase the Chicago White Sox from the Comiskey heirs, Grace and Chuck. Grace, who had inherited 500 more shares than her brother— probably because of his tendency for drinking followed by irresponsibility— was willing to sell her 54 percent. Chuck tried to block the deal in court. He lost yet still refused to give up any of his 46 percent stake or his position as team vice president. He demanded a fifty-fifty split. Nuh-huh, Hank and Veeck said. With their partner Arthur Allyn Jr., they finally wrested control of the club. Veeck ran the club as president; Hank served as treasurer and vice president. Under their ownership, the White Sox won their first pennant in forty years. The Sox lost the World Series to the Los Angeles Dodgers four games to two, but the new owners had made an impressive debut.

---

* The twice-divorced Caral remarried in 1962 to Joseph Lebworth, whom she met through her brother. They remained married forty-six years until his death in May 2008. Caral passed away four months later. Interestingly, in a court case challenging Alabama's quickie divorce racket, a judge ruled that the divorce could be invalid if the plaintiff was not a bona fide resident of the state. That could mean that Hank and Caral never were legally divorced.

The Sox did not repeat in 1960. They finished third, a disappointing ten games back after being in contention until the final two weeks of the season. Football, horse racing and other spectator sports had begun to compete seriously with baseball for spectators, but Veeck managed to whip up interest in his product. The White Sox set a team record for attendance, with Veeck's promotions enticing a league-leading 1,644,460 fans through the turnstiles.

After the 1960 World Series, American League officials approved expansion to Washington (to replace the Senators, who were moving to the Twin Cities) and Los Angeles. They wanted Hank to head the Los Angeles club. When he heard the news, he called his friend Ralph Kiner, saying, "I got it!" Bill Veeck agreed to buy out Greenberg's shares in the White Sox. Hank planned to purchase the Los Angeles club with the profits and be the majority stockholder. Once again, he seemed poised to realize his longtime dream of owning a club in California. In November, Hank traveled to Los Angeles, where he requested a two-year lease on the Coliseum and worked out dates to play there in 1961. He also located a site near the freeway to build a new stadium and retained developer and Yankee owner Del Webb to build it.

But Walter O'Malley, who had recently moved the Dodgers to Los Angeles and was building a new stadium with his own money, opposed the competition from a rival league in his market. Moreover, he objected to one of Hank's partners, C. Arnholt Smith, a banker who owned the San Diego Padres, because Smith's brother had vehemently opposed O'Malley's purchase of the Chavez Ravine site for his stadium. No, said O'Malley, the rules won't allow another team in Los Angeles. Ford Frick, who had succeeded Chandler as commissioner, had frequently referred to Los Angeles as an "open city," same as New York, meaning the rules didn't apply there and both cities could accommodate two teams. (The Yankees had already accepted the expansion Mets in New York.) But when O'Malley objected, Frick buckled. Hank criticized the commissioner for not overruling the Dodgers' owner, but Frick lacked the *cojones* to oppose the most powerful man in baseball. Rather than grovel before O'Malley himself, Hank withdrew his bid for the Los Angeles club. In December, the American League owners backed the singing cowboy Gene Autry and Bob Reynolds, an ex-Stanford football player who ran Autry's chain of radio stations, as new owners of the Los Angeles Angels. Autry and Reynolds agreed to rent the Dodgers' new stadium for their games, O'Malley withdrew his opposition and the deal was done.

Stung, Hank stayed with the White Sox. Veeck didn't. He had developed a nasty cough and permanent headache. Doctors at the Mayo Clinic ruled out lung cancer and a brain tumor. They ultimately decided he had a chronic concussion and demanded he rest, the equivalent of house arrest for the energetic Veeck. Not wanting to be an absentee owner, Veeck sold his shares to Arthur Allyn halfway through the 1961 season. So did Hank, whom Allyn appointed general manager.

Hank commuted from New York, where his children spent the week with Gertrude, the housekeeper who had moved with them, and he returned for the weekends. The regimen exhausted him. With a month left in the 1961 season, the Sox had dropped to fourth place and were virtually eliminated from the pennant race. Hank tendered his resignation on August 27. He agreed to stay on as a director until the year ended. With no specific plans, he went back to New York, "just to breathe," he said.

At times, he had felt excluded as the lone Jewish executive or owner. The other owners met in private clubs that barred Jews. Nate Dolin, one of Hank's fellow owners and backers in Cleveland, said the other owners subjected his group to "a lot of anti-Semitism." During the 1955 World Series, Yankee co-owners Del Webb and Dan Topping along with their general manager George Weiss had joked about Jews among themselves. Despite the supposed attitude of enhanced tolerance following the War, a permissive anti-Semitism prevailed. Hank felt that tide against him. "In many situations I had the feeling that had I not been Jewish I would have been accepted, but instead the door was shut to me," he said.

The close-mindedness and cronyism among the other owners also frustrated Hank. They held back the game, he believed, opposing changes he proposed or supported to strengthen baseball. Sometimes they promised Hank they were behind him, then voted against him. "There was no integrity at all among the owners," Hank wrote. "I reached the conclusion that if I ever needed any help I sure wouldn't get it from my fellow owners. It would be closed ranks against me."

―――――――――∞―――――――――

CHAPTER FIFTEEN

Tennis, Anyone?

Hank bought a town house on the Upper East Side, a beautiful five-story at 123 East 70th Street, between Park and Lexington, decorated by Denning and Fourcade, the top interior design firm of the day. Gertrude, the housekeeper, had her own quarters. Hank also hired a cook, Bunny McManus, who commuted from Harlem. The son of Romanian immigrants had moved up in the world.

His children were growing up without him. Little Hank, who had decided to go by his given name, Glenn, was fourteen, showing his father's size, and had become a promising baseball player at Andover. Steve, thirteen, pitched a no-hitter for his St. Bernard baseball team, striking out ten. Alva, nine, felt out of place among the male-dominated household and, with Hank's blessing, soon moved to her mother's apartment several blocks away.

Hank was competitive with and demanding of his children. He hit two home runs off nine-year-old Glenn in his school's father-son game. Glenn walked him the next time up by rolling four balls to the plate. Later, when Glenn was about thirteen, they were playing touch football, Glenn got physical with his dad. Hank slugged his son. When Alva was older and he caught her smoking, he said, "I'll tan you within an inch of your life if I catch you doing that again." He pushed his kids to do their best, though he did not praise them for their success—that was expected.

He fumbled with instilling in them a sense of their Jewishness. "Dad never told me I was a Jew," Glenn said. "The closest he came to that was when I reached thirteen years of age and he gave me a ring. He said, 'This is the ring my father gave me when I was thirteen. In the Jewish religion, when you turn thirteen you are said to be a man. Now I pass this ring on to you.' It was a reflection of his own confusion."

At Andover, a Congregationalist prep school, Glenn attended the required chapel services where students read the New Testament. He went on to Yale, playing football instead of baseball, and listed on his biographical form under Religious Preference: Congregationalist. He had never known anything else.

One morning, in the fall of 1959, Hank told the children they wouldn't go to school that day. Why not? they asked.

"It's Yom Kippur," he said.

"What's that?"

He explained the Day of Atonement. Instead of taking them to synagogue, he brought them to the Hayden Planetarium, someplace special where they hadn't been, perhaps to give them a sense of awe about the universe. Steve was eleven at the time. "It was several years before I realized that Yom Kippur was not a day that Jews went to the planetarium," Steve said.

Later, in her first year at the University of Pennsylvania, Alva felt embarrassed not to know what it meant culturally and religiously to be a Jew. She asked Hank why he had not taught them more about their religion. He told her that he had seen people of all religions killing each other during World War II, that instead of teaching people how to love one another, religion seemed to have torn them apart.

Hank's Jewishness had framed his baseball career; he let his children find their own identity.

After his divorce, Hank—still handsome, fit, dapper and wealthy—once again became a desirable bachelor, albeit a bit older. Along came Mary Jo DeCicco. A friend had asked Hank for tickets to Game Six when the 1959 World Series returned to Chicago. The tickets were for his wife, Marjie Orbach, and Mary Jo. Hank had met Mary Jo briefly twice before. Four years earlier when her husband, Pat DeCicco, had introduced them before the 1955 World Series, and again in 1958 when Hank had asked her to dance at a studio party hosted by Buddy Adler. Mary Jo was tall, blonde, strikingly beautiful and still in her twenties—twenty-two years Hank's junior. She had a throaty laugh and liked baseball. Mary Jo made an impression on Hank.

A talent scout for Howard Hughes had spotted Mary Jo Tarola in a Tucson hotel lobby when she was seventeen. With no acting experience but excited by the prospect, Mary Jo and her mother accepted the invitation to fly in Hughes's private plane to meet the eccentric millionaire who owned RKO Studios. Mary Jo became Hughes's confidant, though not his mistress— at the time he was infatuated with Janet Leigh—and he cast her in three movies, including *An Affair with a Stranger* with Victor Mature and Jean Simmons. That's when Mary Jo met Pat DeCicco, a charming playboy who had been married to Thelma Todd and Gloria Vanderbilt. Mary Jo gave up acting to marry him in 1953. They lived fast and fun, but their marriage was on the rocks by 1960.

That's when Hank ran into Marjie Orbach at the "21" Club. "Mary Jo DeCicco is coming to town tomorrow, and she's getting a divorce," Marjie said. "Would you like to have lunch with us?"

"Yes."

After lunch, he walked Mary Jo back to the Waldorf Towers, where she and her husband, Pat, were staying in separate rooms. Hank suggested they have a drink in Peacock Alley. The drink lasted hours. About 7:30 p.m., Hank walked her to the elevator.

When the doors opened, there stood Pat DeCicco. He quickly sized up the situation, gave his wife a sharp look, greeted Hank and walked off. "Hank stood there looking very uncomfortable," Mary Jo said. "In my infatuation with Hank, I had totally forgotten about DeCicco. It was the beginning of my relationship with Hank and the end of DeCicco."

Hank had met Louis Marx and his brother David one night in the late Thirties at Toots Shor's restaurant. Hank admired Louis, a self-made multimillionaire with ample intellect and endless energy, and they became good friends. Louis introduced Hank to Caral Gimbel, and Hank was best man at his wedding. Hank also became friends with David Marx, the younger brother who worked with Louis but had more of an interest in the stock market.

After Hank left the White Sox, he and David set up a partnership called MG Securities investing in stocks. They rented an office at 580 Fifth Avenue with a ticker tape machine housed in a six-foot mahogany cabinet. David Greenberg, pushing eighty, would stop by with lunch picked up from a nearby deli, plop in one of the office's stuffed chairs, watch the stock prices stream across the screen and chat with his son. Hank was always glad to see "Pop."*

Hank and David Marx got some early tips on airline stocks and another from Billy Rose, the Broadway producer, who told Hank to buy AT&T. Those tips in a bull market quickly multiplied their initial investment of $100,000 each. Marx remained involved with the toy company, so when the lease expired on their office, they parted amiably, splitting $1.6 million in profits. Hank continued to play the market on his own. Others had often said of Hank that, given his intelligence and work ethic, he could have been successful at whatever he tried. His success with the stock market bore that out.

Friends set him up with dates, but he was smitten by Mary Jo, who divorced Pat in 1960. She idolized Hank. He visited her in California for two to three weeks at a time. She also came to see him in New York. They finally decided in 1966 to marry and eloped to Alexandria, Virginia, for a civil service with one of Mary Jo's friends witnessing. Hank wanted it private. Mary Jo moved into Hank's town house on the Upper East Side.

Bill Veeck, who had recovered from the chronic concussion that had forced him to sell the White Sox, nominated Hank as baseball's commissioner when Ford Frick retired in 1965. Hank had the pedigree as a great player, farm director, general manager and owner with his own capital. "Most important of all, perhaps, he would not be a politician like Frick," Veeck said. "Henry is a blunt, direct man who approaches all problems with the subtlety of an Ohio State fullback hitting over right guard."

But the idea never got serious traction, probably because it was Veeck's. "If Bill Veeck was championing it, that meant he only got one vote," said one baseball insider who insisted on anonymity.

---

* David Greenberg died in 1969. He was eighty-five years old.

Instead, the owners selected William Eckert, a retired Air Force lieutenant. He quickly proved himself unfit for the role, making one *faux pas* after another, and exacerbated tensions between the two leagues. The owners fired him at the end of 1968. Braves owner Bill Bartholomay suggested Greenberg was the man who could tackle baseball's problems. Baseball faced labor issues with Marvin Miller gaining power as the head of the players' association and the umpires organizing; the two leagues stood at loggerheads over expansion and splitting into divisions; and football challenged baseball's status as the national pastime. White Sox owner and Hank's former boss Arthur Allyn believed Hank would project "a wonderful image for baseball."

Hank had been out of baseball basically since 1961 and did not want to leave his lucrative investment business. "I would do anything to help the game, but I can't see myself as the next commissioner," he said. "Let's not kid ourselves. There are too many factions in the game that are competing against one another. The American League owners don't trust the National League owners and vice versa. They have always operated as individuals. They don't think of the welfare of the game as a whole."

Hank's former teammate, submarine pitcher Elden Auker, thought Greenberg had the ideal qualifications with one caveat. "Baseball couldn't conceivably come up with a more ideal person for the job than Greenberg," Auker said. "He was a dedicated player. He's honest, sincere, loyal and highly intelligent. He knows the game from every facet. But if they [the club owners] are looking for a guy to kowtow to them, they've got the wrong guy in Hank Greenberg."

Once again, Walter O'Malley stood in Hank's way. He nominated Bowie Kuhn, a Wall Street attorney who had represented the National League when the city of Milwaukee sued over the Braves' move to Atlanta. When the owners voted in 1983 not to grant Kuhn a third term, Chicago baseball writer Jerome Holtzman, who would become baseball's official historian, again suggested Greenberg take his place, but Hank was not interested in campaigning for the job.

In retrospect, people like Ralph Kiner, former AL president Bobby Brown and current commissioner Bud Selig think Hank would have been a terrific commissioner. Selig said Greenberg influenced him on interleague play and realignment, changes Hank had suggested and Selig had implemented forty years later. "He was right on a lot of issues," Selig said. "He was very progressive in a sport that was very cautious—I'm trying to be kind in how I saw that. He would have been marvelous as a commissioner."

Hank respected that the pitching and fielding had improved since his playing days. He also thought players deserved to be paid more—unless he was the one paying them—until free agency inflated salaries to exorbitant levels. When that happened, he became so disillusioned he hardly watched games on television any longer. He thought games dragged on too long and that there wasn't as much action anymore—prior to the mound being lowered, pitching had become too dominant. By the Seventies, he didn't like the way expansion diluted the talent pool, long-term contracts reduced incentive and artificial turf teased once routine ground balls into base hits. He also bemoaned the fact that the best athletes migrated toward professional football and basketball rather than baseball, like they had in his day. But he admired Willie Mays, whom he called "the most exciting ballplayer of all time."

Hank was not in a role to effect change but could still influence the game by speaking up. In 1970, he did so on behalf Curt Flood, a black player who had stood up to major league baseball. After twelve years with the Cardinals, Flood objected to being treated like a "piece of property to be bought and sold irrespective of my wishes," i.e., a slave, when St. Louis traded him to the lowly Phillies. He sued for his freedom, challenging baseball's revered reserve clause. While others sympathized with him—and the players stood to benefit from his victory—few spoke up for him. Among baseball's ranks, only Hank, Jackie Robinson, Veeck and retired pitcher Jim Brosnan testified on Flood's behalf. "The reserve clause is obsolete and antiquated," Hank said. "Owners and players must go forward together harmoniously, and the first step is to abolish the existing reserve clause and work out a substitute. I'd rather see the owners do it voluntarily than in court, but it has to be worked out somehow."

The U.S. Supreme Court ultimately ruled in the owners' favor, and Flood sat out the 1970 season. Two years later, at Jackie Robinson's funeral, Hank regretted that he had not done more to promote the civil rights of African-American ballplayers. He admitted to a reporter that he had been aware of conditions being different for black ballplayers but never considered what it was like from their perspective. He had not pondered the effects of segregation on them as individuals and had been blind to the social structures that perpetuated the injustice. "It leaves me with a deep guilt complex," he said. "A guilt of insensitivity."

Hank did not enjoy old-timers' games. He played in several, including one in Detroit in 1958, when he liked joking with former teammates in the dugout. But he did not fare well in the contests. Seemed everybody else would get a hit but him. Former Yankee catcher Bill Dickey called Hank the worst-looking old-timer he ever saw. In one game at Shea Stadium, after Hank had spent a month getting in shape and traveled 3,000 miles, he took one swing and popped the ball up to the catcher. "Drop it," Hank yelled. "Drop it!" Much to Hank's dismay, Sal Yvars caught it. The games frustrated him. He didn't want to be remembered—or, worse, introduced to a new generation of fans—as a doddering old-timer. After a game at Dodger Stadium, when he could barely walk, he told Mary Jo, "No more. I'm not going to make a fool out of myself."

Hank remained a celebrity in New York. People waved or stopped him on the street. One time, on the way to Yankee Stadium with his cab stuck in traffic, Hank stuck his head out of the window. An older traffic cop recognized Greenberg and ushered his cab onto the sidewalk past the line of gridlocked cars. Barry Goldwater stopped by Hank's table at "21" to ask for an autograph. So did Punch Sulzberger, owner of the *New York Times*. Ed Sullivan asked Hank to give batting tips on his television show in a May 27, 1962, episode that also featured Milton Gross, Red Buttons and Connie Francis. Hank liked being greeted by Toots Shor at his restaurant. He also enjoyed a good steak at Danny's Hideaway, Trader Vic's, Al Schacht's and Gino's on Lexington and 61st. Gino's was always crowded. Even Frank Sinatra had to wait for a table. But when Hank walked in, the owner immediately seated him. "Gino had a thing with him," Hank's longtime friend Dick Savitt said. "Everybody loved the guy."

Hank did not want to give that up, but Mary Jo did not feel at home in New York. Her friends were back in California. True, Hank had long entertained the idea of living there himself, but he didn't like the idea of being three hours behind when the stock market opened on the East Coast. With his children grown—Alva was in a McLean boarding school, Steve and Glenn had both graduated from Yale and married—Hank finally agreed to sell his Manhattan town house and move to Los Angeles in 1974. He and Mary Jo bought a house in Beverly Hills, a half-mile up from Sunset Boulevard. Hank continued to dabble in the market, but he devoted more time to his second love: tennis.

Hank had taken to tennis in the service. After he stopped playing baseball, tennis became his primary means of keeping in shape and satisfying his competitive jones. He played regularly at the Town Tennis Club and Vanderbilt Club in Manhattan. He was constantly challenging friends to games. Invited to play one day while out of town, he bought a racquet and tennis outfit on the spot. Still fit and trim in his sixties, he dominated celebrity events, especially the popular Dewar's Celebrity Tennis Tournament, where he won two singles titles and five doubles titles, beating professional football and basketball players half his age like O. J. Simpson, Lynn Swann, Ken Anderson, Julius Erving, Earl Monroe and Rick Barry.

Hank had never taken lessons, though he wished he had. What he lacked in formal instruction, he made up for in native intelligence. "He knew what he could and couldn't do," said his friend and sports psychologist Allen Fox, who was ranked No. 4 among U.S. male tennis players in 1962. "You could see how baseball carried over to tennis. He never tried to do things he couldn't do well like a lot of not very smart players do. You could see the wheels turning in his brain as he was working people around the court."

Hank knew he could not hit the white tennis ball with the power he hit a baseball, so he relied on finesse—he still had great hand-eye coordination—and cunning, outlasting his opponents with steady, well-placed ground strokes until they made an error. He went for every ball, never gave up. He didn't choke under pressure. He hit over the middle of the net, where it was lower, knowing that improved his percentage of making the shot. Sometimes he yelled, "Watch out!" like his opponent was trying to catch a foul pop-up. "I used to tell him you can't do that in tennis," said his friend Savitt, the only Jew to win Wimbledon. "He would say, 'Okay, I won't,' but he was so competitive and wanted to win so badly, he'd do it again."

Given Hank's success, others wanted to be paired with him. His doubles partners at Dewar's included Monroe, Satchel Paige and Olympic high-jumper Dwight Stones. But his desire to win sometimes wore down his partners, whom he admonished, "Get your first serve in!" "The only thing worse than playing against Hank in tennis was playing with him in doubles," Kiner said. "He was really demanding."

In Los Angeles, Hank joined the Beverly Hills Tennis Club, where he played with Pancho Segura, Bobby Riggs, Arthur Ashe and Jimmy Connors, who hung around the club during his prime when he wasn't on tour. Hank bet Jimmy fifty dollars he could beat him with the left-handed Connors playing right-handed. Hank did, taking three of five sets off the reigning U.S. Open champ in 1979 when Hank was sixty-eight, but Connors welshed on the bet.

Riggs, the top-ranked player in the world in the late Forties, was Hank's equal in competitiveness and the consummate hustler. They played together often, Bobby often adopting various handicaps like wearing a raincoat and carrying a bucket of water. He always won. One day Riggs crowed, "Hundred bucks says I can beat you with two chairs on my side of the court."

"Make it park benches," Hank countered. "Only I get to place them."

Despite the odds against him, Riggs was so much better—and such a gambler—he took the bet. He scrambled around the benches, even returned shots that ricocheted off them. He kept it close, but Hank eventually won the hundred dollars.

Hank followed pro tennis closely, attended Wimbledon and played five, six days a week. He found the camaraderie courtside that he often missed in the baseball clubhouse, where he seldom partook in the banter and pranks, more focused on his play or interested in serious discussions about a particular aspect of the game. Age had mellowed him. And, of course, taken off the pressure. At the Beverly Hills Tennis Club, he had become more comfortable in the presence of his contemporaries, needling them, telling baseball stories when prodded. Others at the club gravitated toward him. They found him good company. "When he was around, you had a smile," Fox said. "He had this attitude that he was going to have fun, and he was going to tease you. He was a very lovable character."

Actor Walter Matthau grew up during the Thirties reading about Hank in the newspapers and idolizing him. "When you're running around the jungle of the ghetto on the Lower East Side, you couldn't help but be exhilarated by the sight of one of our guys looking like a Colossus," Matthau said. "He eliminated for me all those jokes which start out: 'Did you hear the one about the little Jewish gentleman?'"

Matthau didn't play tennis, but he joined the Beverly Hills Tennis Club so he could meet Hank. They became friends and often ate lunch together, discussing sports, movies and Jews. "I asked him a lot of stupid questions," Matthau admitted. "He always replied with great patience and courtesy, even though his equanimity must have been rattled on more than one occasion."

Greenberg had become the elder his Beverly Hills Tennis Club buddies turned to for advice. Richard Mosk, a judge who served on the Warren Commission, had a son who wanted to attend a baseball game on one of the lesser Jewish holidays, but his mother didn't think he should. Mosk asked Hank for advice. Hank told him about the rabbi who cited children playing in the street after Hank had played on Rosh Hashanah. Mosk let his son go to the baseball game.

Tennis put Hank back into the spotlight, with newspapers and magazines around the country running columns about the baseball star who had reinvented himself as a tennis player in his golden years and showing him in his tennis whites slicing a backhand with his T200. Hank did not mind the attention, especially at the annual Dewar's event. "This is my one moment of glory all year," he said. "All those other guys are heroes all year round."

He continued to observe Yom Kippur in his own quiet way. He did not attend synagogue, but on the Day of Atonement he stayed home instead of playing tennis.

Mary Jo and Hank lived happily in California. They ate quiet dinners Mary Jo cooked at home. They traveled to the Caribbean. They enjoyed evenings at the homes of close friends, such as the journalist Karl Fleming and his wife, Anne Taylor Fleming, a writer and radio and television commentator. They occasionally got together with other ballplayers from Hank's playing days, like the night they had dinner at an Italian restaurant on Sunset Boulevard with Joe DiMaggio and Marilyn Monroe. She was fascinated that Howard Hughes had pursued Mary Jo as an actress. Hank did not like it when people bothered him during a meal for autographs, but that evening the other patrons left him alone. "No one was looking at Hank that night," Mary Jo said.

On the coast opposite of where he grew up, and with his playing days receding farther into the past, Hank's celebrity dwindled outside of the immediate circles he occupied. People didn't stop him on the street; they left him alone in restaurants. Then, in the early Eighties, he noticed an increase in fan mail, people sending him trading cards to sign, five and ten at a time. Flattered and pleased to be remembered, he obliged—until Ralph Kiner told him that the letter writers weren't admirers, they were opportunists selling his autograph. Hank started charging for his signature, one of the first players to do so, and donated the money to charity.

Most of Hank's charitable donations went to Jewish causes. He believed that Jews should help their own. In the same spirit, he contributed generously to the ballplayers' retirement fund. But for his autographs, he picked a neutral charity, Pets Adoption. Mary Jo, who saw herself as an animal lover rather than an actress, had tapped a soft spot in Hank for animals. One day when they were still living in New York, Mary Jo told Hank about the young woman she had come across on the street sobbing because she was leaving town and couldn't take her Yorkshire Terrier, Daisy, with her. Mary Jo promised the young woman they would take the dog. Hank consented. He had not been a dog person, but he grew attached to Daisy. They brought the dog with them when they moved to Los Angeles. Daisy eventually got sick and died. That was one of only two times Mary Jo saw Hank cry. He did not tell the autograph hawks that he matched every autograph donation dollar for dollar.

Hank read voraciously, mostly histories and biography. He loved Michener and was fascinated by World War II. He delighted in arguing politics, smoking good cigars and telling self-deprecating stories. He played backgammon to win—there was no other way for him—and made side bets when watching World Series games on television. Ever the guess hitter, he would wager the next pitch was a curve or slider. He complained about taxes and supported Israel unconditionally. Hank equated any challenge to Israel with anti-Semitism. His rigidity on that position caused a rift with his son Glenn. Hank argued about the Mideast at a Manhattan restaurant with Glenn's wife, Judy, a social worker who helped Palestinian women.

When Hank refused to apologize, Glenn and Judy walked out. Hank didn't speak to his son for five years.

Glenn had graduated from Yale and, after teaching for a short spell, earned a master's in literature from New York University, an MBA at Columbia University and co-founded an investment advisory firm in Manhattan, Chieftain Capital Management, recently renamed Brave Warrior Advisors when he split with his founding partner, John Shapiro. Glenn also became a two-time New York state squash champion.

Alva graduated from Kenyon College in Ohio, then went into business, buying a majority stake in the *Old Lyme Gazette*, a Connecticut newspaper. She eventually followed in her mother's footsteps when she opened an art gallery in New London.

After being an All-America goalie on the Yale soccer team in his junior year, Steve captained the varsity baseball team his senior year. The Washington Senators, who would soon become the Texas Rangers, picked him in the college draft in 1970. Steve had wanted to be a baseball player since his childhood days playing pepper at the Cleveland stadium with Rocky Colavito and Herb Score. Hank had not pressured him, other than to give him some pointers along the way. The six-foot, two-inch, 195-pound Ivy League English major spent five years in the Rangers' farm system, three of those in AAA, where he played first and third base and hit .277, but he was forever dogged by the tag, "son of Hall of Famer Hank Greenberg," a kid with potential but not quite the skills of his old man. "I wanted to give baseball a try, but I wasn't going to embarrass my father," Steve had said. "I told him I'd quit if I couldn't make the majors." When Texas management sold him to the White Sox, whose general manager told Steve his chances of making the team in 1974 were less than fifty percent, Steve left baseball to put his other talents to use.*

---

* Hank used to tell Steve half-jokingly, "I didn't send you to college to become a baseball player." He also said, once Steve made it to the minor leagues: "With all those stocks and bonds in his name, he can make more money any night when he's asleep than he can playing baseball." But Steve did find a career and a way to make money—lots of it—in sports. After graduating from UCLA Law School, he became a sports agent, served as deputy commissioner to Fay Vincent, launched the Classic Sports Network, made the MLB Network happen, brokered regional television deals for several teams, negotiated huge naming rights contracts and was recently dubbed by *Fortune* magazine the "King of the Sports Deal."

Hank's children married and raised their own children. All told, they gave Hank eight grandchildren.

Hank and Bill Veeck remained close friends. When Veeck pursued the Washington Senators, Hank was ready to invest. He said he wouldn't consider going into baseball with anybody but Veeck. The Senators' deal did not go through, but Hank did buy a small stake in the White Sox when Veeck bought back the team in 1975. That kept Hank's hand in the game.

Veeck had battled back from countless injuries and ailments since being wounded in the war, but he finally met his match in lung cancer. His four-pack-a-day cigarette habit had caught up with him. Hank visited his friend when he was dying. He admired Veeck's *joie de vivre* until the end. "He never complained, he was never down, he was always cheerful and optimistic and friendly," Hank wrote.

The Tigers invited Greenberg back to Detroit for a special ceremony on June 12, 1983, to retire his No. 5 along with Charlie Gehringer's No. 2. Since Briggs had sold him to the Pirates, Hank had been back to Detroit only a few times—most notably in 1968 when he threw out the first pitch for Game Four of the World Series from his box seat alongside Jackie Robinson and Vice President Hubert H. Humphrey. By then, Walter O. Briggs Sr. had been dead sixteen years, and his family no longer owned the team. Sunday afternoon, between games of a doubleheader against the Indians, Hank paused on the top step of the dugout and gazed over the field, the broad expanse of green grass and infield dirt that always looked much longer from this view. The years had changed so much. Briggs Stadium had become Tiger Stadium. The park's forest green color had given way to Tiger blue, the bases had hardened from stuffed sacks to molded lumps, large light standards rose from the rooftop and a mammoth television screen dominated the scoreboard over the center field bleachers. But the grass and the dirt, they were still there, and they whispered their memories. His Rosh Hashanah double-home-run day, Dizzy Dean on the mound, that hero's welcome and home run the first game back from the service . . .

Hank, now seventy-two, and Charlie, eighty, walked across the grass to the folding chairs set up for them in the infield. Hank wore a powder blue suit, checked shirt and navy tie with a gold clip. Though still trim, he no longer resembled a ballplayer, stooped and graying as he was. The crowd of 34,124 fans "embraced them warmly, respectfully, but without the wild enthusiasm one might have expected," *Detroit Free Press* columnist George Puscas observed. The majority had never seen the two Hall of Famers perform their heroic feats nearly fifty years earlier on that infield.

But the grass and dirt released some of their secrets when George Kell, Tiger star during the postwar years, introduced his former teammate. Two-time MVP, two-time World Series champion, twice led the league in runs scored, twice led the league in doubles, four-time American League home run king, four AL RBI titles, a .313 lifetime batting average—polite applause. Slugged fifty-eight home runs in a single 154-game season; knocked in 183 runs in another. At that, an audible gasp issued from the stands. *One hundred eighty-three runs batted in!* That figure seemed too large to get their minds around. The Royals' Hal McRae had led the major leagues the year before with 133. Over twenty years had passed since someone hit more than 150.* No one had hit more than 160 since the year after Hank hit his 183.† Those who hadn't known already realized then they were in the presence of greatness.‡

Hank was touched by the ceremony. The Tigers gave Gehringer and Greenberg framed replicas of their uniforms. Chrysler CEO Lee Iacocca donated new LeBaron convertibles to parade the legends around the field. Hank's old Detroit friends Lou Blumberg and Harold Allen attended and took him to dinner afterward. His son Steve was there to share the day with him.

When Hank took his turn at the microphone, he told the assembled, "Little did I dream that fifty-three years ago when I first played in Navin Field and popped up to Tony Lazzeri of the Yankees that I would come back here for such a day as this one."

He walked off the field for the final time with the best feeling Detroit had given him in many, many years.

---

* The Dodgers' Tommy Davis with 153 in 1962.
† Jimmie Foxx, 175, 1938.
‡ Sixty-five years after his retirement, Greenberg still holds the Tigers' single-season records for doubles, home runs, extra-base hits, total bases, RBI and slugging percentage; he holds the career record for slugging percentage and OPS.

Another healing moment occurred for Hank the following year. American League president Bobby Brown needed to select an honorary captain for his league's All-Star team. The National League had chosen Willie McCovey, the former Giant great, for the game to be played in San Francisco. Brown had a long list of distinguished candidates to choose from, including Mickey Mantle, Joe DiMaggio, Bob Feller, Ted Williams and Brooks Robinson. Greenberg was Brown's first choice. On July 10, 1984, at Candlestick Park, Hank joined Rod Carew, Reggie Jackson, Rickey Henderson, Dave Winfield, Eddie Murray, Jim Rice, Phil Niekro, Cal Ripken Jr. and George Brett for the game at Candlestick Park. All future Hall of Famers, none of them hit 58 homers or knocked in 183 runs in a single season. Though they all would play in far more All-Star Games than the two Hank did, only Ripken among them would win two MVP awards. Brown's gesture was a salve to the wound Hank had nursed so long after being snubbed from the 1935 team during his first MVP season and left to sit on the bench in 1937. "I felt they were repaying me for the years I should have gone to the All-Star Game and didn't," Hank wrote.

In October 1984, Lew Matlin, the Tigers' marketing director who had organized the numbers retirement ceremony in June, called Hank in California and invited him to throw out the first pitch at the World Series in Detroit. Hank would have liked that, but he had been having spasms in his back and legs that puzzled the doctors. They ran a battery of tests. He might have peripheral neuropathy, a deficiency in the nervous system. One doctor suggested surgery. Hank did not want people to see him, the once virile athlete, in such a compromised physical condition. *No. No, thanks,* he told Matlin. *Can't do it.*

The spasms had worsened by the following summer. Hank developed a burning sensation in his stomach that made him gag when he tried to eat. He lost weight. Another physician, Dr. Norman Nemoy, a urologist, ran more tests and examined Hank's kidneys. He found a tumor on one. Cancer.

Cancer. Hank couldn't believe it. His physical strength had made him who he was. Now, his body had turned on him.

Steve had been vacationing in Europe with his wife when Mary Jo called him with the news. They flew home right away, and Steve visited his father in Beverly Hills. Hank broke down. It was the first time Steve had seen his father—always the big, strong one—cry.

Hank had his kidney removed on August 21, 1985. He was determined to beat his opponent, cancer. He worked out with light dumbbells. He started to gain back weight.

But the disease had metastasized. Hank's hip ached, and he felt nauseated at times. Trying to stay positive like Veeck had, he summoned his sense of humor whenever he could. Mary Jo tended to him, cooking him three meals a day. She worried through sleepless nights. It pained Hank to see her suffering over his illness.

Hank didn't want anyone to know he was sick. He didn't want others, not even close friends, to see him weak. He didn't want to read about himself dying in the papers. His pride kept him silent. When friends called to play tennis or invite him to dinner, he invented excuses. His back was acting up. He had to go to New York. Mary Jo and Steve, who was living in Los Angeles and working as an agent, helped pull off the charade. Hank looked forward to the day when the doctors cleared him to play tennis again and he could tell his friends, "Yes, sorry. I was sick, but that's over. It was no big deal, really."

New Year's Eve had become a special tradition for Mary Jo and Hank, gathering with close friends to celebrate his birthday and the New Year. As the last day of 1985 approached, Mary Jo worried that her husband would not be up for the evening and that she would break under the emotion of the occasion.

Hank rallied. "With that inner strength and determination, [he] dressed himself up and looked like a million bucks," Mary Jo said. When midnight came, Hank turned seventy-five, exchanged kisses and sang "Auld Lang Syne." Two hours later, he was still regaling the guests with anecdotes and opinions. "They all left our home thinking that there was not much wrong with Hank, just his bothersome back," Mary Jo said.

Two days later, Hank got word that Bill Veeck died.

Steve had long been after his dad to write his life story. Hank had finally agreed several years earlier, dictating into a tape recorder. But he abandoned the project. "I'm not sure I want to do it right now," he explained, "because I'm going to do something great, and I want it to be in the book."

In 1986, when his symptoms worsened, Hank returned to the book. He spent many hours sitting by the pool in his backyard, telling the tape recorder the memories of his life.

As the pain intensified in his back and legs, he needed crutches to move about the house. Going out to a restaurant became a pleasure longed for but not realized. His only comfort seemed to come from Mary Jo, phone conversations with his children, and visits from Steve and his physician and friend Rex Kennamer. In June he tried a radiation treatment. That didn't work. By August, he was surviving only with pain medication, and he could not get out of bed. Nurses tended him around the clock.

The end arrived on Thursday, September 4, 1986. Hank Greenberg, the greatest Jewish ballplayer of all time, went to sleep and did not wake up.

EPILOGUE

———————— ∞ ————————

A man does not expire with his last breath. He lives on in memories and the changes he wrought. Hank Greenberg is not dead. So long as his story is told, he remains with us.

In November 1986, his family held a small memorial service at the Wadsworth Theatre in Los Angeles. Three hundred friends, relatives and fans listened to Ralph Kiner, Walter Matthau, Rex Kennamer, Anne Taylor Fleming and Steve Greenberg reminisce about what Hank had meant to them. They praised his integrity, generosity and drive. Their memories produced tears, and they produced laughs.

Hank touched many lives, but his influence extended well beyond those who knew him—he transformed the national pastime into a true meritocracy, a model of democracy. Just two weeks after Hank's passing, Senator Carl Levin, who as a boy had raced around his living room in glee when Greenberg hit his pennant-clinching grand slam in 1945, proclaimed on the floor of the United States Senate: "Because of people like Hank Greenberg and Jackie Robinson and players like Roberto Clemente and Fernando Valenzuela, we have white kids who grow up idolizing black ballplayers. Christian kids rooting for a Jewish home-run hitter. Anglos cheering on a player from Mexico or the Islands. It isn't much, maybe, but it is a start. It gives a kid the sense that maybe there is something more important than color or religion or national origin—maybe if a player can help the home team win, then that player ought to be admired and accepted for what he can do rather than being rejected because of where he comes from."

Hank's autobiography, *The Story of My Life*, was published in 1989, after Ira Berkow lovingly arranged the memories Hank dictated. Though fraught with inaccuracies, the book gives Hank's voice to his experiences. It has been reissued twice since.

Aviva Kempner's 1998 documentary *The Life and Times of Hank Greenberg* provided context for the events of Hank's playing days and situated him firmly in the pantheon of American heroes. Likewise, Greenberg's story figured prominently in Peter Miller's 2010 documentary *Jews and Baseball: A Love Affair* and in the National Baseball Hall of Fame's symposium on "Jews in Baseball" in 2004. The Hall of Fame even gave Hank his own day in 2008, on the seventy-fifth anniversary of his rookie year.

That is as it should be. Hank Greenberg remains the greatest Jewish baseball player—nay, athlete—of all time. No other Jew has achieved his athletic prowess and cultural significance. He not only batted his way into the Hall of Fame, he showed Jews the way to assimilate and elevated their esteem among their gentile peers. "It's arguable that Hank Greenberg is the most important American Jew to have ever been," baseball scholar Rabbi Michael Paley declares without hyperbole.

Hank's story delivers lessons still relevant today. "Greenberg's experience told the American public that we should challenge our stereotypes, that anyone can participate in sports," says Miller, director of *Jews and Baseball*. "When America operates properly, it is the story of immigrants coming here, overcoming bigotry, stereotypes and poverty and becoming part of the mainstream. Greenberg's influence is a way of helping America understand the humanity of newcomers and helping Americans overcome the bigotry each new group that comes here faces."

Hank Greenberg became a national hero during a dark time. His legacy shines a light for all Americans to follow.

BIBLIOGRAPHY

———————∞———————

First, a note on sources.

Writing the definitive biography of a man who made his mark eight decades ago presented many challenges. Hank Greenberg played in an era when sportswriters often did not interview players but simply made up the quotes they attributed to them. The players themselves embellished anecdotes on the dinner circuit. Time enlarged their legendary exploits on the field. Many of these quotes, anecdotes and exploits were recorded in books as fact. They have subsequently been lifted from those books and disseminated widely on the Internet, again passed off as fact.

There are few spectators and fewer teammates surviving from Hank's playing days. I tracked down as many as I could, though I recognize their memories are challenged by their advanced years and the passage of time (in many cases, sixty to seventy years have passed since certain events transpired). Aviva Kempner, who directed the definitive documentary of Greenberg's playing days, was kind enough to give me transcripts of her interviews with teammates and fans who passed away before I had the chance to interview them. Greenberg's own account—which he dictated in 1986, the summer he was dying, and was published posthumously—is similarly challenged by age and memory, and thus, not surprisingly, riddled with errors (regarding dates, the sequence of events, identities of individuals, specific details, et cetera). Yet his memories have been repeated incessantly on the Internet, in printed articles and even as recently as 2010 in a biography put out by the Yale Press. I've tried to set that all straight here.

Wherever possible, I verified Greenberg's memories and those of other subjects with firsthand accounts. I found these in the *Detroit News* archives; the Ernie Harwell Collection at the Detroit Public Library; the A. Bartlett Giamatti Research Center at the National Baseball Hall of Fame in Cooperstown, New York; the Hennepin County Library in Minneapolis; the Dorot Jewish Division at the New York Public Library; the Historical New York Times' and other publications' archives accessible online; and through the assistance of the University of Minnesota's Interlibrary Loan staff. I sifted through Tiger scrapbooks, team files and official and personal correspondence in the offices of Tigers' owner Mike Ilitch. I scoured Greenberg's personal scrapbooks and correspondence along with mementos he donated at the American Jewish Historical Society. I toured the bat vault and official files of the Louisville Slugger Museum & Factory. Under the Freedom of Information Act, I requested and received Greenberg's military records from the United States Army and his file from the Federal Bureau of Investigation. I obtained the file on Caral Gimbel's divorce from Edward Lasker from the Clark County court; the file of Caral Greenberg's suit for and eventual dismissal of divorce from the Cuyahoga County court; and the file on her divorce from Hank from Cullman County in Alabama. I tracked down family immigration information from Ellis Island and Greenberg's employment file at the Ford Motor Company.

For game accounts and most statistics, I relied on www.baseball-reference.com, the source of choice for Society for American Baseball Research members, and the American League's daily log for Greenberg (though, as SABR member Herm Krabbenhoft discovered regarding Greenberg's 1937 RBI total, these sources are not immune to mistakes either). Newspapers can be a source of misinformation, perhaps best illustrated by the widespread mistakes writers made speculating about Greenberg's annual salary in the days before a players' association tracked those figures. For this information, I relied on the American League's official annual transaction card for Greenberg.

When no official record of events existed, and published and/or oral accounts varied, I used my best judgment to construct events as I figured they were most likely to have occurred.

Despite my best efforts, I recognize that I may have made some mistakes myself. I am committed to correcting them in future printings as soon as they are brought to my attention. My hope is that I've moved the record of Greenberg's life closer to historical accuracy.

As a footnote to that, and since there's more to the story than can be told here, you can see extended notes on events in this book at www.hank-greenberg.net.

Books

Angell, Roger. *Five Seasons: A Baseball Companion.* Lincoln, Nebraska: University of Nebraska, 1977.

Aronoff, Jason. *Going, Going . . . Caught!: Baseball's Great Outfield Catches as Described by Those Who Saw Them, 1887–1964.* Jefferson, North Carolina: McFarland, 2009.

Auker, Elden with Tom Keegan. *Sleeper Cars and Flannel Uniforms: A Lifetime of Memories from Striking Out the Babe to Teeing It Up with the President.* Chicago: Triumph, 2001.

Bak, Richard. *Cobb Would Have Caught It: The Golden Age of Baseball in Detroit.* Detroit: Wayne State Press, 1991.

——. *Henry and Edsel: The Creation of the Ford Empire.* New York: Wiley, 2003.

Barthel, Thomas. *Baseball Barnstorming and Exhibition Games: 1901–1962: A History of Off-Season Play.* Jefferson, North Carolina: McFarland, 2007.

Bedingfield, Gary. *Baseball in World War II Europe.* Charleston: Arcadia, 1999.

Bennett, Harry. *Ford: We Never Called Him Henry.* New York: Tom Doherty, 1987.

Berkow, Ira. *The Corporal Was a Pitcher: The Courage of Lou Brissie.* Chicago: Triumph, 2009.

——. *Hank Greenberg: Hall-of-Fame Slugger.* Philadelphia: The Jewish Publication Society, 1991.

Bevis, Charles. *Mickey Cochrane: The Life of a Baseball Hall of Fame Catcher.* Jefferson, North Carolina: McFarland, 1998.

Bolkosky, Sidney M. *Harmony & Dissonance: Voices of Jewish Identity in Detroit, 1914–1967.* Detroit: Wayne State University Press, 1991.

Borelli, Stephen. *How About That!: The Life of Mel Allen*. Champaign, Illinois: Sports Publishing, 2005.

Boudreau, Lou with Russell Schneider. *Lou Boudreau: Covering All the Bases*. Champaign, Illinois: Sagamore Publishing, 1993.

Boxerman, Burton A. and Benita W. Boxerman. *Jews and Baseball: Volume 1, Entering the American Mainstream, 1871–1948*. Jefferson, North Carolina: McFarland, 2007.

——. *Jews and Baseball: Volume 2, The Post-Greenberg Years, 1949–2008*. Jefferson, North Carolina: McFarland, 2010.

Brody, Seymour. *Jewish Heroes & Heroines of America: 150 True Stories of American Jewish Heroism*. Hollywood, Florida: Lifetime Books, 1996.

Carmichael, John P. *Who's Who in Baseball*. Chicago: Callahan, 1938, 1939, 1944, 1945, 1946 and 1947.

Cochrane, Mickey. *Baseball: The Fan's Game*. New York: Funk & Wagnalls, 1939.

Cohen, Irwin J. *Echoes of Detroit: A 300-Year History*. Haslett, Michigan: City Vision, 2000.

——. *Echoes of Detroit's Jewish Communities: A History*. Haslett, Michigan: City Vision, 2003.

——. *Jewish Detroit*. Chicago: Arcadia, 2002.

——. *Tiger Stadium*. Chicago: Arcadia, 2003.

Cramer, Richard Ben. *Joe DiMaggio: The Hero's Life*. New York: Simon & Schuster, 2000.

Creamer, Robert W. *Stengel: His Life and Times*. New York: Simon & Schuster, 1984.

Daniel, W. Harrison. *Jimmie Foxx: The Life and Times of a Baseball Hall of Famer, 1907–1967*. Jefferson, North Carolina: McFarland, 1996.

Dawidoff, Nicholas. *The Catcher Was a Spy: The Mysterious Life of Moe Berg*. New York: Pantheon, 1994.

Deford, Frank. *The Heart of a Champion: Celebrating the Spirit and Character of Great American Sports Heroes*. San Diego: Tehabi, 2002.

Dorinson, Joseph and Joram Warmund, editors. *Jackie Robinson: Race, Sports, and the American Dream*. Armonk, New York: M.E. Sharpe, 1998.

Eig, Jonathan. *Luckiest Man: The Life and Death of Lou Gehrig*. New York: Simon & Schuster, 2005.

Eisen, George and David K. Wiggins, editors. *Ethnicity and Sport in American History and Culture.* Westport, Connecticut: Greenwood Press, 1994.

Epstein, Leslie. *San Remo Drive: A Novel from Memory.* New York: Handsel, 2003.

Fine, Sidney. *Frank Murphy: The Detroit Years, Volume 2.* Ann Arbor, Michigan: University of Michigan Press, 1975.

Finoli, David. *For the Good of the Country: World War II Baseball in the Major and Minor Leagues.* Jefferson, North Carolina: McFarland, 2002.

Fitzgerald, F. Scott. *The Great Gatsby.* New York: Scribner's, 1925.

Fox, Allen. *The Winner's Mind: A Competitor's Guide to Sports and Business Success.* Vista, California: USRSA, 2005.

Garner, Joe. *And the Crowd Goes Wild.* Naperville, Illinois: Sourcebooks, 1999.

Goldstein, Richard. *Spartan Seasons: How Baseball Survived the Second World War.* New York: Macmillan, 1980.

Greenberg, Hank with Ira Berkow. *Hank Greenberg: The Story of My Life.* Chicago, Triumph, 2001.

Harrigan, Patrick. *The Detroit Tigers: Club and Community, 1945–1995.* Toronto: University of Toronto Press, 1997.

Hawkins, Jim, Dan Ewald and George Van Dusen. *The Detroit Tigers Encyclopedia.* Champaign, Illinois: Sports Publishing, 2003.

Heidenry, John. *The Gashouse Gang: How Dizzy Dean, Leo Durocher, Branch Rickey, Pepper Martin, and Their Colorful, Come-From-Behind Ball Club Won the World Series—and America's Heart—During the Great Depression.* New York: Public Affairs, 2007.

Henrickson, Wilma Wood, ed. *Detroit Perspectives: Crossroads and Turning Points.* Detroit: Wayne State University, 1991.

Higham, Charles. *American Swastika.* New York: Doubleday, 1985.

Hill, Bob. *Crack of the Bat: The Louisville Slugger Story.* Champaign, Illinois: Sports Publishing, 2000.

Hillenbrand, Laura. *Seabiscuit.* New York: Random House, 2001.

———. *Unbroken: A World War II Story of Survival, Resilience, and Redemption.* New York: Random House, 2010.

Hillstrom, Kevin and Laurie Collier Hillstrom. *Industrial Revolution in America, Volume 1.* Santa Barbara: ABC-CLIO, 2006.

Hirsch, James. *Willie Mays: The Life, the Legend.* New York: Scribner, 2010.

Honig, Donald. *Baseball When the Grass Was Real: Baseball from the Twenties to the Forties Told by the Men Who Played It.* Lincoln: University of Nebraska Press, 1975.

James, Bill. *The New Bill James Historical Baseball Abstract.* New York: Free Press, 2001.

Jenkinson, Bill. *Baseball's Ultimate Power: Ranking the All-Time Greatest Distance Home Run Hitters.* Guilford, Connecticut: Lyons, 2010.

Johnson, Harold. *Who's Who in Major League Base Ball.* Chicago: Buxton, 1933.

———. *Who's Who in Major League Base Ball.* Chicago: Callahan, 1935.

Jordan, David M. *A Tiger in His Time: Hal Newhouser and the Burden of Wartime Ball.* South Bend, Indiana: Diamond Communications, 1990.

Karabel, Jerome. *The Chosen: The Hidden History of Admission and Exclusion at Harvard, Yale, and Princeton.* New York: Houghton Mifflin, 2005.

Kavieff, Paul R. *The Purple Gang: Organized Crime in Detroit, 1910–1945.* New York: Barricade Books, 2000.

Kiner, Ralph with Joe Gergen. *Kiner's Korner: At Bat and on the Air—My 40 Years in Baseball.* New York: Arbor House, 1987.

Klein, Clayton. *A Well-Kept Secret: From the Glory Years of the Detroit Tigers.* Manchester, Michigan: Wilderness Adventure Books, 2007.

Koppman, Lionel and Bernard Postal. *Guess Who's Jewish in American History.* New York: Shapolsky Books, 1986.

Kurlansky, Mark. *Hank Greenberg: The Hero Who Didn't Want to Be One.* New Haven: Yale, 2011.

Leavy, Jane. *Sandy Koufax: A Lefty's Legacy.* New York: HarperCollins, 2002.

Levine, Peter. *Ellis Island to Ebbets Field: Sport and the American Jewish Experience.* Oxford and New York: Oxford University Press, 1992.

———, editor. *Baseball History: An Annual of Original Baseball Research.* Westport, Connecticut: Meckler, 1989.

Levitt, Daniel R. *Ed Barrow: The Bulldog Who Built the Yankees' First Dynasty.* Lincoln: University of Nebraska Press, 2008.

Lieb, Frederick. *The Detroit Tigers.* New York: Putnam, 1946.

Lipsyte, Robert and Peter Levine. *Idols of the Game: A Sporting History of the American Century.* Atlanta: Turner, 1995.

Malta, Vince. *A Complete Reference Guide to Louisville Slugger Professional Player Bats.* Concord, California: Black Diamond, 2007.

McCollister, John. *The Tigers and Their Den: The Official Story of the Detroit Tigers.* Lenexa, Kansas: Addax Publishing Group, 1999.

McPhee, John. *Levels of the Game.* New York: Farrar, Straus, Giroux, 1969.

Millikin, Mark R. *Jimmie Foxx: The Pride of Sudlersville.* Lanham, Maryland: Scarecrow Press, 1998.

Montville, Leigh. *The Big Bam: The Life and Times of Babe Ruth.* New York: Doubleday, 2006.

Okkonen, Marc. *Baseball Uniforms of the 20th Century: The Official Major League Baseball Guide.* New York: Sterling, 1991.

Paper, Lew. *Perfect: Don Larsen's Miraculous World Series Game and the Men Who Made It Happen.* New York: New American Library, 2009.

Povich, Shirley. *All Those Mornings . . . at the Post.* New York: Public Affairs, 2005.

Prager, Joshua. *The Echoing Green: The Untold Story of Bobby Thomson, Ralph Branca and the Shot Heard Round the World.* New York: Random House, 2006.

Rampersad, Arnold. *Jackie Robinson: A Biography.* New York, Knopf, 1997.

Ribalow, Harold U. *The Jew in American Sports.* New York: Bloch, 1954.

Ribowsky, Mark. *The Complete History of the Home Run.* New York: Citadel, 2003.

Riess, Steven A., editor. *Sports and the American Jew.* Syracuse: Syracuse University Press, 1998.

Ritter, Lawrence S. *The Glory of Their Times: The Story of the Early Days of Baseball Told by the Men Who Played It.* New York: Macmillan, 1966.

Roberts, Russell. *100 Baseball Legends Who Shaped Sports History.* San Mateo, California: Bluewood Books, 2003.

Rockaway, Robert A. *But He Was Good to His Mother: The Lives and Crimes of Jewish Gangsters.* Jerusalem: Gefen, 2000.

Rossi, John. *A Whole New Game: Off the Field Changes in Baseball 1946–1960.* Jefferson, North Carolina: McFarland & Co., 1999.

Ruggles, William B. *The History of the Texas League of Professional Baseball Clubs.* Dallas: Texas Baseball League, 1951.

Sayers, Michael and Albert E. Kahn. *Sabotage! The Secret War Against America.* New York: Harper & Brothers, 1942.

Sickels, John. *Bob Feller: Ace of the Greatest Generation.* Dulles, Virginia: Potomac Books, 2005.

Skipper, John C. *Charlie Gehringer: A Biography of the Hall of Fame Tigers Second Baseman.* Jefferson, North Carolina: McFarland & Co., 2008.

Slater, Robert. *Great Jews in Sports.* Middle Village, New York: Jonathan David Publishers, 1983.

Smith, Burge Carmon. *The 1945 Detroit Tigers: Nine Old Men and One Young Left Arm Win It All.* Jefferson, North Carolina: McFarland, 2010.

Snyder, Brad. *A Well-Paid Slave: Curt Flood's Fight for Free Agency in Professional Sports.* New York: Plume, 2007.

Stanton, Tom. *Ty and the Babe.* New York: Thomas Dunne Books, 2007.

Sugar, Maurice. *The Ford Hunger March.* Berkeley, California: Meiklejohn Civil Liberties Institute, 1980.

Tebbetts, Birdie with James Morrison. *Birdie: Confessions of a Baseball Nomad.* Chicago: Triumph, 2002.

Tofel, Richard J. *A Legend in the Making: The New York Yankees in 1939.* Chicago: Ivan R. Dee Press, 2002.

Tye, Larry. *Satchel: The Life and Times of an American Legend.* New York: Random House, 2009.

Tygiel, Jules. *Baseball's Great Experiment: Jackie Robinson and His Legacy.* New York: Oxford University Press, 1997.

Vaccaro, Mike. *1941—The Greatest Year in Sports: Two Baseball Legends, Two Boxing Champs and the Unstoppable Thoroughbred Who Made History in the Shadow of War.* New York: Doubleday, 2007.

Vincent, Fay. *The Only Game in Town: Baseball Stars of the 1930s and 1940s Talk About the Game They Loved.* New York: Simon & Schuster, 2006.

Ward, Geoffrey C. and Ken Burns. *Baseball: An Illustrated History.* New York: Knopf, 2000.

Williams, Peter, editor. *The Joe Williams Baseball Reader.* Chapel Hill: Algonquin Books, 1989.

DVDS, Films and Videos

The Life and Times of Hank Greenberg. Directed by Aviva Kempner. The Ciesla Foundation, Washington, D.C., 1999.

Baseball Classics: 1934 & 1935 World Series. Rare Sportsfilms, Inc. Naperville, Illinois, 1997.

Baseball Classics: 1945 World Series. Rare Sportsfilms, Inc. Naperville, Illinois, 2008.

Jews and Baseball: An American Love Story. Directed by Peter Miller. Clear Lake Historical Productions, 2010.

Jews in Baseball Symposium. National Baseball Hall of Fame. Cooperstown, New York, 2004.

The Kid from Cleveland. Directed by Herbert Kline. Herbert Kline Productions, 1949.

Play Ball! 1934 American League Film. Rare Sportsfilms, Inc. Naperville, Illinois, 1997

The Story of America's Classic Ballparks. Media Process Group. Chicago, 1991.

Those Tigers. 1934 Detroit Tigers Season Highlights. Rare Sportsfilms, Inc. Naperville, Illinois.

When It Was a Game. Edited by George Roy. Black Canyon Productions, HBO Video, 1991.

When It Was a Game, 2. Edited by George Roy. Black Canyon Productions, HBO Video, 1992.

Interviews

Martin Abramowitz, Paula Allen, Bill Anderson, Marty Appel, Herbert Aronsson, Jerry Auerbach, Richard Bak, Del Baker Jr., Ralph Berger, Ira Berkow, Dave Blatt, Basil "Mickey" Briggs, Bobby Brown, Dave Bushing, Judith Levin Cantor, Irwin Cohen, Avern Cohn, Harriet Colman, Arnold Edson, Evelyn Eisenstat, Leslie Epstein, Allen Fox, Harvey Frank, Peter Gavrilovich, Phil Gold, Jerry Green, Alva Greenberg, Glenn Greenberg, Mary Jo Greenberg, Steve Greenberg, Jim Hawkins, Bob Hill, Burton Hurshe, Mike Ilitch, Paul Kavieff, Aviva Kempner, Ralph Kiner, Clayton Klein, Herm Krabbenhoft, Ed Kranepool, Gregg Krupa, Max Lapides, Benno Levi, David Lewis, Lew Matlin, Jim McConnell, Ed Mierkowicz, Peter Miller, Johanna Navin Monaghan, Richard Mosk, Jamie Myler, Art Neff, Michael Paley, Jerry Reinsdorf, Fred Rice, Al Rosen, Dick Savitt, Bud Selig, Martha Shanley, Red Simmons, William Simons, Burge Smith, Hope Solinger, Shelley Sommer, Nathan Stalvey, Robert Steinberg, Jeremy Sutton, Keith Thompson, Sam Tolkoff, Virgil Trucks, Mike Veeck, Bill Williams.

Miscellaneous

All-Star Game official game programs 1937, 1940, 1946.

Amman, Larry. "Game Winning Runs Batted In: The Detroit Tigers, 1901–1980." Unpublished study.

Antoinette Kelly letter, March 15, 1936.

Bak, Richard. "The Dark Days of the Black Legion." www.hourdetroit.com.

Bardack, Paul Roitman. "Drash Jews in Major League Baseball." Tifereth Israel Congregation, February 2007.

Baska, Jacob. "I'll Go When They Collar Me: Athletic Heroes, Citizen-Soldiers, and the Press Coverage of Hank Greenberg's 1941 Military Enlistments." April 20, 2009.

Bing Crosby letter, March 29, 1948.

Berger, Ralph. Biographies of Morrie Arnovich, Hank Greenberg, Bobo Newsom and Al Rosen. SABR Bio Project.

Dabscheck, Braham. "Shadows in the Spotlight: Two Jewish American Baseball Players." *Australasian Journal of American Studies*. Vol. 23, No. 1, 2004.

Detroit Baseball Club letter, author unknown, June 27, 1936.

Detroit Tigers press release, June 3, 1983.

Dorinson, Joe. "Baseball's Ethnic Heroes: Hank Greenberg and Joe DiMaggio." *The Cooperstown Symposium on Baseball and American Culture, 2001*. Jefferson, North Carolina: McFarland, 2002.

Doublestein, Matthew G. "Take Me out to the Ball Game: Baseball in Early American Song," *The Bulletin of the Society for American Music*. Vol. XXIX, No. 2, Summer 2003.

Dow, Bill. "The Fascinating Story of Hank Greenberg and Rip Collins." blog.detroitathletic.com.

Frank McKinney telegram, September 2, 1947.

Frank Navin letter, January 24, 1936.

Frank Navin letter, February 29, 1936.

Frederick C. Kidner letters, May 26, June 26, July 21, July 30 and August 13, 1936.

Ginsburg, Daniel. *Biography of Ty Cobb*. SABR Bio Project.

Greenberg, Hank. "Unforgettable Bill Veeck," *Reader's Digest*. July 1986.

Greenberg, Melanie. "Why My Grandpa Was No Hitter on Yom Kippur." *Jewish Daily Forward*. October 10, 2008.

Henry Ford Hospital medical bill submitted to Detroit Baseball Club, August 30, 1939.

Henry Greenberg letters, February 8, 1936; May 10, 1943; November 19, 1946; March 6, 1948; September 16, 1948; December 15, 1948; February 15, 1949; April 13, 1949; June 13, 1958.

Henry Greenberg Major League Baseball Individual Batting and Fielding Records. Daily Log. Bartlett Giamatti Research Center, National Baseball Hall of Fame, Cooperstown, New York.

Henry Greenberg American League transaction card. Bartlett Giamatti Research Center, National Baseball Hall of Fame, Cooperstown, New York.

Henry Greenberg file, Federal Bureau of Investigation, Washington, D.C.

Henry Greenberg file, United States Army, Military Personnel Records, St. Louis, Missouri.

Henry Stimson letter, August 8, 1941.

Hillerich & Bradsby contract with Henry Greenberg, dated September 8, 1934.

Hylton, Gordon. "Regulating the Yankees: Baseball and Antitrust in 1939." http://law.marquette.edu/facultyblog. January 11, 2011.

James Monroe High School yearbook, 1929.

"Jews in Baseball." Panel discussion. National Baseball Hall of Fame. Cooperstown, New York, 2004.

Kempner, Aviva. Transcripts of interviews with Harold Allen, Elden Auker, Flea Clifton, Harold Eisenstat, Charlie Gehringer, Grant Golden, Bert Gordon, Joe Greenberg, Max Lapides, Hal Newhouser, Billy Rogell, Don Shapiro, Birdie Tebbetts.

Kissman, Dr. Joseph. "Romanian Jews in 19th & Early 20th Centuries." *Rom-Sig News.* Volume 1, Number 2, Winter 1992–93.

Krabbenhoft, Herm. "Lou Gehrig's RBI Record." *The Baseball Research Journal.* Society for American Baseball Research, Fall 2011.

Krabbenhoft, Herm. "Hank Greenberg's American League RBI Record." *The Baseball Research Journal.* Society for American Baseball Research, Spring 2012.

Mickey Cochrane letter, February 10, 1936.

McCue, Andy. Biography of Walter O'Malley. SABR Bio Project.

McKenna, Brian. Biography of William Eckert. SABR Bio Project.

Michaels, Leonard. "My Yiddish." *The Threepenny Review.* No. 95, Autumn 2003.

The Modern Millwheel, General Mills employee newsletter, July 1938.

Moynahan, Brian. "The Player Nobody Wanted: Hank Greenberg." www. baseball-almanac.com, 2003.

Norwood, Stephen H. and Harold Brackman. "Going to Bat for Jackie Robinson: The Jewish Role in Breaking Baseball's Color Line. *Journal of Sport History.* Volume 26, Number 1, Spring 1999.

Okkonen, Mark and David Jones. Biography of Frank Navin. SABR Bio Project.

Oliver Labadie letter, March 11, 1936.

Rabinowitz, Bill. "Baseball and the Great Depression." Levine, Peter, editor. *Baseball History: An Annual of Original Baseball Research.* Westport, Connecticut: Meckler, 1989.

Ray, James Lincoln. Biography of Lou Gehrig. SABR Bio Project.

Robert Reynolds letter, July 25, 1941.

Rogers, C. Paul, III. Biography of Hughie Jennings. SABR Bio Project.

Roy McClure letter, May 27, 1940.

Simri, Dr. Uriel. "Jews in the World of Sports: A Historical View." International Jewish Sports Hall of Fame. 1996.

Simons, William B. "Comparative Ethnicity: Joe DiMaggio and Hank Greenberg," *The Cooperstown Symposium on Baseball and American Culture, 2000.* Jefferson, North Carolina: McFarland, 2001.

Simons, William B. "Judaism, Baseball and the American Dream." Paper presented at Cooperstown Symposium on Baseball and the American Culture, 2000.

Simons, William B. "Searching for Hank Greenberg: Aviva Kempner's Mythic Hero and Our Fathers." *The Cooperstown Symposium on Baseball and American Culture, 2001.* Jefferson, North Carolina: McFarland, 2002.

S.K., M.D. letter, October 6, 1936.

Solomon, Eric. "Jews and Baseball: A Cultural Love Story." Edited by George Eisen and David K. Wiggins. *Ethnicity and Sport in American History and Culture.* Westport, Connecticut: Greenwood Press, 1994.

Ted Williams telegram, undated.

Temple Ohabei Shalom flier advertising Greenberg's appearance in December 1935, Brookline, Massachusetts.

Tepperman, Alex. Biography of Izzy Goldstein. SABR Bio Project.

Turbow, Jason, author of *The Baseball Codes*, quoted by dberri.wordpress. com. July 11, 2010.

U.S. Census, Cleveland, 1950.

U.S. Congressional Record, February 7, 1944. Remarks of Hon. Emanuel Celler, of New York.

U.S. Congressional Record, September 17, 1986. Remarks of Senator Carl Levin, of Michigan.

Walter O. Briggs Jr. letter, May 1, 1941.

Wohlgelernter, Elli. Interview with Henry Greenberg on July 25, 1980. New York: American Jewish Committee, Oral History Library, 1981.

Wohlgelernter, Elli. Interview with Shirley Povich on June 5, 1991. New York: American Jewish Committee, Oral History Library, 1991.

World News Tonight, ABC-TV. Interview with Dick Schaap. July 1, 1984.

World Series official game programs 1934, 1940.

Newspapers and News Syndicates

Akron Beacon Journal

American Hebrew

Arizona Republic

Arizona Times

Asahi Evening News

Asbury Park Evening Press

Associated Press

Beaumont Enterprise

Binghamton Press

Boston Evening American

Boston Record–American

Boston Traveler

Chicago Daily News

Chicago Sun–Times

Chicago Tribune

Chicago's American

Christian Science Monitor

Cleveland Call & Post

Cleveland News

Cleveland Plain Dealer

Cleveland Press

Columbus Dispatch

Dallas Times Herald

Dayton Daily News

Dearborn Independent

Detroit Free Press

Detroit Jewish Chronicle

Detroit Jewish News

Detroit News

Detroit Times

Evansville Press

Flint Journal

Fort Lauderdale News and Sun-Sentinel

Forward

Independent Jewish Press Service

Jerusalem Post

Jewish Advocate

Jewish Criterion

Jewish News

Jewish Standard

Jewish Telegraphic Agency

Laredo Times

Las Vegas Review-Journal

Los Angeles Examiner

Los Angeles Times

Memphis Commercial Appeal

Miami Herald

Minneapolis Tribune

New Jersey Jewish Standard

New York American

New York Daily Mirror

New York Daily News
New York Herald Tribune
New York Journal–American Sports
New York Post
New York Sun
New York Times
New York World–Telegram
Newsday
Pacific Stars & Stripes
Peoria Journal–Star
Philadelphia News
Pittsburgh Post–Gazette
Pittsburgh Press
Pittsburgh Sun–Telegraph
Richmond Times
St. Petersburg Times
Savannah News
Seven Arts Feature Syndicate
The Sporting News
Toledo Blade
United Press
USA Today Baseball Weekly
Washington Post
Washington Star
Washington Times–Herald
Washington Tribune
Windsor Daily Star

Periodicals

American Bar Association Journal
Atlantic Monthly
Baseball Digest
Baseball Magazine
Baseball Weekly
B'nai B'rith Magazine

Collier's
Current Biography
Extension
Fortune
Heritage
History Channel Magazine
Huddle
Inside Pitch
Jet
Life
Literary Digest
Look
Memories and Dreams
Minneapolis Review of Baseball
Nevada Life
New Yorker
Newsweek
Oldtyme Baseball News
Ragtyme
Reader's Digest
Saturday Evening Post
Sport
Sports Collectors Digest
Sports Illustrated
Tennis Illustrated
Time
Yank

Web Sites

blogs.wfan.com
jewishmajorleaguers.org
sports.espn.go.com
www.americanthinker.com
www.AncestryLibrary.com
www.baseball-almanac.com

www.baseball-reference.com
www.baseballinwartime.com
www.BaseballLibrary.com
www.bls.gov.data/inflation_calculator.htm
www.coachbuilt.com
www.coinnews.net
www.crosley-field.com
www.deadspin.com
www.espn.com
www.historyplace.com
www.jackhbloom.com
www.jewishgen.org
www.jewishmag.com
www.jockbio.com
www.resurgence.org
www.squashtalk.com
www.weeklystandard.com

ACKNOWLEDGMENTS

There's no I in book; it takes a large supporting cast to uncover the story. I am grateful to all of those people who supported me along the way:

Thank you to Sharon Arend of Ilitch Holdings Inc.; fellow SABR members Bob Bailey, Herm Krabbenhoft, Jack Morris and Lyle Spatz; Gary Bedingfield; Ira Berkow; Freddy Berowski, Jim Gates, John Horne Jr. and Tim Wiles at the A. Bartlett Giamatti Research Center; Mark Bowden at the Detroit Public Library; Mary Burns in the Commissioner's Office; Dave Bushing; Todd Cameron; Irwin Cohen; Harriet Colman; Linda Culpepper, Danielle Kaltz and Wayne Smith at the *Detroit News*; Jan Durecki at the Rabbi Leo M. Franklin Archives; Leslie Epstein; Doak Ewing; Andy Geyer at the Ciesla Foundation; Don Greene and Nathan Stalvey at the Louisville Slugger Museum & Factory; Kim Harbinson at General Mills; Lori Hart; Wayne Hergott; Bob Hill; Terry Hoover at the Edison Institute Ford Archives; Lucille Iasello; Clayton Klein; William LeFevre at Wayne State University's Walter P. Reuther Library; Seymour Manello at the *Detroit Jewish News*; Peter Miller; Maureen Monchamp; Richard Nagler; Shawn Schrager at *The Sporting News*; Amanda Seigel; Mike Skinner; Burge Smith; Keith Thompson; Larry Tye; and Tomi Winters.

Thank you to Patrick Adkins, John Hageman, Alison Rosengren, Brendan Rosengren, Kathy Rysgaard and Mike Sharp for their research help.

Thank you to those who set up and maintained valuable Web sites such as Baseball Reference, Baseball Almanac and Retrosheet, whose previous research and dedicated work made my job so much easier.

Thank you to the University of Minnesota library staff who tracked down my numerous interlibrary loan requests.

A special thank-you to Aviva Kempner, whose wonderful film *The Life and Times of Hank Greenberg* provided a launching pad for this project and whose generous sharing of interview transcripts provided insightful details I would have otherwise missed.

Thank you to Dick Rice for his support from beginning to end.

Thank you to Brent Howard, my editor at New American Library, for his enthusiasm and encouragement with this book.

Thank you to Philip Spitzer, Lukas Ortiz and Luc Hunt at the Philip Spitzer Literary Agency for their early and unfailing belief in this book. Thank you, fellow author Tom Stanton, for recommending Philip and leading me to valuable sources.

Thank you to the Greenberg family for their cooperation and help: Alva, Steve, Glenn and Mary Jo. I hope this book does justice to what a wonderful man your father and husband was.

Finally, thanks to my home team: Maria, Alison and Brendan. I appreciate your belief in me and this book.

INDEX